The Crisis in
Youth Mental Health

Recent Titles in Child Psychology and Mental Health

THE CRISIS IN
YOUTH MENTAL HEALTH

Critical Issues and Effective Programs

Volume 3

Issues for Families, Schools, and Communities

Kristine Freeark and William S. Davidson II

Volume Editors

Hiram E. Fitzgerald, Robert Zucker, and Kristine Freeark

Editors in Chief

Praeger Perspectives
Child Psychology and Mental Health

Hiram E. Fitzgerald and Susanne Ayres Denham, Series Editors

PRAEGER

Westport, Connecticut
London

KH

Library of Congress Cataloging-in-Publication Data

The crisis in youth mental health : understanding the critical issues and effective programs / editors Hiram E. Fitzgerald, Robert Zucker, and Kristine Freeark.
    p. cm.—(Child psychology and mental health)
    Includes bibliographical references and index.
    ISBN 0-275-98480-X (set : alk. paper)—ISBN 0-275-98481-8 (v.1 : alk. paper)—
    ISBN 0-275-98482-6 (v.2 : alk. paper)—ISBN 0-275-98483-4 (v.3 : alk. paper)—
    ISBN 0-275-98484-2 (v.4 : alk. paper) 1. Adolescent psychopathology. 2. Child
psychotherapy. 3. Youth—Counseling of. 4. Community mental health services. I. Fitzgerald,
Hiram E. II. Zucker, Robert A. III. Freeark, Kristine. IV. Series.

RJ503.C76   2006
618.92′8914—dc22   2005030767

British Library Cataloguing in Publication Data is available.

Copyright © 2006 by Hiram E. Fitzgerald, Robert Zucker, and Kristine Freeark

Library of Congress Catalog Card Number: 2005030767
ISBN: 0–275–98480–X (set)
      0–275–98481–8 (vol. 1)
      0–275–98482–6 (vol. 2)
      0–275–98483–4 (vol. 3)
      0–275–98484–2 (vol. 4)
ISSN: 1538–8883

First published in 2006

Praeger Publishers, 88 Post Road West, Westport, CT 06881
An imprint of Greenwood Publishing Group, Inc.
www.praeger.com

Printed in the United States of America

The paper used in this book complies with the
Permanent Paper Standard issued by the National
Information Standards Organization (Z39.48–1984).

10 9 8 7 6 5 4 3 2 1

2|8|07

CONTENTS

SERIES FOREWORD

The twentieth century closed with a decade devoted to the study of brain structure, function, and development that in parallel with studies of the human genome has revealed the extraordinary plasticity of biobehavioral organization and development. The twenty-first century opens with a decade focusing on behavior, but the linkages between brain and behavior are as dynamic as the linkages between parents and children, and children and environment.

The Child Psychology and Mental Health series is designed to capture much of this dynamic interplay by advocating for strengthening the science of child development and linking that science to issues related to mental health, child care, parenting, and public policy.

The series consists of individual monographs, each dealing with a subject that advances knowledge related to the interplay between normal developmental process and developmental psychopathology. The books are intended to reflect the diverse methodologies and content areas encompassed by an age period ranging from conception to late adolescence. Topics of contemporary interest include studies of socioemotional development, behavioral undercontrol, aggression, attachment disorders, and substance abuse.

Investigators involved with prospective longitudinal studies, large epidemiologic cross-sectional samples, intensely followed clinical cases, or those wishing to report a systematic sequence of connected experiments are invited to submit manuscripts. Investigators from all fields in social and behavioral sciences, neurobiological sciences, medical and clinical sciences, and education are invited to submit manuscripts with implications for child and adolescent mental health.

Hiram E. Fitzgerald
Susanne Ayres Denham
Series Editors

ACKNOWLEDGMENTS

This project began at a lunch meeting when Norman Watt, Robert Bradley, Catherine Ayoub, Jini Puma and Hi Fitzgerald concluded that there was a great need for a book that summarized the benefits of early intervention. Shortly after agreeing to pursue such a book, Deborah Carvalko, acquisitions editor at Greenwood Publishing Group, contacted Hi to inquire if he knew anyone who would be interested in editing a series on the Crisis in Youth Mental Health. Bingo! This four-volume set is the result and volume 4 is that original lunch time project. The volumes represent a product forged from the labor and energy of an editorial team composed of long-time and current research and professional colleagues: Catherine Ayoub, Robert Bradley, William Davidson, Hiram Fitzgerald, Kristine Freeark, Whitney LeBoeuf, Barry Lester, Tom Luster, Jini Puma, Francisco Villarruel, Norman Watt, Robert Zucker, and Barry Zuckerman. Each editorial team drafted an extraordinary set of researchers who collectively frame the parameters of the crisis in youth mental health, provide cogent analyses of effective evidence-based preventive-intervention programs, and draw attention to policy implications of their work. Volumes such as these are labors of professional and personal love because the rewards to be gained are only those realized by the impact that words and ideas have on current and future generations of scientists, parents, and policy makers. No one has more passion for bringing science to bear on the problems of society than Lou Anna K. Simon, President of Michigan State University. In her commentary, she eloquently and forcefully articulates the need to forge campus–community partnerships, using evidence-based practices to both understand and resolve community-based problems.

Editors and authors provide the grist for anthologies, but there are many millers that grind the grain and bake it into a final loaf. First to thank is Deborah Carvalko who provided the opportunity to even imagine the project. Lisa Pierce, senior development editor at Praeger Press made sure that this host of contributors met their deadlines. Apex Publishing, assisted by four extremely meticulous and energetic copy editors (Ellie Amico [vol. 1], Bruce Owens [vol. 2], Caryl Knutsen [vol. 3], and Carol Burwash [vol. 4]), moved everyone through a tight time frame for copy editing and page proofs, assured cross-volume uniformity in format and style, removed split infinitives, identified missing references, and translated academic language into a more common prose. Finally, at Michigan State University, Vasiliki Mousouli was the diligent project manager who maintained contact with more than 60 editors, authors, and publishers, organized and tracked all of the manuscript activity, and made final format corrections for APA style. In her spare time she managed to complete her doctoral program requirements in school psychology and successfully defend her doctoral dissertation.

What began as lunchtime table talk, resulted in four volumes that collectively summarize much about the crisis in youth mental health. All involved have our deepest respect and thanks for their contributions.

Hiram E. Fitzgerald
Kristine Freeark
Robert A. Zucker

SPECIAL COMMENTARY: UNIVERSITIES AND THE CRISIS IN YOUTH MENTAL HEALTH

Lou Anna Kimsey Simon
President, Michigan State University

There are at least two key reasons why universities are concerned about the crisis in youth mental health. First, increasing numbers of students matriculating at colleges and universities have mental health problems. Because social and emotional well-being is paramount to academic success and to the ability to negotiate the demands of the workplace, universities must be concerned about student social-emotional health. Second, understanding the causes and life course progression of mental health problems relates directly to the scholarship mission of the university, especially those with historical ties to the land grant system of higher education. Land grant universities, established by the Morrill Act of 1862, were founded to allow all citizens access to higher education and to bind together the scholarships of discovery and application. Thus, land grant universities are about values and beliefs regarding the social role and social responsibility of universities with respect to ameliorating the problems of society.

In 2005, Michigan State University celebrated its 150th anniversary as an academic institution, and in 2012 it will celebrate its 150th anniversary as the first land grant university. We have been actively engaged in a campus conversation concerning the role of land grant institutions in the twenty-first century, and much of that conversation has focused on renewing the covenant between higher education and the public that higher education serves. When land grant institutions were founded, the focus of that covenant was on agricultural production and the mechanical arts. Today, the covenant extends to the broad range of problems in contemporary society, not the least of which are those associated with the causes, treatments, and prevention of mental health problems.

Professional and public documents increasingly draw attention to the pervasive problems affecting children throughout the United States and around the world. Considering all forms of mental illness, recent studies indicate that half of the population will experience a mental health problem sometime during the life course. In the United States, 1 in 10 children and adolescents suffer from mental illness severe enough to cause some level of impairment, but only a fraction of them receive treatment. Most mental health problems are transitory and relatively easily resolved by brief interventions, including support from mental health professionals, friends, family members, or other individuals in one's social support network. Epidemiologists report that approximately 6 percent of the population experiences profound mental health problems and may require psychotropic medications and intense psychotherapy to maintain manageable levels of adaptive behavior. However, an increasing number of individuals deal with mental health problems at a level of severity that falls between the ordinary and the profound. The number of children with learning disabilities, speech and language handicaps, mental retardation, emotional disturbances, poor self-regulatory skills, aggressive behavior, substance abuse disorders, and poor school achievement is increasing at alarming rates. Seventeen percent of all children in the United States have one or more developmental disabilities; 20 percent of all school-age children have attention problems; and the age of first onset of drug use, smoking, and sexual activity continues to spiral downward (Fitzgerald, Lester, & Zuckerman, 2000; Koger, Schettler, & Weiss, 2005).

Collectively, students enrolled in higher education represent the rich spectrum of America's ethnic, racial, political, gender, religious, and physical diversity. If higher education does its job well, students will be challenged to examine their personal beliefs and values against this diversity, arriving at a deeper understanding of their own values as well as those of others, both of which are implicit to sustaining a free, democratic, and diverse society. For many students, such free-ranging discussion and debate is exciting, provocative, and enriching. Other students may encounter diversity that is beyond their prior experience, and public discourse and challenge to their personal beliefs may provoke anxiety and distress. The mental health crisis among America's youth directly translates to a mental health crisis on America's college and university campuses. Increasing numbers of students report suicide ideation, feelings of hopelessness, depression, anxiety, and a sense of being overwhelmed (Kadison & DiGeronimo, 2004). Increasing numbers of these students come from broken families, and many come from stressful neighborhoods and communities. The crisis in youth mental health contributes to the crisis in college student mental health and both challenge university capacity to provide the depth of support necessary to help students maintain psychological and behavioral health in the context of pressures for academic success.

The good news is that prevention specialists from many different disciplines have developed evidence-based programs that not only have positive impacts on child behavior, but also have positive impacts on families and communities. This four-volume set was designed to affirm principles underlying the importance of prevention and the view that individual development is best understood within the framework of systems theory. Systems theory begins with the premise that from the moment of conception, the organism is embedded within an increasingly complex array of systems (family, neighborhood, school, community, society) and that all components mutually transact to shape development over the life course. The contextual embeddedness of mental health problems, therefore, requires perspectives from a broad range of social, behavioral, economic, and biomedical sciences as well as the arts and humanities, in order to understand behavior-in-context. Thus, universities are uniquely positioned to make significant contributions to the understanding and remediation of mental health problems because universities are the repositories of all of the disciplines and can provide the means for interdisciplinary, systemic research and the development and assessment of prevention and treatment approaches. Moreover, from a land grant perspective, such research and development activities gain even greater authenticity when conducted within the context of campus-community partnerships for health and well-being.

Resolving the crisis in youth mental health is essential for the maintenance of a mentally healthy society, because youth comprise society's future policy and political leadership. Universities contribute to the resolution by providing a range of wraparound supportive structures and services and by building stronger campus-community partnerships in health. Equally important for universities is a commitment to search for causal factors that shape developmental pathways that generate mental health problems, to develop biomedical and behavior treatments, and to discover successful ways to prevent or ameliorate mental health problems early in development. The chapters in The Crisis in Youth Mental Health focus attention on each of these objectives.

REFERENCES

Fitzgerald, H.E., Lester, B.M., & Zuckerman, B. (Eds.). (2000). *Children of addiction: Research, health, and policy issues.* New York: Garland.

Kadison, R.D., & DiGeronimo, T.F. (2004). *College of the overwhelmed: The campus mental health crisis and what to do about it.* Boston: Jossey-Bass.

Koger, S.M., Schettler, T., & Weiss, B. (2005). Environmental toxicants and developmental disabilities. *American Psychologist, 60,* 243–255.

Chapter 1

DOMESTIC VIOLENCE AND INFANCY

Alytia A. Levendosky and G. Anne Bogat

Domestic violence, which is defined in this chapter as male violence against their female partners, is a significant public health concern in the United States. Amnesty International (2001) reports that a woman is battered every 15 seconds in the United States. Straus and Gelles (1990) reported that 16 percent of women were abused by their husbands during the past year, with an overall lifetime prevalence rate of 28 percent. Data compiled from the National Crime Victimization Survey revealed that in 1998 nearly 1 million incidents of violence occurred between spouses, dating couples, or cohabiting partners (Rennison & Welchans, 2000). Of these incidents, nearly 85 percent were committed against women. Recently the National Coalition Against Domestic Violence (NCADV) defined battering as "A pattern of behavior used to establish power and control over another person through fear and intimidation, often including the threat or use of violence. Battering happens when one person believes they are entitled to control another" (NCADV, 2003). In fact, 21 to 34 percent of women in the United States are physically assaulted— slapped, kicked, beaten, choked, threatened, and/or attacked with a weapon—by an intimate adult partner during their lifetime (Goodman, Koss, Fitzgerald, Russo, & Keita, 1993). Injuries are a common result of domestic violence and require more medical treatment than rape, auto accidents, and muggings combined (Bureau of Justice Statistics, 1997).

Domestic violence is not, however, restricted to physical abuse; it also includes marital rape and psychological abuse. Marital rape is defined as "being forced into sexual relations in the realization that refusal would lead to further physical abuse and/or psychological harassment" (Shepherd, 1994). Psychological abuse can include "constant verbal abuse, harassment, excessive possessiveness, isolating the woman from friends and family, deprivation of physical and economic resources, and destruction of personal property" (NCDAV, 2003). Finally, domestic violence is not a problem exclusively in the United States; the World Health Organization estimates that 52 percent of women in the world are physically abused by their husbands/partners (Pickup, Williams, & Sweetman, 2001).

Exposure to domestic violence among children is also a significant public health concern. More than half of the women being battered live with children under age 12; thus, about 10 million children in the United States witness domestic violence each year (Straus, 1992). Because battering is more common in younger couples, infants and children to age five are at the greatest risk of exposure (Fantuzzo, Boruch, Beriama, Atkins, & Marcus, 1997). In fact, children's exposure to domestic violence may begin *in utero*. Estimates of women who experience domestic violence during pregnancy range from .9 percent to 20.1 percent (Gazmararian et al., 1996).

Of greatest concern to policymakers and those who work in intervention and prevention is research that indicates an intergenerational transmission of domestic violence. For example, a number of retrospective studies have found that adolescents and young adults who reported exposure to domestic violence as a child are more likely to perpetrate dating aggression (Foo & Margolin, 1995; MacEwan, 1994; O'Keefe, 1998; Wolfe & Wekerle, 1997) and marital aggression (Kalmuss, 1984; Rosenbaum & O'Leary, 1981), although this finding is stronger for males than for females (Caesar, 1988; Doumas, Margolin, & John, 1994; Hotaling & Sugarman, 1986). In addition, retrospective studies have found that women who are victims of domestic violence are more likely to have witnessed parental violence than nonabused women (e.g., Kalmuss, 1984; Walker, 1983). The only prospective study following children from early childhood into young adulthood (Magdol, Moffitt, Caspi, & Silva, 1998) found that only females who experienced domestic violence as children were more likely to be in violent relationships as adults.

The current chapter reviews the research evidence for the negative effects of domestic violence on young children and suggests recommendations for intervention and prevention programs. As part of understanding the impact of domestic violence on young children, the effects of domestic violence on their mothers and parenting is also reviewed. A biopsychosocial model is proposed to explain the variety of effects of domestic violence on young children.

EFFECTS ON YOUNG CHILDREN

Domestic violence can affect children beginning *in utero*. Injury from battering during the pregnancy can cause preterm births, birth complications, low birth weight, and newborn illnesses (Dye, Tollivert, Lee, & Kenney, 1995; Huth-Bocks, Levendosky, & Bogat, 2002; McFarlane, Parker, & Soeken, 1996; Schei, 1991; Valdez-Santiago & Sanin-Aguirre, 1996). Infant health may be compromised by other factors associated with domestic violence, including late entry into prenatal care (Huth-Bocks et al., 2002; McFarlane , Parker, & Soeken, 1996; Taggart & Mattson, 1996). Prenatal and infant health complications are associated with poor outcomes later in life. For example, low birth weight infants are more likely to experience deficits in physical growth, speech and language delays, central nervous system abnormalities, deficits in intelligence and school performance, and health status problems (Lefebvre, Bard, Veilleux, & Martel, 1988; Tomchek & Lane, 1993). In addition, children with poor physical health are at increased risk for problems in psychosocial adjustment compared with healthy peers (Eiser, 1990; Wallender & Varni, 1998).

Studies of normal infant development indicate that infants are able to detect and discriminate facial and vocal emotional expressions during 0–6 months and use significant others' facial and vocal expressions to judge situations during 6–12 months (Walker-Andrews, 1997). Thus, even during the first year of life, infants are acutely aware of the anger and distress of their parents during marital conflict. In one study, infants exposed to more frequent interparental anger over a period of nine months were more likely to become emotionally aroused by displaying anger and distress and to make attempts to comfort or reconcile their angry parents compared with infants exposed to infrequent parental anger (Cummings, Zahn-Waxler, & Radke-Yarrow, 1981). It is likely that infants exposed to violent angry parental interactions will have similar or even heightened reactions. Clinical reports and empirical studies find that infants in battered women's shelters showed weight and eating problems, sleep and mood disturbances, high rates of screaming and crying, problems interacting with peers, post-traumatic stress symptoms, and lacked normal responsiveness to adults (Alessi & Hearn, 1984; Bogat, DeJonghe, Levendosky, von Eye, & Davidson, 2005; Davidson, 1978; Layzer, Goodson, & Delange, 1985; Scheeringa & Zeanah, 1995).

Our own studies indicate that infants exposed to domestic violence are more reactive to adult anger (DeJonghe, Bogat, Levendosky, von Eye, & Davidson, 2005), have higher maternal reported aggressive and negative behavior (Levendosky, Leahy, Bogat, Davidson, & von Eye,

2005), and are more likely to have insecure attachments to their mothers at age one (Huth-Bocks, Levendosky, Bogat, & von Eye, 2004) than infants from households without domestic violence. These infants are also likely to display symptoms associated with post-traumatic stress disorder (PTSD) (Bogat, DeJonghe, Levendosky, von Eye, & Davidson, in press). Other research has also demonstrated that high-risk environments are associated with increased numbers of insecurely attached infants and, in particular, with disorganized attachment (Crittenden, 1985; 1987; Lyons-Ruth, Connell, Zoll, & Stahl, 1987; Main & Solomon, 1990). Attachment is the behavioral manifestation of the level of security in the parent-child relationship. Secure attachment is characterized by the child's confidence in the mother's emotional availability and responsiveness to his or her needs. Insecurely attached children either expect rejection from their mothers or are unsure about her availability; in the case of disorganized attachment, children lack a coherent strategy for coping with the stress of separation from the mother and may show depressed or disoriented behaviors. Disorganized attachment is over-represented in maltreating homes (Carlson, Cicchetti, Barnett, & Braunwald, 1989). A few prospective studies have found that disorganized attachment predicts later aggressive behavior (Hubbs-Tait et al., 1991; Lyons-Ruth, Alpern, & Repacholi, 1993). Thus, attachment quality in infancy may be a precursor to aggressive behavior in children exposed to domestic violence.

In a particularly interesting study of the effects of domestic violence on infant functioning, we staged an angry verbal conflict and videotaped children's responses to it (DeJonghe et al., 2005). As predicted, the infants living in households with domestic violence, compared to those who did not, showed greater distress in response to witnessing the angry verbal conflict. For those children who had not witnessed domestic violence, temperament played an important role in determining their responses—that is, infants who were temperamentally difficult were more likely to show distress when exposed to the verbal conflict in comparison with those who had a more easy-going temperament. However, this difference was not found for infants who had witnessed domestic violence, which suggests that exposure to domestic violence overrides temperament. Infants from domestic violence households who have generalized their distress response to verbal conflict between adults may have reached a ceiling for distress. It is possible that this early sensitivity to conflict demonstrated at age one is then a risk factor for emotional and behavioral problems as the child gets older.

Research has also demonstrated that preschool children who witnessed domestic violence exhibit elevated rates of behavior problems, increased trauma and dissociative symptoms, lower self-esteem, higher levels of depression and anxiety, lower levels of social functioning, and less empathy compared to children from nonviolent families (Davis & Carlson, 1987; Fantuzzo et al., 1991; Graham-Bermann & Levendosky, 1998b; Hinchey & Gavelek, 1982; Hughes, 1988; Jouriles, Pfiffner, & O'Leary, 1988; Levendosky , Huth-Bocks, Semel, & Shapiro, 2002; Stagg, Wills, & Howell, 1989). In a unique observational study of 46 children in the context of a classroom setting, Graham-Bermann and Levendosky (1998a) found that preschoolers who witnessed domestic violence had many more behavioral problems, more negative affect, responded less appropriately to situations, were more aggressive with peers, and had more ambivalent relationships with teachers than those from nonviolent families.

In our own work, we have assessed the post-traumatic stress symptoms of preschool children exposed to domestic violence (Levendosky et al., 2002). All of the children had at least one reported symptom of trauma, and, depending upon the measure used, 3 to 26 percent met the criteria for a traumatic stress disorder. The 3 percent represents the criteria from the Diagnostic and Statistical Manual of Mental Disorders, Version IV (DSM-IV), which is not considered sensitive to the developmental stages of very young infants and children. Based on the criteria from the Diagnostic Manual for Children Ages 0 to 3 (DC: 0–3), 26 percent met the diagnosis of traumatic stress. Furthermore, in this study, more symptoms of post-traumatic stress were associated with increased severity of the domestic violence. Finally, trauma symptoms were associated with externalizing (acting-out) behaviors in the preschool children. Thus, trauma not only impacts children's psychological functioning, but also their interpersonal functioning.

Children living in families with domestic violence may have experienced it prenatally and/or postpartum. Prenatally, the physical trauma itself as well as the biological correlates of maternal stress may affect brain development and thus permanently influence the child's response to stress (see Schore, 2003a). Postnatally, chronic episodes of stressful or traumatic events within the family may negatively affect establishment of stable attachment relationships and psychophysiological (i.e., affect) regulation (Gaensbauer, 1982; 2002). These events also are associated with more infant trauma symptoms (e.g., Bogat et al., 2005; Levendosky, Huth-Bocks, Semel, & Shapiro, 2002), and greater infant sensitivity to adult conflict (e.g., DeJonghe et al., 2005). In addition to the potential direct effects of domestic violence on young children, due to the importance of the mother-child relationship during early childhood, the effects of domestic violence on their mothers may influence children as well.

EFFECTS ON WOMEN

The negative effects of domestic violence on women have been well documented. Depression, low self-esteem, psychological distress, and post-traumatic stress disorder are common among battered women (e.g., Bogat et al., 2003; Cascardi & O'Leary, 1992; Houskamp & Foy, 1991; Kessler, Molnar, Feurer, & Appelbaum, 2001; Levendosky, Bogat, Theran, Trotter, von Eye, & Davidson, 2004; Vitanza, Vogel, & Marshall, 1995). Physical health problems are also prevalent (Eby, Campbell, Sullivan, & Davidson, 1995).

The prevalence of PTSD among battered women is particularly high, ranging from 45 to 84 percent (Houskamp & Foy, 1991; Kemp, Green, Hovanitz, & Rawlings, 1995; Kemp, Rawlings, & Green, 1991; Vitanza et al., 1995). In her work with trauma survivors, Herman (1992) makes a distinction between responses to acute versus ongoing traumatic events. She developed the idea of complex traumatic stress syndrome, which bears similarities to the diagnosis of post-traumatic stress disorder in the DSM-IV TR (American Psychiatric Association, 2000), but also includes additional symptoms (due to the chronic nature of domestic violence) such as depression, somatization, interpersonal sensitivity, and dissociation. She argues that many battered women suffer changes in personality, which leaves them vulnerable to harm. However, Herman (1992) emphasized the perpetrator's actions, rather than the woman's prior psychological functioning, in accounting for these changes.

Bogat et al. (2003) found that a history of exposure to domestic violence as well as domestic violence during pregnancy is negatively related to women's mental health symptoms across diagnostic categories, including depression, anxiety, and PTSD. The number of partners and the timing of this exposure had different effects on the women. Those experiencing chronic domestic violence (across both partners and time) had the worst outcomes. Women who experienced domestic violence recently—during their pregnancies and in the year prior to pregnancy with their current partners—had the next worst outcomes.

Due to the documented impact of domestic violence on women's mental health functioning, it is also important to understand how these effects may influence their parenting. A number of studies have found that parents, under a variety of stressful conditions (e.g., poverty, marital conflict, and divorce), are more likely to be depressed, anxious, hostile, and withdrawn (e.g., McLoyd, 1990). These parents often use harsher punishment, are less warm and nurturing with their children, and are generally less effective; the children of these parents, in turn, are negatively affected (Conger, Conger, Elder, & Lorenz, 1992, 1993; Elder, Conger, Foster, & Ardelt, 1992;

Hetherington, 1991, 1993; Lempers, Clark Lempers, & Simons, 1989). Thus, the negative effects of domestic violence on women's mental health is likely to negatively influence their parenting.

PARENTING AS A MEDIATOR OF THE EFFECTS OF DOMESTIC VIOLENCE ON YOUNG CHILDREN

A number of studies have found that the mother-child relationship is an important mediator of the effects of domestic violence on young children's social-emotional functioning. In other words, young children are not only affected directly by witnessing the violence, but also through the negative effects that the violence has on their mothers' capacities to parent. Mothers who remain affectively attuned and exhibit responsive parenting may protect their young children from some of the impact of this trauma, both physiologically and psychologically. In contrast, mothers who have traumatic responses to domestic violence may function in an impaired capacity as mothers and, thus, negatively influence their children's socio-emotional development (Levendosky & Graham-Bermann, 2000; Scheeringa & Zeanah, 2001).

Parenting begins during pregnancy. It has been documented that exposure to domestic violence during pregnancy has been associated with delayed prenatal care (Dietz et al., 1997; Taggart & Mattson, 1996), which then may have deleterious effects on the fetus and the woman. Another important component of maternal caretaking during pregnancy is the mother's representations of caretaking—the mother's internal parenting schemas of her unborn child. Women develop rich and specific representations/schemas of their infants and their own parenting as pregnancy progresses; these are likely constructed from mothers' own experiences of being parented (e.g., Stern, 1995; Zeanah, Carr, and Wolk, 1990). Representations, derived from semi-structured interviews, can be coded as either *balanced* or two types of *nonbalanced*: *disengaged* or *distorted*. Balanced representations are characterized by the integration of negative and positive emotions about the child, richness of description of the child, and a sense of the mother as absorbed in her relationship with her child. Disengaged representations are exemplified by the mother's cool emotional tone and a lack of emotional and personal involvement with the child. Distorted representations are characterized by inconsistency, inability to focus on the child as a separate individual, and a sense of preoccupation with the child.

In our own work we found that women who had been abused during their pregnancies had significantly more negative schemas/representations of their unborn babies than did nonabused women, and they were more likely to be classified as nonbalanced (either disengaged or distorted) rather than balanced (Huth-Bocks, Levendosky, Theran, & Bogat, 2004). We also examined the stability of maternal representations of caretaking from pregnancy to one year postpartum (Theran , Levendosky, Bogat, & Huth-Bocks, 2005). Women who changed from balanced to nonbalanced were more likely to be abused during pregnancy than were nonabused women. Life event stress was also related to this negative change, and these women were more likely to have sons. Finally, we found that prenatal representations were related to parenting behavior when the children were one year old, such that mothers holding balanced representations exhibited higher levels of positive parenting relative to the two nonbalanced subtypes (Dayton, Levendosky, Bogat, & Davidson, 2005). In addition, mothers holding disengaged representations exhibited higher levels of controlling parenting behaviors, and mothers holding distorted representations exhibited higher levels of covertly hostile behaviors. Thus, the schemas developed during parenting have long-term significant effects on the mother-child relationship.

After the child is born, parenting during early childhood is critical for the formation of the child's self-worth and the child's later functioning in other relationships (e.g., with peers and siblings) as well as normative health and development (Braungart-Rieker, Courtney, & Garwood, 1999; Clarke-Stewart, 1998; Maccoby & Martin, 1983; van Bakel & Riksen-Walraven, 2002). Several studies have documented the negative impact of domestic violence on maternal caretaking and its effects on children's adjustment (Holden & Ritchie, 1991; Holden, Levendosky, Bogat, & Davidson, 1998; Levendosky & Graham-Bermann, 1998, 2000, 2001, Levendosky et al., 2004; Margolin & Gordis, 2003; McCloskey, Figueredo, & Koss, 1995; Wolfe, Jaffe, Wilson, & Zak, 1985). For example, Margolin and Gordis (2003) found that domestic violence was inversely related to consistent and sensitive parenting as well as a mother's ability to provide a structured, organized environment for her children.

Other findings indicate that women who have experienced domestic violence, compared to nonabused women, were more physically aggressive, more inconsistent in their parenting style (Holden et al., 1998), and had greater parenting stress (Levendosky & Graham-Bermann, 1998; Wolfe et al., 1985). Furthermore, maternal caretaking behaviors explain the effects of domestic violence on preschool and school-age children's internalizing and externalizing behaviors (Levendosky & Graham-Bermann, 2001; Levendosky, Huth-Bocks, Shapiro, & Semel, 2003; McCloskey et al., 1995). Observed parenting (using videotaped observations of mother and one-year-old child at play) has also been shown to be negatively affected by domestic violence (Levendosky et al., 2005).

Experiences of domestic violence were negatively related to observed maternal caretaking, including warmth and joy.

Thus, it is clear that domestic violence negatively affects parenting at the first point at which parenting schemas and behavior can be measured—in prenatal schemas/representations, as well as throughout early childhood. Women who experience domestic violence may be psychologically compromised in a number of ways that may then overwhelm their ability to tolerate or relate to their infant in a sensitive and accepting manner (Lieberman & Van Horn, 1998; Zeanah & Scheeringa, 1997). The experience of domestic violence may also activate or reactivate the woman's unresolved thoughts and feelings about her earlier relationships and may alter her conceptualizations of relationships for the worse. This, in turn, may negatively affect the ways in which women conceptualize and organize their perceptions of their young children and themselves as mothers. Domestic violence also affected the stability of mothers' schemas. Interestingly, women whose schemas changed from balanced to nonbalanced from pregnancy to one year after childbirth, were more likely to have sons. Lieberman proposes that mothers may attribute to their sons the same aggressive impulses that abusive partners have; age-appropriate behavior may be misperceived as "malevolent or out-of-control," and mothers may presume that sons will grow up to be violent (Lieberman, 1996, 1997, 1999). This attribution may grow stronger as the children grow into toddlerhood and begin to show normal aggressive behavior.

Thus, while the literature in this area is relatively recent, it is clear that there are a number of documented negative effects of domestic violence on young children, potentially both directly and indirectly through the effects on the mother's parenting. However, the mechanisms through which these effects occur is yet to be understood.

BIOPSYCHOSOCIAL MODEL OF THE IMPACT OF DOMESTIC VIOLENCE ON YOUNG CHILDREN

The authors and their collaborators (Bogat, Levendosky, & von Eye, 2005; Bogat, Levendosky, von Eye, & Seng, 2004) have proposed a biopsychosocial model to explain the wide variety of effects of domestic violence on young children (see Figure 1.1). This theoretical model proposes that prenatally and postnatally through early childhood, the effects of domestic violence on young children are primarily mediated through the mother–child relationship. Beginning prenatally, we argue that exposure to domestic violence, in addition to prior history of victimization (i.e., child abuse) has a direct effect on maternal trauma sequelae. Evidence for this includes our own research that shows that even women who did not experience physical injury as a result of domestic violence exposure still have negative mental health consequences (Bogat et al., 2003; Bogat, Levendosky, DeJonghe, Davidson, & von Eye, 2004), as well as research documenting the negative mental health affects in adulthood of child abuse experiences (e.g., Arata, 1999). In addition, prior history of victimization is a risk factor for adult experiences of domestic violence (Messman-Moore, Long, & Siegfried, 2000; Sandberg, Matorin, & Lynn, 1999). This model also proposes that life events stress may influence maternal trauma sequelae. Chronic stress has been associated with adverse perinatal outcomes, and the course of PTSD also is adversely affected by the chronic stress of disadvantage (Bassuk, Dawson, Rerloff, & Weinreb, 2001; Tolman & Rosen, 2001).

In our model, one example of maternal trauma sequelae is PTSD. It may play a role beginning *in utero* because PTSD is associated with brain functioning dysregulation, as indicated by the low cortisol profiles in PTSD patients (Yehuda, 2001). Both stress and post-traumatic stress are associated with two potential mechanisms that could adversely affect pregnancy and parenting: problematic behavior and neuroendocrine alterations. PTSD is associated with problematic behaviors such as smoking and alcohol consumption. Some risk behaviors can be considered

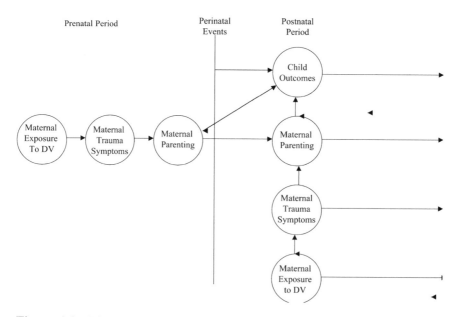

Figure 1.1 Biopsychosocial Model of the Impact of Domestic Violence on Young Children.

poor maternal caretaking because they are known to adversely affect pregnancy outcomes (Chalmers, Enkin, & Keirse, 1989). Domestic violence is associated with greater continuation of substance use despite pregnancy (Grimstad, Backe, Jacobsen, & Schei, 1998; Stevens-Simon & McAnarney, 1994) and with later initiation of prenatal care (McFarlane, Parker, Soeken, & Bullock, 1992). Delaying prenatal care results in missed opportunities for surveillance for obstetric risk and undertaking of preventive care (Merkatz, Thompson, Mullen & Goldenberg, 1990). Maternal and fetal stress modulation systems interact (Blackburn & Loper, 1992), as do maternal and infant affect regulation systems (e.g. Schore, 1994, 2001a, 2001b), such that the mother's dysregulated system could adversely affect both fetal and infant stress regulation. A mother's dysregulated emotional system may result in an impaired attachment after the child is born.

Consider a situation in which an infant is distressed. An available mother can reassure the infant. This helps the infant learn to regulate his or her emotions, and, so, over time, and under future conditions of distress, the infant is more likely to bring his or her emotions under control. Alternatively, if the mother is emotionally unavailable, under conditions of distress, she cannot help the infant modulate his or her emotions. Scheeringa and Zeanah's (1995, 2001) ongoing research shows a strong relationship between infant and caregiver post-traumatic stress disorder. Our own research documents trauma symptoms in infants exposed to domestic violence (Bogat, DeJonghe, Levendosky, von Eye, & Davidson, in press). Almost half (44 percent) of the infants exposed to domestic violence exhibited at least one trauma symptom. There were also significant relationships among infant and mother trauma symptoms, suggesting findings consonant with Scheeringa and Zeanah's (2001) theory of relational PTSD. These authors suggest that infant trauma co-occurs with mother trauma, especially in those situations in which mother's responses are not well-modulated. Young infants, who are kept in close physical proximity to their mothers might be particularly vulnerable. In addition, our findings suggest that female infants may be most vulnerable, possibly because they are held more than male infants (e.g., Benenson, Morash, & Petrakos, 1998).

PTSD appears to affect the body's stress regulation systems differently than chronic stress (Yehuda, 2001), such that levels of estrogen, progesterone, and receptor sites for oxytocin—a hormone critical to labor, lactation, maternal attachment behavior, as well as stress modulation—are altered (Liberzon et al., 1994; Liberzon & Young, 1997; Pedersen, Caldwell, Jirikowski, & Insel, 1992; Young, 1995). Severe stress in pregnancy has the potential to affect infant perinatal outcomes, including lower birth weight and preterm delivery (Murphy, Schei, Myhr, & DuMont, 2001;

Paarlberg, Vingerhoets, Passchier, Dekker, & Van Geijn, 1995). Severe stress could also disrupt hormonal influences on maternal attachment and mothering behaviors after birth (Pedersen et al., 1992).

Various child outcomes (e.g., health, attachment) could also be adversely affected by the intergenerational transmission of PTSD and its associated symptoms (e.g., anxiety). It is known that children of PTSD-affected parents (e.g., Holocaust survivors) develop PTSD symptoms and cortisol profiles similar to their parents without having been exposed to similar trauma (Yehuda, Halligan, & Bierer, 2001). This raises the question of whether PTSD-affected adults' caretaking is characterized by irritable, withdrawn, or anxious behavior, which may be traumatic for the child, or whether there is genetic and/or congenital transmission of a physiological vulnerability to PTSD (see Yehuda et al., 2000).

Our model emphasizes the important influence that maternal caretaking has on child outcomes. For example, maternal caretaking (schemas/representations and behavior) is crucial in the development of the infant's social, emotional, and cognitive functions (Schore, 2003b). The infant's development takes place within a dyadic context, during which critical aspects of brain maturation also occur (Schore, 2003b). From the development of affect synchrony in face-to-face interaction at two months of age to the development of psychological attachment by age one, the mother's ability to establish synchrony and repair asynchrony is critical to the infant's normal development. Attachment is the behavioral manifestation of internal schemas or representations of the relationship with the primary caregiver, usually the mother, and focuses on the emotional security within the context of the parent-child relationship (Bowlby, 1969; Sroufe, Carlson, Levy, & Egeland, 1999). In fact, Emde (1988, p. 32) proposed that "the emotional availability of the caregiver is the most central growth-promoting feature of the early-rearing experience."

We propose that maternal exposure to domestic violence may ultimately impair the developmental processes influencing the socioemotional functioning of the infant—for example, through relational PTSD. In addition, exposure to domestic violence may lead the mother to exhibit frightened/frightening behavior that may arouse the infant's attachment system and lead to the development of attachment disorganization (George & Solomon, 1999). Little research exists on the potential traumatic mother-child relationship in families with domestic violence; however, one study found that women who experienced severe partner violence were more likely to have children with disorganized attachment (Zeanah et al., 1999). In addition, our own work indicates that infants and young children exposed to domestic violence are likely to develop PTSD symptoms (Bogat et al., in press; Levendosky , Huth-Bocks, Semel & Shapiro, 2002).

Thus, the insecure or disorganized attachment developed in the context of the mother-child relationship then serves as a template for the child's interactions with others, including peers and teachers (Bowlby, 1969; Sroufe et al., 1999). The child then evokes particular, predictable behavior from peers and teachers based on the internalized relationship with the mother; for example, the hostility and even aggression expressed by the avoidant child discourages teacher involvement and evokes negative behavior from peers (Sroufe et al., 1999). Thus, through the trauma and resulting emotional system dysregulation, children exposed to domestic violence remain at risk for further problems in later childhood. In fact, the cumulative history of maladaptation is the strongest predictor of children's psychopathology or problems in functioning (Sroufe et al., 1999). Thus, this proposed model takes into account the potential impact of domestic violence on children, beginning during pregnancy, and transmitted through biological, social, and psychological mechanisms. It has yet to be tested. However, understanding gained through this model would help us to develop more effective intervention and prevention programs.

LACK OF KNOWLEDGE AND PROPOSED RESEARCH AGENDA

In summary, the research findings indicate that domestic violence has adverse outcomes for both women's and children's health. Research also indicates that domestic violence negatively affects parenting (maternal representations and behavior) prenatally and during early childhood. Negative effects in children are evident by age one and continue throughout early childhood. However, the mechanisms for these negative effects are not clear. In order to design the most effective intervention and prevention programs, we must have a better understanding of how and why domestic violence negatively impacts young children. The biopsychosocial model proposed above could serve as a framework for prospective longitudinal studies beginning during pregnancy and following families through early childhood.

Some important questions that we need to answer are the following: Is the timing of exposure to domestic violence (e.g., prenatal or postnatal only) important in understanding the effects of domestic violence on children's functioning? How do the mother's trauma sequelae, changing over time, influence her parenting and child outcomes? Is parenting influenced by particular characteristics of the domestic violence—for example, type of abuse, severity, chronicity? Are there characteristics of the child that interact with characteristics of the violence to influence parenting behavior? It is also important to understand whether the effects of domestic violence on young children are ameliorated if their mothers leave the violent relationships. The answers to these questions and others will help guide policy and treatment recommendations. Theoretically guided research, for example, using the model proposed, is a clear priority in this field.

PROGRAMMING AND POLICY CHANGE RECOMMENDATIONS

While the impact of domestic violence on early childhood remains an understudied area, a few clear recommendations have arisen from the findings thus far. First, it is critical to assess for domestic violence during pregnancy because of its prevalence and pervasive negative effects. At this time, however, there is evidence that domestic violence is rarely assessed or identified (American Medical Association, 1992; Naumann, Langford, Torres, Campbell, & Glass, 1999), which places women and infants at risk for future violence and further problems. Routine screening of domestic violence in prenatal health care settings and appropriate referrals and interventions for these women should be mandatory. Prenatal care providers (e.g., nurses, midwives, and doctors) need to be trained to ask about domestic violence. Research indicates that asking multiple times throughout the pregnancy, and using an interview format rather than self-administered questionnaires, increases the likelihood that women will report domestic violence (Gazmararian et al., 1996). Similar methods are likely to be more successful for women after childbirth as well. Part of this assessment should include not only physical abuse, but also sexual and psychological abuse. In addition, since the evidence has demonstrated the importance of maternal schemas for parenting and the maternal-child relationship, prenatal care providers should also be trained to discuss with the mother during pregnancy her ideas about her fetus and her feelings about parenting.

After a thorough assessment, preventive intervention work should begin prenatally with a focus on the mother's parenting schemas. Thus, prenatal care should not be limited to the physical, but also should include psychological care. Clinical work should focus on healing past traumas, as well as coping with current traumas and general distress related to the domestic violence (Groves, Lieberman, Osofsky, & Fenichel, 2000) with the eventual goal of leaving abusive relationships. Finally, clinicians may help mothers understand the origins of their own sense of helplessness and incompetence as caregivers in order to work toward building mothers' confidence and sense of competence. There are currently several models of parent-infant psychotherapy such as those described by Fraiberg (1980) and Lieberman and Pawl (1993), whereby the therapist serves as an available, empathically responsive figure who provides the opportunity for a corrective relationship experience. These models could be adapted for prenatal work.

Interventions conducted postnatally should focus on maternal schemas as well as parent-infant interactive behaviors (Groves et al., 2000; Osofsky, 1999). In the context of parent-infant psychotherapy (e.g., Fraiberg, 1980; Lieberman & Pawl, 1993), clinicians could help the mother understand her responses to and feelings toward the infant. Clinicians should also help the mother feel safe, both in the therapeutic relationship and in her everyday life, by helping to plan active, competent steps to ensure her own safety (Cassidy & Mohr, 2001; Groves et al., 2000). In addition, clinicians should help the mother understand how her own parenting behaviors may be frightening to the child (e.g., by acting aggressively or demonstrating fear of the infant), as well as help her gain empathy for her child's own fear and distress in response to the domestic violence.

It is clear that early intervention is important, given the negative effects on young children found in the research literature. One way to implement early intervention is to have a quick response when women and children are involved in the criminal justice system related to domestic violence. An excellent example of this kind of program is the Violence Intervention Program for Children and Families (Osofsky, 2004). This community intervention effort combines the services of the police, teachers, psychologists, social workers, and community agency leaders. It includes police education on the effects of domestic violence on children and families. A 24-hour hotline is available for families and police to obtain immediate referrals, guidance, or counseling. Finally, there are funds available to provide mental health treatment to children and families who do not have the resources to afford such services. Programs such as these are invaluable to the effort to reduce and eliminate the negative effects of domestic violence on young children and to prevent the cycle of violence.

REFERENCES

Alessi, J.J., & Hearn, K. (1984). Group treatment of children in shelters for battered women. In A. R. Roberts (Ed.), *Battered women and their families* (pp. 49–61). New York: Springer.

American Medical Association, Council on Ethical and Judicial Affairs. (1992). Physicians and domestic violence. *Journal of American Medical Association, 264*, 939–940.

American Psychiatric Association. (2000). *Diagnostic and statistical manual of mental disorders (4th ed – Text revision.)*. Washington, DC: Author.

Amnesty International Publications. (2001). *Broken bodies, shattered minds: Torture and ill treatment of women.* London: Alden Press.

Arata, C. M. (1999). Coping with rape: The roles of prior sexual abuse and attributions of blame. *Journal of Interpersonal Violence, 14,* 62–78.

Bassuk, E. L., Dawson, R., Rerloff, J., & Weinreb, L. (2001). Post-traumatic stress disorder in extremely poor women: Implications for health care clinicians. *Journal of the American Medical Women's Association, 56,* 79–85.

Benenson, J. F., Morash, D., & Petrakos, H. (1998). Gender differences in emotional closeness between preschool children and their mothers. *Sex Roles, 38,* 975–985.

Blackburn, S. T., & Loper, D. L. (1992). *Maternal, fetal, and neonatal physiology: A clinical perspective.* Philadelphia: W. B. Saunders Company.

Bogat, G. A., DeJonghe, E. S., Levendosky, A. A., von Eye, A., & Davidson, W. S. (in press). Trauma symptoms in infants who witness violence towards their mothers. *International Journal of Child Abuse and Neglect.*

Bogat, G. A., Levendosky, A. A., DeJonghe, E., Davidson, W. S., & von Eye, A. (2004). Pathways of suffering: The temporal effects of domestic violence on women's mental health. *Maltrattamento e abuso all'infanzia, 6*(2).

Bogat, G. A., Levendosky, A. A., Theran, S. A., von Eye, A., & Davidson, W. S. (2003). Predicting the psychosocial effects of interpersonal partner violence (IPV): How much does a woman's history of IPV matter? *Journal of Interpersonal Violence, 18,* 121–142.

Bogat, G. A., Levendosky, A. A., & von Eye, A. (2005). The future of research on intimate partner violence (IPV): Person-oriented and variable-oriented perspectives. *American Journal of Community Psychology, 36*(1/2), 49–70.

Bogat, G. A., Levendosky, A. A., von Eye, A., & Seng, J. S. (June, 2004). *DV, trauma, and caretaking: Influence on child outcomes.* Unpublished manuscript.

Bowlby, J. (1969/1982). *Attachment and loss, Vol. 1: Attachment* (2nd ed.). New York: Basic Books.

Braungart-Rieker, J., Courtney, S., & Garwood, M. M. (1999). Mother and father infant attachment: Families in context. *Journal of Family Psychology, 13*(4), 535–553.

Bureau of Justice Statistics. (1997). *Violence related injuries treated in hospital emergency departments.* Washington, DC: U.S. Department of Justice.

Caesar, P. L. (1988). Exposure to violence in the families-of-origin among wife-abusers and maritally nonviolent men. *Violence and Victims, 3*(1), 49–63.

Carlson, V., Cicchetti, D., Barnett, D., & Braunwald, K. (1989). Disorganized/disoriented attachment relationships in maltreated infants. *Developmental Psychology, 25*(4), 525–531.

Cascardi, M., & O'Leary, K. D. (1992). Depressive symptomatology, self-esteem, and self-blame in battered women. *Journal of Family Violence, 7*(4), 249–259.

Cassidy, J., & Mohr, J. J. (2001). Unsolvable fear, trauma, and psychopathology: Theory, research, and clinical considerations related to disorganized attachment across the life span. *Clinical Psychology: Science and Practice, 8*(3), 275–298.

Chalmers, I., Enkin, M., & Keirse, M.J.N.C. (1989). *Effective care in pregnancy and childbirth.* Oxford: Oxford Medical Publications.

Clarke-Stewart, K.A. (1998). Historical shifts and underlying themes in ideas about rearing young children in the United States: Where have we been? Where are we going? *Early Development and Parenting, 7*(2), 101–117.

Conger, R.D., Conger, K.J., Elder, G.H., & Lorenz, F.O. (1992). A family process model of economic hardship and adjustment of early adolescent boys. *Child Development, 63*(3), 526–541.

Conger, R.D., Conger, K.J., Elder, G.H., & Lorenz, F.O. (1993). Family economic stress and adjustment of early adolescent girls. *Developmental Psychology, 29*(2), 206–219.

Crittenden, P.M. (1985). Maltreated infants: Vulnerability and resilience. *Journal of Child Psychology and Psychiatry and Allied Disciplines, 26*(1), 85–96.

Crittenden, P.M. (1987). Non-organic failure-to-thrive: Deprivation or distortion? *Infant Mental Health Journal, 8*(1), 51–64.

Cummings, E.M., Zahn-Waxler, C., & Radke-Yarrow, M. (1981). Young children's responses to expressions of anger and affection by others in the family. *Child Development, 52*(4), 1274–1282.

Davidson, T. (1978). *Conjugal crime: Understanding and changing the wife beating pattern.* New York: Hawthorn.

Davis, L.V. & Carlson, B.E. (1987). Observation of spouse abuse: What happens to the children? *Journal of Interpersonal Violence, 2,* 278–291.

Dayton, C., Levendosky, A.A., Bogat, G.A., & Davidson, W.S. (2005). *The influence of prenatal representations on maternal parenting at one year post-partum.* Unpublished manuscript, East Lansing, MI, Michigan State University.

DeJonghe, E.S., Bogat, G.A., Levendosky, A.A., von Eye, A., & Davidson, W.S. (2005). Heightened sensitivity to adult verbal conflict in infants exposed to domestic violence. *Infant Mental Health Journal, 26,* 268–281.

Dietz, P.M., Gazmararian, J.A., Goodwin, M.M., Bruce, F.C., Johnson, C.H., & Rochat, R.W. (1997). Delayed entry into prenatal care: Effect of physical violence. *Obstetrics & Gynecology, 90*(92), 221–224.

Doumas, D., Margolin, G., & John, R.S. (1994). The intergenerational transmission of aggression across three generations. *Journal of Family Violence, 9*(2), 157–175.

Dye, T.D., Tollivert, N.J., Lee, R.V., & Kenney, C.J. (1995). Violence, pregnancy and birth outcome in Appalachia. *Paediatr Perinat Epidemiol, 9,* 35–47.

Eby, K.K., Campbell, J.C., Sullivan, C.M., & Davidson, W.S. (1995). Health effects of experiences of sexual violence for women with abusive partners. *Health Care for Women International, 16*(6), 563–576.

Eiser, C. (1990). Psychological effects of chronic disease. *Journal of Child Psychology and Psychiatry and Allied Disciplines, 31*(1), 85–98.

Elder, G.H., Conger, R.D., Foster, E.M., & Ardelt, M. (1992). Families under economic pressure. *Journal of Family Issues, 13*(1), 5–37.

Emde, R. N. (1988). Development terminable and interminable: I. Innate and motivational factors from infancy. *International Journal of Psycho-Analysis, 69*(61), 23–42.

Fantuzzo, J., Boruch, R., Beriama, A., Atkins, M., & Marcus, S. (1997). Domestic violence and children: Prevalence and risk in five major U.S. cities. *Journal of the American Academy of Child and Adolescent Psychiatry, 36*(1), 116–122.

Fantuzzo, J. W., DePaola, L. M., Lambert, L., Martino, T., Anderson, G., & Sutton, S. (1991). Effects of interparental violence on the psychological adjustment and competencies of young children. *Journal of Consulting and Clinical Psychology, 59*(2), 258–265.

Foo, L., & Margolin, G. (1995). A multivariate investigation of dating aggression. *Journal of Family Violence, 10*(4), 351–377.

Fraiberg, S. (1980). *Clinical studies in infant mental health.* New York: Basic Books.

Gaensbauer, T. J. (1982). Regulation of emotional expression in infants from two contrasting caretaking environments. *Journal of the American Academy of Child Psychiatry, 21,* 163–171.

Gaensbauer, T. J. (2002). Representations of trauma in infancy: Clinical and theoretical implications for the understanding of early memory. *Infant Mental Health Journal, 23,* 259–277.

Gazmararian, J. A., Lazorick, S., Spitz, A. M., Ballard, T. J., Saltzman, L. E., & Marks, J. S. (1996). Prevalence of violence against pregnant women. *Journal of the American Medical Association, 275*(24), 1915–1920.

George, C., & Solomon, J. (1999). Attachment and caregiving: The caregiving behavioral system. In J. Cassidy & P. R. Shaver (Eds.), *Handbook of attachment: Theory, research, and clinical applications* (pp. 649–670). New York: Guilford Press.

Goodman, L. A., Koss, M. P., Fitzgerald, L. F., Russo, N. F., & Keita, G. P. (1993). Male violence against women: Current research and future directions. *American Psychologist, 48*(10), 1054–1058.

Graham-Bermann, S. A., & Levendosky, A. A. (1998a). The social functioning of preschool age children whose mothers are emotionally and physically abused. *Journal of Emotional Abuse, 1,* 59–84.

Graham-Bermann, S. A., & Levendosky, A. A. (1998b). Traumatic stress symptoms in children of battered women. *Journal of Interpersonal Violence, 13*(1), 111–128.

Grimstad, H., Backe, B., Jacobsen, G., & Schei, B. (1998). Abuse history and health risk behaviors in pregnancy. *Acta Obstetrica Gynecologica Scandinavia, 77,* 893–897.

Groves, B. M., Lieberman, A. F., Osofsky, J. D., & Fenichel, E. (2000). Protecting young children in violent environments—A framework to build on. *Zero to Three, 20,* 9–13.

Herman, J. L. (1992). Complex PTSD: A syndrome in survivors of prolonged and repeated trauma. *Journal of Traumatic Stress, 5*(3), 377–391.

Hetherington, E. M. (1991). Presidential address: Families, lies, and videotapes. *Journal of Research on Adolescence, 1*(4), 323–348.

Hetherington, E. M. (1993). An overview of the Virginia Longitudinal Study of Divorce and Remarriage with a focus on early adolescence. *Journal of Family Psychology, 7*(1), 39–56.

Hinchey, F. S., & Gavelek, J. R. (1982). Empathic responding in children of battered mothers. *Child Abuse and Neglect, 6*(4), 395–401.

Holden, G. W., & Ritchie, K. L. (1991). Linking extreme marital discord, child rearing, and child behavior problems: Evidence from battered women. *Child Development, 62*(2), 311–327.

Holden, G. W., Stein, J. D., Ritchie, K. L., Harris, S. D., & Jouriles, E. N. (1998). Parenting behaviors and beliefs of battered women. In G. W. Holden, R. Geffner, & E. N. Jouriles (Eds), *Children exposed to marital violence: Theory, research, and applied issues.* Washington, DC: American Psychiatric Association.

Hotaling, G. T., & Sugarman, D. B. (1986). An analysis of risk markers in husband to wife violence: The current state of knowledge. *Violence and Victims, 1*(2), 101–124.

Houskamp, B. M., & Foy, D. W. (1991). The assessment of posttraumatic stress disorder in battered women. *Journal of Interpersonal Violence, 6*(3), 367–375.

Hubbs-Tait, L., Eberhart-Wright, A., Ware, L., Osofsky, J., Yocky, W., & Rusco, J. (1991). *Maternal depression and infant attachment: Behavior problems at 54 months in children of adolescent mothers.* Seattle, WA: Society for Research in Child Development.

Hughes, H. M. (1988). Psychological and behavioral correlates of family violence in child witnesses and victims. *American Journal of Orthopsychiatry, 58*(1), 77–90.

Huth-Bocks, A., Levendosky, A., & Bogat, G. A. (2002). The effects of domestic violence during pregnancy on maternal and infant health. *Violence and Victims, 17*(2), 169–185.

Huth-Bocks, A., Levendosky, A., Theran, S., & Bogat, G. (2004). The impact of domestic violence on mothers' prenatal representations of their infants. *Infant Mental Health Journal, 25*(2), 79–98.

Huth-Bocks, A. C., Levendosky, A. A., Bogat , G. A., & von Eye, A. (2004). The impact of maternal characteristics and contextual variables on infant-mother attachment. *Child Development, 75*(2), 480–496.

Jouriles, E. N., Pfiffner, L. J., & O'Leary, S. G. (1988). Marital conflict, parenting, and toddler conduct problems. *Journal of Abnormal Child Psychology, 16*(2), 197–206.

Kalmuss, D. (1984). The intergenerational transmission of marital aggression. *Journal of Marriage and the Family, 46*(1), 11–19.

Kemp, A., Green, B. L., Hovanitz, C., & Rawlings, E. I. (1995). Incidence and correlates of posttraumatic stress disorder in battered women. *Journal of Interpersonal Violence, 10*, 43–55.

Kemp, A., Rawlings, E. I., & Green, B. L. (1991). Post traumatic stress disorder (PTSD) in battered women: A shelter sample. *Journal of Traumatic Stress, 4*(1), 137–148.

Kessler, R. C., Molnar, B. E., Feurer, I. D., & Appelbaum, M. (2001). Patterns and mental health predictors of domestic violence in the United States: Results from the National Comorbidity Survey. *International Journal of Law and Psychiatry, 24,* 487–508.

Layzer, J. I., Goodson, B. D., & Delange, C. (1985). Children in shelters. *Response to the Victimization of Women & Children, 9*(2), 2–5.

Lefebvre, F., Bard, H., Veilleux, A., & Martel, C. (1988). Outcome at school age of children with birthweights of 1000 grams or less. *Developmental Medicine and Child Neurology, 30*(2), 170–180.

Lempers, J. D., Clark Lempers, D., & Simons, R. L. (1989). Economic hardship, parenting, and distress in adolescence. *Child Development, 60*(1), 25–39.

Levendosky, A. A., Bogat, G. A., Davidson, W., & von Eye, A. (2000). *Risk and protective factors for domestic violence* (Grant No. R49/CCR519519–02), Centers for Disease Control and Prevention.

Levendosky, A. A., Bogat, G. A., Theran, S. A., Trotter, J. S., von Eye, A., Davidson, W. S. (2004). The social networks of women experiencing domestic violence, *American Journal of Community Psychology, 34,* 95–109.

Levendosky, A. A., & Graham-Bermann, S. A. (1998). The moderating effects of parenting stress in woman-abusing families. *Journal of Interpersonal Violence, 13*(3), 383–397.

Levendosky, A. A., & Graham-Bermann, S. A. (2000). Parenting in battered women: A trauma theory approach. *Journal of Aggression, Maltreatment, and Trauma, 3,* 25–36.

Levendosky, A. A. & Graham-Bermann, S. A. (2001). Parenting in battered women: The effects of domestic violence on women and children. *Journal of Family Violence, 16,* 171–192.

Levendosky, A. A., Huth-Bocks, A. C., & Semel, M. A. (2002). Adolescent peer relationships and mental health in families with domestic violence. *Journal of Clinical Child Psychology, 31,* 206–218.

Levendosky, A. A., Huth-Bocks, A. C., Semel, M. A., & Shapiro, D. L. (2002). Trauma symptoms in preschool-age children exposed to domestic violence. *Journal of Interpersonal Violence, 17,* 150–164.

Levendosky, A. A., Huth-Bocks, A. C., Shapiro, D. L., & Semel, M. A. (2003). The impact of domestic violence on the maternal-child relationship and preschool-age children's functioning. *Journal of Family Psychology, 17,* 275–287.

Levendosky, A. A., Leahy, K., Bogat, G. A., Davidson, W. S., & von Eye, A. (2005). *The impact of domestic violence on parenting and one-year-old infant functioning.* Unpublished manuscript, East Lansing, MI, Michigan State University.

Levendosky, A.A., Lynch, S.M., & Graham-Bermann, S.A. (2000). Mothers' perceptions of the impact of woman abuse on their parenting. *Violence Against Women, 6,* 247–271.

Liberzon, I., Chalmers, D.T., Mansour, A., Lopez, J.F., Watson, S.J., & Young, E.A. (1994). Glucocorticoid regulation of hippocampal oxytocin receptor binding. *Brain Research, 650,* 317–622.

Liberzon I., & Young, E.A. (1997). Effects of stress and glucocorticoids on CNS oxytocin receptor binding. *Psychoneuroendocrinology, 22,* 411–422.

Lieberman, A.F. (1996). Aggression and sexuality in relation to toddler attachment: Implications for the caregiving system. *Infant Mental Health Journal, 17*(3), 276–292.

Lieberman, A.F. (1997). Toddlers' internalization of maternal attributions as a factor in quality of attachment. In L. Atkinson & K.J. Zucker (Eds.), *Attachment and psychopathology* (pp. 277–291). New York: Guilford Press.

Lieberman, A.F. (1999). Negative maternal attributions: Effects on toddlers' sense of self. *Psychoanalytic Inquiry, 19,* 737–756.

Lieberman, A.F. & Pawl, J.H. (1993). Infant-parent psychotherapy. In C. Zeanah (Ed.), *Handbook of infant mental health* (pp. 427–442). New York: Guilford Press.

Lieberman, A.F., & Van Horn, P. (1998). *Attachment, trauma, and domestic violence. Child and Adolescent Psychiatric Clinics of North America, 7,* 423–443.

Lyons-Ruth, K., Alpern, L., & Repacholi, B. (1993). Disorganized infant attachment classification and maternal psychosocial problems as predictors of hostile-aggressive behavior in the preschool classroom. *Child Development, 64*(2), 572–585.

Lyons-Ruth, K., Connell, D.B., Zoll, D., & Stahl, J. (1987). Infants at social risk: Relations among infant maltreatment, maternal behavior, and infant attachment behavior. *Developmental Psychology, 23*(2), 223–232.

Maccoby, E.E., & Martin, J.A. (1983). Socialization in the context of the family: Parent-child interaction. In E.M. Hetherington (Ed.), *Handbook of Child Psychology: Vol. 4. Socialization, Personality and Social Development.* New York: Wiley.

MacEwen, K.E. (1994). Refining the intergenerational transmission hypothesis. *Journal of Interpersonal Violence, 9*(3), 350–365.

Magdol, L., Moffitt, T.E., Caspi, A., & Silva, P.A. (1998). Developmental antecedents of partner abuse: A prospective-longitudinal study. *Journal of Abnormal Psychology, 107*(3), 375–389.

Main, M., & Solomon, J. (1990). Procedures for identifying infants as disorganized/disoriented during the Ainsworth Strange Situation. In M.T. Greenberg & D. Cicchetti (Eds.), *Attachment in the preschool years: Theory, research, and intervention.* The John D. and Catherine T. MacArthur Foundation series on mental health and development (pp. 121–160). Chicago: University of Chicago Press.

Margolin, G., & Gordis, E. (2003). Co-occurrence between marital aggression and parents' child abuse potential: The impact of cumulative stress. *Violence and Victims, 18*(3), 243–258.

McCloskey, L. A., Figueredo, A. J., & Koss, M. P. (1995). The effects of systemic family violence on children's mental health. *Child Development, 66,* 1239–1261.

McFarlane, J., Parker, B., & Soeken, K. (1996). Abuse during pregnancy: Associations with maternal health and infant birth weight. *Nursing Research, 45,* 37–42.

McFarlane, J., Parker, B., Soeken, K., & Bullock, L. (1992). Assessing for abuse during pregnancy: Severity and frequency of injuries and associated entry into prenatal care. *Journal of the American Medical Association, 267,* 3176–3178.

McLoyd, V. C. (1990). The impact of economic hardship on black families and children: Psychological distress, parenting, and socioemotional development. *Child Development, 61*(2), 311–346.

Merkatz, I. R., Thompson, J. E., Mullen, P. D., Goldenberg, R. L. (1990). *New perspectives on prenatal care.* New York: Elsevier.

Messman-Moore, T. L., Long, P. J., & Siegfried, N. J. (2000). The revictimization of child sexual abuse survivors: An examination of the adjustment of college women with child sexual abuse, adult sexual assault, and adult physical abuse. *Child Maltreatment, 5,* 18–27.

Murphy, C. C., Schei, B., Myhr, T. L., & DuMont, J. (2001). Abuse: A risk factor for low birth weight? A systematic review and meta-analysis. *Canadian Medical Association Journal, 164,* 1567–1572.

National Coalition Against Domestic Violence. (2003). *What is battering?* from *discontinuity of mothers' internal representations of their infants over time.* Unpublished manuscript, Washington, D.C.

Naumann, P., Langford, D., Torres, S., Campbell, J., & Glass, N. (1999). Women battering in primary care practice. *Family Practice, 16,* 343–352.

O'Keefe, M. (1998). Factors mediating the link between witnessing interparental violence and dating violence. *Journal of Family Violence, 13*(1), 39–57.

Osofsky, J. (1999). The impact of violence on children. *The Future of Children, 9,* 33–49.

Osofsky, J. (2004). Community outreach for children exposed to violence. *Infant Mental Health Journal, 25,* 278–287.

Paarlberg, K. M., Vingerhoets, A.J.J.M., Passchier, J., Dekker, G. A., & Van Geijn, H. P. (1995). Psychosocial factors and pregnancy outcome: A review with emphasis on methodological issues. *Journal of Psychosomatic Research, 39*(5), 563–595.

Pedersen, C., Caldwell, J., Jirikowski, G., & Insel, T. (1992). *Oxytocin in maternal, sexual, and social behaviors* (Vol. 652). New York: New York Academy of Sciences.

Pickup, F., Williams, S., & Sweetman, C. (Eds.). (2001). *Ending violence against women: A challenge for development and humanitarian work.* Oxford: Information Press.

Rennison, C. M., & Welchans, S. (2000). *Intimate partner violence.* NCJ 178247. *Hospital Emergency Departments.* Washington, DC: U.S. Department of Justice.

Rosenbaum, A., & O'Leary, K. D. (1981). Marital violence: Characteristics of abusive couples. *Journal of Consulting and Clinical Psychology, 49*(1), 63–71.

Sandberg, D. A., Matorin, A. L., & Lynn, S. J. (1999). Dissociation, posttraumatic symptomatology, and sexual revictimization: A prospective examination of mediator and moderator effects. *Journal of Traumatic Stress, 12*, 127–138.

Scheeringa, M. S., & Zeanah, C. H. (1995). Symptom expression and trauma variables in children under 48 months of age. *Infant Mental Health Journal Special Issue: Posttraumatic stress disorder (PTSD) in infants and young children, 16*(4), 259–270.

Scheeringa, M. S., & Zeanah, C. H. (2001). A relational perspective on PTSD in early childhood. *Journal of Traumatic Stress, 14*(4), 799–815.

Schei, B. (1991). Physically abusive spouse—A risk factor of pelvic inflammatory disease? *Scandinavian Journal of Primary Health Care, 9*(1), 41–45.

Schore, A. N. (1994). *Affect regulation and the origin of the self: The neurobiology of emotional development.* Hillsdale, NJ: Lawrence Erlbaum.

Schore, A. N. (2001a). Effects of a secure attachment relationship on right brain development, affect regulation, and infant mental health. *Infant Mental Health Journal, 22*(21–22), 27–66.

Schore, A. N. (2001b). The effects of early relational trauma on right brain development, affect regulation, and infant mental health. *Infant Mental Health Journal, 22*(21–22), 201–269.

Schore, A. N. (2003a). *Affect dysregulation and the disorders of the self.* New York: Norton Books.

Schore, A. N. (2003b). *Affect regulation and the repair of the self.* New York: Norton Books.

Shepherd, J. (Ed.). (1994). *Violence in health care: A practical guide to coping with violence and caring for victims.* Oxford: Oxford University Press.

Sroufe, L. A., Carlson, E. A., Levy, A. K., & Egeland, B. (1999). Implications of attachment theory for developmental psychopathology. *Development and Psychopathology, 11*, 1–13.

Stagg, V., Wills, G. D., & Howell, M. (1989). Psychopathology in early childhood witnesses of family violence. *Topics in Early Childhood Special Education, 9*(2), 73–87.

Stern, D. (1995). *The motherhood constellation: A unified view of parent-infant psychotherapy.* New York: Basic Books.

Stevens-Simon, C., & McAnarney, E. R. (1994). Childhood victimization and adolescent pregnancy outcome. *Child Abuse and Neglect, 18,* 569–575.

Straus, M.A. (1992). Sociological research and social policy: The case of family violence. *Sociological Forum, 7*(2), 211–237.

Straus, M.A., & Gelles, R. (1990). *Physical violence in American families: Risk factors and adaptation to violence in 8,145 families.* New Brunswick, NJ: Transaction.

Taggart, L., & Mattson, S. (1996). Delay in prenatal care as a result of battering in pregnancy: Cross cultural implications. *Health Care for Women International, 17*(1), 25–34.

Theran, S. A., Levendosky, A. A., Bogat, G. A., & Huth-Bocks, A. C. (2005). Stability and change in mothers' internal representations of their infants over time. *Attachment and Human Development, 7*, 253–268.

Tolman, R.M., & Rosen, D. (2001). Domestic violence in the lives of women receiving welfare: Mental health, substance dependence, and economic well-being. *Violence Against Women, 7*, 141–158.

Tomchek, S.D., & Lane, S.J. (1993). Full-term low birth weight infants: Etiology and developmental implications. *Physical and Occupational Therapy in Pediatrics, 13*(3), 43–65.

Valdez-Santiago, R., & Sanin-Aguirre, L.H. (1996). Domestic violence during pregnancy and its relationship with birth weight. *Salud. Publication Mexico, 38*, 352–362.

van Bakel, H.J.A., & Riksen-Walraven, J.M. (2002). Quality of infant parent attachment as reflected in infant interactive behaviour during instructional tasks. *Journal of Child Psychology and Psychiatry and Allied Disciplines, 43*(3), 387–394.

Vitanza, S., Vogel, L.C., & Marshall, L.L. (1995). Distress and symptoms of posttraumatic stress disorder in abused women. *Violence and Victims, 10*(1), 23–34.

Walker, L. E. (1983). Victimology and the psychological perspectives of battered women. *Victimology, 8*, 82–104.

Walker-Andrews, A.S. (1997). Infants' perception of expressive behaviors: Differentiation of multimodal information. *Psychological Bulletin, 121*(3), 437–456.

Wallender, J. L., & Varni, J. W. (1998). Effects of pediatric chronic physical disorders on child and family adjustment. *Journal of Child Psychology and Psychiatry, 39*, 29–46.

Wolfe, D.A., Jaffe, P., Wilson, S.K., & Zak, L. (1985). Children of battered women: The relation of child behavior to family violence and maternal stress. *Journal of Consulting and Clinical Psychology, 53*(5), 657–665.

Wolfe, D.A., & Wekerle, C. (1997). Pathways to violence in teen dating relationships. In D. Cicchetti & S.L. Toth (Eds.), *Developmental perspectives on trauma: Theory, research, and intervention.* Rochester symposium on developmental psychology, Vol. 8 (pp. 315–341). Rochester, NY: University of Rochester Press.

Yehuda, R. (2001). Biology of posttraumatic stress disorder. *Journal of Clinical Psychiatry, 62*, 41–46.

Yehuda, R., Bierer, L. M., Schmeidler, J., Aferiat, D. H., Breslau, I., & Dolan, S. (2000). Low cortisol and risk for PTSD in adult offspring of holocaust survivors. *American Journal of Psychiatry, 157,* 1252–1259.

Yehuda, R., Halligan, S. L., & Bierer, L. M. (2001). Relationship of parental trauma exposure and PTSD to PTSD, depressive and anxiety disorders in offspring. *Journal of Psychiatric Research, 35,* 261–270.

Young, E. A. (1995). The role of gonadal steroids in hypothalamic-pituitary-adrenal axis regulation. *Critical Reviews in Neurobiology, 9,* 371–381.

Zeanah, C. H., Carr, S., & Wolk, S. (1990). Fetal movements and the imagined baby of pregnancy: Are they related? *Journal of Reproductive and Infant Psychology, 8*(1), 23–36.

Zeanah, C. H., Danis, B., Hirshberg, L., Benoit, D., Miller, D., & Heller, S. S. (1999). Disorganized attachment associated with partner violence: A research note. *Infant Mental Health Journal, 20*(1), 77–86.

Zeanah, C. H., & Scheeringa, M. S. (1997). The experience and effects of violence in infancy. In J. D. Osofsky (Ed.), *Children in a violent society* (pp. 97–123). New York: Guilford Press.

Chapter 2

THE ROLE OF PEDIATRICIANS IN U.S. CHILD MENTAL HEALTH CARE

Sheila Gahagan and Alane Gahagan

We would like to thank my partners (S.G.) at Ypsilanti Health Center, Dr. William Chavee, Dr. Terrence Joiner, Dr. Layla Mohammed, and Dr. Sharon Swindell for their contributions to this chapter. We also thank our patients for all that we have gained in caring for them.

We dedicate this chapter to the memories of our beloved father and brother, Thomas and Brian Gahagan, who we believe would be alive today if they had had access to compassionate and competent mental health care.

INTRODUCTION

Mental health disorders in children are common, yet often go unrecognized and untreated, due to a fragmented and often inaccessible mental health "system" organized by mechanisms of payment and availability of providers, rather than by levels of care and the needs of the child (U.S. Public Health Service, 2000). Whether it is by default or by choice, pediatricians are an integral, if unofficial, source of child mental health care in the United States. Primary care physicians provide mental health services in the form of screening, diagnosis, referral, and treatment. The term primary care physician refers to pediatricians, family physicians, internists, and gynecologists who provide preventive, acute, and chronic illness care to patients who identify the physician as their regular doctor. Subspecialists in those specialties, such as cardiologists, gastroenterologists, or nephrologists typically do not provide primary care. In this chapter, we concentrate on mental health care provided by pediatricians and touch on the commonalities and differences between the care provided by pediatricians and family physicians. This chapter is based, in part, on my (S.G.) experience as a practicing primary care pediatrician in four culturally diverse, low-income communities over 20 years and as an academic, developmental-behavioral pediatrician with responsibility for pediatric resident training. My experience as a pediatrician on the Navajo reservation (1984–1989) working within the Indian Health Service, a single payor health system, continues to influence my public health perspective. The coauthor is my sister, a child psychotherapist, who treats children in an inpatient mental health care setting. Her experience in caring for children who have often had inadequate evaluation and treatment prior to hospitalization and in arranging outpatient mental health services for her patients (at the time of discharge) highlights the current crisis in mental health care for children as well as the importance of the role of the pediatrician.

PEDIATRICIANS PROVIDE MENTAL HEALTH CARE TO MANY CHILDREN IN THE UNITED STATES

There are approximately 60,000 pediatricians in the United States, serving 85 million children from birth to 21 years of age, of whom 7–12 million have a mental health disorder at any point in time. The average pediatric practitioner cares for a patient panel of 1,500 patients (Bocian, Wasserman, Slora, Kessel, & Miller, 1999) . Access to pediatric care varies by geographic location with 92 percent of pediatricians practicing in urban areas. The ratio of primary care physicians to children is 1/8,300 in rural areas compared to 1/2,500 in cities (Randolph & Pathman, 2001). Based on these numbers, the average pediatrician in an urban practice could expect to have 150 to 300 patients, each with a diagnosable, mental health disorder. Pediatricians practicing in rural areas may be called upon to provide care for more children with a broad range of cognitive, emotional, behavioral, and mental disorders.

Mental health disorders in children are common and demand attention from primary care physicians. In a recent study of 21,150 visits to 401 pediatricians (from primarily urban U.S. practices), the physicians identified mental health or behavioral problems in *one quarter* of the children, ranging from self-limited to severe and debilitating (Rushton, Bruckman, & Kelleher, 2002) . Examples of self-limited problems include infant sleep problems, adaptation to a new sibling, problem toddler behavior such as temper tantrums, and adolescent limit-testing. While almost all children with an identified psychosocial problem were initially managed by the primary care physician, 16.2 percent were referred to a mental health provider at the initial visit, and 27.4 percent were referred at either the initial or follow-up visit. Therefore, approximately 7 percent of this unselected sample of children were referred for mental health services. In addition to identification and referral, the pediatricians provided counseling (33.4 percent), medication (32.2 percent), and watchful waiting. They were most likely to provide counseling and/or medication for the children who were referred for mental health services. This finding suggests that the children did not have immediate access to mental health care.

In contrast to the relative abundance of pediatricians, child psychiatrists are an elite group. There are 6,500 members of the American Academy of Child and Adolescent Psychiatry (AACAP), some of whom are general psychiatrists with an interest in child and adolescent psychiatry. The ratio of members of the AACAP to children in the United States is 1/13,000. Geographic maldistribution is an even greater problem for psychiatrists than for pediatricians, with child and adolescent psychiatrists being concentrated in urban areas and more affluent communities. For example, there are approximately 18.9 child psychiatrists per 100,000 youths in Massachusetts compared to 0.8 child psychiatrists per 100,000 youths in Mississippi (Thomas & Holzer, 1999) . Prevalence rates for serious emotional disturbance are twice as high in low socioeconomic groups as in high socioeconomic groups. Therefore, the tendency for child psychiatrists to work in metropolitan centers and areas with lower rates of child poverty exacerbates the poor access to mental health services for the neediest children.

While child mental health services are provided by social workers, psychologists, and mental health technicians, prescribing of psychopharmacologic agents requires a medical license (M.D., D.O., nurse practitioner, or physician's assistant) (Jellinek, Patel, & Froehle, 2002). Therefore, in many low-income or rural communities, pediatricians are heavily called upon to prescribe medication for children with attention deficit hyperactivity disorder (ADHD), depression, pervasive developmental disorders, and sleep disorders. Pediatricians are therefore integral providers in the system of care for children with mental health disorders in the United States. We will explore the strengths, weaknesses, and opportunities inherent in the role of the pediatrician as one type of mental health provider for U.S. children.

SCREENING AND IDENTIFICATION OF MENTAL HEALTH DISORDERS

The pediatrician is commonly the first professional to know that a child is suffering emotional distress. There are three reasons that this is true. (1) Pediatricians see children and their families frequently in the first years of life. (2) Pediatricians screen for developmental and behavioral disorders. (3) Families often feel comfortable disclosing a mental health concern to a known and trusted pediatrician.

Pediatricians providing primary health care are well acquainted with the families in their practice. Health care maintenance visits are scheduled six times in the first year of life and three times in the second year of life. Most children make yearly "well child visits" thereafter, which are augmented by numerous sick visits for colds, ear infections, injuries, etc. During these crucial early months, the pediatrician may be the first to identify a regulatory disorder in the infant, such as primary excessive crying, a feeding disorder, or a sleep problem. Pediatricians also have a window into a family's coping style in meeting the challenges of their infant's temperament and adaptation to life. The pediatrician is often aware of maternal depression as well as other family mental health disorders, including substance abuse and family violence. The relationship forged between pediatrician and parents during the dynamic period of early growth and development provides a foundation on which to promote infant and family mental health (Jellinek et al., 2002). Pediatricians are therefore well situated to screen for and identify mental health disorders in the children and families in their practice.

Screening for developmental and behavioral problems is now a routine component of pediatric practice. The Accreditation Council for Graduate Medical Education (ACGME) requires that pediatric residents have adequate training to recognize internal and external determinants of behavior as well as to identify normal and abnormal child mental health (ACGME, 2003). During the three-year post-medical school training, pediatric residents develop skills in child and parent interviewing and the use of psychosocial and developmental screening instruments. Behavioral counseling is a core competency requirement for certification. Pediatricians are expected to differentiate behavior problems appropriate for pediatric management from those appropriate for referral to mental health specialists. In addition, pediatricians in training learn about community agencies, including early intervention, special education, community mental health, and child abuse and prevention services. Screening for mental health disorders in the pediatric office is performed by open-ended questions, targeted questions about specific behaviors, and the use of specific screening tools. Most important for identification of mental health problems in children is the availability of the pediatrician as a professional with whom a parent can discuss even the most trivial concern. Pediatricians must know when to reassure and when to proceed with assessment. Ideally, reassurance is not offered before a concern is given serious consideration through interview and the use of appropriate evaluation instruments.

When a family suspects that their child needs mental health evaluation, they are often confused about where to seek help. The primary care physician is known to the family and in many communities is highly trusted and admired. Families often feel that there is lower stigma attached to addressing these problems with their own doctor than that associated with going to a psychiatrist or other mental health professional. Furthermore, many families are unwilling to go to an identified mental health facility, yet will accept mental health services from their pediatrician or from a mental health professional in the pediatrician's office. The stigma of mental illness is related to an ancient, yet still pervasive, belief that mental illness is a sign of poor character, weakness, or a bad family (Brunton, 1997; Hirschfeld et al., 1997). Parents often feel extreme guilt about their child's mental illness, believing that if they had parented differently their child would be well (Pejlert, 2001; Singh, 2004). Pediatricians are ideally situated to help families understand the interplay of genetic predisposition to mental illness and external stressors that can trigger these problems. Families can be helped to understand which stressors are within and which are beyond their control, giving families the power to help their child and to accept the reality that some life circumstances are not of their own making.

The role of the pediatrician as first responder and coordinator of mental health services is supported by pediatric advocacy for a "Medical Home" for all children. In 1992, the American Academy of Pediatrics (AAP) defined the Medical Home as care in a "partnership of mutual responsibility and trust" by a well-trained primary care physician known to the child and family in a setting that is "accessible, continuous, comprehensive, family-centered, coordinated, compassionate and culturally effective" (American Academy of Pediatrics, 2002). The physician and staff, within the Medical Home, manage and facilitate all aspects of pediatric care, including mental health care. While there are many barriers to achieving this goal, the Medical Home is highly desirable for quality of care and cost containment. The Medical Home increases both patient satisfaction and professional reward, but it requires adequate staffing for care coordination and a health care system that allows and reimburses mental health screening, assessment, treatment, and care coordination in the primary care setting.

ARE PEDIATRICIANS PART OF THE MENTAL HEALTH SYSTEM?

Pediatricians identify children with mental health disorders according to family concern, school report, or by screening. When a concern is raised, the physician categorizes the concern into: (1) normal variant; (2) a behavioral problem linked to family functioning or external stressors; or (3) a mental health disorder that is intrinsic or of genetic origin (see Figure 2.1). This is obviously an oversimplification because intrinsic disorders are triggered by environmental conditions. Most pediatricians provide care for children who have behavioral concerns, but without frank mental health disorder. For children with behavior disorders, the pediatrician considers whether the condition is of low or high severity (see Figure 2.2). Low-severity conditions are often managed by the pediatrician, although additional mental health counseling or consultation may be required. High-severity conditions are referred to a mental health professional. It is at this point that the pediatrician struggles alongside the family to access appropriate services for a child, from a system that is not organized to provide easily accessible compassionate care to those who need it most.

In the United States, mental health care is provided by a variety of professionals who work through privately or publicly funded systems.

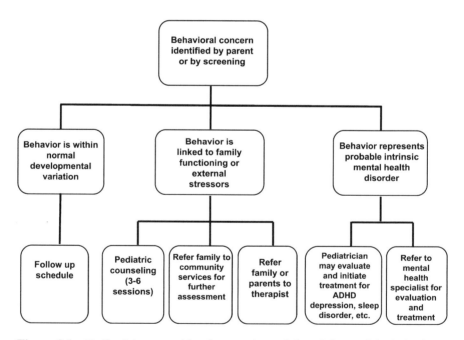

Figure 2.1 Pediatricians consider the severity and the etiology of the behavioral concern in deciding whether to provide evaluation or treatment services in the pediatric office or to refer to a mental health specialist for further evaluation and/or treatment.

At the most private level, individuals with unlimited resources can pay fee-for-service for evaluation and treatment from psychiatrists, psychologists, and social workers. While this system is common for mental health providers, pediatricians rarely provide mental health services through personally paid fee-for-service. For most children, mental health services are financed through insurance, primarily purchased by their parents' employers. Insurance companies typically contract separately for physical and mental health services, perpetuating the Western medical supposition that mental and physical health function separately, without interaction (Kleinman, 1995). This practice of funding mental health separately (often referred to as a mental health carve out) creates difficulty for pediatric reimbursement for mental health services. In many insurance systems, pediatricians are not reimbursed for mental health counseling and medication management even for common mental health disorders such as ADHD and depression. The insurance agency typically pays a set contracted fee to the mental health provider. This system actually forces rationing of services due to underestimation of the need for child mental

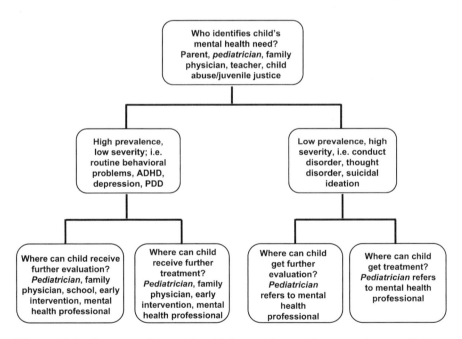

Figure 2.2 System of care for high-prevalence, low-severity conditions, including routine childhood behavioral problems, ADHD, and depression, and low-prevalence, high-severity conditions, including conduct disorder, thought disorder, and suicidal ideation.

health services. A system designed to meet the needs of children would reimburse care for high-prevalence, low-severity mental health disorders by a skilled pediatrician in a comfortable setting, close to home.

Children with private insurance usually have access to mental health providers designated by the insurance company. This fragments service from the pediatrician's perspective. An ideal system for delivering child mental health care would allow the pediatrician to select a known and highly regarded mental health provider. Because most pediatricians care for children from a variety of different health plans, the physician does not personally know the mental health professional to whom they are referring. Furthermore, many health plans require that patients self-refer into mental health services, eliminating the pediatrician's ability to directly communicate concerns about the child (except through a written referral). This organizational structure isolates pediatricians and interferes with collaboration in the care received by the children with serious mental illness. A study of child mental health referral by primary care physicians found that there was direct communication in only 12 percent of referrals (Rushton et al., 2002; Rushton, Clark, & Freed, 2000). Just as communication from pediatrician to mental health professional is problematic, communication back from mental health provider to pediatrician is often lacking. Because mental health records are highly confidential, pediatricians often receive no information about their patient's progress until they are asked to prescribe psychoactive medication for the child's ongoing treatment.

Publicly funded mental health programs for children on Medicaid or state child health insurance programs are organized by community mental health agencies in most states. This adds to the complexity of the system for pediatricians who care for children from several different counties. Knowing where to refer for each county may be difficult; personally knowing the providers at each of the agencies may be impossible. Identifying mental health services for children without insurance is extremely difficult. Therefore, pediatricians provide some mental health services to uninsured children for little or no reimbursement.

In an ideal health care system, pediatricians and other first responders would have access to mental health professionals of varying levels of expertise, specialty, and skill within a geographical accessible area, organized around the needs of the child. For example, a child with poor school performance after the death of a parent could be referred to a child psychotherapist with expertise in grief. Another child with longstanding school failure and minor neurologic findings could be referred, first, to a neuropsychologist for evaluation. A third child with social difficulties that interfere with school performance and a family history of obsessive compulsive disorder (OCD) could be referred to a psychiatrist with interest and expertise in the evaluation and treatment of OCD. The ideal system would promote and facilitate communication between professionals at every level of care.

INTERFACE BETWEEN PEDIATRICIANS AND PSYCHIATRIC HOSPITAL PATIENTS

From the perspective of the inpatient mental health service provider, there is often a treatment gap between care in the hospital and what is needed in the community at discharge. Pediatricians can (and often do) provide services that ensure continuation of care during the period after psychiatric hospitalization. Due to the shortage of child psychiatrists, patients are often subjected to long waiting periods for routine follow-up visits for monitoring of psychotropic medications prescribed in the hospital. At discharge from inpatient care, a child is typically required to have an outpatient psychotherapy appointment within one week and a physician's appointment within one month. Inpatient hospitalization often gives priority status, allowing a child to leapfrog the extensive waiting list of overburdened outpatient mental health clinics. However, all too often, a clinic cannot guarantee essential medication management within the first month after discharge. The following example shows the importance of pediatric collaboration in arranging post hospital care for a boy with a serious mental health disorder.

Recently the mother of A.B., an 11-year-old boy with a psychotic disorder who had been discharged one month previously, called the inpatient therapist asking if she could obtain a prescription for the boy's antipsychotic medication. She informed the therapist that she could not get a psychiatry appointment at her outpatient clinic for two more months. The clinic was contacted and echoed this request to the hospital psychiatrist. Unfortunately, the psychiatric facility was not local to the family, who had no transportation except for the weekly hospital bus which was not scheduled to make the trip before the prescription had expired. The hospital therapist contacted the boy's pediatrician who had been involved in the child's referral to the hospital. The pediatrician stated that he felt comfortable caring for him until the start of outpatient psychiatric treatment. Since the mother had a long-term trusting relationship with the pediatrician, and the pediatrician was interested in forming a partnership with A.B.'s mental health team, a successful solution resulted.

Children coming out of inpatient psychiatric hospitalization have more severe mental health problems than those typically treated by pediatricians. Many of these children possess co-morbid diagnoses that require intricate and often changing formulations of medications. It is therefore understandable that many pediatricians feel that the ongoing mental health treatment of these children is out of their realm. However, some patients do well with a discharge plan of psychotherapy plus medication management by a pediatrician who is well versed in mental health care. This is especially true when the psychiatric disturbance is coupled with physical symptoms. The following example illustrates the importance of pediatric collaboration in the care of a child with a mental health disorder that affected her physical health.

K.L. was a 10-year-old girl referred for inpatient psychiatric care when she was seen at her pediatrician's office for complete food refusal over a period of one month. The parents were reluctant to allow inpatient treatment, insisting on finding a physical cause for her problem. During the inpatient stay, K.L. was diagnosed with an anxiety disorder and responded well to treatment. Upon discharge, a therapist who specialized in anxiety and phobias in children was located for continued outpatient treatment. In this case, it was appropriate for K.L. to continue monthly visits to her pediatrician for medication and for monitoring her weight and other physical concerns. The treatment initially went very well.

A sad postscript highlights the complexity of caring for children with mental illness and their families. K.L. ultimately left both the therapist's and the pediatrician's care due to her parents' inability to accept a mental illness diagnosis as the cause of their daughter's problems. In a follow-up call by the inpatient therapist, the mother reported that a "Lyme disease specialist" had diagnosed K.L. with Lyme disease. The family now believed that this accounted for all of her symptoms, even though Lyme disease had been considered and ruled out by the pediatrician, as well as by the hospital medical staff, during her inpatient treatment. The stigma of mental illness and mental health treatment was certainly an important component in this turn of events. One can only hope that if K.L. needs further mental health treatment, their good experiences with the pediatrician and the successful inpatient mental health treatment will allow the family to resume appropriate mental health care.

In severely emotionally disturbed (SED) children, physical and mental well-being is intertwined in a fragile balance. SED children are at greater risk for physical problems due to psychosocial factors in their lives (Cohen, Pine, Must, Kasen, & Brook, 1998). They are also at increased risk for injuries due to dangerous behaviors related to their psychological condition. Pediatricians who are alert to these co-morbidities can play an important role in assuring that these children get needed care before and after hospitalization.

SUPPORT, GUIDANCE, AND CONTINUING EDUCATION FOR PEDIATRICIANS PROVIDING MENTAL HEALTH SERVICES

The past decade has seen the development of new resources and tools to support the primary care physician in the provision of evidence-based mental health services. Many organizations have provided technical assistance and support in this endeavor. The AAP has been a leader in this endeavor by including mental health topics in all general continuing education activities and offering pediatric conferences with specific mental health focus dedicated to improving the physical and mental health of children and adolescents through the promotion of research, teaching, and clinical practice in developmental and behavioral pediatrics. The AAP was a partner with 52 other organizations in the development of the two-volume *Bright Futures in Practice: Mental Health Practice Guide and Tool Kit* (Jellinek, Patel, & Froehle, 2002). This initiative was funded by the Maternal and Child Health Bureau and the U.S. Department of Health and Human Services, confirming that in today's complex society many problems brought to primary health care professionals are related to developmental, psychosocial, and specific mental health problems. This resource provides tools to assist the busy health professional in identifying, evaluating, and sometimes treating child mental health disorders.

In addition, the AAP, in partnership with the National Initiative for Child Health Quality developed an ADHD toolkit for primary care physicians that contains evaluation instruments, forms for communicating with school personnel, and resources for families (AAP, 2002). Methods to assist families in establishing behavioral goals for the child at home and at school are included. Behavioral strategies and psychopharmacological treatments are documented and agreed upon by the child, parent, and physician. The toolkit provides a structure for tracking the child's response to intervention.

The Society for Developmental and Behavioral Pediatrics has 750 members who promote the training of pediatricians to provide high-quality care for children with behavioral concerns and disorders. The inaugural board certifying exam was offered in November 2002, resulting in the first pediatricians with subspecialty certification in Developmental-Behavioral (D-B) Pediatrics. D-B pediatricians provide subspecialty pediatric care for children with behavioral problems including ADHD, depression, disorders of feeding and sleeping, and developmental problems including autism, cerebral palsy, and language and sensory disorders. Children who have chronic symptoms such as headaches, constipation, and bed-wetting are also commonly treated by D-B pediatricians. The work of D-B pediatricians overlaps with that of several other subspecialists, including child neurologists, specialists in pediatric physical medicine and rehabilitation, and child psychiatrists. D-B pediatricians often care for children who have both biomedical and behavioral disorders.

Another example of a Continuing Medical Education (CME) program directly aimed at improving pediatricians' skill in caring for children with behavioral disorders is the Maternal Child Health Bureau–funded Collaborative Office Rounds . This forum for pediatricians to partner with psychiatrists in small discussion groups is regarded as the most beneficial and satisfying of all continuing medical education venues by the participants, many of whom have been participating for over a decade.

FAMILY PHYSICIANS PROVIDE MENTAL HEALTH SERVICES FOR CHILDREN AND ADOLESCENTS

Family physicians (physicians with three years of post–medical school residency training in the care of the entire family) have a scope of practice similar to that of pediatricians in child mental health. They are involved in screening, evaluation, referral, and treatment of children with mental illness. Their residency and continuing medical education training differs from that of pediatricians in being more focused on family systems. This can be a strong advantage for understanding both the etiology of a behavioral disorder and in implementing management strategies appropriate for a particular family. Family physicians may also have a stronger bias toward a biopsychosocial model of health than many pediatricians. On the other hand, the training of family physicians in specific child mental health disorders is extremely variable depending largely on the faculty in their residency program and the availability in their area of high-quality continuing medical education in child mental health (Rushton et al., 2000).

A study of self-reported management strategies for child and adolescent depression by pediatricians and family physicians (in North Carolina) found that both specialties were likely to refer depressed youth for treatment in the mental health system (Rushton et al., 2000). However, family physicians were at least twice as likely as pediatricians to prescribe serotonin reuptake inhibitors (SSRIs) for adolescents in their practice (18 percent versus 9 percent) and were often comfortable prescribing medication prior to referral into the mental health system. Most pediatricians in the survey had never prescribed SSRIs and cited inadequate time available as a barrier to treating depression in the office. We suspect that family physicians have become comfortable prescribing SSRIs in adults and therefore feel confident about their ability to treat depression in their adolescent patients. Conversely, pediatricians have little experience prescribing SSRIs during training or practice.

Evidence-based guidelines for evaluation and treatment of ADHD were published by the AAP in 2000 and 2001. These guidelines were also published in the *American Family Physician* in 2001. A study of 723 Michigan primary care physicians, equally divided between pediatricians and family physicians, found that most physicians in both specialties were aware of the published guidelines. However, pediatricians were more likely than family physicians to be familiar with the recommendations and to have incorporated them into their practice (Rushton, Fant, & Clark, 2004). It is possible that the time from dissemination of these guidelines to implementation in practice will take longer in family physicians' practices because a smaller percentage of their practice is devoted to children and there are many competing demands for their attention.

EXAMPLES OF MENTAL HEALTH CONDITIONS THAT COMMONLY PRESENT TO THE PEDIATRICIAN'S OFFICE

Infantile Colic

Infantile colic or primary excessive crying is an example of a biobehavioral condition that requires the primary care physician to think about biomedical etiologies, infant regulatory disorders, and family psychosocial functioning in order to provide optimal care for the infant and family. Infants and their families rarely enter a designated mental health system for excessive crying, and therefore primary care physicians and visiting nurses provide most of the care for this condition. While infantile colic is sometimes related to food intolerance, hunger, or pain, most often it is "idiopathic," meaning that there is no identified medical cause (Barr, Hopkins, & Green, 2000). Parental knowledge about normal infant crying and expectations for their own parenting and the infant's behavior are important determinants of their current and ultimate perceptions of their child and themselves. When pediatricians take excessive crying as an opportunity to address psychosocial functioning of the family, they signal that mental health functioning is part of the realm of pediatric practice and that the family can bring future similar concerns to their attention.

Care for colic involves evaluating the family for contributing causes, including parental exhaustion, depression, and stress. It is important that pediatricians have a plan for intervention when a psychosocial contributor is identified. Pediatric counseling can help the family identify mechanisms by which to get extra help and support, to reduce demands at home and at work, and to take practical actions such as sleeping when the baby sleeps.

Failure To Thrive

Failure to thrive is another condition that challenges pediatricians to think about biomedical, psycho-developmental, and family functioning in an integrated way. While few cases of failure to thrive relate to serious diseases such as cystic fibrosis and celiac disease,[1] even fewer are caused by outright child neglect or starvation. Almost all cases of failure to thrive relate to an infant or toddler who is vulnerable to developing poor feeding in a family that does not understand, interpret, or respond appropriately to his or her needs (Gahagan & Holmes, 1998). The pediatrician takes a comprehensive approach to understand the child's health status and possible underlying medical conditions and to simultaneously understand the family's economic, social, and psychological health.

Maternal depression is a common contributing condition to failure to thrive (Singer, Song, Hill, & Jaffe, 1990). The mechanism that leads to poor feeding in the child relates to the mother's lack of awareness and inability to interpret the baby's hunger cues and perhaps her lack of energy to respond. In the most severe cases, the mother may not care that the infant is hungry or may have altered perceptions of ideal body habitus for an infant. Even more common than maternal depression is a layering of multiple minor conditions that predispose the infant to poor feeding, including prematurity, recurrent ear infections, early gastroesophageal reflux, infection, or discomfort combined with a vulnerable family environment. A family may be vulnerable because of work demands, attention to other children, life stress, or mental health disorders. The pediatrician learns about various risk factors and helps the family to understand the infant's need for greater nutrition. Together with the family, the pediatrician begins to understand the barriers operating to prevent the child from attaining adequate calories. The infant may have developed feeding refusal, which will require that the parents use highly skilled feeding strategies.

Preschool-age children may have internal psychodynamic reasons for refusing food. For example, a four-year-old boy whose sister had cancer consumed inadequate amounts of food. It was difficult to determine whether he felt guilty for being well or whether food refusal was a strategy to get some of his parents' attention away from his sister. As in the previous discussion of primary excessive crying, the pediatrician may need to refer the family of a child with failure to thrive to a mental health provider. Accessing appropriate services is often difficult. Ideally, a child with failure to thrive is cared for by a pediatrician who is expert in growth, a mental health professional who understands family systems and disorders of attachment, and a professional who can work directly with the family to train the child to eat in an age-appropriate manner. Disordered eating is often seriously entrenched. One of the obvious problems with the current organization of physical and mental health is that children with failure to thrive need intervention from professionals in both medical and mental health specialties. Because the health financing systems separate these professionals, it is very difficult to build collaborative partnerships and teams that bridge these complex biopsychosocial needs.

Maternal Depression

Maternal depression, including postpartum depression, is associated with the following adverse child health and developmental outcomes: lower cognitive function; somatic symptoms, including headache and stomachache; and increased risk for child maltreatment (Downey & Coyne, 1990; Field, 1995; Galler, Harrison, Ramsey, et al., 2000; Gelfand & Teti, 1990; Hay, et al., 2001). Maternal depression is common when children are young. Depressive symptoms are reported in 5 to 25 percent of women during the postpartum period and in 20 percent of women whose children are not yet in elementary school (Georgiopoulos, Bryan, Wollan, & Yawn, 2001; Nielsen Forman, Videbech, Hedegaard, Dalby Salvig, & Secher, 2000; O'Hara, 1996; Yonkers et al., 2001). While the risk is increased in unmarried, minority, lower-income/-education women and those who have positive drug screens, maternal depression occurs in women of all races and socioeconomic levels (Flynn, Davis, Marcus, Cunningham, & Blow, 2004; Kemper & Babonis, 1992).

Maternal depression is easily ascertained at child medical visits. This is true for health care maintenance, emergency care, and ill visits. Seeking care in the emergency room and multiple doctor visits for minor complaints (in addition to health care maintenance) may indicate maternal anxiety or depression (Flynn et al., 2004). Ascertainment is greatly enhanced by the use of screening tools at specific visits, including the six-week newborn visit and yearly visits for the first three years. For example, the Edinburgh Postnatal Depression Scale has been proposed as a well-standardized instrument for routine use at the six-week newborn visit . The response to a positive depression screen or concern about the mother's affect or symptoms should lead to referral for further evaluation and treatment. Ideally, the pediatrician would have an identified mental health provider to call in the case of suspected maternal depression. Because the current system is complicated and fragmented, it is common for pediatricians to suggest that the parent call the mental health number on their insurance card for access to care. This impersonal approach leaves the pediatrician out of the initial communication with the mental health provider. Another approach is to suggest that the mother seek care from her own physician. There are pitfalls to each of these approaches. A seriously depressed woman may not have the energy to pursue the pediatrician's suggestions. Therefore, it would be preferable for an appointment to be made at the time of a positive screen. Pediatricians should be well-versed in treatment options in order to explain how treatment will help mother and baby.

In addition to referral, some treatment begins in the pediatrician's office. Professional support is a form of treatment that pediatricians are qualified to provide. This includes weekly follow-up phone calls or visits. Helping the mother identify sources of support (both informal and professional) is a simple intervention easily employed by pediatricians. Some pediatricians, particularly those with developmental-behavioral pediatric training, can provide cognitive behavioral or brief solution-focused therapy. Rarely, some pediatricians prescribe antidepressant medication for the mother as a temporizing measure until she accesses mental health care. Suicide risk associated with starting SSRIs as well as excretion of psychotropic medications in breast milk are important concerns when initiating psychopharmacologic treatment in the pediatrician's office. Furthermore, antidepressant action does not begin for several weeks. Therefore, beginning medication could create an unwarranted sense of security. Screening, referral, and supportive treatment for maternal depression may be the most important mental health treatment offered by pediatricians.

Attention Deficit Hyperactivity Disorder

ADHD is the most common mental health disorder cared for by pediatricians. It is a high-prevalence condition, with 5 to 10 percent of children 4 to 15 years old exhibiting symptoms of hyperactivity, inattention, and or distractibility. Published guidelines and practical tools for providing evidence-based care in the primary care setting have improved the quality of care given in the primary care setting and increased the number of pediatricians who feel qualified to provide this care (American Academy of Pediatrics, 2000). More than half of children diagnosed with ADHD are never evaluated or treated by a mental health professional (Hoagwood, Kelleher, Feil, & Comer, 2000). My primary care pediatric partners report feeling more comfortable evaluating and treating children for ADHD than they do evaluating and treating other mental health disorders, including depression, bipolar disorder, oppositional defiant disorder, and conduct disorder (Joiner, Mohammed, & Swindell, 2005). This is a reflection of the high prevalence of ADHD, the excellent treatment guidelines and assessment and monitoring tools, and the excellent response to treatment of children with uncomplicated ADHD.

Unfortunately, it is very challenging for a pediatrician to create an office system that allows appropriate time for each step of ADHD evaluation and treatment. Pediatric visits range from 7 minutes for acute visits to 20 minutes for health care maintenance visits. Initial evaluation of ADHD in mental health settings can take from two and a half to eight hours (Robin, 1998). A streamlined approach has been described for primary care settings, which calls for two 45-minute visits (Block, 1998). Additional time is needed for scoring of parent and teacher checklists that collect the behavioral history in a standardized format. Some practices use ancillary personnel to assist in the collection, scoring, and collation of the assessment packet. A recent study of this practice found that scoring required approximately 41 minutes and contacting parents and teachers to prompt them to return their packets took approximately 20 minutes per patient (Leslie, Weckerly, Plemmons, Landsverk, & Eastman, 2004).

Poor reimbursement for ADHD evaluation and treatment perpetuates the practice of scheduling inadequate time for appropriate evaluation, patient education, and counseling. Even as many pediatricians struggle to learn the proper diagnostic codes for billing and how to bill for using diagnostic tools, some health insurance plans do not pay primary care physicians at all for evaluation and treatment of mental health conditions, including ADHD. Adequate reimbursement is the solution to time constraints in the pediatric practice. If a pediatrician is reimbursed for a mental health visit at a level equivalent to reimbursement for five or six acute care visits (such as for colds and ear infections), then an hour can be justified for the mental health visit.

In addition to time constraints and reimbursement problems, pediatricians cite other barriers to providing excellent quality of care to children with ADHD. Collaborating with schools is challenging because of communication barriers. The medical and educational professions may have differing goals and perspectives relating to child behavior and psychosocial functioning. The physician must carefully adhere to diagnostic criteria and this may create frustration for teachers and other educators. Another barrier to high quality care of children with ADHD in the primary care office is that these children often have co-morbid mental health conditions, including tic disorders, oppositional defiant disorder, and learning disabilities. The pediatrician may not have adequate training to consider these diagnoses. Furthermore, when these diagnoses are present, the child may not have access to adequate mental health services for their care. For some pediatricians, the fear of missing an important diagnosis is a barrier to including the care of ADHD in their practice. Some children with ADHD need behavioral therapy, and most pediatricians do not have training in psychotherapy, family systems therapy, or cognitive behavioral therapy.

When the counseling needs are greater than typical pediatric counseling, it may be difficult to access appropriate therapy for the child.

Another difficulty for the pediatrician and family in the care of children with ADHD is that the commonly used stimulant medications are highly controlled by the U.S. Drug Enforcement Agency. This means that the patient is required to present for a medication refill each month. The pediatrician is faced with the dilemma of requiring a brief visit and billing the patient (or the insurance company) each month, or writing a prescription without monitoring the patient or getting reimbursed for the care. This is very difficult for families, as even presenting to the office to pick up a prescription may necessitate missing work and school. It would certainly be preferable for patients who are doing well on medication to allow refills for six months' duration. However, because of the small abuse potential of stimulant medications, the law requires monthly prescribing.

Child and Adolescent Depression

Adolescent depressive symptoms are common and increase with age. A school-based study of 11- to 15-year-old children found that one in six U.S. youths reported depressive symptoms, and the prevalence of these symptoms increased between sixth and tenth grade (Saluja et al., 2004). Girls were more likely than boys to report depressive symptoms (34.3 percent versus 13.6 percent in the tenth grade). Suicidal ideation is also common in teens, with 24 percent of teens in grades 9 through 12 indicating that they had seriously considered attempting suicide during the previous 12 months (American Academy of Pediatrics, Committee on Adolescence, 2000). Despite the fact that depressive symptoms and suicidal ideation are commonly reported by adolescents, the vast majority of pediatricians do not feel adequately trained in the management of childhood depression. In a recent survey of 595 primary care pediatricians in North Carolina, approximately one third reported that "managing depression is too time-consuming for my office schedule" (Rushton et al., 2000). Responding to a national survey of pediatricians, 90 percent agreed that "recognizing childhood and adolescent depression" is their responsibility (Olson et al., 2001). While there are no population-based studies evaluating actual ascertainment of depression in the pediatric primary care practice, published reports suggest that only a fraction of child and adolescent depression is identified in this venue (Costello et al., 1998). Despite pediatricians' intent to identify depression, some practices do not routinely screen for depressive symptoms at health care maintenance visits. Unfortunately, some adolescents never present for routine visits. However, the primary care pediatrician does have contact with most adolescents, as 70 percent are seen each year by a primary care provider for a health care maintenance, acute care, or chronic illness visit (Singh, 2002). Adolescents who do receive some primary care each year come to the doctor an average of three times per year. So efforts at uniform screening in primary care practices or in schools would go a long way toward identifying this common adolescent disorder.

There are other barriers to care of depressed adolescents in the primary care pediatrician's office. In addition to inadequate training, time pressure, and lack of routine visits for many adolescents, pediatricians are often poorly reimbursed for this service. Furthermore, the systems of mental health care are complex, and pediatricians often have difficulty assisting adolescents in accessing caring behavioral health services. Pediatricians are less likely to actively screen for a condition if they do not know exactly how to treat or where to refer. Depression currently fits into this category for many pediatricians.

While pediatricians have become increasingly comfortable prescribing psychopharmacologic agents for ADHD, they do not have the same level of comfort prescribing antidepressants (Rushton, Clark, & Freed, 2000). New concerns about increased suicide risk with antidepressants, and general heightened fears about the safety of all medications, are influencing many pediatricians to exercise extreme caution in prescribing antidepressants, if they do it at all.

The lack of experience and training for psychological counseling for depression is another impediment to the treatment of adolescent depression in the pediatric practice. Furthermore, many pediatricians have difficulty scheduling appointments that are long enough for counseling. While some children with ADHD can be successfully treated with medication alone, pediatricians are not convinced that the same is true for depression. In addition, the risks associated with depression are higher than the risks associated with ADHD. Adolescents do not die of ADHD, but suicide is the third leading cause of death among youth 15 to 19 years old (American Academy of Pediatrics—Committee on Adolescence, 2000).

Because of the high prevalence of depressive symptoms in adolescents, it is critical to develop a system of universal mass screening for these symptoms in U.S. adolescents. This screening could be organized through health care systems or through schools. In either structure, well-trained primary care physicians could provide the first step in evaluation of an adolescent who has a positive screen. In order for this to be feasible, resident training in the primary care specialties will need to include competencies for evaluation, initial treatment, and referral of adolescents with depression.

Mental Heath Care for Children with Chronic Medical Conditions

All childhood chronic medical conditions have mental health consequences. Adaptation to chronic illness is a challenging process for adults, and it is even more complicated during childhood, because children are expected and assumed to be healthy. Pediatricians support the child and family as they adapt their daily routines to medication and limitations of illness. The physician is alert for the development of maladaptive family patterns, including parental overprotection or extreme denial. Asthma is the most common chronic medical condition among children. It affects 7 percent of children under 16 years and has higher morbidity for African American children. Childhood obesity—which has shown a dramatically increasing prevalence over the past several decades—is a chronic condition with important implications for mental health. Congenital heart disease, juvenile rheumatoid arthritis, and inflammatory bowel disease are other examples of chronic conditions of childhood. All of the conditions mentioned may be associated with decreased physical activity levels, increased school absence, and family stress (Newacheck, McManus, & Fox, 1991). All of these consequences can interfere with optimal mental health functioning of the child, parents, and siblings.

Conversely, mental health problems can also exacerbate chronic medical conditions. For example, anxiety can worsen asthma. This is mediated through the biologic pathways that cause tightening of the muscles in the bronchial tree. It is now understood that chronic muscle tensing can cause muscle pain and tenderness, which can exacerbate already painful conditions such as arthritis and inflammatory bowel disease. Another example of mental illness worsening a physical problem is the negative influence of depression on physical activity, which thereby worsens obesity. The pediatrician can be instrumental in alerting the child and the family to these mind-body interactions. Additionally, the pediatrician helps the family to find coping strategies that enhance health for all members of the family.

Adherence to medical regimens may be adversely affected by mental health problems. Denial, while adaptive at some levels, may interfere with taking medications and following other recommendations such as avoiding cigarette smoke, pet dander, and dust. Depression may also interfere with a family taking control of the life changes necessary for thriving with a chronic condition. The pediatrician's role is to monitor both the physical condition and mental health of the child and family. Educating families about the complex interactions between body and mind, as well as the importance of the mental health of parents and siblings, serves to demystify the mental health connection to chronic disease. Attention to the whole child, within the whole family, signals that this is all in the pediatrician's domain. Families become comfortable seeking help for the mental health aspects of chronic disease along with the medical care.

MENTAL HEALTH CARE FOR DIFFERENT CULTURES IN THE UNITED STATES

Navajo

I (S.G.) lived and worked on the Navajo reservation from 1984 to 1989. I learned a great deal about the diversity of health beliefs in the United States during the time that I practiced pediatrics on the reservation. It is important to state that, as in other cultures, there are diverse views within the Navajo population. There is therefore no attempt, on my part, to stereotype Navajo people and their health beliefs.

It was unusual for parents to seek care from the Indian Health Service (IHS) pediatricians for behavioral disorders in their children. There are probably many reasons for this. Because the mental health department was well known and easy to access, pediatricians did not serve as the gatekeepers to mental health services for children. Mental health was connected to Community Health Services, which was staffed by Community Health Representatives (CHRs) and visiting nurses. The CHRs were paraprofessionals from the community, trained in health education. These individuals provided advice about when to seek care from IHS, as well as transportation when necessary. A child in the community with mental health problems might be identified by a CHR and referred into mental health services directly. It is possible that we were not viewed as the professionals that care for behavioral health concerns. It is also possible that just as "Navajos tend to put up with ailments that cause little discomfort and do not impair function" (Kunitz, 1983) until the pain is great, Navajos may not seek care for children with mental health disorders until the symptoms are severe. Another factor in the lack of demand for behavioral health services in the Navajo pediatric clinic may relate to the greater degree of autonomy given to each individual (including children) in this culture. Individual differences in temperament and ability were not only accepted but valued. So, during the years that I practiced there, I was rarely asked to evaluate a child for colic or ADHD.

In contrast to the low demand for behavioral health services, I found that Navajo families were very accepting of mental health referrals and diagnoses. The psychiatrist was called "the talking doctor," and his ability to provide relief was as acceptable as our ability to treat infections with antibiotics. My patients did not view the physical, mental, and spiritual parts of the person as separate. In other words, mental health care did not carry the stigma previously discussed in this chapter.

Traditional Navajo belief attributes some symptoms to the supernatural (this is common in many religious and health belief systems). I became aware of this concern when a family raced more than 20 miles over dirt roads in their pickup truck to bring their five-year-old daughter to the hospital, after she awoke during the night acting strangely. Her medical evaluation revealed no disease. After a careful history, I concluded that she had experienced a night terror. Night terrors are arousals that occur in stage III or IV sleep, typically an hour after falling asleep. The child appears awake and terrified but has no recollection of the event in the morning. The family was reluctant to take their daughter home, based on traditional beliefs about the cause of her symptoms. "According to Navajo belief, disease may be contracted by soul loss, intrusive object, spirit possession, breach of taboo and witchcraft" (Kunitz, 1983). Our willingness to keep the child in the hospital until a traditional healing ceremony was arranged was instrumental in supporting the family's ability to cope with the child's symptoms. It also reinforced our culturally respectful, collaborative caring relationship with them.

Mexican American

Between 1989 and 1995, my work took me to a Mexican American community in Phoenix, Arizona. In that setting, I began to learn how a different low-income minority population approached behavioral health disorders in their children. The Mexican American families that I worked with were, characteristically, highly respectful to me and the other health care professionals who worked at the county hospital. They expressed this respect by dressing very nicely for their visits, waiting patiently when we were late, and uniformly expressing their intention to always follow our recommendations. Asking for another opinion or questioning a treatment plan was not done. However, alternative care was commonly sought from *curanderas* in the community, as well as from a variety of faith healers. These families valued putting their best foot forward and saving face for the doctor, such that we did not always know the full story.

The following case is an extreme example of the consequences of seeking alternative care and not revealing some of the facts to medical professionals. A 13-year-old girl was brought to the emergency department by paramedics. The girl's mother had called them when her daughter had a seizure that did not resolve spontaneously. She was at a neighbor's house at the time of the seizure. After stabilization by the emergency medical technicians in the field, the child was heavily sedated with anticonvulsant medication and required assisted ventilation for breathing. She was admitted to the pediatric intensive care unit. The family did not reveal any prior developmental or behavioral concerns. She was taken off the ventilator on the second hospital day. I was asked to evaluate her because her speech was slurred, and she picked at her clothes and pulled at her hair. She exhibited increasingly bizarre behavior, including jumping on top of her hospital roommate and grabbing at a nurse's breasts. The mother revealed that her daughter had displayed bizarre behavior and had been having difficulty in school for several months. She was confused, emotionally labile, and avoided bathing. On the day of the seizure, the girl had been found in the street, calling their neighbors to come out into the street to pray for her. The seizure activity occurred during a religious ceremony designed to drive away evil. After this history was obtained, we suspected that the child had experienced pseudo-seizures rather than an actual seizure. Her brain function as measured by an electroencephalograph was normal. We also learned that there was a family history of schizophrenia, in a first cousin and in a nephew. The family was experiencing considerable discord, including domestic violence. The mother believed that her daughter's strange behavior was punishment for her own marital infidelity. The child was discharged from the hospital with psychiatric follow-up and without anticonvulsant medication. This case is not meant to imply that faith healers or exorcisms are commonly used in the Mexican American community. Rather, it is presented as an example of misunderstandings that can occur when families, albeit well-meaning, conceal information from health care providers. In addition, this case illustrates pediatric involvement at the interface between physical and mental health.

Arabic Immigrants

I was asked to consult on a seven-month-old baby who presented with feeding refusal. She was a full-term baby whose birth weight was 10 pounds 9 ounces. She was born to an educated family who had immigrated to Michigan from Baghdad. Two older brothers had no medical or behavioral problems. The baby girl breast fed very poorly and slept most of the time, from the first days of life. The infant also vomited occasionally and was mildly developmentally delayed. At four months of age, she weighed only two ounces more than she had at birth. Beginning at four months, her pediatrician recommended gavage feeding by a tube though her nose into her stomach. Her mother was trained to insert the tube for feeding. The developmental-behavioral pediatric evaluation revealed that the maternal grandmother (who was in her 40s) had died in Iraq during the mother's pregnancy with this baby. The mother had infrequent telephone contact with her family during this time but had a premonition that her mother had died. Because she felt that it would be harmful to the baby if she learned of her mother's death during the pregnancy, she chose not to communicate with her family for the remainder of her pregnancy. She was told by a cousin of her mother's death after the baby was born. I noted significant anxiety in the mother and was very concerned about maternal depression. The mother was unwilling to engage in mental health evaluation or treatment because of the severe stigma associated with mental illness in her culture. At this point, the infant had been fed by a nasogastric tube for longer than typically recommended. Because there was little progress with the behavioral feeding intervention, the medical team recommended a gastrostomy tube through the skin and directly into the stomach, which is much more comfortable for the child. Additionally, it is hidden from view in comparison to a nasal tube. The parents felt that making a surgical incision into her abdomen would be permanently disfiguring and therefore unacceptable. The infant was fed through a nasogastric tube for two years until her eating disorder had gradually resolved and she was able to eat enough for adequate growth. In this case, pediatric involvement in the child's mental health and behavioral condition was essential because mental health care was not acceptable to the family.

CONCLUSION

In this chapter, we have described the roles that pediatricians play in caring for children with mental health concerns. Their functions in both the provision of care and referral into specialized mental health services have been examined. The current child mental health system is fragmented, geographically maldistributed, and often inaccessible to children with mental illness. Furthermore, the role of pediatricians is not always officially recognized or adequately reimbursed, which leads to inadequate time budgeted for mental health evaluation. These deficiencies not only cause frustration, but also place pediatricians in the role of providing mental health care without adequate support by other mental health providers. The less-than-optimal coordination of care with other mental health care providers can be dangerous for children with worsening mental health problems who do not have access to the official mental health care system. Nonetheless, in an ideal health care system, pediatrician involvement in screening, diagnosis, counseling, prescribing, and referring for child mental health problems would ultimately improve the care of children and their families.

NOTE

1. Celiac disease is a rare condition characterized by a gastrointestinal inflammatory reaction to the ingestion of wheat and associated with poor growth.

REFERENCES

Accreditation Council of Graduate Medical Education. (2003). Program requirements for resident education in pediatrics. Retrieved February 24, 2005, from http://www.acgme.org/acWebsite/downloads/RRC_progReq/320pr701.pdf.

American Academy of Pediatrics—Committee on Adolescence. (2000). Suicide and suicide attempts in adolescents. *Pediatrics, 105,* 871–874.

American Academy of Pediatrics—Medical Home Initiatives for Children with Special Needs Project Advisory Committee. (2002). Policy statement. The Medical Home. *Pediatrics, 110*(1), 184–186.

American Academy of Pediatrics. (2000). Clinical Practice Guideline: Diagnosis and evaluation of the child with attention deficit/hyperactivity disorder. *Pediatrics, 105,* 1158–1170.

American Academy of Pediatrics. (2002). Caring for children with ADHD: A resource tool kit for clinicians. Retrieved February 24, 2005, from http://www.aap.org/moc/ADHD/adhdmaterials.htm.

Barr, R. G., Hopkins, B., & Green, J. A. (2000). *Crying as a sign, a symptom and a signal.* London: Mac Keith Press.

Block, S. (1998). Attention deficit disorder: A paradigm for psychotropic medication intervention in pediatrics. *Pediatric Clinics of North America, 45,* 1053–1083.

Bocian, A., Wasserman, R., Slora, E. J., Kessel, D., & Miller, R. S. (1999). Size and age-sex distribution of pediatric practice: A study from pediatric research in office settings. *Archives of Pediatric and Adolescent Medicine, 153*(1), 9–14.

Brunton, K. (1997). Stigma. *Journal of Advanced Nursing, 26*(5), 891–898.

Cohen, P., Pine, D. S., Must, A., Kasen, S., & Brook, J. (1998). Prospective associations between somatic illness and mental illness from childhood to adulthood. *American Journal of Epidemiology, 147*(3), 232–239.

Costello, E., Edelbrock, C., Costello, A., Dulcan, M., Burns, B., & Brent, D. (1998). Psychopathology in the pediatric primary care: The new hidden morbidity. *Pediatrics, 82,* 415–424.

Downey, G., & Coyne, J. (1990). Children of depressed parents: An integrative review. *Psychological Bulletin, 108*(1), 50–76.

Field, T. (1995). Infants of depressed mothers. *Infant Behavior and Development, 18,* 1–13.

Flynn, H., Davis, M., Marcus, S., Cunningham, R., & Blow, F. (2004). Rates of maternal depression in pediatric emergency department and relationship to child service utilization. *General Hospital Psychiatry, 26*(4), 316–322.

Gahagan, S., & Holmes, R. (1998). A stepwise approach to evaluation of under-nutrition and failure to thrive. *Pediatric Clinics of North America, 45*(1): 169–187.

Galler, J., Harrison, R., Ramsey, F., et al. (2000). Maternal depressive symptoms affect infant cognitive development in Barbados. *Journal of Child Psychology and Psychiatry, 41*(6), 747–757.

Gelfand, D., & Teti, D. (1990). The effects of maternal depression on children. *Clinical Psychology Reviews, 10,* 329–353.

Georgiopoulos, A., Bryan, T., Wollan, P., & Yawn, B. (2001). Routine screening for postpartum depression. *Journal of Family Practice, 50*(2), 117–122.

Hay, D., Pawlby, S., Sharp, D., Asten, P., Mills, A., & Kumar, R. (2001). Intellectual problems shown by 11-year old children whose mothers had postnatal depression. *Journal of Child Psychology and Psychiatry, 42*(7), 871–889.

Hirschfeld, R. M., Keller, M. B., Panico, S., Arons, B. S., Barlow, D., Davidoff, F., et al. (1997). The National Depressive and Manic-Depressive Association consensus statement on the undertreatment of depression. *Journal of the American Medical Association, 277*(4), 333–340.

Hoagwood, K., Kelleher, K., Feil, M., & Comer, D. (2000). Treatment services for children with ADHD: A national perspective. *Journal of the American Academy of Child & Adolescent Psychiatry, 39,* 198–206.

Jellinek, M., Patel, B., & Froehle, M. (2002). *Bright futures in practice: Mental health volume I. Practice guide.* Arlington, VA: National Center for Education in Maternal Child Health.

Joiner, T., Mohammed, L., & Swindell, S. (2005). Personal communication.

Kemper, K., & Babonis, T. (1992). Screening for maternal depression in pediatric clinics. *American Journal of Diseases of Children, 146*(7), 876–878.

Kleinman, A. (1995). *Writing at the margin: Discourse between anthropology and medicine.* (p. 30). Berkeley: University of California Press.

Kunitz, S. (1983). *Disease change and the role of medicine: The Navajo experience.* Berkeley: University of California Press.

Leslie, L., Weckerly, J., Plemmons, D., Landsverk, J., & Eastman, S. (2004). Implementing the American Academy of Pediatrics attention-deficit/hyperactivity disorder diagnostic guidelines in primary care settings. *Pediatrics, 114,* 129–140.

Newacheck, P. W., McManus, M. A., & Fox, H. B. (1991). Prevalence and impact of chronic illness among adolescents. *American Journal of Diseases of Children, 145*(12), 1367–1373.

Nielsen Forman, D., Videbech, P., Hedegaard, M., Dalby Salvig, J., & Secher, N. (2000). Postpartum depression: Identification of women at risk. *British Journal of Obstetrics and Gynaecology, 107*(10), 1210–1217.

O'Hara, M. (1996). Rates and risk of postpartum depression: A meta-analysis. *International Reviews in Psychiatry, 8,* 37–54.

Olson, A., Kelleher, K., Kemper, K., Zuckerman, B., Hammond, C., & Dietrich, A. (2001). Primary care pediatricians' roles and perceived responsibilities in the identification and management of depression in children and adolescents. *Ambulatory Pediatrics, 2,* 91–98.

Pejlert, A. (2001). Being a parent of an adult son or daughter with severe mental illness receiving professional care: Parents' narratives. *Health & Social Care in the Community, 9*(4), 194–204.

Randolph, G., & Pathman, E. (2001). Trends in the rural-urban distribution of general pediatricians. *Pediatrics, 107*(18-DOI:10.142/peds107), E18.

Robin, A. (1998). *ADHD in adolescents: Diagnosis and treatment.* New York: Guilford Press.

Rushton, J., Bruckman, D., & Kelleher, K. (2002). Primary care referral of children with psychosocial problems. *Archives of Pediatric and Adolescent Medicine, 156,* 592–598.

Rushton, J., Clark, S., & Freed, G. (2000). Primary care role in the management of childhood depression: A comparison of pediatricians and family physicians. *Pediatrics, 150*(4S2), 957–962.

Rushton, J., Fant, K., & Clark, S. J. (2004). Use of practice guidelines in the treatment of children with attention deficit/hyperactivity disorder. *Pediatrics, 114*(1e), 23–28.

Saluja, G., Iachan, R., Scheidt, P., Overpeck, M., Sun, W., & Giedd, J. (2004). Prevalence of and risk factors for depressive symptoms among young adolescents. *Archives of Pediatric & Adolescent Medicine, 158,* 760–765.

Singer, L. T., Song, L., Hill B. P., & Jaffe, A. C. (1990). Stress and depression in mothers of failure to thrive children. *Journal of Pediatric Psychology, 15*(6), 711–720.

Singh, I. (2004). Doing their jobs: Mothering with Ritalin in a culture of mother-blame. *Social Science & Medicine, 59*(6), 1193–1205.

Singh, N. (2002). The evolving role of the primary care practitioner in adolescent depression screening and treatment. *Minnesota Medicine, 5*(8), 33–35, 37–38.

Thomas, C., & Holzer, C. I. (1999). National distribution of child and adolescent psychiatrists. *Journal of the American Academy of Child & Adolescent Psychiatry, 38*(1), 9–16.

U.S. Public Health Service. (2000). *Report of the Surgeon General's Conference on Children's Mental Health: A national action agenda.* Washington, DC: U.S. Department of Health and Human Services.

Yonkers, K., Ramin, S., Rush, A., Navarrete, C., Carmody, T., March, D., et al. (2001). Onset and persistence of postpartum depression in an inner-city maternal health clinic system. *American Journal of Psychiatry, 158*(11), 1856–1863.

Chapter 3

CHILDHOOD OBESITY PREVENTION: RESPONSIBILITIES OF THE FAMILY, SCHOOLS, AND COMMUNITY

Julie Lumeng

Childhood obesity is a growing public health problem. The rates of childhood obesity have more than doubled in the past 30 years, with most of the increase occurring in just the last 10 (Strauss & Pollack, 2001). Obesity is the final common pathway for an imbalance between energy consumed and energy expended. To this extent, it represents a dysregulation of the balance of eating and exercise. When children's lives are dysregulated in one area, they are often dysregulated in others. It is therefore not surprising that researchers have documented a number of interconnections between children's mental health or emotional regulation and a predisposition to obesity (Whitaker, 2004). Children with behavioral problems are more likely to become obese (Lumeng, Gannon, Cabral, Frank, & Zuckerman, 2003), as are depressed adolescents (Goodman & Whitaker, 2002). It is evident that affect and obesity are closely connected, but it is much less apparent *how* they are connected. Children living in poverty (Strauss & Pollack, 2001) and children in homes with less stimulating environments (Strauss & Knight, 1999) are at higher risk for obesity. The common denominator among children who have developed obesity seems to be dysregulation, whether it is in the form of a mental health disorder, chronic stress caused by poverty or understimulating environments, or any of these factors impacting the parent. Thus, as with all issues affecting the well-being of children, society as a whole has a responsibility to ensure that all children grow up in environments with the greatest financial resources, mental health supports, and education that we are able to provide. Children's overall well-being could be viewed, however, as the most distal contributor to a complex problem, and recommending that children's overall well-being be improved has limited immediate practical applicability. This discussion, therefore, will focus on issues more proximal to the problem which can be considered reasonable targets for intervention programs.

SCOPE OF THE PROBLEM

Although rates of childhood obesity are increasing across populations, as with most health-related issues, the epidemic is not blind to socioeconomic status and race. The relationship is complicated and is an interaction between ethnicity/race, socioeconomic status, and gender. Study after study has confirmed that the groups generally at highest risk for childhood obesity are low-income minority children. An oft-cited example of the divergence in obesity rates based on socioeconomic status and ethnicity is the fact that over the past 10–15 years, rates of obesity in upper-income white girls have remained essentially unchanged at about 6 percent. Rates of obesity in lower-income black boys, in contrast, have ballooned from 6 percent to more than 25 percent in the same time period (Strauss & Pollack, 2001). A clear explanation for this dramatic and growing disparity has yet to be identified.

Just as there is no debate surrounding the dramatic increase in the prevalence of childhood obesity, there is no debate over the fact that the adverse health and psychological consequences of childhood obesity are protean. Obesity in childhood is associated with high cholesterol, high blood sugar (a precursor or sign of diabetes), and high blood pressure (Steinberger, 1995). Obesity in childhood increases the risk of obesity in adulthood (Whitaker, Wright, Pepe, Seidel, & Dietz, 1997), and adolescent obesity increases the risk of a variety of adverse health outcomes in adulthood, regardless of adult weight status (Must, Jacques, Dallal, Bajema, & Dietz, 1992).

Although increasing rates of obesity begin to emerge in the preschool years, prevalence really begins to surge between the ages of 6 and 11 years, across ethnic and socioeconomic groups (Hedley et al., 2004). By the teenage years, it appears that lifelong behavioral patterns with regard to exercise and eating have been established and are unlikely to change. Teenagers who are obese are at least 15 times more likely to be obese adults than teenagers who are not obese (Whitaker et al., 1997). Focusing resources on obesity prevention and treatment in childhood is worthwhile. Obesity that develops during childhood is much more amenable to intervention than obesity that develops in adulthood.

A third of children who participated in a weight loss program in one study maintained the weight loss 10 years later (Epstein, Myers, Raynor, & Saelens, 1998). The numbers are not nearly as encouraging in adults (NIH Technology Assessment Conference Panel, 1993). These findings are a compelling reason to focus obesity prevention and intervention efforts in the childhood years. Since obesity develops over time, it is also logical to focus these efforts beginning in early childhood, when behavioral patterns around eating and exercise are being established.

The rapid increase in obesity prevalence in the population over the past 30 years is not due to genetics, but is due to the environment. Genes simply do not change rapidly enough to account for the rapid increase. Although genes certainly may contribute to the way we interact behaviorally with our environment (i.e., some of us seem to enjoy sweets more and long-distance running less than others), it is the multiple changes in the environment that have led to the rise in obesity prevalence. It is also clear that obesity is not the result of a single risk factor (i.e., obesity has not been caused by either the proliferation of fast food restaurants or the birth of cable television alone). A large number of contributors with a complex interplay have contributed to the epidemic.

The problem, defined as more calories being consumed than expended, is deceptively simple. How this imbalance occurs over a period of years is a more complex question. In the final equation, efforts at obesity prevention and treatment need to reduce calories consumed and increase calories expended—although, as any dieter knows, this is a task more easily said than done. Stemming the obesity epidemic will require interventions on multiple levels and from multiple angles and perspectives. No single change in a single setting (i.e., making school lunches healthier or increasing the amount of time in physical education) will be fully effective.

It is worth defining several terms and mentioning several caveats. Body fatness is measured with the "body mass index," which is equal to weight in kilograms divided by height in meters squared. Body fatness varies throughout childhood, with children reaching their natural thinnest between about 4 and 7 years of age. Therefore, a single cutoff value for body mass index (BMI) in children is not appropriate. BMI in children is plotted for age on gender-specific growth charts (provided by the National Center for Health Statistics of the Centers for Disease Control (CDC) and accessible at (www.cdc.gov/growthcharts). Children with a BMI greater than or equal to the 95th percentile are those described in the popular press and by the public as "obese." It is important to note, however, that the official term recommended by the CDC is "overweight" for these children. In official CDC terminology, no child is ever described as "obese." For the sake of this discussion, however, we will use the terminology commonly used and understood by the public, and refer to the children in this group (who comprise more than 15 percent of U.S. children today) as "obese."

LAYERS OF INTERVENTION: FROM CONGRESS TO THE SCHOOL LUNCHROOM

Childhood obesity can be addressed by policy change at a national level. Prior examples of public health initiatives that have been extremely successful and had profound effects on the nation's health include automobile safety and tobacco use. The federal government has cited its successful campaign to reduce tobacco use as being a "comprehensive approach—one that optimizes synergy from a mix of educational, clinical, regulatory, economic, and social strategies" (Department of Health and Human Services, 2004). Childhood obesity must be addressed with the same degree of national commitment and should be a national public health priority. The federal government has a long history of successfully addressing nutritional deficiencies in the U.S. population going back to the 1930s after the Depression. We are at a turning point as a nation when equally aggressive, far-reaching, and innovative programs need to be implemented to address obesity. The responsibility extends beyond the reach of the federal government, however. The design of neighborhoods and the choices of foods served during school lunches are in the domain of local communities. From the U.S. congressperson, to the city council member, to the school board, all policymakers have a responsibility to recognize the factors impacting on childhood obesity in their communities and to address them with the best available evidence. Equally important as the policymakers are the individuals on the front lines working with children on a daily basis, such as educators and health care providers. These individuals provide a critical voice for children's needs, have a unique understanding of factors impacting the children they care for, and can provide an authoritative voice to influence change.

There are seven common triggers for public action in response to a public health problem (Kersh & Morone, 2002), and three of these have occurred in relation to the obesity epidemic: (1) social disapproval of the issue (social approval of smoking has changed significantly over the past 40 years, and social approval of fast food appears to be declining); (2) evidence-based medical research (evidence is beginning to emerge over the past decade for the efficacy of a variety of interventions); and (3) the emergence of self-help movements for individuals with the health problem. Other triggers have not yet come to fruition with the obesity epidemic: (1) a widespread and coordinated campaign; (2) a fear of the culture related to the health problem (e.g., fear of the drug culture related to substance abuse); (3) coordinated interest group advocacy; and (4) a targeting of groups or industries related to the problem. Most of these triggers have emerged or are in the process of emerging in relation to childhood obesity, and thus one may predict that intensive public action is not too far in the future (Kersh & Morone, 2002).

DIFFICULTIES IN MAKING FIRM RECOMMENDATIONS

Prior to making recommendations regarding what types of interventions would be effective, it is first prudent to review prior efforts at community intervention programs that have been carefully studied for their efficacy. We could then make recommendations based on the available reliable evidence. Unfortunately, a review of the literature reveals that we have little to go on. Research on intervention programs is extremely limited. The federal government recognizes this, and billions of dollars in federal funds are now dedicated to studying the efficacy of various obesity prevention and intervention programs. Unfortunately, results are several years away, and preventing childhood obesity is not a problem that can wait years. Thus, we must make our best judgments based on the currently available evidence.

The last several years have marked a crossroads in the synthesis of evidence that has occurred on a national level addressing obesity prevention. A variety of expert panels have been convened, with resulting evidence-based syntheses of the data on which policymakers and community groups can rely when considering a particular program. The recommendations set forth in this chapter represent a synthesis of the recommendations of these expert panels. These key informational resources include the Cochrane Databases, *The Community Guide,* and the Institute of Medicine.

The Cochrane Databases

The Cochrane Databases continuously review evaluation research on the efficacy of treatment or prevention of medical problems. They are updated and published four times per year and are available at medical libraries and online at www.cochrane.org. We will briefly review the most recent conclusions on obesity prevention and intervention programs for children from the Cochrane Databases.

The Community Guide

Another source of carefully reviewed evidence for the efficacy of community-based interventions targeting nutrition and physical activity is

The Community Guide, which can be accessed at www.thecommunityguide. org. *The Community Guide* is researched and compiled by the Task Force on Community Preventive Services, which is an independent task force appointed by the director of the Centers for Disease Control. The task force's membership is multidisciplinary and includes perspectives representative of state and local health departments, managed care, academia, behavioral and social sciences, communications sciences, mental health, epidemiology, quantitative policy analysis, decision and cost-effectiveness analysis, information systems, primary care, and management and policy. The group's charge is to provide leadership in the evaluation of community, population, and healthcare system strategies to address a variety of public health and health promotion topics such as physical activity. Although convened by the U.S. Department of Health and Human Services, the task force is an independent decision-making body.

The Institute of Medicine

The largest, most up-to-date, and comprehensive review of the available evidence for the treatment and prevention of childhood obesity is that of the Institute of Medicine (IOM). IOM is a component of the National Academy of Sciences and works outside the framework of government to provide unbiased, evidence-based, and authoritative information and advice concerning health and science policy to policymakers, professionals, leaders in every sector of society, and the public at large on issues pertinent to the nation's health. The IOM is composed of 1,400 national and international expert scientists who volunteer to serve on committees that address specific scientific questions posed to them by federal government. On September 30, 2004, the IOM published "Preventing Childhood Obesity: Health in the Balance" in response to a request for recommendations from the U.S. Congress (Koplan, Liverman, & Kraak, 2005). The full report can be accessed via the IOM Web site: www.iom.edu. The IOM begins its report by frankly acknowledging the clear lack of data in the area of childhood obesity prevention. However, it also emphasizes that we must use our best available information to implement changes now.

A FRAMEWORK FOR DISCUSSION OF PREVENTION AND INTERVENTION PROGRAMS

There are two ways to approach combating any health problem. One is to intensively target those at highest risk (or who already have the problem) with comprehensive and resource-intensive programs. The second is to implement small changes that affect the entire population. The data for the efficacy of either approach at this juncture are so limited as to prevent any conclusions regarding which method is best. A combination of both comprises the multilayered approach that is likely necessary to address the issue. The remainder of our discussion will therefore focus first on the evidence for the comprehensive and resource-intensive programs. We then go on to review evidence for the more limited, but directed changes targeted at single behaviors, moving from the level of the family, to the schools, and finally to the community. We conclude with a synthesis of the discussion in which we provide specific recommendations.

COMPREHENSIVE, RESOURCE-INTENSIVE PROGRAMS FOR CHILDHOOD OBESITY

Prevention Programs

Studies of childhood obesity prevention programs meeting rigorous criteria for inclusion that extend to one year of follow-up (including the intervention phase), number only seven in all of the medical literature—a testament to our extremely limited knowledge of how to tackle this problem. Three of these studies were conducted in the United States, the remainder in four other countries. They all focused on various combinations of dietary modification (e.g., fat intake and fruit and vegetable consumption) and changes in physical activity level. They varied as to whether their targeted site for intervention was the home or school, what type of adults were enlisted to help (e.g., only parents or school staff as well), and the targeted age ranges spanned from 3 to 14 years of age. Although a full analysis of their various methods is not possible here, the most significant conclusions from the different findings will be presented.

The combination of increased physical activity and improved nutrition was not consistently shown to prevent excessive weight gain via school-based programming (Donnelly et al., 1996; Gortmaker et al., 1999; Mueller, Asbeck, Mast, Lagnaese, & Grund, 2001; Sahota et al., 2001). We must consider how school-based intervention programs can be shaped to become more effective, or how their reach can be extended. Two studies evaluated the effect of dietary education (to parents or via schools) alone. The programs in each study were effective, though their effects were small (Epstein et al., 2001; Simonetti et al., 1986). Changing eating behaviors to result in marked change in obesity prevalence requires a high intensity of intervention with the dietary education messages delivered through multiple avenues repeatedly. This finding again speaks to the intensity of resources at multiple levels that will need to be simultaneously committed to this problem. Finally, the single study of a program focused on physical activity alone demonstrated no effect (Mo-Suwan, Pongprapai, Junjana, & Peutpaiboon, 1998). Physical activity interventions in isolation appear unlikely to address the problem. Successful prevention requires both an improvement in dietary composition and an increase in physical activity levels.

Treatment Programs

It is worthwhile to evaluate the effect of treatment programs for children who are already obese, as these programs would likely also be effective at preventing obesity in non-obese children. The literature in this area, however, is also extremely limited. Just 18 studies in the medical literature meet criteria for rigorous scientific review for the evaluation of obesity treatment programs in children. Dropout rates from these obesity treatment programs were high. In half the studies, more than one in five of the participants dropped out (Summerbell et al., 2004). Thus, one of the first and perhaps most insurmountable goals in comprehensive programs with this level of intensity is maintaining the involvement of both child and family. The high dropout rate is one reason for targeting programs and resources broadly at the population via schools and communities, reaching children and families where they live as opposed to requiring them to come into (usually) the tertiary care medical center to address a lifestyle problem.

Five studies focused on increasing physical activity or reducing sedentary behavior in obese children, and all found improvement in weight loss, at least in the short term (Epstein et al., 1995; Epstein, Wing, Koeske, & Valoski, 1985; Epstein, Wing, Penner, & Kress, 1985). Studies evaluating the efficacy of psychological interventions have demonstrated mixed results. Behavioral interventions consisting of training in self-monitoring, stimulus control strategies, family support, cognitive restructuring, peer relations, and maintenance strategies have not been consistently found to be any more effective than simple dietary and exercise instruction alone (Epstein, Wing, Woodall et al., 1985; Graves, Meyers, & Clark, 1988). Similarly, coaching parents and children in problem-solving situations that contribute to the child's obesity in daily life has had mixed results (Epstein, Paluch, Gordy, Saelens, & Ernst, 2000; Graves et al., 1988). A relatively intensive adolescent intervention that included a variety of cognitive and behavioral techniques showed an effect of the intervention, but it was relatively modest: a loss of 3.1 pounds in the intervention group versus a loss of 2.4 pounds in the control group (Mellin, Slinkard, & Irwin, 1987). Efforts at using cognitive behavioral therapy to effect weight loss have not been found to be any more effective than a relaxation control group (Duffy & Spence, 1993; Warschburger, Fromme, Petermann,

Wojtalla, & Oepen, 2001). In summary, although the data are mixed, interventions that focus on psychological techniques to alter behavior patterns do not appear to have the power to overcome the drive to remain sedentary and eat high-calorie foods in excessive quantities. Understanding the psychological and behavioral contributors to weight loss is critical, and all intervention programs must be based in sound behavioral modification theory. However, individual work with a therapist to change the way an individual family or child functions with regard to food and exercise does not appear to provide much additional effect.

Family therapy and parent involvement have been found to have inconsistent effects (Flodmark, Ohlsson, Ryden, & Sveger, 1993; Golan, Fainaru, & Weizman, 1998; Wadden et al., 1990). In reality, although involving the parent heavily in implementing the weight loss program has been shown to have a variable degree of efficacy, it is illogical to create any intervention program addressing a child's health problem that does not include the parent in some way. Interventions that occur in schools alone are not effective, likely because they do not reach into the home. Likewise, interventions with families and parents alone are also unlikely to be effective, because they do not reach into the schools where children spend most hours of their day. In addition, the degree of parental involvement that is needed or is most effective is also going to be a function of the age of the child: younger children will be entirely reliant on the parent for behavior change, and older children will be reliant to the extent that the parent generally purchases and supplies the food in the home.

In summary, very few conclusions can be drawn from the scientific literature to date regarding treatment of obesity in children. The best studies show mixed results and have very small samples of children; therefore, it is difficult to know how generalizable these results are. Second, many of these samples were drawn from hospital-centered weight loss clinics, in which the participants (both parent and child) were already quite motivated. Effecting weight loss in the general population, in which levels of motivation are undeniably much lower, is likely a more difficult endeavor.

These sparse findings, indicating the very limited efficacy of a variety of intensive and multifaceted interventions, reflect the reality that modifying human behavior around eating and physical activity is an extremely formidable goal. Behavior modification techniques that would typically be effective for other behaviors with adverse health consequences have limited efficacy. This is likely due to the fact that these efforts at behavior change are working against the profound influence of biology. From an evolutionary standpoint, humans (and all animals) are biologically programmed to consume calories and conserve energy. We are therefore left to ponder how to change the environment in small ways, but at a population level, such that the obesity epidemic can be slowed or halted.

TARGETING INDIVIDUAL BEHAVIORS VIA FAMILIES, SCHOOLS, AND COMMUNITIES

Addressing the childhood obesity epidemic will be, by necessity, a multifaceted and many-layered endeavor. We begin by discussing the role of the family, the microcosm of the child's life, and extend our reach progressively to the schools and then to the community. The number of potential interventions grows from few within the family to a relatively large number in the community. This variation of influences and environments in a child's life illustrates that obesity is a public health problem over which parents have relatively limited power. Parents are the agents of change within the home, and the goal should be to support parents in that role. However, policymakers and community leaders are the primary agents of change in schools and communities, and therefore carry arguably the vast majority of responsibility in addressing the problem.

The Family

Children spend a great deal of time outside the home, or outside the supervision of their parents. From a public health perspective, the home and family are much less accessible than a variety of other venues, such as schools, community centers, and the media and advertising. Thus, although parents certainly exert a great deal of control over a variety of behaviors that unfold in the home, it should be recognized that parents have a limited ability to battle the myriad adverse influences on their child's weight status outside the home. Efforts at obesity prevention should provide support to families through a variety of venues, encouraging parents' efforts to raise healthy children and recognizing that in children who struggle with obesity, there are many factors contributing to weight gain that fall outside of the parent's control.

Children are inherently reluctant to try new foods, particularly vegetables. Because increased fruit and vegetable intake is associated with decreased risk of obesity, encouraging children's fruit and vegetable intake is a public health goal. Not surprisingly, children will eat more fruits and vegetables at home when they are more readily available (Cullen et al., 2003). Children are more likely to accept vegetables to which they have been exposed repeatedly, so it is the responsibility of parents to ensure that a wide variety of vegetables are offered at meals repeatedly (and it can require up to 5 to 10 exposures to induce acceptance of a new food).

Parents are also responsible for portion size in the home. Portion sizes have increased over the past 20 years, and beginning at about age five, children begin to eat more in response to a larger portion size (younger children simply stop eating when they are satiated) (Rolls, Engell, & Birch, 2000). Notably, when children are allowed to serve themselves, they will take a smaller and more appropriate portion size. In contrast, when adults serve children, they typically give the children a larger portion size and the children eat more (Fisher, Rolls, & Birch, 2003). These findings suggest that, in addition to parents limiting portion sizes, letting children serve themselves may also be effective. It should be recognized, however, that when children serve themselves, they are more likely to choose the high-fat, salty or sweet, highly palatable foods on the table. Therefore, giving children control over portion size is warranted, but limiting the availability of less healthy foods at the table is also necessary. It is also important for parents to help children recognize their own hunger cues and to respond to them appropriately. For example, rewarding a child for eating a food or using food as a reward dissociates eating with hunger cues and should be avoided. All recommendations about shaping children's eating behavior, however, should be regarded cautiously given that nearly all of the research in this area has been conducted in middle- to upper-class white children, mostly girls. Therefore, the ability to confidently extrapolate the findings to other populations is very limited.

Parents are also in a position to influence children's physical activity levels. Although it is tempting to surmise that more active parents will have more active children, in reviews of the available evidence, there is actually a low correlation between the two (Sallis, Prochaska, & Taylor, 2000). It does appear to be true, however, that parental support for physical activity is a significant predictor. Thus, providing children and adolescents with the *opportunity* to participate does result in increased activity levels in children. Not surprisingly, higher socioeconomic status is associated with greater physical activity in both parents and children (Gordon-Larsen, McMurray, & Popkin, 2000). Parents who have the time and resources to join a gym are more likely to have the ability to transport their children to organized sports practices and other activities. Therefore, as with most issues affecting child well-being, poverty plays a key role. Reducing the number of children living in poverty is clearly an overarching policy issue. For the time being, finding ways to enable low-income families to get more exercise should be a priority (to be discussed later). One of the greatest correlates of physical activity in children is the amount of time spent outdoors. Thus, increasing time outside (especially in lieu of watching television or other sedentary activities) is an important intervention for parents to implement.

It has been demonstrated repeatedly that the more television children watch, the more likely they are to be obese (Andersen, Crespo, Bartlett, Cheskin, & Pratt, 1998). Children who watch more than four hours per day are at particularly high risk. Efforts focused solely on reducing the amount of television children watch (without aiming to replace it with physical activity) have had a significant impact on obesity. Thus, encouraging parents to limit the amount of time children spend watching television, on the computer, or playing video games is important.

Schools

Discussing the role of schools in helping to stem the childhood obesity epidemic is an endeavor fraught with conflict due to the financial constraints and myriad pressures schools today face. All public schools have limited funds and often must make difficult choices in prioritizing the many needs of their students. Many educators express concern that schools are being expected to do more and more to ensure the well-being of U.S. children. Just as they are being asked to provide increasing mental health, health, and social services to students, academic standards are also being raised and more strictly regulated. Suffice it to say that involving schools in childhood obesity prevention efforts must be done with sensitivity to the multiple demands placed on staff and administrators in these settings.

School Lunches

The dietary composition of meals provided to children at school is clearly an important point for intervention. However, the issue is much more complicated than what might be surmised. The National School Lunch Program (NSLP) was established in 1946 and provides reduced cost or free lunch to children based on income, while also regulating the content of the meals. NSLP lunches are required by law to adhere to certain nutritional standards (which are generally agreed upon as being appropriate), and studies show that most do (United States Department of Agriculture, 2001). Children who are given the meal as provided by the NSLP have healthier diets than children who eat the other foods provided in many school cafeterias. Children who have access to non-NSLP foods in their cafeterias eat fewer NSLP lunches and have less healthy diets. The other foods provided in school cafeterias are largely problematic; non-NSLP foods are typically served through vending machines or at snack bars. In order to compete with NSLP lunches, they are typically substantially higher in fat, salt, and sugar and are best characterized as junk food. Schools sell these foods in order to finance their lunch programs. Currently, NSLP programs are not self-supporting; therefore, the schools must be able to fund their facilities and staff time independently.

Federal legislation that would increase the funding of the NSLP would eliminate the need for non-NSLP foods in the schools, but there are clearly significant financial, and therefore political, disincentives for doing so. There is currently no federal legislation that limits the number or type of non-NSLP foods in school cafeterias, although carbonated beverages and candy cannot be sold within the confines of the cafeteria during the lunch period (they can be sold outside the front door and at times other than the meal hours in the cafeteria). States and local communities have created their own policies to limit the sale of non-NSLP foods within schools. For example, the sale of soft drinks has been banned at all Los Angeles City Public Schools since 2001. The state of West Virginia does not allow the sale in schools of any food with more than 40 percent of its calories from added sugar or 8 grams of fat per ounce. Programs similar to these around the nation will require broad-based community support, primarily in the form of taxpayer dollars to replace revenue lost by the schools.

Physical Education

The content of physical education classes has also been a topic of research. It is generally agreed that increasing the time spent in physical education, and increasing the amount of time spent in moderate to vigorous physical activity while in physical education class, are worthwhile interventions. Several studies have shown that children typically are engaged in physical activity less than a third of the time they spend in physical education classes (Koplan et al., 2005).

Weight Screening

While 70 percent of schools routinely conduct hearing and vision screens, just 25 percent weigh and measure children, and only 60 percent of those provide these reports to parents. At least one study has shown that when parents receive information about their child's height and weight status, they are more likely to consider intervention than if they receive no information (Chomitz, Collins, Kim, Kramer, & McGowan, 2003). Unfortunately, providing parents with the information that their child is overweight cannot be accompanied by an easy prescription to the parent (e.g., glasses for the failed vision screen). Thus, it arguably places undue burden (and possibly blame) on parents without offering them any reasonable intervention tools. At the least, monitoring the weight status of children in individual schools can help focus school staff, school boards, and communities on how significant the problem is locally and how it is changing, and therefore may serve as an impetus to change or create community programs to address the problem.

The Community

Obesity prevention is most likely to be effective at the community level. Far-reaching changes in community design, media, and the food system are just a few examples of the systematic alterations in our environment that are necessary to change the trajectory of the obesity epidemic.

Opportunities for Physical Activity

To the surprise of many, adults report about 40 hours more per week of "free time" (time not spent at work, sleeping, or completing meal preparation or household chores) today than 20 years ago (Sturm, 2004). In contrast, children have significantly fewer of these hours than they did in the early 1980s, primarily because they are spending more time at school or in after-school programs. Children today do, however, spend significantly more time in organized sports activities than they did 20 years ago (Sturm, in press). Thus, the data suggest that parents, contrary to popular belief, have more time in which to engage their children in physical activity than ever before. The fact that children have fewer of these hours confirms the validity of prior recommendations that much of children's physical activity will need to occur during school or in after-school programs. Special efforts must be made to ensure that the limited leisure time children do have is not spent watching television or in other sedentary activities.

The community environment is an important predictor of childhood activity patterns. The more time children spend outdoors, the more active they are, and children's highest activity levels are located at community parks. Thus, designing communities so that parks are easily and safely accessible to children should be a priority. Not surprisingly, communities with higher incomes have more locations that provide opportunities for physical activity. Minority communities in particular have few locations for physical activity, or the community is not perceived as safe. There are many communities where the major preventive strategy that needs to be addressed is the accessibility of green spaces and facilities to engage in exercise (Powell, Slater, & Chaloupka, 2004).

Physical Transportation

Another important area for intervention is encouraging children to walk or bike to school. Only 19 percent of children walk to or from school at least once a week (Centers for Disease Control, 2002). Of children who do not walk to school, about half of respondents noted that this was because the distance was too far. Other reasons included that traffic was too dangerous (40 percent) or crime and safety concerns (18 percent). A variety of interventions across the nation have already been effective at increasing the number of children who walk to school. For example, in the city of Chicago, more than 90 percent of 422,000 public school students now walk to school. New school construction nationally totals in the billions of dollars. Given the amount of resources invested in constructing new schools each year, a focus on building these schools in locations where students who attend them can walk from home is warranted. Schools and police departments also need to partner to ensure student safety by providing crossing guards and other safety measures before and after school.

There are also relatively simple evidence-based interventions communities can implement to improve physical activity patterns among their residents. "Point of decision prompts" are signs placed by elevators and stairs that remind and encourage people to take the stairs to improve health. On average, stair use increases by about 50 percent when signs are posted (United States Preventive Services Task Force, 2004). In some studies, stair use increased by nearly 150 percent (for example, at malls). The fact that many malls today do not even have stairs as an option (only escalators or elevators) raises another design issue that is a potential point of intervention. Social groups that promote physical activity in different settings have also been found to be effective (Prevention, 2003). For example, setting up walking groups over the lunch hour in the workplace is simple and practical. Finally, providing individuals greater access to opportunities for physical activity in some form results in a roughly 25 percent increase in the likelihood that they will exercise three or more time per week (United States Preventive Services Task Force, 2004). This encouragement can take the form of gym equipment at the workplace or reduced rates for joining health clubs or other local fitness facilities as a benefit to employees who work for large companies.

Food Security

"Food security" is defined as having access at all times to adequate food for a healthy and active lifestyle. In 2002, more than 1 in 10 U.S. households were food insecure (Nord, Andrews, & Carlson, 2003). In households with children, the rate was nearly 1 in 6. It has been hypothesized that parents in low-income families are more likely to purchase high-fat, highly palatable foods than high-fiber, low-fat, less-palatable foods, because the cost per calorie is lower for the high-fat foods (Drewnowski &

Specter, 2004). Thus, in families where inadequate food and children's hunger are concerns, parents are likely to buy cheap, high-fat items to ensure that their children are full and seemingly well fed. Studies attempting to make this link, however, have been inconclusive, and more research needs to be done.

It is relatively well documented that individuals who live closer to supermarkets have healthier diets, presumably because they have ready and convenient access to a range of healthy, fresh foods (Morland, Wing, & Roux, 2002). The number of supermarkets per capita, however, is much higher in affluent white suburbs than in low-income, primarily minority communities. In fact, regardless of socioeconomic status, communities that are primarily minority have fewer supermarkets per resident. At the same time, these communities have experienced a proliferation of fast food restaurants and other outlets for cheap, energy-dense foods (e.g., convenience marts). Local communities around the nation have taken a variety of steps to address these issues—for example, providing grants to promote the establishment of grocery stores in urban, underserved areas and supporting the development of community gardens and farmers' markets. In addition, recent federal legislation has provisions to promote the transmission of locally grown produce to area schools.

Food Industry

Retail establishments and industry are also part of the community. Sweets and desserts, sugared beverages, and salty snack foods comprise nearly 30 percent of the average American's daily caloric intake (Block, 2004), and nearly a third of the calories that children consume are eaten outside the home (e.g., at restaurants) (Lin, Guthrie, & Frazao, 1999). Analyses of the children's menus of full-service restaurants indicate (to no parent's surprise) that the majority of them offer French fries as the only side dish for children and no other vegetable. Developing palatable but healthy foods has been a challenge for the food industry. If parents and communities make it clear to area restaurants that they want other options for their children, the industry will respond. Companies and restaurants that offer foods to children have recently begun to make changes to their menus (Hurley & Liebman, 2004). These establishments are therefore increasingly considered to have a responsibility to alter the options available to children. By purchasing healthy food products and encouraging their consumption, communities can support the efforts of the food industry in delivering these products, and thereby promote their proliferation.

Retail establishments and food producers need to experiment with providing more appropriate portion sizes, especially for children. Unfortunately, consumers are generally driven to purchase meals that they view as an economic value, and this typically translates into getting a large amount of food (though more than a child can reasonably consume) for their money. It is an economic challenge for the food industry to reduce portion sizes for fear that consumers will feel (even at lower total cost) that they are not getting their money's worth. If consumers and communities demand more appropriate portion sizes at a reasonable relative price, changes may begin to occur. There has also been an ongoing request for restaurants to be required to provide standardized nutritional information on their menus (just as packaged food items at the grocery store do), but this has not yet been implemented as a policy due to financial considerations. Some communities have involved public health nutritionists to evaluate the food offerings at community restaurants in order to provide nutritional information to customers; this may be an option for some communities in the interim.

Health Care Providers

Another area in the local community that can be a point for obesity prevention is the health care provider. Seventy-five percent of children have seen a health care provider in the last six months (Dey, Schiller, & Tai, 2004). For adults, brief counseling regarding weight in primary care has been found to be effective. At present, the evidence for the efficacy of obesity screening and provision of brief counseling about behavior and lifestyle changes in children is currently inconclusive. But, given that pediatric health care providers already routinely measure weight and height, calculating body mass index and providing this information to parents during routine visits with brief counseling about its interpretation, implications, and what families can try to do to change it is warranted.

Thus, communities play a key role in obesity prevention, and individuals throughout the community can contribute. Coalitions of community leaders can serve to coordinate the efforts of multiple institutions and agencies, bringing together individuals with a broad array of expertise and opinions. This has begun to occur in many communities across the nation, with increasingly effective public health prevention programs likely not too far in the future.

SUMMARY

The contributors to childhood obesity are complex and multifactorial. Various contributors impact individuals and communities differently. It is the responsibility of individual policymakers to understand their own

Table 3.1

Proposed Interventions to Combat Childhood Obesity for Which There is Evidence or Expert Consensus Regarding Adequate Efficacy to Warrant Immediate Implementation

Families

1. Reduce the amount of time children spend watching television, working at the computer, or other "screen time" activities to less than two hours per day. Children spending more than four hours per day in these activities are at particularly high risk for obesity.
2. Reduce the number of meals children eat outside the home, particularly at fast food restaurants. Meals eaten outside the home have lower nutrient value and higher caloric density.
3. Promote children's recognition of hunger and satiety cues. Avoid rewarding children for eating or using foods as rewards.
4. Ensure that healthy and palatable food options are available in the home, to the best of the family's financial ability.
5. Provide opportunities for exercise and increased time outdoors, to the best of the family's ability given available resources.
6. Monitor children's weight status as a component of children's health through regular visits to a pediatric health care provider for annual checkups.

Schools

1. Provide increased opportunities for physical activity. Children should spend a minimum of about 60 minutes per day in at least moderate physical activity, and providing at least half of this during school hours would begin to address this goal.
2. Improve the palatability of healthy school lunches, and eliminate the availability of "junk" food, sweetened beverages, and other unhealthy foods on school campuses.
3. Monitor rates of obesity in school children in individual schools as a way of tracking the extent of the problem and the degree of efficacy of programs already in place.
4. Do not advertise "junk" food directly to children within school buildings. Just as tobacco or alcohol would not be advertised within school walls, nor should food with low nutritional content and high caloric value.

Communities

1. Increase the availability of fresh fruit and vegetables in communities currently with limited access by promoting connections to area farmers, supporting farmer's markets, and creating community gardens.
2. Communicate the need for the food industry to reduce portion sizes for children both at restaurants and in prepackaged foods purchased at the grocery store.
3. Communicate the need for the food industry to continue to develop healthy food products with high palatability for consumers.
4. Change zoning in such a manner that walking is promoted. For example, allow a corner store to be built in a residentially zoned area, or ensure that there are sidewalks or bike paths along busy roads.
5. Encourage large companies to provide opportunities for their employees to exercise through increased access to facilities or equipment.
6. Implement "point of decision" prompts to encourage individuals to choose stairs instead of escalators or elevators.
7. Increase the number of grocery stores in low-income, minority neighborhoods.
8. Create community coalitions to bring together a diversity of ideas to address the problem.

communities well enough to understand where interventions may best be focused. For example, a paucity of community recreation resources and parental perception that neighborhoods are unsafe may significantly affect obesity rates in inner-city, impoverished neighborhoods. In a wealthy suburb, the focus might instead be the composition of meals in school cafeterias and encouraging children to walk to school.

As with many movements, change begins at the grassroots level. Many innovative programs across the nation are attempting to address the obesity epidemic in individual communities (see Table 3.1). Evaluating the efficacy of these efforts, and then tying those that are effective together and spreading them across the nation, is a goal in the years to come. As with all issues affecting child well-being, addressing this problem is indeed the responsibility of every level of our society: the family, the school, and the community.

REFERENCES

Andersen, R., Crespo, C., Bartlett, S., Cheskin, L., & Pratt, M. (1998). Relationship of physical activity and television watching with body weight and level of fatness among children: Results from the third national health and nutrition examination survey. *Journal of the American Medical Association, 279*(12), 938–942.

Block, G. (2004). Food contributing to energy intake in the U.S.: Data from the NHANES III and NHANES 1999–2000. *Journal of Food Composition Analysis, 17*(3), 439–447.

Centers for Disease Control. (2002). Barriers to children walking and bicycling to school—United States, 1999. *Morbidity and Mortality Weekly Report, 51*, 701–704.

Chomitz, V., Collins, J., Kim, J., Kramer, E., & McGowan, R. (2003). Promoting healthy weight among elementary school children via a health report card approach. *Archives of Pediatrics and Adolescent Medicine, 157*(8), 765–772.

Cullen, K., Baranowski, T., Owens, E., Marsh, T., Rittenberry, L., & Moor, C. (2003). Availability, accessibility, and preferences for fruit, 100% fruit juice, and vegetables influence children's dietary behavior. *Health Education and Behavior, 30*(5), 615–626.

Dey, A., Schiller, J., & Tai, D. (2004). Summary health statistics for U.S. children: National Health Interview Survey, 2002. *Vital Health Statistics, 10,* 221.

Donnelly, J., Jacobson, D., Whatley, J., Hill, J., Swift, L., Cherrington, A., et al. (1996). Nutrition and physical activity program to attenuate obesity and promote physical and metabolic fitness in elementary school children. *Obesity Research, 4*(3), 229–243.

Drewnowski, A., & Specter, S. (2004). Poverty and obesity: The role of energy density and energy costs. *American Journal of Clinical Nutrition, 79*(1), 6–16.

Duffy, G., & Spence, S. (1993). The effectiveness of cognitive self management as an adjunct to a behavioural intervention for childhood obesity: A research note. *Journal of Child Psychology and Psychiatry, 34*(6), 1043–1050.

Epstein, L., Gordy, C., Raynor, H., Beddome, M., Kilanowski, C., & Paluch, R. (2001). Increasing fruit and vegetable intake and decreasing fat and sugar intake in families at risk for childhood obesity. *Obesity Research, 9*(3), 171–178.

Epstein, L., Myers, M., Raynor, H., & Saelens, B. (1998). Treatment of pediatric obesity. *Pediatrics, 101*(3), 554–570.

Epstein, L., Paluch, R., Gordy, C., Saelens, B., & Ernst, M. (2000). Problem solving in the treatment of childhood obesity. *Journal of Consulting and Clinical Psychology, 68*(4), 717–721.

Epstein, L., Valoski, A., Vara, L., McCurley, J., Wisniewski, L., Kalarchian, M., et al. (1995). Effects of decreasing sedentary behaviour and increasing activity on weight change in obese children. *Health Psychology, 14*(2), 109–115.

Epstein, L., Wing, R., Koeske, R., & Valoski, A. (1985). A comparison of lifestyle exercise, aerobic exercise, and calisthenics on weight loss in obese children. *Behaviour Therapy, 16,* 345–356.

Epstein, L., Wing, R., Penner, B., & Kress, M. (1985). Effect of diet and controlled exercise on weight loss in obese children. *Journal of Pediatrics, 107,* 358–361.

Epstein, L., Wing, R., Woodall, K., Penner, B., Kress, M., & Koeske, R. (1985). Effect of family-based behavioual treatment on obese 5- to-8-year-old children. *Behaviour Therapy, 16,* 205–212.

Fisher, J. O., Rolls, B., & Birch, L. (2003). Children's bite size and intake of an entree are greater with larger portions than with age-appropriate or self-selected portions. *American Journal of Clinical Nutrition, 77*(5), 1164–1170.

Flodmark, C., Ohlsson, T., Ryden, O., & Sveger, T. (1993). Prevention of progression to severe obesity in a group of obese schoolchildren treated with family therapy. *Pediatrics, 91*(5), 880–884.

Golan, M., Fainaru, M., & Weizman, A. (1998). Role of behaviour modification in the treatment of childhood obesity with the parents as the exclusive agents of change. *International Journal of Obesity, 22*(12), 1217–1224.

Goodman, E., & Whitaker, R. (2002). A prospective study of the role of depression in the development and persistence of adolescent obesity. *Pediatrics, 110*(3), 497–504.

Gordon-Larsen, P., McMurray, R., & Popkin, B. (2000). Determinants of adolescent physical activity and inactivity patterns. *Pediatrics, 105*(6), E83.

Gortmaker, S., Peterson, K., Wiecha, J., Sobal, A., Dixit, S., Fox, M., et al. (1999). Reducing obesity via a school-based interdisciplinary intervention among youth. *Archives of Pediatrics and Adolescent Medicine, 153*(4), 409–418.

Graves, T., Meyers, A., & Clark, L. (1988). An evaluation of parental problem solving training in the behavioral treatment of childhood obesity. *Journal of Consulting and Clinical Psychology, 56*(2), 246–250.

Hedley, A., Ogden, C., Johnson, C., Carroll, M., Curtin, L., & Flegal, K. (2004). Prevalence of overweight and obesity among US children, adolescents, and adults, 1999–2002. *Journal of the American Medical Association, 291,* 2847–2850.

Hurley, J., & Liebman, B. (2004). *Kids' cuisine: What would you like with your fries?* Nutrition Action Healthletter (March 2004), Washington, DC:

Kersh, R., & Morone, J. (2002). How the personal becomes political: Prohibitions, public health, and obesity. *Studies in American Political Development, 16,* 162–175.

Koplan, J., Liverman, C., & Kraak, V. (Eds.). (2005). *Preventing childhood obesity: Health in the Balance.* Washington, DC: Institute of Medicine of the National Academies Press.

Lin, B., Guthrie, J., & Frazao, E. (1999). *Away-from-home foods increasingly important to quality of American diet.* Washington, DC: U.S. Department of Agriculture, Economic Research Service.

Lumeng, J., Gannon, K., Cabral, H., Frank, D., & Zuckerman, B. (2003). The association between clinically meaningful behavior problems and overweight in children. *Pediatrics, 112,* 1138–1145.

Mellin, L., Slinkard, L., & Irwin, C. (1987). Adolescent obesity intervention: Validation of the SHAPEDOWN program. *Journal of the American Dietetic Association, 87*(3), 333–338.

Morland, K., Wing, S., & Roux, A.D. (2002). The contextual effect of the local food environment on residents' diets: The atherosclerosis risk in communities study. *American Journal of Public Health, 92*(11), 1761–1768.

Mo-Suwan, L., Pongprapai, S., Junjana, C., & Peutpaiboon, A. (1998). Effects of a controlled trial of a school-based exercise program on the obesity indexes of preschool children. *American Journal of Clinical Nutrition, 68,* 1006–1111.

Mueller, M., Asbeck, I., Mast, M., Lagnaese, L., & Grund, A. (2001). Prevention of obesity—more than an intention. Concept and first results of the Kiel Obesity Prevention Study (KOPS). *International Journal of Obesity, 25,* S66-S74.

Must, A., Jacques, P., Dallal, G., Bajema, C., & Dietz, W. (1992). Long-term morbidity and mortality of overweight adolescents: A follow-up of the Harvard Growth Study, 1922–1935. *New England Journal of Medicine, 327,* 1350–1355.

NIH Technology Assessment Conference Panel. (1993). Methods for voluntary weight loss and control. *Annals of Internal Medicine, 119,* 764–770.

Nord, M., Andrews, M., & Carlson, S. (2003). *Household food security in the United States, 2002.* Washington, DC: United States Department of Agriculture.

Powell, L., Slater, S., & Chaloupka, F. (2004). The relationship between community physical activity settings and race, ethnicity, and socioeconomic status. *Evidence-based Preventive Medicine, 1*(2), 135–144.

Rolls, B., Engell, D., & Birch, L. (2000). Serving portion size influences 5-year-old but not 3-year-old children's food intakes. *Journal of the American Dietetics Association, 100*(2), 232–234.

Sahota, P., Rudolf, M., Dixey, R., Hill, A., Barth, J., & Cade, J. (2001). Randomised controlled trial of primary school based intervention to reduce risk factors for obesity. *British Medical Journal, 323,* 1029–1032.

Sallis, J., Prochaska, J., & Taylor, W. (2000). A review of correlates of physical activity of children and adolescents. *Medicine and Science in Sports and Exercise, 32*(5), 963–975.

United States Department of Agriculture. (2001). School nutrition dietary assessment study II: Summary of findings. Alexandria, VA: United States Department of Agriculture.

Simonetti, D., Tarsitani, G., Cairella, M., Siani, V., DeFilippis, S., Mancinelli, S., et al. (1986). Prevention of obesity in elementary and nursery school children. *Public Health, 100,* 166–173.

Steinberger, J. (1995). Relationship between insulin resistance and abnormal lipid profile in obese adolescents. *Journal of Pediatrics, 86,* 697–706.

Strauss, R., & Knight, J. (1999). Influence of the home environment on the development of obesity in children. *Pediatrics, 103*(6), E85.

Strauss, R., & Pollack, H. (2001). Epidemic increase in childhood overweight. *Journal of the American Medical Association, 286*(22), 2845–2848.

Sturm, R. (2004). The economics of physical activity: Societal trends and rationales for interventions. *American Journal of Preventive Medicine, 27*(3S), 126–135.

Sturm, R. (2005). Childhood obesity—What can we learn from existing data on societal trends, part 1. *Preventing Chronic Disease.* Accessed January 2005 at http://www.cdc.gov/pcd/issues/2005/jan/04_0038.htm.

Summerbell, C., Ashton, V., Campbell, K., Edmunds, L., Kelly, S., & Waters, E. (2004). Interventions for treating obesity in children. *Cochrane database of systematic reviews, 4.*

United States Preventive Services Task Force. (2004). *The guide to community preventive services.* Accessed December 2004 at http://www.thecommunityguide.org.

U.S. Department of Health and Human Services. (2004). *The health consequences of smoking: A report from the Surgeon General.* Washington, DC: U.S. Department of Health and Human Services.

Wadden, T., Stunkard, A., Rich, L., Rubin, C., Sweidel, G., & McKinney, S. (1990). Obesity in black adolescent girls: A controlled clinical trial of treatment by diet, behaviour modification and parental support. *Pediatrics, 85*(3), 345–352.

Warschburger, P., Fromme, C., Petermann, F., Wojtalla, N., & Oepen, J. (2001). Conceptualization and evaluation of a cognitive-behavioural training programme for children and adolescents with obesity. *International Journal of Obesity, 25,* S93–S95.

Whitaker, R. (2004). Mental health and obesity in pediatric primary care: A gap between importance and action. *Archives of Pediatrics and Adolescent Medicine, 158,* 826–828.

Whitaker, R., Wright, J., Pepe, M., Seidel, K., & Dietz, W. (1997). Predicting obesity in young adulthood from childhood and parental obesity. *New England Journal of Medicine, 337,* 869–873.

Chapter 4

FAMILY AND SCHOOL SUPPORT FOR HEALTHY RACIAL IDENTITY DEVELOPMENT IN AFRICAN AMERICAN YOUTH

Stephanie J. Rowley, Shauna M. Cooper, and Yvette C. Clinton

Adolescence is a time of both vulnerability and opportunity for all youth. Studies have clearly demonstrated that the transition from childhood to adolescence is often marked with decreases in self-esteem, academic achievement, and psychological well-being and that youth of color are most likely to be vulnerable during this transition. In addition to these intrapsychic changes, the transition to adolescence also brings changes in important external systems of influence, including increased conflict with parents (Arnett, 1999) and less supportive school environments (cf. Gutman & Midgley, 2000). Despite these risks associated with adolescence, most youth make the transition successfully (Arnett, 1999). Thus, many scholars have sought to highlight factors that may promote positive outcomes and buffer ethnic minority adolescents through this critical period in life. Racial identity has been posited as one factor that influences psychological, emotional, and academic well-being both directly and indirectly for adolescents of color.

In this chapter we build the argument that a healthy racial identity can help youth of color be resilient through this time of risk and that families and schools are agents that can help to foster success in these groups. In doing so, we acknowledge the valid reluctance of families, schools, and communities to promote group differences because of concerns over divisiveness and offer suggestions of how to simultaneously build healthy identities and healthy communities.

ADOLESCENCE AS A TIME OF RISK

As noted, adolescence can be a time of great risk for youth of color. Increasing awareness of negative societal stereotypes (Rowley, Kurtz-Costes, Mistry, & Feagans, in press) and discrimination (Quintana, 1998) are occurring during the transition to middle school, which has been associated with diminishing well-being for youth of all ethnicities (Gibbons, Gerrard, Cleveland, Wills, & Brody, 2004; Romero & Roberts, 2003; Simons et al., 2002). A number of characteristics of middle schools may negatively affect the self-views and well-being of youth of color. For instance, middle schools are more likely to be ethnically diverse than neighborhood elementary schools, making social comparisons of academic performance more likely. In addition, middle school teachers tend to be less emotionally supportive than elementary school teachers (Eccles, Lord, Midgley, 1991; Eccles & Midgley, 1990), leaving all youth more vulnerable during difficult emotional experiences. Finally, middle schools are characterized by more explicit tracking and public discussion of performance than are elementary schools, which may raise awareness of racial differences in performance. Thus, rapidly developing awareness of stereotypes and discrimination coincide with a school context that is more competitive and less warm, leaving youth of color in a vulnerable position.

Family life during adolescence also tends to present more challenges. An important developmental task is for adolescents to begin the process of individuation, becoming more independent from parents and often more dependent on peers (Arnett, 1999). Depending on the characteristics of the peer group, youth may find that this leaves them vulnerable to negative peer pressure or to bullying and discriminatory experiences. Moreover, disagreements about appropriate levels of adolescent autonomy are associated with increasing conflicts at home and less positive well-being (Demo & Acock, 1996).

Additionally, racial identity is forming during this time of transition. Quintana (1998) suggested that early adolescence is a time when cognitive skills, such as perspective-taking, allow individuals to be truly reflective about their identity and to understand the social significance of race. Cross and Fhagen-Smith (2001) purported that whereas childhood racial views are shaped by parents, neighborhood influences, schools, and church settings, adolescence is a time to take ownership of this early identity by exploring its meaning and challenging a formerly foreclosed, but possibly healthy, identity. In the next section we discuss relevant literature that supports a direct relationship between adolescent racial identity and several indices of psychological well-being.

RACIAL IDENTITY AND ADOLESCENT WELL-BEING

Racial identity is one of several factors that may promote healthy outcomes in youth of color (Wong, Eccles, & Sameroff, 2003). This chapter focuses on the function of racial identity in the lives of African American youth, although we believe that the same concepts can apply to other youth of color. We will discuss the growing evidence that racial identity has a direct and positive influence on adolescent well-being, which we define as positive academic achievement, self-esteem, mental health, and lack of engagement in risky behaviors. We also will discuss the importance of racial identity as a buffer of well-being and a factor in the resilience of adolescents of color.

ACADEMIC ACHIEVEMENT

As it relates to the academic domain, there has been an ongoing discussion on whether racial identity has positive effects on individuals' academic engagement and subsequent performance. Assertions by Ogbu (1986) and Fordham and Ogbu (1986) suggested that the African American social identity is negatively related to academic achievement. This literature focused mainly on an oppositional Black identity that associated doing well in school with White culture, leading to underachievement in African American students. Although these assertions have been widely discussed in mainstream media, an extensive body of research indicates that quantitative measures of racial identity that emphasize group pride, connections to other group members, and values for group cultural processes relate positively to academic achievement.

Several studies have suggested that racial identity positively affects the academic outcomes of minority adolescents both directly and indirectly (Ford, Harris, & Schuerger, 1993; Sellers, Chavous, & Cooke, 1998). Feeling close to other African Americans and prideful in one's group membership has been associated with positive educational values (Chavous et al., 2003), a sense of efficacy over academic outcomes (Oyserman, Harrison, & Bybee, 2001), educational aspirations (O'Connor, 1997), being identified as intellectually gifted (Ford & Harris, 1997), and more positive achievement outcomes (i.e., school grades;) (O'Connor, 1997; Smith, Atkins, & Connell, 2003; Sellers, Chavous, & Cooke, 1998; Wong, Eccles, & Sameroff, 2003).

In addition, one study found that children who had stronger beliefs in assimilation (i.e., beliefs that African Americans should de-emphasize race and emphasize their Americanness) received lower grades (Sellers et al., 1998). Similarly, Spencer, Noll, Stoltzfus, and Harpalani (2001) found that lower achievement was associated with high Eurocentric racial attitudes, suggesting that a strong African American identity promotes academic success. There are many mechanisms that might explain these effects. Youth with higher scores on racial identity scales may be more aware of positive contributions of members of the African American community, leading to a desire to emulate these role models. Youth of color, particularly African American youth, may also develop a sense of self-pride from their sense of pride in their racial group.

Adolescents with a positive racial identity also tend to score higher on measures of self-esteem and self-worth (Crocker, Luhtanen, Blaine, & Broadnax, 1994; McMahon & Watts, 2002; Paschall & Hubbard, 1998; Rowley, Sellers, Smith, & Chavous, 1998; Umana-Taylor, 2004). Some suggest that this effect reflects the sense of belonging that racial identity affords (Wong et al., 2003). Having a sense of connectedness to a racial group and pride in one's membership in that group seems to be associated with a more positive sense of self. Rowley and colleagues (1998) and Cross and Fhagen-Smith (2001) caution researchers, though, that racial identity is not the only route to positive self-views. Some studies show relatively little relationship between racial identity and self-esteem (e.g., Wong et al., 2003) and others show small effects. The relatively modest relationships between racial identity variables and self-esteem suggest that other aspects of identity (Cross, [1991] suggests gender, sexual orientation, or religion) may also serve a similar function. Nevertheless, promoting positive racial identity development will likely increase achievement and other achievement-related outcomes for youth of color.

RISKY BEHAVIORS

Racial identity has also been related to less engagement in risky behaviors in African American adolescents and adolescents from other ethnic backgrounds. For instance, African American youth with more positive racial identity are less likely to report engaging in violent and aggressive behavior (McMahon & Watts, 2002; Paschall & Hubbard, 1998) and hold more negative views toward fighting (Arbona, Jackson, McCoy & Blakely, 1999). In addition, adolescents more strongly espousing Afrocentric values and more positive views about being African American have healthier attitudes about drug use (Belgrave, Cherry, Cunningham, & Walwyn, 1994) and are less likely to use drugs (Brook, Balka, Brook, Win, & Gursen, 1998).

MENTAL HEALTH

In addition to self-esteem and general well-being, racial identity has been directly related to the mental health of youth of color. More positive scores on measures of racial identity have been related to lower levels of depressive symptoms (Arroyo & Zigler, 1995; McMahon & Watts, 2002; Roberts et al., 1999), loneliness (Roberts et al., 1999), and anxiety (Caldwell, Zimmerman, Bernat, Sellers, & Notaro, 2002). As with self-esteem, however, some studies find weak connections between racial identity and mental health (Caldwell et al., 2002; Wong et al., 2003), suggesting that other factors may also be at work.

RACIAL IDENTITY AS A PROTECTIVE FACTOR

In addition to the strong evidence that racial identity promotes well-being in a number of domains for youth of color, racial identity may also protect these adolescents from the effects of being a member of an oppressed social group. A protective factor is an influence that diminishes the effect of a risk factor on outcomes (Garmezy, Masten & Tellegen, 1984; Jessor, Van Den Bos, Vanderryn & Costa, 1995). A number of studies have found that racial identity also protects youth of color from negative outcomes associated with racial discrimination and negative stereotyping. In this section, we explore racial identity's role in buffering the self-views and mental health of youth of color in the face of racial discrimination. Cross and Strauss (1998) suggests that this buffering function is the primary function of racial identity.

A number of studies have shown that racial identity protects adolescents from the risks associated with racial discrimination. Studies with adults and adolescents have shown that racial discrimination is related to depressive symptomatology (Kessler, Mickelson, & Williams, 1999; Noh, Beiser, Kaspar, Hous, & Rummens, 1999), psychological stress (Sellers, Caldwell, Schmeelk-Cone, & Zimmerman, 2003; Wong et al., 2003), lower self-esteem (Romero & Roberts, 2003; Simons et al., 2002), decreased achievement outcomes (Brown & James, 2004; Taylor, Casten, Flickinger, Roberts, & Fulmore, 1994; Wong, Eccles, & Sameroff, 2003), and increased involvement in risky behaviors (Caldwell, Kohn-Wood, Schmeelk-Cone, Chavous, & Zimmerman, 2004 ; Gibbons et al., 2004; Guthrie, Young, Williams, Boyd, & Kitner, 2002). However, recent research also notes that individuals with certain racial identity profiles are less affected by experiences with racial discrimination. For example, research by Caldwell and colleagues (2004) suggests that identification with a racial group, such as is found in those who view race as central to their self-concept (racial centrality) and those who are aware that society views Blacks negatively (public regard), is protective. They studied the connection between perceptions of racial discrimination in late adolescence and violent behavior in early adulthood. Their results showed that perceptions of racial discrimination in males was associated with violent behaviors in early adulthood for individuals with low levels of racial centrality (i.e., the relative importance of race) and high levels of public regard (i.e., the belief that others view African Americans positively). However, this connection was significantly weaker for those for individuals who reported that their race was more central to the self-concept and those who felt that society viewed African Americans more negatively. Other studies show that racial centrality buffers the association between racial discrimination and mental health (Sellers et al., 2003; Sellers & Shelton, 2003) as well as the incidence of problem behaviors, self-competence ratings, and school achievement (Wong et al., 2003).

Scholars of racial identity have offered several hypotheses for how this buffering function of racial identity works. In general, racial identity may be conceptualized as a form of social support (Scheier, Botvin, Diaz, & Ifill-Williams, 1997). Wong and colleagues (2003) noted that racial identity may provide youth of color with a sense of group affiliation that buffers them psychologically. Cross and Strauss (1998) posited that when race is important to an individual's self-concept (high race salience), he or she may dismiss discriminatory experiences and not internalize them. Cross similarly noted that when individuals are low in race salience they may be unprepared or confused by discriminatory experiences and therefore be less able to cope effectively with the insult. Racial identity may also offset the sense of stigmatization and marginalization experienced by many African American males (Caldwell et al., 2004).

Although the literature clearly points to the adaptive function of racial identity, some parents report that they are concerned that socialization focusing on race will make their children paranoid and overly sensitive to racial dynamics (Sanders Thompson, 1994; Stevenson, 1998). In some ways, their fears are borne out by research. A number of studies have shown that racial identity measured in a variety of ways is positively related to perceived discrimination (Operario & Fiske, 2001; Sellers & Shelton, 2003; Sellers et al., 2003). Youth who feel more connected to their racial group also may be more likely to interpret ambiguous events as discriminatory (Rowley, Burchinal, Robert, & Zeisel, 2005). These same studies, however, noted that racial identity also buffers the relationship between racial discrimination and various outcomes, such that when racial identity is high, racial discrimination may have a less negative impact on outcomes than when racial identity is low. This protective effect may be important for youth living in a society that consistently devalues and underestimates them.

HOW CAN FAMILIES AND SCHOOLS FOSTER POSITIVE RACIAL IDENTITY DEVELOPMENT?

Racial identity development represents an important individual characteristic that can be enhanced in an effort to promote well-being among adolescents of color (Caldwell et al., 2002). Parents, schools, and communities can all play a role in fostering healthy identities as a way of increasing youths' positive feelings about themselves, sense of psychological well-being, academic achievement, and healthy behavior. In the sections that follow, we suggest ways that these agents can work to support racial identity development.

The primary manner in which parents and families can support racial identity development is through racial or ethnic socialization. Although race-related socialization can take numerous forms, many parents use it as a way to buffer their children from an oppressive world (Brega & Coleman, 1999; Murray, Stokes, & Peacock, 1999). The literature in this area tends to focus on four types of race socialization messages:

1. Cultural socialization that emphasizes pride in and the history of the group;
2. Preparation for bias socialization aimed at making children aware of potential discrimination and supporting the development of racial coping skills;
3. Promotion of mistrust socialization that encourages children to mistrust whites and other non-Blacks; and
4. Egalitarian socialization that emphasizes tolerance of others.

With the exception of promotion of mistrust, each of these socialization messages helps to prepare youth for life in a multicultural society. Relatively few parents report actively encouraging their children to mistrust people of other ethnic groups (Hughes & Chen, 1997).

Racial socialization has also been directly related to healthy outcomes such as self-esteem (Constantine & Blackmon, 2002; Phinney & Chavira, 1995), adaptive coping strategies (Scott, 2003; Stevenson, 1998), problem solving (Caughy, O'Campo, Randolph, & Nickerson, 2002), fewer behavior problems (Caughy et al., 2002), and positive academic achievement (Bowman & Howard, 1985; Sanders, 1998). Race socialization also attenuates the negative effects of perceived discrimination (Fischer & Shaw, 1999. These effects are most likely indirect, via race socialization's relationship to racial identity (Marshall, 1995; Thompson, Anderson, & Bakeman, 2000).

Socialization aimed at encouraging group pride is associated with positive outcomes for African American youth (Murray et al., 1999). When parents discuss the achievements of the group and involve their children in activities that support that message (e.g., visits to cultural museums, buying African American toys, attending community cultural events), children develop a sense of pride in their own accomplishments and positive self-views.

Socialization emphasizing the reality of racial discrimination and offering ways to cope with discrimination is also related to positive outcomes (Murray & Mandara, 2002). For instance, Bowman and Howard (1985) found that youth who reported that their parents discussed discrimination with them had higher grades than those whose parents did not discuss discrimination. Others have found that discrimination socialization is associated with more positive self-esteem (Murray & Mandara, 2002) and stronger academic values (Bowman & Howard, 1985; Sanders, 1997).

These positive effects of race socialization have led intervention scientists to develop programs aimed at increasing race socialization in families of color (Brody et al., 2004; Coard, Wallace, & Stevenson, 2004). In one intervention, parenting that included race socialization was associated with increases in factors that protect youth from risky behavior and poor mental health (such as negative attitudes about alcohol and early sexual initiation), a planful, goal-directed future orientation, and acceptance of parents' views about alcohol use (Brody et al., 2004).

It is important to note that not all aspects of race socialization are associated with positive outcomes. For instance, one study found that whereas socialization emphasizing culture and pride were positively related to self-esteem, socialization that focused more on contributions of mainstream America and assimilation were negatively associated with self-views (Constantine & Blackmon, 2002). Others have found that promotion of mistrust socialization may undermine cross-race friendships (O'Connor, Brooks-Gunn, & Graber, 2000) and self-esteem (Murray & Mandara, 2002). There is also some evidence that parents who socialize their children about negative aspects of the Black community or emphasizing negative stereotypes of Blacks (e.g., Blacks are lazy or unintelligent) tend to have the worst outcomes (Cooper, 2004). Therefore, we recommend that parents emphasize pride in the group, respect and tolerance for all, and awareness of discrimination.

Although most African American parents do discuss race with their children, a sizable minority do not (Murray et al., 1999). Some parents are concerned that discussing race too much may make children paranoid or bitter (Sanders Thompson, 1994; Stevenson, 1998). They may also be concerned that emphasizing race may be divisive, diminishing the possibility of cross-race friendships. Other parents may accept the negative societal views of African Americans or believe that discrimination is no longer an issue (Stevenson, 1998). Many empirical studies on the topic, though, suggest that not discussing race may leave children ill prepared to deal with racial discrimination and confused when they encounter discriminatory experiences (Bowman & Howard, 1985; Feagin, 1991). Children may also miss out on the benefits of the sense of community that racial identity might afford. Still, empirical investigations of the role of race socialization have not explored other explanations for the negative outcomes associated with lack of race socialization. It is likely that parents who do not talk about race with their children take a less active role in their children's socialization more generally.

In summary, the literature clearly supports the value of proactive, balanced racial socialization for African American youths' self-concept, academic achievement, and mental health. Additional research must be conducted on potentially negative effects of certain socialization messages and the absence of race socialization. We concur with recent research that suggests that parental race socialization may be an ideal way to intervene on behalf of youth at risk for a host of negative outcomes.

SCHOOLS

Sheets (1999) asserted that racial identity often begins and develops in private homes. However, it is often displayed in institutional settings, such as schools. American children are more likely to come into contact with adults and children of other ethnicities in school than they are in their neighborhoods. This means that schools may also play a central role in supporting or undermining healthy racial identities. There are many ways in which schools can encourage healthy racial identities. Some of these methods are structural. That is, by emphasizing equity and access, schools can improve the ways that students of color view their group and others. Other strategies entail programming initiatives that improve the school climate and promote healthy relationships. All of these strategies must be executed with the particular school context in mind. The most effective strategies will vary according to the school's racial composition, location, and size.

School desegregation was originally offered as a way to improve the racial identities of African American students. Kenneth Clark's classic doll studies were interpreted as evidence that systematic segregation of African American students damaged Black children's self-concepts. Clark's finding that some African American children preferred White dolls to Black dolls was said to reflect "Negro self-hatred" or even a desire to be White (Cross, 1991); segregation led African American children to view African Americans negatively. Clark testified in the *Brown v. Board of Education* Supreme Court trial, suggesting that desegregation of American schools was the only route to saving the damaged self-views of African American students.

More contemporary research has actually found just the opposite; that African American students' self-esteems (Rosenberg & Simmons, 1971) and racial identities (Ford, Harris, Webb, & Jones, 1994) are less positive in integrated settings. Rosenberg (1981) suggested that being in closer proximity to whites leads to negative social comparisons that are less likely in segregated environments. Rather than interpreting these results as evidence in support of the widespread re-segregation that the U.S. is experiencing, we see it as evidence in favor of structural school reform. That is, having contact with other ethnic groups is not the problem. The issue, rather, is the lack of equal status accorded to African American students in some American schools (Ferguson, 2003).

There are a number of structural changes that schools could enact to improve the self-views of African American students. The first is improving equity and access in the process of identifying gifted students of color. As long as African American and Latino students fail to see students like themselves in college-bound and gifted courses, there will be a tendency to associate high achievement with whites. Oyserman, Harrison, and Bybee (2001) have identified an aspect of racial identity that is defined by the belief that scholastic excellence benefits the community. One way to improve African American students' belief that education is valued by the community is to increase the visibility of high-achieving students of color. This strategy may also decrease the development of oppositional identity. Donna Ford (Ford & Harris, 1994; Ford & Webb, 1994) has conducted several systematic studies of gifted referral procedures in different schools. She has found that African American students with identical credentials are less likely to be identified as gifted by teachers than their European American counterparts (Ford & Harris, 1994). She suggested that teachers are more likely to value the cultural manifestations of giftedness in European American students than in African American students. For instance, use of African American vernacular English rather than standard English may be confused with low levels of intelligence. In most school systems, teachers are the agents who initiate the gifted referral process. Ford also notes that standardized tests—which have been shown to underestimate African American students' abilities—are most likely to be used as the sole or primary criteria for gifted referral. Finally, her research finds that some African American students eschew participation in gifted classes because of fear of isolation from other students.

In recent years the popular media have reported on Fordham and Ogbu's (1986) "acting white" phenomenon to explain poor achievement of African American students. Fordham and Ogbu suggest that African American students sometimes underperform to avoid being viewed as too smart by their peers. Moreover, years of racial discrimination and oppression have led African Americans to link behaviors associated with success in the mainstream with whites. Therefore, high-achieving African American students are teased for "acting white." Steinberg and his colleagues (1992) found that adolescents of all ethnicities are teased to some degree when they do well in school. They suggested that this teasing becomes more problematic for African American students who have less access to a high-achieving peer group who might buffer them from these assaults than European American students do. Therefore, high-achieving African American students may be more likely to withdraw from school in the face of such teasing, while European American students may retreat to their high-achieving peer group. Greater identification of African American gifted students and the creation of a critical mass in gifted courses may provide a buffer for high-achieving African American students (Rowley & Moore, 2002).

Although less research has investigated the effects of special education referral on identity development in African American youth, a similar argument may be made. It is logical to think that widespread overidentification of Black students for special education could lead to the belief that being African American should be associated with low achievement. This issue is especially egregious for Black males who are most likely to be identified for special education services (Smith, 2004). It is not surprising to find that even African American male students view African American males as least intelligent (Graham, Taylor, & Hudley, 1998; Hudley & Graham, 2001) and most likely to have behavioral problems. Therefore, this group may be most at risk of developing an oppositional identity in which achievement is viewed as incongruous with a strong racial identity.

Although no studies linking teacher race to racial identity development could be identified, it stands to reason that students who have contact with more teachers of color should feel better about being a member of their racial group. Teachers of color may also be more likely to include culturally relevant topics in the classroom. This is not to say that European American teachers cannot support healthy identities. The following recommendations related to programming initiatives should be of value to teachers of any race.

Intervention scientists suggest that prejudice and discrimination are reduced when members of different groups interact on an equal plane (Ladson-Billings, 2002). Cooperative learning in the classroom is one way to achieve such interactions. Regular interactions in classes in which members of different ethnic groups collaborate on projects may decrease prejudice and oppositional identities and increase the sense of group pride that is associated with positive outcomes. Just as research suggests that parenting that embraces and celebrates race is most effective, some suggest that teachers who include race as part of their daily activities and who reflect on the meaning of race in their own lives foster the healthiest identity outcomes for all children (Ladson-Billings, 2002).

Schools can also support healthy racial identities through a truly integrative multicultural curriculum that goes beyond Black History Month and pat discussions of slavery. Literature on multiculturalism suggests that one way to reduce prejudice and increase healthy identities in youth of color is by including people of color in everyday discourse, rather than ghettoizing these discussions by relegating them to one week or one month a year (Swetnam, 2003; Williams-Carter, 1999). We expect that schools that promote race pride and proactive discussion may help students in the same ways that parental race socialization does. Schools that attempt to adopt race-neutral or "colorblind" policies may be more likely to silently accept low expectations and negative stereotypes of youth of color (Lewis, 2001). Students of color may internalize these messages, leading to oppositional identity or attempts to deny racial group membership.

To summarize, schools can support healthy racial identities by creating an environment in which youth of color feel good about group membership. This can be accomplished by improving equity and access to gifted and college preparatory tracks (or ending tracking completely), supporting racially equivalent classroom interactions, and incorporating multiple racial and ethnic perspectives in classrooms.

CONCLUSION

Although youth of color face many challenges as they move into and through their teen years, pride in and connection to their racial group can act as a buffer against the many risks that all adolescents face. This chapter presents a variety of ways that racial identity is related to positive youth development. More research on the mechanisms by which racial identity affects development will help to better shape interventions aimed at youth of color. It is likely that youth who feel that they have a connection to a social group benefit from an increased sense of belonging and from pride in group membership. Awareness of the contributions of the group may encourage positive behavior and may shield individuals from the negative effects of discrimination and negative stereotypes.

Because families and schools are the settings in which adolescents are most likely to develop and enact racial identities, these are ideal contexts for encouraging support of positive identities. Parents can support healthy racial identities by discussing the accomplishments of the group, exposing children to group-related cultural experiences, and preparing their children for possible discrimination. Concern that discussing race leads to paranoia or divisive social interactions appears to be largely unfounded. Instead, open, honest communication about race seems most helpful. Still, parents should avoid negative socialization that denigrates the group and socialization that encourages negative views of out-groups.

Our recommendations for ways in which schools can support racial identity focus on creating an environment of equity and fairness in which students of color and white students can all feel good about the accomplishments of their group and feel that their own accomplishments are rewarded with opportunities. This strategy is particularly effective when students also see members of their group represented in the schools' faculty, administration, and programming.

Although we reviewed these literatures separately, it is clear that families, schools, and communities interact in complex ways to produce outcomes. Interventions must be aimed at the whole child as he or she is embedded in various contexts. Socialization agents from different contexts may have very different expectations regarding the identities viewed as appropriate or desired. Lewis's (2001) research in a suburban school district suggests that many teachers aim to adopt a "colorblind" racial ideology. It is likely that these teachers encourage the same aims in their students. Research on parents of color, on the other hand, suggests that discussions about race and ethnicity are critical aspects of socialization and that identification with one's racial group is important (Hughes & Chen, 1997). In addition, identities that develop in one context are enacted in other contexts where they may be more or less adaptive. For example, some of the discussion on Black-White achievement differences has focused on the connection between language use and identity (see Perry, 2004, for a discussion). Although use of Black English may be valued and promoted at home, it is often less well received in the classroom (Williams, 1997). Some even suggest that there is a type of Black racial identity that is enacted through Black English use that is specifically designed to antagonize teachers (Fordham, 1999). At the very least, African American students must learn to negotiate these different contexts.

The complexity of identity development for youth of color makes it difficult to make broad prescriptions for interventions. Parents, teachers, and school administrators must be sensitive to the competing demands on adolescents and not try to develop one-size-fits-all programs.

REFERENCES

Arbona, C., Jackson, R. H., McCoy, A., & Blakely, C. (1999). Ethnic identity as a predictor of attitudes of adolescents toward fighting. *The Journal of Early Adolescence, 19*(3), 323–340.

Arnett, J. J. (1999). Adolescent storm and stress, reconsidered. *American Psychologist, 54,* 317–326.

Arroyo, C. G., & Zigler, E. (1995). Racial identity, academic achievement, and the psychological well-being of economically disadvantaged adolescents. *Journal of Personality and Social Psychology, 69*(5), 903–914.

Belgrave, F. Z., Cherry, V. R., Cunningham, D., & Walwyn, S. (1994). The influence of Africentric values, self-esteem, and Black identity on drug attitudes among African American fifth graders: A preliminary study. *Journal of Black Psychology, 20*(2), 143–156.

Bowman, P. J., & Howard, C. (1985). Race-related socialization, motivation, and academic achievement: A study of Black youths in three-generation families. *Journal of the American Academy of Child Psychiatry, 24,* 134–141.

Brega, A. G., & Coleman, L. (1999). Effects of religiosity and racial socialization on subjective stigmatization in African American adolescents. *Journal of Adolescence, 22,* 223–242.

Brody, G. H., Murry, V. M., Gerrard, M., Gibbons, F. X., Molgaard, V., McNair, L., Brown, A. C., Wills, T. A., Spoth, R. L., Zupei, L., Chen, Y., & Neubaum-Carlan, E. (2004). The strong African American families program: Translating research into prevention programming. *Child Development, 75*(3), 900–917.

Brook J. S., Balka E. B., Brook, D. W., Win, P. T., & Gursen, M. D. (1998). Drug use among African Americans: Ethnic identity as a protective factor. *Psychological Reports, 83*(3), 1427–1446.

Brown, W. T., & Jones, J. M. (2004). The substance of things hoped for: A study of future orientation, minority status perceptions, academic engagement, and academic performance of Black high school students. *Journal of Black Psychology, 30*(2), 248–273.

Caldwell, C. H., Kohn-Wood, L. P., Schmeelk-Cone, K. H., Chavous, T. M., & Zimmerman, M. A. (2004). Racial discrimination and racial identity as risk or protective factors for violent behaviors in African American young adults. *American Journal of Community Psychology, 33*(1–2), 91–105.

Caldwell, C. H., Zimmerman, M. A., Bernat, D. H., Sellers, R. M., & Notaro, P. C. (2002). Racial identity, maternal support, and psychological distress among African American adolescents. *Child Development, 73*(4), 1322–1336.

Caughy, M. O., O'Campo, P. J., Randolph, S. M., & Nickerson, K. (2002). The influence of racial socialization practices on the cognitive and behavioral competence of African American preschoolers. *Child Development, 73*(5), 1611–1625.

Chavous, T. M., Bernat, D. H., Schmeelk-Cone, K., Caldwell, C. H., Kohn-Wood, L., & Zimmerman, M.A. (2003). Racial identity and academic attainment among African American adolescents. *Child Development, 74*(4), 1076.

Coard, S. I, Wallace, S. A., & Stevenson, H. C. (2004). Towards culturally relevant preventive interventions: The consideration of racial socialization in parent training with African American families. *Journal of Child and Family Studies, 13*(3), 277–293.

Constantine, M. G., & Blackmon, S. M. (2002). Black adolescents' racial socialization experiences: Their relations to home, school, and peer self-esteem. *Journal of Black Studies, 32*(3), 322–335.

Cooper, S. M. (2004). The stories they tell: Racial socialization in the academic engagement and academic performance of African American boys and girls. Paper presented at the Society for Research on Adolescence, Baltimore, MD.

Crocker, J., Luhtanen, R., Blaine, B., & Broadnax, S. (1994). Collective self-esteem and psychological well-being among White, Black, and Asian college students. *Personality and Social Psychology Bulletin, 20*(5), 503–513.

Cross, W. E. (1991). *Shades of black: Diversity in African American identity.* Philadelphia: Temple University Press.

Cross, W. E., Jr., & Fhagen-Smith, P. (2001). Patterns of African American identity development: A life span perspective. In C. L. Wijeyesinghe & B. W. Jackson, III (Eds.), *New perspectives on racial identity development: A theoretical and practical anthology* (pp. 243–270). New York: New York University Press.

Cross, W. E., Jr., & Strauss, L. (1998). The everyday functions of African American identity. In J. Swim & C. Stangor (Eds.), *Prejudice: The target's perspective* (pp. 267–279). San Diego, CA: Academic Press, Inc.

Demo, D. H., & Acock, A. C. (1996). Family structure, family process, and adolescent well-being. *Journal of Research on Adolescence, 6,* 457–488.

Eccles, J., Lord, S., & Midgley, C. (1991). What are we doing to early adolescents? The impacts of educational contexts on early adolescents. *American Journal of Education, 99*(4), 521–542.

Eccles, J., & Midgley, C. (1990). Changes in academic motivation and self-perception during early adolescence. In R. Montemayor (Ed.), *Early Adolescence as a Time of Transition* (pp. 1–29). Beverly Hills, CA: Sage.

Feagin, J. R. (1991). The continuing significance of race: AntiBlack discrimination in public places. *American Sociological Review, 56*(1), 101–116.

Ferguson, R. (2003). Teachers' perceptions and expectations and the black–white test score gap. *Urban Education, 38*(4), 460–507.

Fischer, A. R., & Shaw, C. M. (1999). African Americans' mental health and perceptions of racist discrimination: The moderating effects of racial socialization experiences and self-esteem. *Journal of Counseling Psychology, 46*(3), 395–407.

Fisher, C. B., Wallace, S. A., & Fenton, R. E. (2000). Discrimination distress during adolescence. *Journal of Youth & Adolescence, 29*(6), 679–695.

Ford, D. Y., & Harris, J. J. (1994). Promoting achievement among gifted Black students: The efficacy of new definitions and identification practices. *Urban Education, 29*(2), 202–229.

Ford, D. Y., & Harris, J. J. (1997). A study of the racial identity and achievement of Black males and females. *Roeper Review, 20,* 105–110.

Ford, D. Y., Harris, J. J., & Schuerger, J. M. (1993). Racial identity development among gifted Black students: Counseling issues and concerns. *Journal of Counseling and Development, 71*(4), 409–417.

Ford, D. Y., & Webb, K. S. (1994). Desegregation of gifted educational programs: The impact of Brown on underachieving children of color. *Journal of Negro Education, 63*(3), 358–375.

Fordham, S. (1999). Dissin' "the standard": Ebonics as guerrilla warfare at Capital High. *Anthropology & Education Quarterly, 30*(3), 272–293.

Fordham, S., & Ogbu, J. U. (1986). Black students' school success: Coping with the burden of "acting white". *Urban Review, 18*(3), 176–206.

Garmezy, N., Masten, A. S., & Tellegen, A. (1984).The study of stress and competence in children: A building block for developmental psychopathology. *Child Development, 55*(1), 97–111.

Gibbons, F. X., Gerrard, M., Cleveland, M. J., Wills, T. A., & Brody, G. (2004). Perceived discrimination and substance use in African American parents and their children: A panel study. *Journal of Personality and Social Psychology, 86*(4), 517–529.

Graham, S., Taylor, A. Z., & Hudley, C. (1998). Exploring achievement values among ethnic minority early adolescents. *Journal of Educational Psychology, 90*(4), 606–620.

Guthrie, B. J., Young, A. M., Williams, D. R., Boyd, C. J., & Kitner, E. K. (2002). African American girls' smoking habits and day-to-day experiences with racial discrimination. *Nursing Research, 51*(3), 183–190.

Gutman, L. M., & Midgley, C. (2000). The role of protective factors in supporting the academic achievement of poor African American students during the middle school transition. *Journal of Youth and Adolescence, 29*(2), 223–248.

Hudley, C., & Graham, S. (2001). Stereotypes of achievement striving among early adolescents. *Social Psychology of Education, 5*(2), 201–224.

Hughes, D., & Chen, L. (1997). When and what parents tell children about race: An examination of race-related socialization among African American families. *Applied Developmental Science, 1,* 200–214.

Jessor, R., Van Den Bos, J., Vanderryn, J., Costa, F. M., & Turbin, M. S. (1995). Protective factors in adolescent problem behavior: Moderator effects and developmental change. *Developmental Psychology, 31*(6), 923–933.

Kessler, R. C., Mickelson, K. D., & Williams, D. R. (1999). The prevalence, distribution, and mental health correlates of perceived discrimination in the United States. *Journal of Health and Social Behavior, 40*(3), 208–230.

Ladson-Billings, G. (2002). But that's just good teaching! The case for culturally relevant pedagogy. In S. Denbo and L. M. Beaulieu (Eds.), *Improving schools for African American students: A reader for educational leaders* (pp. 95–102), Springfield, IL: C. Thomas.

Lewis, A. E. (2001). There is no "race" in the schoolyard: Color-blind ideology in an (almost) all-white school. *American Education Research Journal, 38*(4), 781–811.

Marshall, S. (1995). Ethnic socialization of African American children: Implications for parenting, identity development, and academic achievement. *Journal of Youth and Adolescence, 24,* 377–396.

McMahon, S. D., & Watts, R. J. (2002). Ethnic identity in urban African American youth: Exploring links with self-worth, aggression, and other psychosocial variables. *Journal of Community Psychology, 30*(4), 411–432.

Murray, C. B., & Mandara, J. (2002). Racial identity development in African American children: Cognitive and experiential antecedents. In H. P. Mcadoo (Ed.), *Black children: Social, educational, and parental environments* (pp. 73–96). Thousand Oaks, CA: Sage.

Murray, C. B., Stokes, J. E., & Peacock, M. J. (1999). Racial socialization of African American children. In R. L. Jones (Ed.), *African American Children, Youth, and Parenting* (pp. 209–229). Hampton, VA: Cobb and Henry Publishers.

Noh, S., Beiser, M., Kaspar, V., Hou, F., & Rummens, J. (1999). Perceived racial discrimination, depression, and coping: A study of Southeast Asian refugees in Canada. *Journal of Health and Social Behavior, 40*(3), 193–207.

O'Connor, C. (1997). Dispositions toward (collective) struggle and educational resilience in the inner city: A case analysis of six African-American high school students. *American Education Research Journal, 34*(4), 593–629.

O'Connor, L. A., Brooks-Gunn, J., & Graber, J. (2000). Black and White girls' racial preferences in media and peer choices and the role of socialization for Black girls. *Journal of Family Psychology, 14*(3), 510–521.

Ogbu, J. (1986). The consequences of the American caste system. In U. Neisser (Ed.), *The school achievement of minority children: New perspectives* (pp. 19–56). Hillsdale: Eribaum.

Operario, D., & Fiske, S. T. (2001). Ethnic identity moderates perceptions of prejudice: Judgments of personal versus group discrimination and subtle versus blatant bias. *Personality and Social Psychology Bulletin, 27*(5), 550–561.

Oyserman, D., Harrison, K., & Bybee, D. (2001). Can racial identity be promotive of academic efficacy? *International Journal of Behavioral Development, 25*(4), 379–385.

Paschall, M. J., & Hubbard, M. L. (1998). Effects of neighborhood and family stressors on African American male adolescents' self-worth and propensity for violent behavior. *Journal of Consulting & Clinical Psychology, 66*(5), 825–831.

Perry, T. (2004). Competing theories of group achievement. In T. Perry, C. Steele, & A. Hilliard (Eds.), *Young gifted and Black* (pp. 52–87). Boston, MA: Beacon Press.

Phinney, J. S., & Chavira, V. (1995). Parental ethnic socialization and adolescent coping with problems related to ethnicity. *Journal of Research on Adolescence, 5*(1), 31–53.

Quintana, S. M. (1998). Children's understanding of ethnicity and race. *Applied and Preventive Psychology, 7*(1), 27–45.

Roberts, R. E., Phinney, J. S., Masse, L. C., Chen, Y. R., Roberts, C., & Romero, A. (1999). The structure of ethnic identity of young adolescents from diverse ethnocultural groups. *The Journal of Early Adolescence, 19*(3), 301–322.

Romero, A. J., & Roberts, R. E. (2003). The impact of multiple dimensions of ethnic identity on discrimination and adolescents' self-esteem. *Journal of Applied Social Psychology, 33*(11), 2288–2305.

Rosenberg, M., & Simmons, R. G. (1971). *Black and White self-esteem: The urban school child.* Arnold and Caroline Rose Monograph Series. Washington, D.C: American Sociological Association.

Rowley, S. J., Burchinal, M. Roberts, J., & Zeisel, S. (2005). Racial identity and race-related social cognition in African Americans during middle childhood. Paper presented at the semi-annual meeting of the Russell Sage Social Identity Consortium, Ann Arbor, Michigan.

Rowley, S. J., Kurtz-Costes, B., Mistry, R., & Feagens, L. (in press). Children's beliefs about stereotypes: Age, gender, and race differences in social stereotypes. *Social Development.*

Rowley, S. J., & Moore, J. (2002). Racial identity in context for the gifted African American student. *Roeper Review, 24*(2), 63–67.

Rowley, S. J., Sellers, R. M., Smith, M. A., & Chavous, T. M. (1998). The relationship between racial identity and self-esteem in African American high school and college students. *Journal of Personality and Social Psychology, 74*(3), 715–724.

Sanders, M. G. (1997). Overcoming obstacles: Academic achievement as a response to racism and discrimination. *Journal of Negro Education, 66*(1), 83–93.

Sanders, M. G. (1998). The effects of school, family, and community support on the academic achievement of African-American adolescents. *Urban Education, 33*(3), 385–409.

Sanders Thompson, V. L. (1994). Socialization to race and its relationship to racial identification among African American. *Journal of Black Psychology, 20*(2), 175–188.

Scheier, L. M., Botvin, G. J., Diaz, T., & Ifill-Williams, M. (1997). Ethnic identity as a moderator of psychosocial risk and adolescent alcohol and marijuana use: Concurrent and longitudinal analyses. *Journal of Child & Adolescent Substance Abuse, 6*, 21–47.

Scott, L. D. (2003). The relation of racial identity and racial socialization to coping with discrimination among African American adolescents. *Journal of Black Studies, 33*(4), 520–538.

Sellers, R. M., Caldwell, C. H., Schmeelk-Cone, K. H., & Zimmerman, M. A. (2003). Racial identity, racial discrimination, perceived stress, and psychological distress among African American young adults. *Journal of Health and Social Behavior, 44*(3), 302–317.

Sellers, R. M., Chavous, T. M., & Cooke, D. Y. (1998). Racial ideology and racial centrality as predictors of African American college students' academic performance. *Journal of Black Psychology, 24*(1), 8–27.

Sellers, R. M., & Shelton, J. N. (2003). The role of racial identity in perceived discrimination. *Journal of Personality and Social Psychology, 84*(5), 1079–1092.

Sheets, R. H. (1999). Human development and ethnic identity. In R. H. Sheets and E. R. Hollins (Eds.), *Racial and ethnic identity in school practices: Aspects of human development* (pp. 91–101). Mahwah, NJ: Lawrence Erlbaum.

Simons, R. L., Murry, V., McLoyd, V. C., Lin, K., Cutrona, C., & Conger, R. D. (2002). Discrimination, crime, ethnic identity, and parenting as correlates of depressive symptoms among African American children: A multilevel analysis. *Development and Psychopathology, 14,* 371–393.

Smith, E. P., Atkins, J., & Connell, C. M. (2003). Family, school, and community factors and relationships to racial-ethnic attitudes and academic achievement. *American Journal of Community Psychology, 32*(1–2), 159–173.

Smith, R. A. (2004). Saving Black boys. *The American Prospect, 15*(2), 49–51.

Spencer, M. B., Noll, E., Stoltzus, J., & Harpalani, V. (2001). Identity and school adjustment: Revisiting the "acting white" assumption. *Educational Psychologist, 36*(1), 21–30.

Steinberg, L., Dornbusch, S. M., & Brown, B. B. (1992). Ethnic differences in adolescent achievement. *American Psychologist, 47,* 223–229.

Stevenson, H. C. (1998). Raising safe villages: Cultural-ecological factors that influence the emotional adjustment of adolescents. *Journal of Black Psychology, 24*(1), 44–59.

Swetnam, L. A. (2003). Lessons on multicultural education from Australia and the United States. *The Clearinghouse, 76*(4), 208.

Taylor, R. D., Casten, R., Flickinger, S. M., Roberts, D., & Fulmore, C. D. (1994). Explaining the school performance of African American adolescents. *Journal of Research on Adolescence, 4,* 21–44.

Thompson, C. P., Anderson, L. P., & Bakeman, R. A. (2000). Effects of racial socialization racial identity on acculturative stress in African American college students. *Cultural Diversity and Ethnic Minority Psychology, 6*(2), 196–210.

Umana-Taylor, A. J. (2004). Ethnic identity and self-esteem: Examining the role of social context. *Journal of Adolescence, 27*(2), 139–146.

Williams, R. L. (1997). The ebonics controversy. *Journal of Black Psychology, 23*(3), 208–214.

Williams-Carter, D. (1999). Do we need multicultural education? Paper presented at the annual meeting of the Mid-South Education Research Association, Point Clear, AL.

Wong, C. A., Eccles, J. S., & Sameroff, A. (2003). The influence of ethnic discrimination and ethnic identification on African American adolescents' school and socioemotional adjustment. *Journal of Personality, 71*(6), 1197–1231.

Chapter 5

UNDERSTANDING THE PSYCHOLOGICAL DEVELOPMENT OF AFRICAN AMERICAN CHILDREN: THE IMPACT OF RACE, CLASS, AND SOCIAL INEQUALITY

Jonathan Livingston

> Those of us who are black can not think of our children without thinking about our families. We can not think about black children and black families without thinking about black communities. We can not think about black children, black families, and black communities without, at the same time, realizing that this entire configuration of blackness is surrounded by a white, racist society ... which devalues everything black. (Barnes, 1991, p. 667)

How healthy psychological functioning and development occur for African Americans has been a topic of debate for decades (Franklin, 1991; Grier & Cobbs, 1968; Kardiner & Ovessey, 1951; King, Dickson, & Nobels, 1976; Parham & Helms, 1985; Thomas & Sillen, 1972). Given the social and structural impingements on Black life in America, many question whether psychological health is even possible for African Americans. This has raised the questions: How does one raise a psychologically healthy Black child; is it possible given the conditions in which Black people exist?

The purpose of the present chapter is to highlight the mental health challenges and factors that are associated with the psychological development of African American children. This chapter also provides a historical and ecological understanding of issues that shape the world in which these children are reared and, subsequently, impact their psychological health and development.

MENTAL HEALTH AMONG BLACK CHILDREN

According to Spencer, Kohn, and Woods (2002), over the past 10 years, increased attention has been given to the assessment and diagnosis of children's mental health problems. Research on the influence of poverty on children's neurological development, the impact of medication, and the development of new treatment methods have all been aimed at improving the lives of children (Conger et al., 1992; Shore, 1997). However, despite these developments, a number of issues in regard to services for African American children still need to be addressed (Spencer et al., 2002). Issues of access to mental health services, the differential availability of these services, the lack of health insurance to cover costs, and negative interactions between Black families and service providers have all been cited as barriers to children's receiving mental health services (Richardson, 2001). Additional factors that may hinder Black families from utilizing mental health services are:

1. fear of the added stigmatization that mental health diagnoses can bring upon a child,
2. lack of trust of healthcare professionals, and
3. the belief that mental health practitioners do not understand and are not sensitive to the social and cultural factors that affect a Black child's life.

As a result, reluctance to use outpatient services (i.e., counseling, medication, group therapy, etc.), may lead to late detection, more severe mental health outcomes, and an eventual need for long-term hospitalization (Spencer et al., 2002). Since official mental health service utilization statistics are often used for epidemiological purposes, the differential use patterns summarized here may render such information useless. Therefore, developing an accurate picture of the mental health needs of African American children is problematic.

To date, few studies have assessed the prevalence of mental illness among Black children. Those that have been conducted comparing Black and White children have provided inconclusive results (Costello et al., 1988, 1996; Valleni-Basile et al., 1996). Much of what is known about the prevalence of mental illness among African Americans has been collected on institutionalized adults. Furthermore, there exist limited longitudinal data on rates of mental illness across the lifespan prior to institutionalization. As a result, there is a lack of understanding of the probable ecological factors that may impact healthy development and lead to maladjustment (Spencer et al., 2002).

Chronic poverty, family instability, and exposure to violence are all factors that may impact how Black children shape their social and psychological worlds (Children's Defense Fund, 2004). These factors, combined with the barriers to services for African Americans and the effects of racism suggest that a structural or ecological analysis is warranted to better understand the mental health needs of Black children.

A review of inpatient mental health facilities and other residential institutions suggests that Blacks are disproportionately represented (Snowden, 2003). The overrepresentation of African American children in inpatient mental health facilities may be explained, or impacted, by social and economic factors (i.e., stigmatization, lack of trust, lack of insurance), which may eventually lead to more severe diagnoses. Any critical assessment of mental health issues as they relate to Black children must address the degree to which poverty, chronic unemployment or underemployment, family instability, and social inequalities affect their lives (Office of the Surgeon General, n.d.; Snowden, 2003; Vega & Rumbaut, 1991).

In addition to rates of incarceration, various data indicate high rates of school dropout, increasing rates of suicide, in particular among young Black boys, and increasing incarceration rates among young Black females. These trends should be of grave concern for human service and mental health professionals. Therefore, more comprehensive assessments of the mental health needs of Black children must be undertaken. Such an assessment should include factors that may prevent Black parents from utilizing services as well as how ecological factors impact Black child development.

Gaining an accurate picture of the mental health needs of African Americans and understanding the barriers to African Americans' seeking mental health services for their children are cumbersome tasks. Traditionally, African Americans have neither been accustomed to utilizing mental health services nor divulging their mental health needs. Moreover, African American families experiencing stressors and other psychological problems have relied on community religious leaders or an extended social support network of friends and family members (Neighbors, Jackson, Bowman, & Gurin, 1993). Given that a good deal of epidemiological research is conducted in traditional mental health treatment settings, a skewed picture may have been developed.

Social scientists seeking information on the mental health needs of the African American community must first educate the community about mental illness and the need for mental health services. They will have to dismantle negative stereotypes associated with mental illness and improve the relationship between the research community and the Black community.

To gain access to the African American community, researchers will have to be visible and become abreast of the social and cultural makeup of the Black community by establishing relationships with the community and its respective stakeholders (i.e., elected officials, community center directors, health professionals, clergy) and institutions (i.e., churches, social organizations). Through community forums, focus groups, and information booths at annual cultural events, human service and mental health professionals can increase visibility, inform, and establish better relationships with Black communities. Such efforts will not only improve the relationship between the mental health research community and the Black community, but they will also create a context in which African Americans are more apt to discuss their mental health needs.

SELF-ESTEEM AND DEVELOPMENT

I'm Black. I'm dirty, and I will never be anything. (eight-year-old Black boy after losing a math competition during summer camp)

There has long been a discussion of self-esteem as a key variable in mental health. Although much contemporary research suggests that Black children's self-esteem is equal to or higher than their White counterparts (Twenge & Crocker, 2002), a number of Black children continue to negotiate low self-esteem and a negative self-concept. To assume that all Black children can develop positive self-esteem and not be impacted by the negative stereotypes associated with being Black in this culture is illogical and wishful thinking, at best. The many negative stereotypes associated with being Black and the significance of skin color in America have a profound influence on the psychology of the Black community and, subsequently, the psychological development of Black children. Not only do these stereotypes affect how Black parents raise their children, but they also impact Black children's self-esteem and the value they place on being a member of the Black community.

Self-esteem is defined as an individual's subjective evaluation of the self. Self-esteem includes one's feelings of self-worth, judgment, and perceptions of one's values, morals, and personal attitude (Wells, 1978). According to the Social Looking Glass and Generalized Significant Other theories proposed by Cooley (1902) and Mead (1934), one's perception of self is influenced by how it is reflected through the eyes of one's significant others. Therefore, if the significant others (i.e., community or society at large) reflect negative and derogatory images of Blacks to the Black child, then the child will internalize this negative view of self and develop a negative self-concept and, consequently, lower self-esteem.

Moreover, depending on the context for social comparison, Black children who see themselves through the eyes of Whites have no choice but to view themselves negatively and devalue themselves as human beings, given the negative stereotypes associated with being Black in U.S. culture. Such stereotypes as Blacks being lazy, less intelligent, and of low moral character are pervasive throughout various institutions in American culture. These views can be transmitted to young children through various social institutions (i.e., media, school) and even the Black community.

This devaluing of Black people and the color black pervades Western culture and is transmitted through the language and symbolism of the culture as a whole (Murray & Mandara, 2002). For example, as Black children begin to read and acquire language, they soon learn that black is associated with everything bad, dirty, and evil (i.e., black cat, blackmail, black ball, black knight, black hole), and white is associated with everything good, clean, and pure (i.e., Snow White, white knight, white lie). Black children who internalize these negative stereotypes and use the White community as a point of social comparison are at higher risk of developing low self-esteem. Empirical support for this relationship was found in Clark and Clark's (1947) and Stevenson and Stewart's (1958) classic doll studies, which supported the notion that African American children, who preferred White dolls, suffered from low self-esteem and wished to be White. Cross (1985), Semaj (1985), and Spencer (1984) each found that some Black children, when given a choice, did not like being called black and preferred lighter skin to darker skin.

Such findings are not surprising given the negative stereotypes associated with being Black in U.S. culture. However, such findings must be viewed with a great deal of caution, given that not all Black children use the White community as a point of social comparison, and some parents' socialization practices instill positive messages about Black people and the Black community. Parent socialization practices that cultivate a strong racial identity through racial awareness and pride have been found to buffer children from the negative stereotypes associated with race (Boykins & Toms, 1985).

IDENTITY AND DEVELOPMENT

Hell, if they are going to treat me like a criminal, then I am going to act like one. (15-year-old Black male returning to school after serving two months in a juvenile detention center)

According to Erikson (1968), the development of a sense of identity for a child is key in establishing psychological health. For Black children, developing a sense of who they are can be a challenging task, given the negative stereotypes and social and structural impingements that characterize Black life. Black children, unlike their White counterparts, have the added task of trying to negotiate identity and decide what they want to become in a context that consistently reflects negative images of what it means to be Black. Thus, identity exploration for African American children can be a tenuous process, given the negative social expectations or assumptions of who they are and how they will behave (Erikson, 1968; Kunjufu, 2001). For example, African American boys are consistently reminded of how they're seen in the context of this culture by the White community, schools, and, in particular, the police. The sight of women clutching their purses and the sound of doors being locked as young Black boys walk past Whites are reminders of their perceived social status. These experiences, and other overt and subtle experiences of racism and prejudice, can greatly influence how young Black children see themselves and, subsequently, may determine the life choices they perceive to be possible. As a consequence, the development of a positive identity can be very difficult to achieve for many Black children. This may especially be true for those children who don't have positive Black role models or positive experiences that reinforce positive perceptions and views of being Black.

Positive racial identity development. From a review of the research on racial identity and the history of Blacks in America, identity development for Black children has unfolded in the context of two competing processes (Cross, Parham, & Helms, 1991):

1. "de-racination," which was an attempt of American culture to erase African consciousness from newly arrived African slaves and the contemporary need for some African Americans to identify with mainstream culture, or

2. "racial awareness/consciousness," which is the successful cultivation of a Black identity through the awareness of one's African or African American culture and heritage and a firm understanding of issues facing the African American community.

Both processes of identity development have social and political implications for Black families. They directly affect the social and psychological development of Black children. Each process impacts the social context (i.e., parenting practices and values articulated and transmitted by family members) in which the child is reared and identity formed. Racial identity in African Americans is defined as the significant and qualitative meaning that individuals attribute to their membership within the Black community

(Cross, 1971; Parham & Helms, 1985; Sellers et al., 1998). The definition proposed addresses two important questions for the Black child: (1) How important is race to the individual's perception of self? and (2) What does it mean to be a member of one's respective racial group (Sellers, Smith, Shelton, Rowley, & Chavous, 1998)? Given the importance of history and culture on an individual's conception of self and construction of race, the use of an ecological analysis to understand identity for African American children is of critical importance.

The development of a positive identity for any child is dependent upon the degree to which positive messages about one's race are articulated by parents and the community and the degree to which one's membership and heritage are celebrated, affirmed, and reinforced. To understand identity development in Black children, the social history of African Americans in the United States cannot be overlooked. A careful review of the history suggests that there was a deliberate attempt to de-culturalize Africans and their descendents. For example, newly arrived Africans were given Christian names and, by law, were forbidden from using their native languages or participating in rituals or customs that affirmed their culture and reinforced positive identity development (Kambon, 1992). The outcomes of such social practices over time have not only led to a lack of appreciation for and confusion about African culture but leave African Americans to ponder the questions "Who am I?" and "Am I a person of value, given the significance of race and skin color in this culture?" Bringing clarity to these questions is essential in any assessment of Black psychological functioning and healthy development for Black children.

Over the past 20 years, a number of studies have been conducted on racial identity. Contemporary studies suggest that the development of a strong identity may protect African Americans from the negative effects of racism and may be related to better psychological outcomes (Carter, 1991; Chambers et al., 1998; Munford, 1994; Sellers et al., 1998). However, many of the studies have only been conducted on African American adolescents and adults. Thus, contemporary research yields very little information about racial identity in preadolescent Black children. Among African American adolescents and young adults, positive racial identity has been related to high academic performance (Baldwin, Duncan, & Bell, 1987) and higher levels of self-esteem (Rowley, Sellers, Chavous, & Smith, 1998). Lower levels of racial identity have been related to depression, alcoholism, and low self-esteem (Caldwell, Sellers, Bernat, & Zimmerman, 2004; Carter, 1991; Munford, 1994).

Research on racial identity among young African American children has produced mixed results. Some studies have suggested that Black children who have a stronger racial identity also have higher levels of self-esteem (Akbar, Chambers, & Sanders-Thompson, 2001) and better academic outcomes (Newsom, 2004). Others have found that Black children are reluctant to identify with being Black due to the stigma associated with the color black or being a member of that racial group (Murray & Mandara, 2002). Still others suggest that Black children, depending upon context, acculturation, and degree of racial socialization, may simultaneously have a positive concept of self while not identifying with the Black community (McAdoo, 1985; Spencer, 1984). Although a number of studies report the protective nature of racial identity in Black adolescents and adults, there exist little conclusive data about whether racial identity is related to positive outcomes among young Black children. However, we do know that race is a significant factor in determining how Black children construct their identities and perceptions of self. Thus, further research is needed to understand the significance of racial identity among Black children. Inquiry concerning its significance is warranted in any therapeutic, preventive, or programmatic context given the importance of race in American culture.

REARING AFRICAN AMERICAN CHILDREN: RACIAL SOCIALIZATION

African American families face a unique set of experiences in regard to rearing children. Also, it is no secret that Black families experience a great amount of stress. The impact and significance of race and social inequality on Black children in America cannot be overlooked. Thus, raising a Black child becomes a psychologically challenging task. Moreover, the task of parenting and raising Black children is usually undertaken by a number of family members (i.e., uncles, aunts, grandparents). Each adult is cognizant of the importance of imparting information needed to develop into a competent and productive adult, as well as imparting information about their history and culture (Peters, 2002; Stevenson, Reed, Bodison, & Bishop, 1997). It is vital to communicate information about how to navigate a culture that devalues their race and skin color. Therefore, many Black parents are active in socializing their children about race. At a very young age, some Black children receive messages about race and their social location in this culture. Later, in childhood or adolescence, they are taught abstractions for understanding social relationships in the context of race. To cultivate positive views about their race and the Black community, some Black families may expose their children to cultural events (Kambon, 1992) that affirm and reinforce the significance of African culture. Children are often required to read books on African and African American history. Additionally, Black parents, grandparents, aunts, and uncles may discuss Black history and current issues that affect the Black community. These practices become a part of parenting in an effort to instill racial pride, prepare the child for future discrimination, and protect the child from the negative stereotypes associated with being Black in America (Stevenson et al., 1997).

According to Stevenson and colleagues (1997), some Black children are taught that they have to work twice as hard as Whites to obtain just a small amount of the material wealth that Whites obtain. This is seen in such messages articulated by Black parents and elders as:

> "You have to be twice as smart as Whites if you are going to make it in this world" and

> "You have to get an education because it will open doors for you, and it's the one thing they (Whites) can't take away from you."

Research on racial socialization and child rearing practices among Black parents suggests that racial socialization, which instills pride and recognition of one's racial and social contexts, is related to more positive outcomes for Black children (Stevenson et al., 1997). Although such practices are pervasive among many Black parents, some may not feel the need to socialize their children about race and, instead, may adopt a parenting style that de-emphasizes the significance and importance of race. These parents, likened to parents who articulate positive messages about their race, may feel that the negation of race and acceptance of mainstream values, transmitted in their rearing practices, may protect their children from the negative assumptions and stereotypes associated with being Black (Peters, 2002). Despite differences in racial socialization practices among African American families, the values that families feel are important and the messages transmitted about race have an impact on the child's psychological development and how the child interacts with his or her environment (i.e., family, community, society, and culture).

EXPERIENCES OF RACISM: INTERPERSONAL AND INSTITUTIONAL

> It is utterly exhausting being Black in America—physically, mentally, and emotionally … there is no respite or escape from your badge of color. (Edelman, 1992)

Any discussion of African American mental health or child development would not be complete without bringing clarity to the psychological and social residuals of slavery, the continued overt and institutional racism, and their impact upon the African American community. Continued racial profiling by law enforcement, disproportionate rates of incarceration, and political and economic isolation all suggest that racism is still a salient part of Black life in America. The degree to which African American families cope with racism and the social and psychological resources (i.e., religion, extended family, social network) they have to buffer them from its effects determine how racism affects the Black child. Black children today may not experience as many overt instances of racism and discrimination as African Americans born prior to the Civil Rights movement and before integration; yet the influence of institutional racism and racism directly experienced by their parents do impact their lives. Although each Black parent may negotiate experiences of racism differently, it is a part of most Black parents' lives, regardless of status or socioeconomic background (Murray & Brody, 2002). Overt experiences with racism, such as racial epithets or slurs at work or being followed in stores by clerks or security guards, are daily experiences African American parents must endure. The cumulative effects of these experiences can be overwhelming for some Black parents and compromise their ability to effectively nurture their child (Peters, 2002). Black parents who consistently experience racism may have to expend a lot of psychological energy trying to evaluate whether an uncomfortable encounter with a White individual is due to racism or some other factor. The experiences of racism and the consistent need to appraise such encounters can lead to anger, confusion, depression, or hostility among Black parents, and some may seek to engage in maladaptive behaviors (i.e., alcohol or drug use) in an effort to cope with these experiences of racism (Wilson, 1991). Research on the impact of racism on parenting practices among Black parents suggests that racism not only can influence socialization practices among Black parents, but it can also compromise the parents' psychological well-being and alter parental esteem and self-perception (Murray & Brody, 2002; Peters, 2002). Although Black parents report periods of being depressed and angry, many are cognizant of the need to not impose these stressors upon their children. They may instead seek to use these experiences as opportunities to socialize their children about racism and educate them about the systemic racism that the child will encounter as he or she enters the adult world (Peters, 2002; Richardson, 1981).

Systemic, or institutional, racism, although not as identifiable as the racism Blacks experienced prior to the 1960s and 1970s, has had a negative impact upon the Black community, Black families, and, subsequently, Black children. Unfair hiring practices, discrimination in lending and housing, and inequities in sentencing in the criminal justice system have all adversely affected the Black community (Ladd, 1998; National Urban League, 2002; Watts & Nightingale, 1996). The cumulative effects of these factors have geographically and politically isolated some Black communities in America and created a context, and culture, of persistent poverty in which a disproportionate number of Black children are being reared (Wilson, 1991). Therefore, addressing the question of how the aforementioned factors impact Black children may entail employing a structural or ecological approach.

THE ECOLOGY OF BLACK CHILD DEVELOPMENT: A STRUCTURAL APPROACH

A good deal of evidence suggests that Black children experience a great number of challenges. Disproportionate rates of incarceration, poverty, and violence all speak to the need for a holistic approach to understanding and addressing the problems that Black children face (Hawkins, Laub, Lauritsen, & Cothern, 2000). An ecological, or structural, approach advances the importance not only of social scientists and human service professionals working in the Black community, understanding of the influences of family and community on Black child development, but also their understanding of the effects of institutions, culture, and subsequent policies and values that negatively impact and shape the social world of Black people (Livingston, Hines, & Nahimana, 2004). An ecological approach attempts to explain the effects that structural and environmental factors have upon a Black child's life and development. Employing this approach will assist the social scientists, human service professionals, and all those individuals concerned with the well-being of Black children in understanding that their behavior and development do not occur in isolation, and the Black child responds to and is impacted by a larger social or ecological system (Bronfenbrenner, 1979; Holliday, 1985). Therefore, the development of any interventions to address the challenges that these children face must account for these environmental influences. For example, those interested in developing interventions or creating policies regarding Black families and Black children must be able to understand the intersection of race, class, and social inequality and how unemployment and poverty due to economic shifts may have deleterious effects on Black families. Moreover, they must be able to explain or address the cumulative effects of unemployment and poverty on Black communities and how these conditions are related to increased violence, high incarceration rates, poor school performance, and negative behavioral outcomes for Black children.

Unemployment

As for all American families, the ability to secure and maintain stable employment is a cornerstone in creating the family stability needed to rear children. Historically, Black parents, in particular Black men, have experienced disproportionate rates of unemployment in the United States (National Urban League, 2002). For the past six years, unemployment rates for African American men over the age of 25 have been almost twice the rate of their White counterparts (U.S. Census Bureau, 2003). In many urban areas, such as New York, Philadelphia, New Jersey, and Washington, DC, where many African American families reside, 15–35 percent of African American men and women are unemployed (National Urban League, 2002).

These increases in unemployment affect Black families and children in a number of ways (Horn & Bush, 1997, Loury, 2000). Unemployment for Black families not only causes family instability (i.e., eviction, constant moving, utility disconnection), which all impact children's well-being, but it also compromises parents' psychological well-being (Rodriguez, Allen, Frongillo, & Chandra, 1999) and strains interpersonal relationships within the family. The stress created by unemployment may impact the amount of parental attention and support Black children receive (Hankins-Jarrett, 1997). Moreover, the tension created by a lack of employment can lead to frustration, depression, drug use as a coping mechanism, increased violence between the parents, and, in some cases, verbal and physical abuse toward the child (Ceballo & McLoyd, 2002). Children reared in families plagued by unemployment experience problems that may have long-term effects on their behavior, development, and psychological functioning (Edelman, 1985; Children's Defense Fund, 2004). The frustration experienced by parents can lead to a nihilistic attitude toward life and work and can manifest into low aspirations among Black children. The anger and frustration experienced due to chronic unemployment can cause parents to become hostile or depressed (Rodriguez et al., 1999).

Children observing this behavior in their parents may become fearful and detached from them. This detachment from parents, although typical at some point for any young child, can be more problematic for Black children, considering the context and challenges that many low-income Black children have to negotiate. Black children living in low-income communities and who are detached or alienated from their parents may be drawn to and become more susceptible to the added pressures of gang involvement and drug trafficking, which may be pervasive in low-income neighborhoods (Wilson, 1991). Given the importance of adequate employment and its influence upon family functioning, human services and mental health professionals have to begin to understand the cumulative psychological impact of chronic unemployment on Black communities, Black families, and Black children.

Poverty

One of the logical outcomes of chronic unemployment is poverty. Although not all African American families experience unemployment and poverty, African American children represent a disproportionate number of the children in poverty (Children's Defense Fund, 2004; McLoyd, 1998). An overwhelming proportion of the individuals living in poverty in the United States are, in fact, Black children. In fact, 34.1 percent of Black children live in poverty (Children's Defense Fund, 2004). Data on poverty suggest that 26 percent of Black families live below the poverty level, compared to 6 percent of White families (National Urban League, 2002). Despite America's economic success over the past decade and the gains in education made by Blacks during this period, many Blacks continue to earn less than their White counterparts (National Urban League, 2002). The impact of poverty on Black families affects many life domains for Black parents and Black children. Families that live in poverty either experience chronic homelessness or reside in low-income communities plagued by substandard housing that can not only be deleterious to a child's psychological well-being but can stifle his or her mental and physical development. For example, 28.4 percent of low-income African American children have had lead poisoning, compared to 9.8 percent of low-income White children (Kay, 2003). African Americans who live in substandard housing are far more likely than Whites to live close to uncontrolled hazardous waste sites (74 percent compared to 54 percent) (Kay, 2003). Such toxic conditions in many low-income Black communities have been related to respiratory and asthma-related problems among Black children. Currently, the asthma-related hospitalization rate for African Americans is three to four times the rate for Whites (Kay, 2003).

The impact of poverty on Black children can be multifaceted and have long-term effects on the child's development. Children who live in poverty are at a greater risk of being malnourished and may not receive or have access to adequate healthcare, which can lead to long-term health problems (Institute of Medicine, n.d.). Lack of proper diet and medical attention can hinder intellectual development and school performance. Children who are reared in poverty are more likely to lack skills necessary for school readiness and, therefore, be labeled as learning disabled and experience school failure (Children's Defense Fund, 2004). The impact of poor school performance leads to decreased future employment options for Black children and an increased likelihood that the child will experience poverty and, in the future, rear a child in poverty, thus creating a cycle of poverty, which is pervasive among low-income Blacks in urban communities.

Violence and Incarceration

High rates of violence and incarceration are pervasive in some low-income and poverty-stricken communities. Statistics on homicide reveal that African American males between the ages of 18 and 25 are six times more likely to be killed than their White counterparts (Watts & Nightingale, 1996). In urban cities, such as Washington, DC, 1 out of every 12 Black men is a victim of homicide (Kunjufu, 2001). Although many social scientists and legislators have discussed the economic impact of the loss of Black men from many families, little has been done to address the social and psychological effects that crime and high Black male incarceration rates have on Black families and, consequently, on Black children.

This removal of young men from the Black community, whether it is through incarceration or homicide, creates feelings of fear and hopelessness, which eventually lead to many young Black children in those communities not envisioning themselves living beyond age 18. The emotional pain, trauma, and scars they experience from witnessing violence are eventually replaced with a social apathy, hostility, and an aggressive bravado posture, which contemporary urban youth articulate as being "hard" or "thug" (Wilson, 1991). Black children in low-income or poverty-stricken communities who experience a lot of violence may also become desensitized toward violence and view it and aggression as normative behavior, which can lead to behavioral problems in school and increased likelihood that they will engage in criminal behavior (Wilson, 1991). Disproportionate rates of unemployment, poverty, violence, and poor living conditions can leave very few perceived positive life choices for Black children in these communities, and for many of these children, going to prison has become a rite of passage.

A review of incarceration rates suggests that African American children are disproportionately represented in juvenile detention centers (Hawkins et al., 2000). African American children, like African American adults, receive more severe sentences and are labeled as criminals once they return to their communities and seek employment or attempt to further their education. Early incarceration among African American children increases the likelihood of recidivism and further reduces their life choices and opportunities for success and advancement (Kunjufu, 2001; Wilson, 1991). Black children who grow up in such environments, at an early age realize that they are not valued members of society and their existence has little meaning or significance to the dominant culture. They become cognizant of this through the negative images of Black people portrayed in the media and the inequities they see when they venture into White and more affluent communities. The cumulative effects of racism, poverty, and violence shape the child's perception of self and can lead to negative identity development, behavior, and psychological outcomes (Kunjufu, 2001; Wilson, 1991).

Although each of these factors can have a dynamic impact upon Black families and children, it is important to note that unemployment and poverty do not equal pathology. Many Black families in these same communities have been able to raise productive Black children despite these economic and social challenges. Therefore, mental health professionals and those seeking to develop interventions among these communities have to understand the resiliency among Black families and their children. Understanding the roles of religion, support provided by one's social or extended network, and parent socialization practices may shed light on how some Black parents are able to rear healthy children even in poverty-stricken communities. African American family reliance on extended family and the faith-based community is well documented (Martin, 2001). The church, for many African American families, is part of their extended family and provides solace and a therapeutic context wherein African Americans go to express and release through testimonials and devotionals the challenges they face during the week. Young children observing these testimonials and church practices begin to recognize religion as a coping mechanism and the church as a context wherein Black people can talk about their pains and sorrows without ridicule. Moreover, the church community provides an extended family network for Black children and young families not only by providing them examples of normative Black family life, but also the elders of the church can assist the parents in rearing and socializing children about race and providing support and counsel for families in times of need (Christian & Barbarin, 2001; Martin, 2001). The therapeutic context and the extended network provided by the church can provide some protection and guidance for Black children as they develop and navigate the social world. Understanding the context in which many Black children develop, the structural factors that influence or shape their social world, and the strengths or protective factors in the Black community can assist social scientists, human service professionals, and educators in developing interventions that adequately address and speak to the needs of Black children.

CONCLUSION

Given the social and economic challenges that Black families face and the impact that they have upon the development and well-being of Black children, mental health and human service professionals and social and behavioral scientists are at somewhat of an impasse. They can no longer continue to conduct assessments of Black children without understanding the cumulative effects of race and social inequality on the African American community. This suggests that there is a need for a new approach that addresses the intersection of race, class, and social inequalities and its impact upon the development and well-being of Black children in America. Thus, an ecological approach in research and practice may be needed to understand not only the cumulative and structural effects of racism on Black communities and families but also the effects of mainstream cultural values and subsequent institutional policies that have shaped the social world that Black children have to navigate.

Understanding and addressing mental health and other needs among Black children will, again, require mental health and human service professionals to shift their thinking in terms of research, practice, and policy. In regard to research, the mental health research community must engage in practices that will increase the likelihood that African Americans will participate in research. The mental health research community will first have to improve their relationships with the Black community and educate African Americans on mental illness and the importance of children's social and emotional health. Community information booths and community-wide focus groups and forums will increase service provider visibility and provide opportunities for researchers to gain valuable information on Black children's mental health needs. Additionally, research on Black children must be able to explain the influences of racial socialization, poverty, and racism on identity development and psychological health. Therefore, research conducted on Black children must be able to assess how they construct identity and the value they place on being a member of the Black community, as well as how experiences of racism have affected them and their families.

Research on Black families and Black children must become more comprehensive in that broader sampling techniques must be employed to secure a larger and more representative sample of African Americans. Although a number of African Americans are low-income and experience some of the life conditions expressed above, their experiences do not explain the totality of Black life. Hence, gaining data from working class, middle class, and even more affluent African Americans will be key in understanding Black child psychological development in America.

Improving relationships, educating African Americans about the importance of psychological health, and conducting more comprehensive and multilevel research in Black communities, although key, must be accompanied by a shift in practice among human service and mental health professionals. Those professionals seeking to work with Black children must be culturally competent and receive continuous training, education, and consultation regarding the social world in which Black children are reared. According to the Council of the National Psychological Advancement of Ethnic Minority Issues (2003), clinicians, as well as human service professionals, must have a knowledge, appreciation, and understanding of African American culture, values, beliefs, and world view, as well as the ecological and historical influences that impact and shape the social and psychological worlds of African Americans. As a result, mental illness and pathology among African American children should be understood and evaluated vis-à-vis their social location within American culture and what is considered normative in the context of their respective community. Employing such an approach will improve communication between human service providers and the Black community, as well as lead to more accurate diagnoses, treatments, and better outcomes for Black children.

In regard to policy, according to McAdoo (2002), there is a need for research that will document the impact of policy changes (i.e., welfare reform, No Child Left Behind Act, etc.) on human service agencies and the Black community and their affect upon Black families and Black children. Such an effort will allow for policies that negatively affect Black families to be reevaluated and revised in an attempt to better serve Black communities. Moreover, in an effort to create better policies that accurately reflect the Black community and the lives of Black children, community advocates, human service professionals, and government administrators must begin to work with constituents in the African American community (i.e., churches, parents, children, politicians, social organizations) and the research community to devise strategic, long-term plans to address issues that affect Black children. Community collaboratives that include the perspectives of Black parents and children must be established to address disproportionate rates of school failure and high school dropout, juvenile delinquency, poverty, and unemployment. These collaboratives must be vigilant in advocating for the needs of Black children in each social institution that the children have to navigate (i.e., schools, social service agencies, etc.), while also understanding that the problems that African American children face do not occur in isolation but are a part of the social fabric in which they exist (Powell, 2004). Thus, an ecological approach that assesses the intersection of race and social inequality will be needed to improve the lives of Black children.

REFERENCES

Akbar, M., Chambers, J.W., & Sanders-Thompson, V.L. (2001). Racial identity, Africentric values, and self-esteem in Jamaican children. *Journal of Black Psychology, 27*(2), 341–358.

Baldwin, J., Duncan, J.A., & Bell, Y.R. (1987). Assessment of African self-consciousness among Black students from two college environments. *Journal of Black Psychology, 13*(2), 27–41.

Barnes, E.J. (1991). The Black community as the source of positive self-concept for Black children: A theoretical perspective. In R.L. Jones (Ed.), *Black Psychology* (pp. 667–692). New York: Harper & Row.

Boykins, W.A. & Toms, F. (1985). Black child socialization: A conceptual framework. In H.P. McAdoo & J.L. McAdoo (Eds.), *Black Children: Social, educational, and parental environment* (pp. 35–51). Beverly Hills, CA: Sage.

Brofenbrenner, U. (1979). *The ecology of human development: Experiments by nature and design.* Cambridge, MA: Harvard University Press.

Caldwell, C.H., Sellers, R.M., Bernat, D.H., & Zimmerman, M.A. (2004). Racial identity, parental support, and alcohol use in a sample of academically at-risk African American high school students. *American Journal of Community Psychology, 34*(1–2), 71–82.

Carter, R.T. (1991). Racial identity attitudes and psychological functioning. *Journal of Multicultural Counseling and Development, 19,* 105–114.

Ceballo, R., & McLoyd, V.C. (2002). Social support and parenting in poor, dangerous neighborhoods. *Child Development, 73*(4), 1310–1321.

Chambers, J.W., Jr., Kambon, K., Birdsong, B.D., Brown, J., Dixon, P., & Robbins-Brinson, L. (1998). Africentric cultural identity and the stress experience of African American college students. *Journal of Black Psychology, 24*(3), 368–396.

Children's Defense Fund. (2004). Retrieved January 14, 2005, from http://www.childrensdefense.org.

Christian, M.D., & Barbarin, O.A. (2001). Cultural resources and psychological adjustment of African American children: Effects of spirituality and racial attribution. *Journal of Black Psychology, 27*(1), 43–63.

Clark, K.B., & Clark. M.P. (1947). Racial identification and preference in Negro children. In T.M. Newcomb and E.L. Hartley (Eds.), *Readings in social psychology* (pp. 169–178). New York: Holt.

Conger, R.D, Conger, K.J., Elder, G.H., Lorenz, F.O., Simons, R.L., & Whitbeck, L.B. (1992). A family process model of economic hardship and adjustment of early adolescent boys. *Child Development, 63,* 526–541.

Cooley, C.H. (1902). *Human nature and social order.* New York: Scribner.

Costello, E., Arnold, A., Burns, B., Stangl, D., Tweed, D, Erkanli, A., & Worthman, C. (1996). The great smokey mountain study of youth: Goals, design, methods, and prevalence of DSM-IIIR disorders. *Archives of General Psychiatry, 53,* 1129–1136.

Costello, E.J., Costello, A.L., Edelbrock, C., Burns, B.J., Dulcan, M.K., Brent, D., & Janiszewski, S. (1988). Psychiatric disorders in primary care: Prevalence and risk factors. *Archives of General Psychiatry, 45,* 107–166.

Council of the National Psychological Advancement of Ethnic Minority Issues. (2003). *Psychological treatment of ethnic minority populations.* Washington, DC.

Cross, W. (1985). Black identity: Rediscovering the distinction between personal identity and reference group orientation. In M. Spencer, G. Brookins, & W. Allen (Eds.), *Beginnings: the social and affective development of black children,* (pp. 155–171). Hillsdale, NJ: Lawrence Erlbaum.

Cross, W.E. (1971). The Negro-to-Black conversion experience. *Black World,* 13–27.

Cross, W.E., Parham, T., & Helms, J.E. (1991). The stages of black identity development: nigrescence models. In R.L. Jones (Ed.), *Black Psychology* (pp. 319–338). New York: Harper & Row.

Edelman, M.W. (1985). The sea is so wide and my boat is so small: Problems facing black children today. In H.P. McAdoo & J.L. McAdoo (Eds.), *Black children: Social, educational, and parental environments* (pp. 72–82). Beverly Hills, CA: Sage.

Edelman, M.W. (1992). *The measure of our success: A letter to my children and yours.* Boston: Beacon.

Erikson, E.H. (1968). *Identity: Youth and crisis.* New York: Norton.

Franklin, A.J. (1991). An index of psychological well-being among African Americans. *Handbook of Tests and Measurements for Black Populations,* 587–595.

Grier, W.H., & Cobbs, P.M. (1968). *Black rage.* New York: Bantam Books.

Hankins-Jarrett, S. (1997). *Welfare reform, domestic violence, and the African American community.* Retrieved January 14, 2005, from http://www.dvinstitute.org/Proceedings/1997/welfare.pdf.

Hawkins, D.F., Laub, J.H., Lauritsen, J.L., & Cothern, L. (2000). Race, ethnicity, and serious and violent juvenile offending. *National Criminal Justice Reference Service.* Department of United States Justice.

Holliday, B.G. (1985). Developmental imperatives of social ecologies: Lessons learned from black children. In H.P. McAdoo & J.L. McAdoo (Eds.), *Black children: Social, educational, and parental environments* (pp. 53–69). Beverly Hills, CA: Sage.

Horn, W., & Bush, A. (1997). Fathers and welfare reform. *Public Interest, 129,* 38–49.

Institute of Medicine. (n.d.). Retrieved December 6, 2004, from http://www.iom.edu.

Kambon, K.K. (1992). *The African personality in America: An African-centered framework.* Tallahassee, FL: Nubian Nations Publications.

Kardiner, A., & Ovessey, L. (1951). *The mark of oppression.* New York: World.

Kay, V. (2003). *Creating regional equity for families and children.* Institute on Race and Poverty.

King, L.M., Dickson, V.J., & Nobels, W.W. (Eds.). (1976). *African philosophy: Assumptions and paradigms for research on Black persons.* Los Angeles: Fanon R & D Center.

Kunjufu, J. (2001). *State of emergency: We must save African American males.* Chicago: African American Images.

Ladd, H.F. (1998). Evidence on discrimination in mortgage lending. *Journal of Economic Perspectives, 12*(2), 41–62.

Livingston, J., Hines, R., & Nahimana, C. (2004, September). *Understanding the etiology of health disparities from an ecological approach.* Poster session presented at the Innovative Approaches to Eliminate Racial and Ethnic Health Disparities conference, Ann Arbor, MI.

Loury, G. (2000). Twenty-five years of Black America: Two steps forward and one step back? *Journal of Sociology and Social Welfare, 27*(1), 19–52.

Martin, P.P. (2001). *The African American church and African American parents: Examining the relationships between racial socialization practices and racial identity attitudes.* Unpublished doctoral dissertation, Michigan State University.

McAdoo, H.P. (1985). The development of self-concept and race attitudes of young black children over time. In H.P. McAdoo & J.L. McAdoo (Eds.), *Black children: Social, educational, and parental environments* (pp. 213–242). Beverly Hills, CA: Sage.

McAdoo, H.P. (2002). Diverse children of color: Research and policy implications. In H.P. McAdoo (Ed.), *Black children: Social, educational, and parental environments* (2nd ed., pp. 13–26). Thousand Oaks, CA: Sage.

McLoyd, V.C. (1998). The impact of economic hardship on black families and children: Psychological distress, parenting, and socioeconomic development. *Child Development, 61,* 311–346.

Mead, G.H. (1934). *Mind, self, and society.* Chicago: University of Chicago Press.

Munford, M.B. (1994). Relationship of gender, self-esteem, social class, and racial identity to depression in Blacks. *Journal of Black Psychology, 20*(2), 157–174.

Murray, C.B., & Mandara, J. (2002). Racial identity development in African American children: Cognitive and experiential antecedents. In H.P. McAdoo (Ed.), *Black children: Social, educational, and parental environments* (2nd ed., pp. 73–96). Thousand Oaks, CA: Sage.

Murray, V.M., & Brody, G.H. (2002). Racial socialization processes in single-mother families: Linking maternal racial identity, parenting, and racial socialization in rural, single-mother families with child self-worth and self-regulation. In H.P. McAdoo (Ed.), *Black children: Social, educational, and parental environments* (2nd ed., pp. 97–115). Thousand Oaks, CA: Sage.

National Urban League. (2002). Annual Report. Retrieved December 6, 2004, from http:/www.nul/org/publications/index.htm.

Neighbors, H.W., Jackson, J.S., Bowman, P.J., & Gurin, G. (1983). Stress, coping, and Black mental health: Preliminary findings from a national study. *Prevention in Human Services, 2*(3), 5–29.

Newsom, K.C. (2004). The relationship between ethnic identity development and self-concept of African American preadolescent youth. *Dissertation Abstracts International, 65*(2-B), 1053.

Office of the Surgeon General. (n.d.). *Mental health care for African Americans: The need for mental health care* (United States Department of Health and

Human Services). Retrieved December 6, 2004, from http://www.mentalhealth.org.

Parham, T.A., & Helms, J.E. (1985, March). Attitudes of racial identity and self-esteem of Black students: An exploratory investigation. *Journal of College Student Personnel, 26*(2), 143–147.

Peters, M.F. (2002). Racial socialization of young black children. In H.P. McAdoo (Ed.), *Black children: Social, educational, and parental environments* (2nd ed., pp. 57–72). Thousand Oaks, CA: Sage.

Powell, J. (2004, June). *Reconceptualizing early childhood education and care: A atructural approach.* Presented at the Michigan Legislative Black Caucus Summit Early Childhood Education and Care. Lansing, MI.

Richardson, B.B. (1981). Racism and child-rearing: A study of Black mothers. *Dissertation Abstracts, 42*(1), 125-A.

Richardson, L.A. (2001). Seeking and obtaining mental health services: What do parents expect? *Archives of Psychiatric Nursing, 15,* 223–231.

Rodriguez, E., Allen, J.A., Frongillo, E.A., & Chandra, P. (1999). Unemployment, depression, and health: A look at the African American community. *Journal of Epidemiology and Community Health, 53,* 335–342.

Rowley, S.J., Sellers, R.M., Chavous, T.M., & Smith, M.A. (1998, March). The relationship between racial identity and self-esteem in African American college and high school students. *Journal of Personality & Social Psychology, 74*(3), 715–724.

Sellers, R.M., Smith, M.A., Shelton, J.N., Rowley, S.J., & Chavous, T.M. (1998). Multidimensional model of racial identity: A reconceptualization of African American racial identity. *Personality and Social Psychology Review, 2*(1), 18–39.

Semaj, L.T. (1985). Afrikanity, cognition, and external self-identity. In M. Spencer, G. Brookins, & W. Allen (Eds.), *Beginnings: The social and affective development of Black children* (pp. 59–72). Hillsdale, NJ: Lawrence Erlbaum.

Shore, R. (1997). *Rethinking the brain: New insights in early development.* New York: Families and Work Institute.

Snowden, L.R. (2003, February). Bias in mental health assessment and intervention: Theory and evidence. *American Journal of Public Health, 93*(2), 239–243.

Spencer, M.B. (1984). Black children's race awareness, racial attitudes, and self-concept: A reinterpretation. *Journal of Child Psychology and Psychiatry, 25*(3), 433–441.

Spencer, M.A., Kohn, L.P., & Woods, J.R. (2002). Labeling vs. early identification: The dilemma of mental health service under-utilization among low-income African American children. *African American Research Perspectives, 8*(2), 1–14.

Stevenson, H.C., Reed, J., Bodison, P., & Bishop, A. (1997). Racism stress management: Racial socialization beliefs and the experience of depression and anger in African American youth. *Youth and Society, 29,* 197–219.

Stevenson, H.W., & Stewart, E.C. (1958). A developmental study of racial awareness in young children. *Child Development, 29,* 399–410.

Thomas, A., & Sillen, S. (1972). *Racism and psychiatry.* New York: Bruner/ Mazel.

Twenge, J., & Crocker, J. (2002, May). Race and self-esteem: Meta-analyses comparing Whites, Blacks, Hispanics, Asians, and American Indians and comment on Gray-Little and Hafdahl. *Psychological Bulletin, 128*(3), 371–408.

United States Census Bureau. (2003, April). *The Black population in the United States: March 2002.* Retrieved January 14, 2005, from http://www.census. gov/prod/2003pubs/p20–541.pdf.

Valleni-Basile, L.S., Garrison, C.Z., Waller, J.L., Addy, C.L., McKeown, R.E., Jackson, K.L., & Cuff, S.P. (1996). Incidence of obsessive-compulsive disorder in a community sample of young adolescents. *Journal of the American Academy of Child and Adolescent Psychiatry, 35,* 898–906.

Vega, W.A., & Rumbaut, R.G. (1991). Ethnic minorities and mental health. *Annual Review of Sociology, 17,* 351–383.

Watts, H., & Nightingale, D.S. (1996). Adding it up: The economic impact of incarceration on individuals, families, and communities. *Oklahoma Criminal Justice Research Consortium Journal.* Oklahoma City: Oklahoma Criminal Justice Research Consortium.

Wells, E.E. (1978). *The mythical Black self-concept.* San Francisco: R & E Research Associates.

Wilson, A.N. (1991). *Understanding Black adolescent male violence: Its remediation and prevention.* Brooklyn, NY: Afrikan World InfoSystems.

Chapter 6

ADOPTION AND YOUTH: CRITICAL ISSUES AND STRENGTHS-BASED PROGRAMMING TO ADDRESS THEM

Kristine Freeark

> The ultimate aim of adoption is to enable children to tell their own story in their own way. (Hart & Luckock, 2004)

Adoption has been a suspect and stigmatized institution in American society, and, although some argue that the situation is improving (Pertman, 2000), others point out that the predominant portrayal of adoption in the United States is still wary, marginalizing, and one involving less-than-"real" family ties (Brodzinsky, Smith, & Brodzinsky, 1998; Wegar, 2000). Americans' strong belief that "blood is thicker than water" and in family relationships being constituted by shared genetics leave adoption regarded as "second best." In contrast, other societies and even some subcultures within America have a kinship-based model of family that emphasizes the roles people adopt toward one another, rather than their biological relatedness, in defining family (Leon, 2002). Grotevant and Kohler (1999) have suggested that adoptive families be considered as a "yoked" family form, with the adopted child functioning as a connection between two families—birth and adoptive—producing a complex adoptive kinship network.

How does the experience of wearing the label "adopted" impact the adjustment and identity of an adopted person as he or she grows up? How do adopted adolescents integrate into their self-image what the fact of having been adopted means about them and all of their relatives—adoptive and birth? Does it place adopted children at risk, or is their resilience combined with a supportive and nurturant environment sufficient to buffer against significant difficulties? These questions have been evaluated and debated in the field of adoption for years.

This chapter explores the tension between the resilience and vulnerability of adopted youth and highlights the contextual factors that facilitate healthy exploration of an identity as an adopted person. It reviews the demographics of adoption as they are relevant to understanding the social milieu of adopted adolescents. Public attitudes and stereotypes about adoption are detailed. The chapter outlines the unique developmental tasks of adopted adolescents and their families, as well as the interpersonal challenges they often encounter. It summarizes research findings on the adjustment of adopted children and adolescents as well as the complexities and limitations of that research. The roles of clinical services and family relationships in the adaptation of adopted youth are considered. Finally, we address the potential for innovative, strengths-based programming for adopted youth. One program is presented in detail to illustrate creative partnerships between adopted youth, the adoption community, and local communities.

The involvement of adopted youth in ventures of this sort shows great promise for facilitating identity exploration and challenging negative stereotypes. Promoting a public image of adoption that highlights strengths and opportunities, rather than stigma and loss, is a goal with significant implications for adopted individuals and their families, and also for children in the foster care system.

THE DEMOGRAPHICS OF ADOPTION

The 2000 census was the first time that adoption had ever been directly included as a form of family creation in the United States census (Kreider, 2003); it was also the first time in 25 years that the government had systematically gathered adoption statistics (Grotevant & Kohler, 1999). The census established that roughly 2.5 percent (1.6 million) of all children under 18 living in their parents' household had been adopted. Among those over 18 still living with their parents, the same percentage was adopted. This figure corroborated what had been estimated (2–4 percent) in prior demographic analyses (Brodzinsky et al., 1998) and means that there are roughly 2 million adopted children or adolescents living with their parent(s). While there were minor geographic variations, the census report concluded that "adoption is a family-building process which takes place in all states in about the same proportions" (Kreider, 2003).

At 2.5 percent of the population, adopted children and adolescents are a very small minority. By way of comparison, the representations of several racial/ethnic minorities among the general population are: Hispanic or

Latino, 12.5 percent; African American, 12.3 percent; Asian, 3.6 percent; biracial or multiracial, 2.4 percent (U.S. Census Bureau, 2001). If one projects 2.5 percent onto a hypothetical U.S. high school of 1,200 students, only 30 would be adopted (7 or 8 per graduating class). In a typical classroom of 30 students, an adopted adolescent would almost certainly be the sole representative of this minority group. Yet his or her minority status might not be known by anyone else in the class. Despite the visibility of transracial and international adoptions, the majority of adoptions in the U.S. are within race (U.S. Census Bureau, 2001). Adolescents long so deeply to fit in and belong that the rarity of adoption and the embarrassment about standing out in that way lead many adopted adolescents to hide or downplay their adoptive status (Brodzinsky, Schechter, & Henig, 1992).

Two recent trends in adoption have made it more public and less secretive. The biggest demographic change in adoption patterns in recent years has been the increase in intercountry adoption; the number of immigrant visas issued to foreign-born children being adopted by U.S. citizens increased by more than two and a half times between 1990 and 2000. In 2000, 13 percent of adopted children were foreign-born. Given that 81 percent of these intercountry adoptions are of children born in Asian and Latin American countries and adopted by Caucasian parents, differences in physical appearance has made adoption more visible as a social phenomenon. Another change in adoption practice since the 1970s has been the move toward open adoption, an arrangement between birth parents and adoptive parents that involves mutual sharing of identifying information and a plan of some sort for ongoing contact between them (Brodzinsky et al., 1998). Both of these trends have made adoption a more public and visible type of family formation. Yet it can't be assumed that the increased visibility and attention that adoption has received necessarily means that Americans are embracing adoption (Melosh, 2002) or that adopted adolescents will necessarily be more forthright about their adoptive status. Because the community of adopted children is so small and many of them will hesitate to identify themselves as adopted, the opportunities for one adopted child to look at others and conclude that they all collectively look like "average kids" is extremely limited.

PUBLIC ATTITUDES TOWARD ADOPTION

Evidence of the complex attitudes held toward adoption in the United States came from the first national survey on adoption attitudes, sponsored by the Evan B. Donaldson Adoption Institute (1997). The survey found that 59 percent of Americans have some personal connection to adoption, such as knowing a family member or friend who is a member of an adoptive family. Seventy-eight percent of the respondents believed that adoption served a useful purpose in our society, and 90 percent had a somewhat or very favorable opinion of adoption. Thirty-six percent of those polled reported having considered adopting either somewhat or very seriously. These findings suggest reasonably high levels of acceptance of adoption as a social institution, and some openness to considering kinship alongside biology as grounds for defining the family unit.

Perceptions of adopted children, however, reflected more ambivalence. A majority of respondents viewed adopted children as well adjusted (76 percent) and secure (68 percent), but roughly one-third believed that adopted children were more likely to have problems than their nonadopted peers. Thirty-nine percent anticipated more behavior problems, 35 percent more school problems, and 28 percent more problems with drugs and alcohol. Beliefs about the adjustment of foreign-born adopted children were even more pessimistic: 52 percent of respondents believed that foreign-born children were more likely to have emotional problems than would children born within the United States and adopted domestically. Thus, while there was support of the institution of adoption and an acknowledgement of its benefits and accomplishments, at the level of perceptions of the adopted child's experience, more than one in three people expected to see an adopted child struggle.

The Adoption Institute survey results (Adoption Institute, 1997) also provided information about the origins of these public attitudes. The media (newspapers, books, magazines, movies, etc.) were cited as a source of information about adoption by 52 percent of those surveyed, while 45 percent cited personal sources such as friends and family. The particular source of adoption information influenced the image held of adoption: Of those polled who were classified as "full supporters" of adoption, almost three-quarters received their information about adoption from family and friends. In contrast, "marginal supporters" were more likely to learn about adoption from the media. Clearly, a substantial portion of the population is being influenced by images of adoption that are removed from the day-to-day experiences and relationships of adoptive families and their children. The sensationalistic publicity of two recent television specials has been vehemently criticized (Pertman, 2004; Schram, 2004).

Not only do the media sensationalize adoption, but more authoritative sources such as college-level textbooks either overlook it or portray it negatively (Fisher, 2003). Fisher's survey of 37 textbooks and anthologies published between 1998 and 2001 for use in undergraduate courses in the family confirmed that coverage of adoption continues to be very poor. Nineteen percent of the books didn't address adoption at all. In anthologies, adoption was typically only mentioned in passing; less than

1 percent of the anthology selections addressed adoption in any depth. Fisher analyzed the statements that were made about adoption for their positive and negative portrayals: Nearly twice as many negative points as positive ones were made. He also found that the negative coverage did not accurately represent the current state of knowledge in the field of adoption research. Sixty-seven percent of these books either didn't address adoption or portrayed it negatively.

If popular media coverage of adoption is making the public wary, and more accurate portrayals are not being provided in higher education, then there is a great need for other avenues of influence to impact people's consideration of adoption as a viable route to family creation. The Adoption Institute (2002) makes the point that if just 1 in 500 of the adults who their surveys indicate have considered adopting, would adopt, all of the children in the United States foster care system would have permanent families.

DEVELOPMENTAL TASKS OF ADOPTED ADOLESCENTS AND THEIR FAMILIES

Adopted children grow up amid these contradictory messages. They either unwittingly internalize them or, through the help of their families and adoptive communities, become consciously aware of them and are able to sort them out and evaluate their relevance to their own life stories (Steinberg & Hall, 2000).

During adolescence one of the primary developmental tasks for all young people is to sift through and begin to organize the various elements of an identity, some of which are ascribed (e.g., adopted), others chosen (e.g., soccer player, clarinetist) (Grotevant, Dunbar, Kohler, & Lash Esau, 2000). Gains in cognitive abilities make it possible for adolescents to reason more abstractly about how they see themselves and their place in the world; for adopted adolescents, thinking more abstractly about adoption entails understanding its legal, sexual, relational, and societal dimensions (Grotevant et al., 2000).

This task of identity organization is more complex for adopted adolescents because their life story must incorporate belonging to one family and disconnection from another. It also contains questions about who one takes after and who one will turn out to be like. Often feelings of abandonment, rejection, anger, shame, and divided loyalty need to be dealt with. Ties to two ethnicities, nations, or races can create the additional challenge of incorporating two cultures, with different values and social status, into that self-definition. An adopted adolescent must also grapple with negative societal messages about adoption, both as they reflect on individuals (e.g., birth parents) and on family bonds. Sorting out the pieces of a complex life puzzle and recognizing the image of self that emerges can be a profound and challenging process for an adopted adolescent. Working to organize the pieces and fit them in place taps an adolescent's strength and vulnerability, capacity for connection and separateness, autonomy, and reliance on others.

Middle- to late-adolescence is also a stage of family life when a major renegotiation of family relationships takes place. An adopted adolescent's increasing separateness and individuation from his or her adoptive family can challenge both child's and parents' confidence in their connection over time (Rosenberg, 1992). Whether the normative adolescent challenging of parental values or expectations will lead to an unhealthy urge to embrace aspects of the birth parents' lives—real or imagined—can create suspense and battles for control within adoptive families (Rosenberg, 1992). Peer relationships and other connections outside the family typically play a central role in helping adolescents to define themselves as different from and independent of their families (Grotevant et al., 2000). By moving between family and broader contexts (e.g., peer, school, community), the adolescent defines who he or she is. A preoccupation with the birth family can become the counterpoint to the adoptive family ties, but there are other alternatives. Open communication and productive points of connection available to the adopted adolescent can enhance family security rather than challenge it. The adoptive family's ability to tolerate the tension of that individuation and maintain trust in the strength of their psychological connections to one another are a major factor in how the adolescent years unfold (Rosenberg, 1992).

INTERPERSONAL CHALLENGES EXPERIENCED BY ADOPTED YOUTH

Adopted children grow up not only facing their own questions about their life story but also fielding other people's questions. They encounter other people's projections onto them regarding how it must feel to have been adopted and the struggles and problems that are imagined to result. A New Yorker cartoon depicts two women in ancient Egypt kneeling by the side of a river carefully placing a baby swaddled in a woven basket into the water. One says to the other, "He'll have abandonment issues!" This caricature of Moses' relinquishment perfectly captures the widely held assumption that the fact of having been placed for adoption will overshadow all other life events in shaping one's personality. To imagine the profound vulnerability and existential helplessness entailed in being separated early in life from one's biological parents seems to evoke an instinctive reaction in others that centers on loss, blame, or misfortune.

Adopted persons from an early age are stereotyped and depersonalized as they interact with others around the topic of their life story and how they came to join their family. The following account from a transracially adopted young woman portrays a typical encounter:

> All my life, I've known that I'm different because I am an Asian adoptee. As a server at a restaurant, I always have my customers guessing my nationality and commenting on how good my English is. Some ask nosy questions like if I'm adopted and if I know my birth mother. I've gotten better with my responses but it still makes me uneasy to tell absolute strangers my personal history. In a way, my sharing of my experiences can hopefully shed a new perspective into their narrow one. One day a customer actually asked me if I was Oriental and I really wanted to bark back to him, "No, I'm not a rug"! It never ceases to amaze me how ignorant people can be. (Cronican-Walker, 2004, p. 9)

Adopted children function as blank screens onto which individuals, professionals, the media, and society project their fear, shame, pity, or unsettling awareness of the complexity and fragility of family relationships. While this may occur more frequently in transracial adoptions, adopted children who are of the same race as their parents are not immune to alienating experiences. Others' misunderstanding of their experience, insensitivity, and stigmatization of adoption have been reported by adopted adolescents as being the main reasons that they would hesitate to ask for help at times when it might be useful (Ryan & Nalavany, 2003; Smith & Howard, 1999).

EVIDENCE ABOUT THE ADJUSTMENT OF ADOPTED CHILDREN AND YOUTH

The diversity of adoptive experiences as well as the reality that adoption is a lifelong process with unique aspects to its developmental course make summarizing adoption outcomes a complex undertaking. Psychodynamic theory and accounts of clinical work with adopted children dominated the literature on adoption for many decades, despite the fact that the assumptions about intrapsychic processes are difficult to test and largely empirically unproven (Brodzinsky et al., 1998). Characterizing the experience of adoption from clinical accounts was problematic and limited in several ways: (1) they emphasized the pathology, turmoil, and losses experienced by members of adoptive families; (2) they were either single case descriptions or based on very small and nonrepresentative samples; (3) they confounded the effects of psychological problems with the experience of adoption; and (4) they were used to overgeneralize from a clinical population onto the experiences of the larger majority of people who have not sought therapy.

The picture of adoption as drawn by clinicians was eventually balanced by empirical research based on larger samples of adopted children drawn from the community rather than clinicians' offices. One challenge in studying groups of adopted children is the heterogeneity of adoption in the United States. There are wide variations in adopted child characteristics and in the circumstances of their adoption (e.g., adopted as a newborn versus school-age child, birth in a foreign country versus months or years spent in U.S. foster care). Combining such varied adoption situations provides a better sample size for quantitative analysis, but it is very likely to be mixing apples and oranges. Overall, these studies have shown that the vast majority of adopted children function in the normal range (Brodzinsky et al., 1998); when there are significant differences between adopted and nonadopted groups, they are most often in the areas of externalizing (acting out) problems (as opposed to internalizing problems such as anxiety and depression), academic problems, or attentional problems. Research findings may inaccurately estimate risk (either over- or underestimate) to a particular group of adopted children if they are based on a highly disparate group (Haugaard, 1998). Not surprisingly, given the predominance of clinical reports and the stigma associated with adoption, most of the research has been framed to find out whether adopted children fare worse than their nonadopted peers.

Community-based studies and analysis of adopted-nonadopted differences in national survey samples have reached less dire conclusions. These findings have provided evidence that the vast majority of adopted children are well adjusted and that where differences do exist favoring nonadopted children, the differences were not large enough to be clinically meaningful (Benson, Sharma, & Roehlkepartain, 1994; Brodzinsky et al., 1998; Juffer & van Ijzendoorn, 2005). A recent meta-analysis including the data from 98 adoption studies from around the world recently concluded that the difference in behavior problems between adopted and nonadopted children, favoring the nonadopted, is small (Juffer & van Ijzendoorn, 2005). In comparing the adjustment of internationally versus domestically adopted children they found, contrary to their hypothesis and public perception, that the internationally adopted children had fewer behavior problems than their domestically adopted peers. Some studies have found that adopted youth functioning surpasses that of comparison groups in some areas (Benson et al., 1994; Brodzinsky et al., 1998; Haugaard, 1998).

Haugaard attempted to reconcile the inconsistency in the field between reports that adopted children have more significant difficulties than nonadopted peers and those that show few significant differences. By exploring various models of adopted-nonadopted group differences and comparing them to the most solid research findings, he showed that with as little as 10 percent of adopted children having clinically significant problems, the average adjustment level of the other 90 percent would appear worse than that of a nonadopted comparison group. The implication is that for every one problematic adoption story that people hear and remember, there could easily be nine that are far from problematic.

Recent analyses of the National Longitudinal Survey of Adolescent Health (commonly referred to as Add Health) have shed new light on the adjustment of adopted adolescents and, inadvertently, on the stereotyping to which they are subject. The Add Health Survey has a scope that exceeds all previous attempts at assessing adolescent well-being at a national level (Feigelman, 2001). It surveyed over 90,000 7th- through 12th-graders at school and then followed up to interview more than 20,000 of them at home with their parents. Adopted adolescents self-identified on the school survey, and their adoptive status was then confirmed in the course of the home interview. One initial analysis of the school survey data comparing adopted to nonadopted groups concluded that adopted adolescents were "at higher risk in all of the domains examined, including school achievement and problems, substance use, psychological well-being, physical health, fighting and lying to parents" (Miller et al., 2000, p. 1458).

When this same research group attempted to corroborate adoptive status between what respondents reported at school and what their parents reported in the home, they found a major discrepancy (Fan et al., 2002): 19 percent of the adolescents who had identified themselves as adopted were not adopted, according to their parents. And these "jokesters" provided "mischievous or dishonest" reports of their adjustment. After identifying this jokester phenomenon, the authors concluded that "the extreme responses of the jokesters appear to have resulted in substantial overstatement about the differences between the adopted and non-adopted groups," (p. 20). A reanalysis of the data based only on the reports of true adopted adolescents versus their nonadopted peers showed very small differences in adjustment.

This important discovery only corrected inaccurate conclusions about the adjustment difficulties of adopted youth after the original paper had been published in *Child Development. Child Development* is not only one of the most influential journals in the field of developmental and educational psychology, but it is also read by a large audience, many of whom know very little about adoption. The correction that was published in an issue of the journal two years later is unlikely to have been spotted by the readers who had formerly incorporated the more dire findings into their understanding of adopted adolescents. The paper that fully explained how the error came about and corrected the conclusions to be drawn was published in *Adoption Quarterly,* a journal with a fraction of *Child Development*'s readership and an already more adoption-informed audience. This is unfortunately a prime example of how incorrect adoption stereotypes get perpetuated despite the fact that science is disproving them.

The jokester phenomenon also revealed the negative tenor of associations to adoption that are likely to exist in a high school setting. The fact that this small group of high school students would choose to misrepresent themselves first as adopted, and second with major adjustment, school, and family problems, confirms the risk that adopted adolescents might be taking to be more open in acknowledging adoptive status in the high school setting.

Researchers in adoption have also argued that comparing adopted youth only to peers who have grown up with two biological parents is stacking the deck from the start. Another Add Health analysis (based on data gathered in the home interview) compared three groups of adolescents: those living in two-parent biological families, those living in divorced or remarried families with one biological parent, and adopted adolescents living in two-parent families (Feigelman, 2001). The adolescents whose parents had divorced showed far greater adjustment problems than the other two groups. In contrast to the public perception that adopted youth would be more likely to have trouble with substance abuse, it was the biologically related/intact family group that reported the highest rates of drug use. The adopted adolescents differed very little from the nonadopted/intact group in the level of problem behavior.

The three areas of adopted/nonadopted difference that were both statistically significant and were reported often enough to reveal a common pattern were that: (1) adopted youth were more likely to have run away from home; (2) they were less motivated to go to college, though they did intend to get a college education; and (3) they were more likely to be in counseling. The first two findings, running away and difficulty beginning the transition to college, may not be as reflective of individual psychopathology as they are the complexity of negotiating separation-individuation within adoptive families during adolescence. Running away can be a way of testing family bonds. The prospect of leaving for college may raise the question of whether adoption has served its purpose once the child is old enough to move out from under the family roof; fantasies that college matriculation signifies an end to the family relationships may well create anxiety. If challenging situations are viewed in light of the unique developmental tasks for adoptive families, they can be understood as part of a process to be managed rather than a deficit in either the adolescent or his or her family. (The finding on the prevalence of counseling will be considered in greater depth in the next section.)

Feigelman's findings illustrate the importance of considering adoption as one example along a continuum of life challenges and advantages faced by young people. Divorce appears to disrupt adolescents' lives more than having been adopted, but the fact that divorce is so much more common than adoption normalizes the image of adolescents of divorce.

THERAPY AS CONFIRMATION OF PSYCHOPATHOLOGY OR A CONTEXT FOR IDENTITY EXPLORATION?

There is ample evidence of the overrepresentation of adopted children and adolescents in a range of settings that provide psychological services such as outpatient psychotherapy, inpatient services, and residential school placements. Clinicians have reported rates ranging from one and a half to five times higher in outpatient settings for adopted children than for their nonadopted peers (Grotevant & McRoy, 1990; Miller et al., 2000) and five to seven times higher in residential care and psychiatric inpatient settings (Brodzinsky, 1993). In a careful review of several studies of inpatient clinical samples conducted between the 1960s and 1980s, adopted children constituted 9 to 21 percent of the recipients of services (Haugaard, 1998). A parallel analysis of outpatient settings between the 1950s and 1980s found adopted children represented at rates ranging from 1 to 7 percent. Given that the rates of nonrelative adoption have always been estimated at around 1 to 2 percent, these indicators of high rates for utilization of mental health services made it appear that adopted children were at substantial risk for psychological problems. Haugaard noted that in all of the studies he reviewed, children with widely varying adoption histories were combined together; "children who were abused and neglected for 6 years before adoption, for example, are considered with newborns adopted from a mother who provided a good prenatal environment." (p. 51). He went on to point out that the generalizability from such findings about psychopathology and use of clinical services to any specific subgroup of the adopted population was fraught with error. One cannot tell whether it is adoption itself that places children at risk, or the preadoption circumstances that some children experience that later accounts for the need for treatment. Juffer and van Ijzendoorn (2005) found that although the level of differences in behavior problems between adopted and nonadopted groups was small, the difference in use of mental health services by adoptees was large and not at all in proportion to their adjustment difficulties. Lively debate in the field of adoption research has centered on the following question: If adopted children are not markedly different from their nonadopted classmates, neighbors, and friends, why are so many of them receiving psychological services? While many in the adoption field have said it is because adopted children are more vulnerable due to factors such as genetics, prenatal care, or the trauma of separation from their birth parents, others have found a referral bias due to adopted status (Miller et al., 2000).

Many have made the case that adoptive parents have a lower referral threshold (Ingersoll, 1997), referring their adopted children for milder difficulties than a nonadoptive parent might. Several explanations for this overreferral phenomenon have been posited: (1) adoptive parents are more worried about what their child's struggles might develop into; (2) normative crises for adopted children, such as mourning the loss of birthfamily, might be misperceived as behavior problems and a cause for referral; (3) they are more socioeconomically advantaged and can afford psychological care more readily; or (4) they might be more accustomed to turning to professional help to treat their children, just as they did to become parents in the first place (Brodzinsky, 1990; Miller et al., 2000). It is not only adoptive parents who are more likely to refer adopted children to treatment; the same readiness has been reported in professionals (Brodzinsky et al., 1998). The expectation that adopted children will have greater difficulty during the course of their youth is believed to influence the readiness of a range of adults to refer them for psychological services.

Because mental health services, like adoption, are stigmatized, the suggestion that an adopted adolescent needs therapy could obviously meet substantial resistance. It could also undermine the adolescent's confidence in his or her own psychological well-being and adjustment. Wegar (2000) has argued that many adopted children and youth are either in need of therapy or simply end up in therapy because of the adoption stigma they encounter, rather than because of their psychopathology. One group of researchers has concluded that, despite the advances in adoption research, "the end result is that there is very little good information about the functioning of U.S. adopted persons. In the absence of this information, the scientific treatment of adopted persons is often characterized by stereotypy and hearsay" (Sharma, McGue, & Benson, 1998). When adopted children and youth then encounter those who have been misinformed, they see themselves reflected in a distorted mirror that casts doubt and difficulty on their adjustment, life story, and family ties.

If one views psychotherapy as a process through which people construct a story of their life (Lieblich, McAdams, & Josselson, 2004), then the overrepresentation of adopted children and adolescents even in the absence of significant adjustment problems, begins to make sense. Adopted children do have a more complex life narrative to construct, and many parents are aware of this. Ideally, the adoptive family functions as a context for story-building by adopted children in early childhood (Watkins & Fisher, 1993) and continues to help them add depth to the story through middle childhood. But during adolescence, the adopted child's need to differentiate him- or herself from parents becomes necessary in order to make developmental gains. A site for life story creation apart from home and family might be necessary. Entering therapy may be one solution. Community programming to fill that need is almost nonexistent. In the absence of alternative settings (with peers, in high school, etc.) in which to undertake this life story construction, mental health settings might be the default. What is needed are ways for adopted youth to present their own story of their adoptive experience, a picture that reflects their reality.

STEREOTYPING AND STRENGTHS OF ADOPTIVE FAMILIES

Negative stereotypes about adoptive family relationships continue to be promoted, and they subtly undermine the status of adopted children (even as adults) and the legitimacy of family ties created through adoption. Adoptive families experience insensitive and sometimes intrusive comments from others that question the strength and legitimacy of their family ties. Adoptive parents also encounter projections from other people that imply that they have adopted out of some altruistic motive rather than to simply become a parent, or that they are parenting in spite of the fact that their children are not "their own"; for example, "You are so courageous to raise someone else's child. I don't think I could do it" (Brodzinsky, 1990, p. 17). The more visible the adoption is (e.g., transracial) and the more open a family is about being an adoptive family, the greater the likelihood that such comments will occur. The more actively the family works as a unit to develop a perspective and coping strategies for other people's skepticism about their bonds, the better the child's feelings about adoption and him- or herself (Brodzinsky, 1990).

For the last 40 years it has been acknowledged that adoptive families have several unique developmental tasks in addition to those of biologically related families (Kirk, 1964) by virtue of the "role handicap," and that these differences unfold over time and have a normative developmental course (Rosenberg, 1992). Adoption is not a one-time event for either a child or a family, but instead a joining together on a journey.

Multiple influences have made adoptive parents question their ability to become fully adequate parents. Psychoanalytic writing suggested that the origins of infertility were psychological and resided in women's ambivalence about mothering (Brinich, 1990). When adopted children had behavioral or emotional problems, the supposition was that the parents' (meaning mother's) inability to truly love the child was the explanation (Brinich, 1990). Although we now know much more about the complexities of reproductive capacity for men and women and the predominance of physical origins of infertility, those early parent-blaming (and particularly mother-blaming) beliefs have not disappeared .

The adoption process itself can reinforce this sense of skepticism about adequacy to parent. In order to adopt, a couple or single parent must undergo a home study, an assessment by a social worker designed to evaluate the potential adoptive parents' clarity about what they are undertaking, their motivations to adopt, and their suitability to become parents. Although the home study process can be anxiety-producing for couples in the midst of it, once completed it in effect issues a "stamp of approval" for parents (Rosenberg, 1992) and might even become a source of validation. In fact, a variety of findings about adoptive parents culled from research reports over the years suggest that adopted children benefit from a family context that is at least as nurturing and stable as those created solely by birth (Cohen, Coyne, & Duvall, 1996). However, because most research on adoption is problem-focused rather than strengths-focused, the evidence about the protective and growth-promoting sides of adoptive family life receive less attention. They often emerge from studies that have focused on strain and difficulty.

The Search Institute survey (Benson et al., 1994) of randomly selected adoptive families with adolescent children in four states was designed to identify the mental health and service needs of these families; each family had a child who had been placed with them before 15 months of age. The survey also included instruments that assessed developmental assets, defined as protective influences that promote well-being and minimize risky behaviors. The adopted adolescents were compared to both their nonadopted siblings and a national sample of 51,000 public school students. The adopted adolescents scored higher on many of the developmental assets and lower on a parallel measure of high-risk indicators. Out of 16 indicators of well-being (ranging from educational commitment, connectedness, support, caring, optimism, and social competence), the adopted adolescents averaged nearly even with their nonadopted siblings (11.1 versus 11.5), and both sibling groups averaged higher than the public school sample (10.3). The difference between the adoptive family members and the public school students was large enough to be statistically significant. Seventy-three percent of the adopted adolescents had 10 or more of the well-being indicators as opposed to 62 percent of the public school students. Assessment of 20 high-risk indicators (e.g., substance use, sexuality, depression, antisocial behavior) yielded an average of 1.95 for adopted adolescents compared to 2.89 for the public school sample.

Like much other adoption research, the Search Institute's participant base somewhat limits generalizability, but the study's outcomes emphasized positive adjustment rather than negative. It broke new ground in documenting that adopted adolescents do flourish and may even surpass the adjustment of their nonadopted peers.

What family characteristics contribute to the well-being of so many adopted youth? Findings from the Search Institute's survey, along with other studies (as cited), have identified the following dimensions of family functioning that shape positive outcomes for adopted adolescents:

1. A strong emotional attachment between parent and child, felt in both directions.

2. A goodness-of-fit from the child's perspective between his or her worldview and that of the parents'. This is not surprising, considering that parental perception of incompatibility with the child has been identified as the strongest predictor of parental report of behavior difficulties of both an internalizing (depression, anxiety, etc.) and externalizing (aggressive, oppositional, etc.) nature (Grotevant & Kohler, 1999).

3. Positive family dynamics characterized by warmth, cohesion, and a democratic style. Young adults whose adoptive parents have been firm and willing to accept responsibility for making (sometimes unpopular) family decisions, have been found to have higher levels of self-control and moral self-approval (Kelly, Towner-Thyrum, Rigby, & Martin, 1998).

4. A positive family stance regarding adoption, including open communication (Wrobel, Kohler, Grotevant, & McRoy, 2003).

5. A positive perception of adoption on the child's part with adoptive status accepted as a part of their self-definition but not so exclusively that it is solely defining or preoccupying.

6. Parental support of ethnic and/or racial socialization in international or transracial families (Yoon, 2000). This kind of support is related to both a positive parent-child relationship and the adolescent's ethnic pride and ethnic involvement.

As the earlier discussion of possible overreferral of adopted children to therapy would imply, adoptive parents are very attentive and invested in their children's well-being. If their concern takes the form of overreaction or overprotection, this could prove detrimental to their children's adjustment, but if on the other hand, it takes the form of investment in their lives and activities, it could lead to a greater sense of family cohesion.

As suggested, the field has just begun to address the possibility that there may be gains in adoption—not just gains over what life would be for a child orphaned and without a family, but gains that might evolve out of the synergy of having a family unit that had consciously committed to and worked at creating a sense of belonging to one another. Similarly, sensitivity and maturity may be produced by grappling with a more complex identity, with ties to multiple families, ethnicities, races, and/or communities (Smith, Surrey, & Watkins, 1998).

ALTERNATIVE CONTEXTS FOR NORMALIZING ADOPTIVE EXPERIENCES

Protecting youth from high-risk behaviors and promoting positive attitudes and adjustment is an undertaking that requires the nurture of developmental assets within young people, as well as outside them, in their families, schools, and communities (Benson, Scales, Leffert, & Roehlkepartain, 1999). As adopted adolescents address identity questions and negotiate an increased separateness and individuation from their families, the school and community contexts become more central to their adjustment than they were at younger ages. Yet programming for adoptive families by post-adoption agencies and adoptive family organizations is heavily geared to families of young children.

Strengths-based Programming for Adopted Adolescents

Programming designed specifically to address the aforementioned issues for adopted adolescents is rare (Theodore, 2000a). Finding an activity that intrigues adolescents and also assists them in forming a positive identity by embracing adoptive experiences, rather than pushing them away, can be challenging. When it succeeds, it creates an adoption "neighborhood" for the adolescents involved, connecting them with adopted peers they might not have come to know. Linking that neighborhood to other groups outside itself simultaneously benefits the members of the neighborhood and rewrites the one-sided image of adoption held by the nonadoptive community. Following are descriptions of three types of programming that utilize these approaches.

Culture camps: Culture (or heritage) camps (Steinberg & Hall, 2000) for internationally adopted children often succeed at recruiting adopted adolescents of a particular heritage as staff for their child-focused camp. Over the typically week-long camp, the adolescents learn and teach about their birth heritage, but the content is typically geared to the younger children. The adolescents also interact with both adopted and nonadopted staff members of their own ethnic or racial group.

The Lost and Found Company©: One program has utilized drama to engage adolescents. Theodore (2000b) founded a performance company for adolescents who were adopted or in foster care because of the way that acting had helped her through her own adolescence. As a clinician, educator, youth worker, and performer, she recognized the overrepresentation of members of "this culture" in clinical settings and the absence of alternative programming. Theodore explains her use of the term culture in this way:

> I say culture, because regardless of race or ethnicity, adoptees and fostered people share much. We are an "invisible" population that shares much pain and possibility. We may require support and connection with peers to help common feelings of isolation in the span of a lifetime, particularly at the salient developmental time of life where being a part of something larger than our family, however someone is defining "family", is crucial. (Theodore, 2000a)

The Lost and Found Company was a troupe for 12- to 19-year-olds that taught dramatic skills, creative writing, background research, and technical production. The troupe's goals were:

1. to affirm this "invisible population";
2. to acknowledge their resilience and unique life skills gained through their experiences;
3. to encourage self-exploration outside of a therapeutic context;
4. to provide a forum for them to tell their stories and "re-story themselves in creative ways" (Theodore, 2000b, p. 10);
5. to build resilience by providing new avenues of coping and growth; and
6. to provide a cohort of other adolescents with similar life experiences.

Theodore explains the role of strengths-based programming and its advantages over traditional therapeutic approaches very eloquently:

> No teen that I have met relishes the thought of speaking one on one to an adult or even in a peer group about why she is "different" or "problematic". I feel that this is why many therapy situations or "rap groups" are difficult arenas into which to draw struggling teens.... There is no need to reach adulthood without discovering *with* peers, that you may not be as alone as you think. These kids can then, on their own terms, define and redefine themselves in relation to a larger whole, thereby remaining faithful to the normative teen mantra: I am a unique design and please let me be like all my friends. (Theodore, 2000a)

Theodore stipulated that adolescents participating in the troupe were to be "clinically supported" in order to provide an adjunct setting in which they could explore and process the discoveries and reactions that emerged from their dramatic involvement.

The Latino Photojournalism Projects:[1] Photography is a medium that fascinates children and serves as a unique mode of self-expression. It can promote literacy and engage children directly in social issues (Ewald, 1985; Kauffman & Briski, 2004; Strack, Magill, & McDonagh, 2003). Growing up as a member of a minority group, and particularly a racially stereotyped and stigmatized group, creates challenges to self-esteem, formation of a positive identity, and belief that one is a valued member of society (Bernal & Knight, 1993). While Latino children who have been adopted by non-Latino families are protected from many of the hardships that many (nonadopted) Latino youth experience on a daily basis, they also share experiences of racial prejudice, negative stereotypes, and marginalization (Steinberg & Hall, 2000). For adopted Latino youth, especially during adolescence, a sense of disconnection from one's birth country, ethnic group, and cultural heritage can complicate identity formation and increase the risk of identity confusion (Cedarblad, Hook, Irhammar, & Mercke, 1999).

The FOLK Photojournalism Project (Freeark, 1999) was initially funded through a grant program aimed at serving transracially adopted children and their families; innovative programs that would promote a direct connection between adopted children and adults of their race were funded. The project was designed and directed by the author, an adoptive mother and clinical psychologist. It featured a collaboration between an adoptive family group (Families of Latin Kids; FOLK) and the Latino Students' Psychological Association (LSPA) at the University of Michigan. The photojournalists-in-training were adopted Latino early adolescents and Latino graduate students, learning and practicing as a cohort.

The project's aims were:

1. to teach skills and develop a unique area of competence in photography and interviewing;
2. to establish personal relationships with Latino role models and Latino peers;
3. to provide adopted Latino children with connections to cultural and historical information about their birth countries through learning of the life experiences of other Latinos;
4. to encourage family discussion and collaboration around the topic of Latino identity and adoptive status; and
5. to present the experiences, accomplishments, and strengths of adopted youth and Latinos to the community.

Elaboration on the project's means to achieving each of these aims follows:

Developing competence. The participants learned the basic skills of portrait photography and interviewing during six workshops. The workshops, co-led by a professional photographer and the director/psychologist, included a short didactic presentation and hands-on practice with taking pictures, critiquing photo contact sheets, and recording sample interviews.

Establishing personal relationships with other Latinos. The participants practiced photography and interviewing using each other as subjects, getting to know one another in the process. Workshops were structured to maximize small group interaction (e.g., critiquing contact sheets in teams) and informal socializing so that the participants gradually became aware of their common interests and experiences (music, dancing, birth countries, etc.).

Connecting with cultural and historical information. Eventually the participants conducted interviews of Latinos of their choice (ranging in age from 12 to 70). The collection of interviews covered an array of cultural, historical, and biographical topics (e.g., immigration stories, adoption stories, cultural and family customs, career choice, educational background). The photojournalists were encouraged to interview about any topics that piqued their curiosity. Some of the interviewees were adopted, but most were not.

Encouraging discussion of adoption and collaboration with family and friends. Homework assignments structured the participants' practice of the concepts and techniques that had been taught and also prompted interaction with family members and friends about the project itself. For example, by asking a nonadopted friend whether she would agree to pose for a photograph for a project, the adolescent would be sharing information about this adoption-related project and thereby addressing both her Latino heritage and her adoption. Family involvement was also subtly integrated into the project: for example, the adolescents and their parents were responsible for the transcription and editing of their interviews, thereby prompting collaboration and discussion of cultural topics.

Presenting adoption and Latinos in a positive light to the community. Each interview, accompanied by the chosen photographs, was constructed as a display, and exhibits of the collection of interviews were held in venues targeted toward different audiences. The local library held an exhibit during Hispanic/Latino Heritage Month; the university hosted an exhibit in the student union. Exhibits at the local Festival Latino brought the project to the attention of the Latino community. The Latino graduate students, who were soon to become doctoral-level psychologists, became acquainted with adopted youth in a setting that emphasized their individuality, the integration of a bicultural identity, and their successful adjustment. It changed their views of adoption.

EVIDENCE FOR INTEGRATION OF LATINO AND ADOPTIVE IDENTITIES

Several of the adolescents invited their nonadopted friends to the reception at the public exhibit. This reflected a level of comfort in integrating two sides of their social identities and friendship networks. The adolescents were assigned the role of hosts at the reception and they proudly and graciously welcomed guests, explained the project to them, and then promptly returned to socializing with their friends.

A filmmaker friend of one of the graduate students heard of the project and was interested in making a short documentary. Because he was working with digital equipment, the process of filming was very casual and unobtrusive. The teens were excited, but nervous, at the prospect of being on camera and deciding what they might choose to share about themselves. The group (teenagers and graduate students) decided that rather than doing individual interviews, they would all talk together and have their informal discussion filmed. Their two-hour discussion touched on Latino identity, adoptive identity, religious identity, what participating in the project meant to them, what they thought it had meant for their families, and more. They then agreed to meet with the filmmaker a second time to provide some different footage. The openness with which they discussed all of this with one another was just as striking as the fact that they would do it on camera. The short documentary exists as firsthand evidence of the project's success at facilitating an integration of a multilayered identity with footage of the group discussion interspersed with clips that reflected other aspects of their lives and identities, like talents, hobbies, and extended family.

The Latino Photojournalism Project (Freeark, 2003) was a second phase of the program that aimed to consolidate the earlier learning and broaden the project's scope. With these adolescent photojounalists now quite accomplished at photography and collecting narratives, the project had too much potential to draw to a close. Funding for this second phase was obtained from the University of Michigan's Arts of Citizenship program, an initiative aimed at building university-community partnerships and service learning opportunities through the arts and humanities. The design of this second phase of the project centered around three aims:

1. to provide these adolescents with the opportunity to teach and mentor a younger "generation" of children in what they had learned;

2. to broaden the diversity of the young people participating so that both the personal connections and cultural exposure would be more varied; and

3. to integrate more of the university community into the project and thereby broaden exposure to two marginalized groups, Latinos and the adopted.

Elaboration of the methods for achieving these aims follows:

Teaching and mentoring. More than half of the teen photojournalists volunteered to continue as staff for this new project. Becoming teachers and role models to a younger generation consolidated their learning, provided a leadership opportunity, and formalized their acquired expertise. Given that adopted adolescents have indicated twice as much interest in mentoring younger adopted children as they have in any other type of adoption-related activity (Benson et al., 1994), the project's two-tiered approach that turns students into teachers holds great promise for engaging adopted youth. It also exposes the younger children to local youth who view their birth heritage with pride, who are vivid examples of integrating two cultures into their life, and who are active citizens within their community.

Creating broader community connections. Increased diversity of the new generation of photojournalist trainees was accomplished by recruiting both through FOLK and through a bilingual academic enhancement program called Asociación Latina Alcanzado Sueños (ALAS). Many of the children participating in ALAS are members of families that have immigrated recently to the United States and are primarily Spanish-speaking; the children may be more fluent in English than their parents and many participate in English as a second language programming at school. ALAS children and their parents were eager to participate in the photojournalism project because it would simultaneously teach the children new skills and honor their family heritage. The ALAS- and FOLK-affiliated children were from very different cultural worlds and socioeconomic backgrounds; they would not have been likely to meet if not for this program. Fascination with cameras and an engaging and motivated staff of undergraduate and high school students, led by a Mexican photographer, became bridges between these two worlds.

Greater integration of the university community. Learning and exposure were accomplished at multiple levels: The college students learned about the interface of developmental tasks, minority experiences, and group dynamics. The children and adolescents from FOLK and ALAS learned more about the realities of each other's lives, cultures, and communities. The exhibit and reception for this collection of interviews was attended by a very diverse group of guests from the adoption, Latino, university, and local communities. It was an event that bridged different worlds, challenged stereotypes, and facilitated introductions. The talents of Latino youth and the richness of Latino lives, both adopted and nonadopted, took center stage.

Photography is a powerful tool for empowerment and validation. All the young photojournalists had the opportunity to view their heritage, family history, and life experiences through a lens of pride. They valued the educational potential of their work, realizing that public exhibits of the collection of interviews would teach those who came to see them aspects of the Latino experience that they might not otherwise know.

Applied to the context of transracial adoptive identity, portrait photography has a distinctive power to cultivate pride and neutralize stigma. In contrast to constantly feeling noticed for not matching one's family, the adopted adolescent is the one who is looking and capturing not only the physical features of his or her subject (which bear a resemblance to his or her own), but also the psychological essence of the person as it might be conveyed in setting, pose, props, or expression. The process of interviewing also reworks the common experience of helplessness or embarrassment in the face of someone else's questions about one's life story or family life. The opportunity to formulate questions of interest to oneself and figure out how to ask them in a way that elicits a detailed narrative is a very useful social and professional skill, and it also builds confidence. It also seemed in many cases to be a safely displaced way to ask another Latino the kind of questions one might wish to ask the members of one's own birth family about their life, values, and customs.

CONCLUSIONS

Adolescence is a time of change, self-discovery, and spheres of newly acquired competence. For an adopted adolescent, this includes sorting out and organizing the pieces of a complex life story and developing a "coherent autobiographical self in the context of adoption" (Hart & Luckock, 2004, p. 191). While the majority of adopted adolescents complete this story-building successfully, they are not the ones whose trajectories have been widely reported or studied. The dominant focus in adoption research, policy, and post-adoption practice has been on the problematic side of this identity formation process. In contrast, creative programming tailored to the developmental tasks of adopted youth and built on their strengths and unique perspective is a relatively unplumbed resource. Community-based efforts to channel adolescent energy, curiosity, and self-reflection into a constructive experience is extremely rare (Benson et al., 1994). I have argued that the overrepresentation of adopted children and youth in traditional mental health settings may occur because a strengths-based approach to facilitating adoptive identity exploration has not been provided.

Beginning with strengths and successful adaptation is essential. "It is too easy to assume that nontraditional... implies abnormal or unhealthy (Grotevant & Kohler, 1999, p. 186). In addition to benefiting individual adolescents and engaging their families, a strengths-based perspective also provides opportunities to improve the public perception of adoption. By providing adopted young people with a way to embrace the unique perspective they have gained by virtue of adoption, these programs empower new leaders who can model strength and confidence for younger members of marginalized groups. Programming that explores adoptive identity while developing areas of competence and expertise should be supported and expanded. Efforts must also be made to research its impact both cross-sectionally and longitudinally so that the critical elements of such programs and their mechanisms for change can be identified. This will require partnerships between the research, adoption, and service communities and mutual regard for each community's skills, tools, and orientation. The most compelling voices to speak to the realities of growing up as an adopted person are those of the adopted themselves.

NOTE

1. These projects were funded by a Transcultural Mini-Grant from Pact, An Adoption Alliance, under federal grant # 90-CO-0846 from the Children's Bureau of Administration of Children Youth and Families (ACYF) and the Arts of Citizenship Program at the University of Michigan.

REFERENCES

Adoption Institute. (1997). *Benchmark adoption survey: Report on the Findings.* Princeton Survey Research Associates for The Adoption Institute. Washington, D.C.: Princeton Survey Research Associates.

Adoption Institute. (2002). *Landmark study shows vast majority of Americans support adoption.* Retrieved January 3, 2005, from http://www.adoptioninstitute. org.survey/press_release.html.

Benson, P.L., Scales, P.C., Leffert, N., & Roehlkepartain, E.C. (1999). *A fragile foundation: The state of developmental assets among American youth.* Minneapolis: Search Institute.

Benson, P.L., Sharma, A.R., & Roehlkepartain, E.C. (1994). *Growing up adopted: A portrait of adolescents and their families.* Minneapolis: Search Institute.

Bernal, M.E., & Knight, G.P. (Eds.). (1993). *Ethnic identity: Formation and transmission among Hispanics.* Albany: State University of New York Press.

Brinich, P. M. (1990). Adoption from the inside out. In D. M. Brodzinsky & M. D. Schechter (Eds.), *The psychology of adoption* (pp. 42–61). New York: Oxford University Press.

Brodzinsky, D. M. (1990). A stress and coping model of adoption adjustment. In D. M. Brodzinsky & M. D. Schechter (Eds.), *The psychology of adoption* (pp. 3–24). New York: Oxford University Press.

Brodzinsky, D. M. (1993). Long-term outcomes in adoption. In R. E. Behrman (Ed.), *The future of children: Adoption* (pp. 153–166). Los Altos, CA: Center for the Future of Children, the David and Lucile Packard Foundation.

Brodzinsky, D. M., Schechter, M. D., & Henig, R. M. (1992). *Being adopted: The lifelong search for self.* New York: Doubleday.

Brodzinsky, D. M., Smith, D. W., & Brodzinsky, A. B. (1998). *Children's adjustment to adoption: Developmental and clinical issues* (Vol. 38). Thousand Oaks, CA: Sage.

Cedarblad, M., Hook, B., Irhammar, M., & Mercke, A. M. (1999). Mental health in international adoptees as teenagers and young adults: An epidemiological study. *Journal of Child Psychology and Psychiatry, 40*(8), 1239–1248.

Cohen, N. J., Coyne, J. C., & Duvall, J. D. (1996). Parents' sense of "entitlement" in adoptive and nonadoptive families. *Family Process, 35,* 441–456.

Cronican-Walker, A. (2004 Fall). A journey of two hearts: Part II: Aeranie's journey. *FAC Sheet, 8,* 9.

Ewald, W. (1985). Portraits and dreams: Photographs and stories by children of the Appalachians. New York: Writers and Readers Publications.

Fan, X., Miller, B. C., Christensen, M., Park, K., Grotevant, H. D., van Dulmen, M., et al. (2002). Questionnaire and interview inconsistencies exaggerated differences between adopted and nonadopted adolescents in a national sample. *Adoption Quarterly, 6*(2), 7–27.

Feigelman, W. (2001). Comparing adolescents in diverging family structures: Investigating whether adoptees are more prone to problems than their non-adopted peers. *Adoption Quarterly, 5*(2), 5–36.

Fisher, A. P. (2003). A critique of the portrayal of adoption in college textbooks and readers on families, 1998–2001. *Family Relations, 52,* 154–160.

Freeark, K. (1999). *The F.O.L.K. Photojournalism Project* (unpublished grant proposal). Ann Arbor: Families of Latin Kids.

Freeark, K. (2003). *The Latino Photojournalism Project* (unpublished grant proposal). Ann Arbor: Center for Human Growth & Development, University of Michigan.

Grotevant, H. D., Dunbar, N., Kohler, J. K., & Lash Esau, A. M. (2000). Adoptive identity: How contexts within and beyond the family shape developmental pathways. *Family Relations, 49*(4), 379–387.

Grotevant, H. D., & Kohler, J. K. (1999). Adoptive families. In M. E. Lamb (Ed.), *Parenting and child development in "nontraditional" families* (pp. 161–190). Mahwah, NJ: Lawrence Erlbaum.

Grotevant, H. D., & McRoy, R. G. (1990). Adopted adolescents in residential treatment: The role of the family. In D. M. Brodzinsky & M. D. Schechter

(Eds.), *The psychology of adoption* (pp. 167–186). New York: Oxford University Press.

Hart, A., & Luckock, B. (2004). *Developing adoption support and therapy: New approaches for practice.* London: Jessica Kingsley.

Haugaard, J. J. (1998). Is adoption a risk factor for the development of adjustment problems? *Clinical Psychology Review, 18*(1), 47–69.

Ingersoll, B. D. (1997). Psychiatric disorders among adopted children: A review and commentary. *Adoption Quarterly, 1*(1), 57–73.

Juffer, F., & van Ijzendoorn, M. H. (2005). Behavior problems and mental health referrals of international adoptees. *Journal of the American Medical Association, 293*(20), 2501–2533.

Kauffman, R., & Briski, Z. (2004). Born into brothels. Accessed September 2005, from http://www.kids-with-cameras.org/bornintobrothels/.

Kelly, M. M., Towner-Thyrum, E., Rigby, A., & Martin, B. (1998). Adjustment and identity formation in adopted and nonadopted young adults: Contributions of family environment. *American Journal of Orthopsychiatry, 68*(3), 497–500.

Kirk, H. D. (1964). *Shared fate.* New York: Free Press.

Kreider, R. M. (2003). *Adopted children and stepchildren: 2000* (No. CENSR-6RV). Washington, DC: U.S. Census Bureau.

Leon, I. G. (2002). Adoption losses: Naturally occurring or socially constructed? *Child Development, 73*(2), 652–663.

Lieblich, A., McAdams, D. P., & Josselson, R. (Eds.). (2004). *Healing plots: The narrative basis of psychotherapy.* Washington, DC: American Psychological Association.

Melosh, B. (2002). *Strangers and kin: The American way of adoption.* Cambridge, MA: Harvard University Press.

Miller, B. C., Fan, X., Grotevant, H. D., Christensen, M., Coyl, D., & van Dulmen, M. (2000). Adopted adolescents' overrepresentation in mental health counseling: Adoptees' problems or parents' lower threshold for referral? *Journal of the American Academy of Child and Adolescent Psychiatry, 39,* 1504–1511.

Pertman, A. (2000). Adoption nation: How the adoption revolution is transforming America. New York: Basic Books.

Pertman, A. (2004). *The "daddy" of TV tastelessness.* Retrieved January 27, 2005, from http://www.adoptioninstitute.org/commentary/20041221_latimes_oped.html.

Rosenberg, E. B. (1992). The adoption life cycle: The children and their families through the years. New York: Free Press.

Ryan, S. D., & Nalavany, B. (2003). Adopted children: Who do they turn to for help and why? *Adoption Quarterly, 7*(2), 29–52.

Schram, K. (2004). *Shame on ABC and Barbara Walters.* Retrieved May 14, 2004, from http://www.komotv.com/news/printstory.asp?id = 31028.

Sharma, A. R., McGue, M. K., & Benson, P. L. (1998). The psychological adjustment of United States adopted adolescents and their nonadopted siblings. *Child Development, 69*(3), 791–802.

Smith, B., Surrey, J.L., & Watkins, M. (1998). "Real" mothers: Adoptive mothers resisting marginalization and re-creating motherhood. In C.G. Coll, J.L. Surrey, & K. Weingarten (Eds.), *Mothering against the odds: Diverse voices of contemporary mothers:* New York: Guilford Press.

Smith, S.L., & Howard, J.A. (1999). *Promoting successful adoptions: Practice with troubled families.* Thousand Oaks, CA: Sage.

Steinberg, G., & Hall, B. (2000). *Inside transracial adoption.* Indianapolis, IN: Perspectives Press.

Strack, R.W., Magill, C., & McDonagh, K. (2003). Engaging youth through Photovoice. *Health Promotion Practice, 5*(1), 49–58.

Theodore, E. (2000a, June 9–10). *Adoption from an adolescent's perspective: Adolescents in improvisational theater.* Paper presented at Psychotherapy and the Adoption Triangle, Boston.

Theodore, E. (2000b). The Lost and Found Company. *Children's Group Therapy Association Newsletter.*

U.S. Census Bureau. (2001). *Population by race and Hispanic or Latino origin for the United States: 1990 and 2000.* Retrieved December 15, 2004, from http://www.census.gov/population/www/cen2000/briefs.html#sr.

Watkins, M., & Fisher, S. (1993). *Talking with young children about adoption.* New Haven, CT: Yale University Press.

Wegar, K. (2000). Adoption, family ideology, and social stigma: Bias in community attitudes, adoption research and practice. *Family Relations, 49*(4), 363–370.

Wrobel, G.M., Kohler, J.K., Grotevant, H.D., & McRoy, R.G. (2003). The Family Adoption Communication (FAC) model: Identifying pathways of adoption-related communication. *Adoption Quarterly, 7*(2), 53–84.

Yoon, D.P. (2000). Causal modeling predicting psychological adjustment of Korean-born adolescent adoptees. *Journal of Human Behavior in the Social Environment, 3*(3), 65–82.

Chapter 7

ASSET STRATEGIES FOR COMMUNITY YOUTH DEVELOPMENT: LESSONS FROM THE YES WE CAN! PROJECT

Melissa S. Quon Huber, Laurie A. Van Egeren, Pennie Foster-Fishman, and Tara Donahue

In the past decade, communities have begun to refocus on their health and vitality in two important ways that impact youth. First, a growing number of communities have implemented a Community Youth Development approach in an effort to improve the quality of life for youth. This approach recognizes that youth development does not occur in isolation, but rather in all the multifaceted and interconnected contexts in which youth find themselves, including home, school, work, neighborhoods, and communities. Furthermore, it approaches youth development from an asset framework rather than with a problem or deficit focus (Villarruel, Perkins, Borden, & Keith, 2003). This asset focus has become increasingly important as research has linked both the quality and quantity of development assets as a predictor of youth thriving and reduced risk behavior (Keith, Huber, Griffin, & Villarruel, 2001; Scales, Benson, Leffert, & Blyth, 2000).

Second, a growing number of comprehensive community building initiatives (CBIs) have been developed and implemented to improve the context in which individuals, families, children, and youth reside. These initiatives, while varied in scope, focus on improving outcomes such as education, health, employment, and poverty in specific geographically bounded areas by including multiple sectors within a community, building partnerships, strengthening local capacity for change, and working to improve service integration (Kingsley, McNeely, & Gibson, 1997). CBIs recognize that the qualities of neighborhoods are important factors in the health and well-being of families, children, and youth (Shonkoff & Phillips, 2000). Advocates of these place-based initiatives suggest that these approaches are more holistic and thus more likely to succeed than individually based interventions because they consider the complex and interconnected nature of social issues (Kingsley et al., 1997; Kubisch, Weiss, Schorr, & Connell, 1995).

Of particular note is the fact that many comprehensive community building initiatives adopt Community Youth Development strategies in the design and implementation of their efforts. Most seek to mobilize and engage youth and adult residents in the work at hand, involving them in designing the initiative, governing the efforts, and even implementing and evaluating change pursuits (Smock, 1997; Traynor, 1995). In this chapter, we review three youth asset building strategies that are often found in CBIs and that have exceptional promise for promoting youth outcomes. These include out-of-school programs, mentoring, youth governance, and youth-adult partnerships. We then describe how one CBI—the Yes We Can! initiative in Battle Creek, Michigan, funded by the W. K. Kellogg Foundation—utilized a community youth development approach that incorporated elements of these three strategies. We first describe the dreams that this community had for their children that pointed to resident awareness (including adult and youth) of the need for increased youth involvement in out-of-school activities, mentoring, and governance. Then we present a case study of some of the strategies that were adopted to foster youth development and the lessons learned from this process.

ASSET STRATEGIES: EMERGING BEST PRACTICES

Out-of-School Time

Out-of-school activities have emerged as an increasingly important factor in youth outcomes. The diversity of out-of-school time activities provides youth with many different options. For instance, youth may participate in community-based programs or in school-based programs. The foci of these activities also differ. Some programs specialize in tutoring or academic services, while others offer enrichment or recreation. Many communities have sought to increase the availability of out-of-school activities in response to concerns about the amount of time youth spend unsupervised—time in which youth are more likely to become injured, engage in drug or alcohol consumption, or engage in other delinquent behaviors (Carnegie Council on Adolescent Development, 1992).

Time spent in out-of-school programs has been found to be a contributor to positive outcomes for youth (Cooper, Valentine, Nye, & Lindsay, 1999; Miller, 2003; Scales & Leffert, 1999; Schinke, Cole, & Poulin, 2000). The amount of time spent in youth programs has been found to be a consistent predictor of youth assets such as school performance, ability to overcome adversity, efforts to help others, development of leadership qualities, and efforts to maintain good physical health (Scales et al., 2000). Furthermore, youth have been found to experience the highest levels of intrinsic motivation and concentration when they are in structured out-of-school experiences compared to when they are in school or with peers (Larson, 2000).

Although many positive outcomes of structured out-of school experiences have been observed, ways in which these experiences interact with individual youth development and directly translate into positive youth outcomes is less clear. Observers have noted that out-of-school programs offer youth a variety of opportunities to increase knowledge and skills through experiential learning, develop goal-directed abilities that support success (e.g., planning, problem-solving, decision-making), encourage self-exploration and creativity, and build relationships in a context of affirmation and respect (Eccles & Barber 1999; Hart, 1992; Whalen & Wynn; 1995). However, it is not clear to what extent any specific element of these experiences or how much a certain amount of an activity fosters specific outcomes for youth (Larson, 2000).

In addition, the out-of-school needs of youth with different demographic characteristics are not entirely understood. Barriers to involvement in these out-of-school experiences may be different for youth of varying ages, backgrounds, and communities (Quinn, 1999). For example, youth characteristically decrease participation in these activities as they reach middle school and high school (Sipe, Ma, & Gambone, 1998). Accessibility may be a hindrance for individuals from low-income backgrounds and those geographically isolated from programs. Programs may not exist, or there may be challenges in accessing existing programs due to costs or transportation (Huber & Kossek, 1999; Markstrom, 1999).

Youth workers and researchers are becoming aware of the expanding needs of an increasingly ethnically diverse population of youth. Youth of different ethnic groups participate in out-of-school activities at different rates, with the lowest rates found among non–European American populations (Brown & Evans, 2002). Furthermore, youth of varied ethnic backgrounds have different priorities and restrictions for their involvement in such activities. Parents of color have been found to more highly favor activities with strong educational components (Le Menestrel, 2003). Male and female youth from multiple ethnic groups—including African American, Latina/o, Arab, and Chaldean—have reported family restrictions that impede their ability to participate in out-of-school activities, although the restrictions vary by gender and are more limiting for girls, particularly among first-generation immigrants (Perkins, Borden, Villarruel, Carlton-Hug, & Stone, under review). For example, some Middle Eastern cultures prohibit mixed gender groups beyond adolescence, which prevents them from participating in many out-of-school programs since boys and girls are integrated (Ziazi, 2003).

These findings suggest that more learning is required about specific processes through which different types of out-of-school experiences contribute to particular youth outcomes. Although out-of-school activities keep participants engaged in structured activities, little is known about which activities prove most effective for desired outcomes. For instance, what enrichment activities lead to better motivation in students? Which academic activities help improve the intellectual development of students? Although answers to these questions are yet unknown, out-of-school experiences have great potential for youth development. It is a direction that many communities are pursuing to improve the quality of youth time out of school.

Mentoring

Youth of today have more time unsupervised and alone than any previous generation and spend less time in positive interactions with adults (Hersch, 1998). It has thus become even more important to provide opportunities for youth to engage in caring, meaningful interactions with adults. Mentoring is one forum for these interactions. Mentoring is a sustained relationship between an adult and a young person in which the adult provides support and guidance (Jekielek, Moore, Hair, & Scarupa, 2002). It has been associated with positive outcomes such as improved school attendance, post–high school education pursuits, improved attitudes toward school, decreased substance abuse, reduced levels of some forms of delinquency, and positive relationships and social attitudes (Jekielek et al., 2002). While mentoring occurs most frequently in settings outside of school, in-school mentoring is showing promise as well (Herrera, Sipe, McClanahan, Arbreton, & Pepper, 2000).

However, the quality of mentoring relationships differ, and these differences impact youth experiences and outcomes. Quality mentoring that has been linked to positive outcomes has been characterized by long-term, positive relationships (12 months or more) in which the adult and youth share interests and a focus on the needs and interests of the youth (Grossman & Rhodes, 2002). In addition, mentor support, including supervision, support, and training (six hours or more), is required from the program to develop high-quality mentoring (Herrera et al., 2000; Jekielek et al., 2002).

The most successful programs overall have strong relationships between mentors and youth and use best practices (Dubois, Holloway, Valentine, & Cooper, 2002). To ensure strong relationships, several background factors for volunteers should be considered. Prior experience can be a strong indicator of which mentors will be most likely to form a strong relationship (DuBois et al., 2002; Sipe, 2002). Mentors must also be responsible for establishing trust with the youth (Sipe, 2002). Setting achievable mentoring goals also leads to more effective mentoring relationships.

The research on mentoring indicates that strong relationships between youth and adults can have positive effects. Duration and strength of the relationship are two important factors in successful relationships. Setting goals and developing trust at the onset of the relationship are essential components to a quality mentoring relationship. While mentoring is one method of interacting with youth, there are other forms of youth-adult interactions in which youth and adults have equal positions in the relationship.

Youth-Adult Partnerships and Youth Governance

Youth-adult partnerships are similar to mentoring in that a positive relationship is essential to the partnership; however, these partnerships are characterized by a mutuality that is not present in mentoring relationships (Camino, 2000a). In this type of partnership, adults work alongside youth in the community in a context of mutual teaching, learning, and action (Zeldin, McDaniel, Topitzes & Lorens, 2001). For instance, this type of partnership can exist when both youth and adults serve together on a board of directors or co-design and implement a project in the community. This mutuality is also consistent with a *youth governance* approach in which youth and adults work together rather than in separate decision-making or advising committees. Youth governance is defined by "those situations where youth work—often in partnership with adults—to set the overall policy direction of organizations, institutions, and coalitions ... and often refer to young people working on boards of directors, sanctioned committees, planning bodies, and advisory groups" (Zeldin, McDaniel, Topitzes, Calvert, 2000, p. 3). This approach can be applied to informal activities and community coalition work as well as formal boards of directors for public, private, or nonprofit firms.

Successful youth-adult partnerships seek to overcome past failures in which adult leaders *did things for* youth, often without seeking youth input. They also attempt to avoid adult *abandonment* of youth in the name of youth empowerment, where youth undertake efforts without adult support or assistance (Hart, 1992). Current partnership approaches recognize that both youth and adults make critical contributions to the relationship and the organization or group. These partnerships recognize that everyone will benefit from greater youth participation.

Organizations and communities increasingly recognize the need for increased youth participation. This includes participation on the board of directors of nonprofit and government agencies that make financial or programming decisions affecting youth, in neighborhood and community development change efforts, and in community research and evaluation (Beker, Eisikovits, & Guttmann, 1987; Checkoway, 1998; Young & Sazama, 1999; Zeldin et al., 2001). Many states have lowered the legal age at which someone can become a voting member of a board to 16 to accommodate this growing trend (Young and Sazama, 1999). Although the impetus for this shift originated primarily out of ethical concerns in which youth felt they had the right to be heard and recognized as decision-makers (Hoover & Weisenbach, 1999), benefits clearly exist for youth, adults, and organizations when youth governance strategies are employed.

Youth benefit in many ways from such partnerships. Research indicates that decreased risk behaviors, positive communication skills, and enhanced self-esteem and competence are linked to youth involvement in these positive partnerships with adults (Camino, 2000b; Kirby & Coyle, 1997). Meaningful participation in community efforts has also been associated with increased youth empowerment and decreased alienation from their communities (Calabrese & Schumer, 1986).

Involved adults, organizations, and communities also benefit from youth governance approaches. Not only do communities and organizations receive tangible benefits from the additional human resources youth provide (Beker, Eisikovits, & Guttmann, 1987), but programs and initiatives are strengthened from youth involvement. The design, implementation, and evaluation of youth programs become more relevant, effective, and credible to youth when youth are involved in these stages (Klindera & Menderweld, 2001). Youth involvement helps organizations to solidify commitments to diversity, to become more responsive in meeting the needs of the community while employing a more diverse set of strategies in meeting those needs, and to enhance the credibility of their programs to funders in showing a clear commitment to youth development (Zeldin et al., 2000). Adults have also benefited from youth-adult partnerships; adults have reported feeling more connected, purposeful, and energized from the passion and insight of youth members (Zeldin et al., 2000).

Yes We Can!, a CBI targeting improved educational and economic success through resident mobilization, involved residents in identifying key issues around which the community might mobilize to affect change—and the need for increased youth opportunities to achieve bright futures emerged as a primary motivating force. By first asking resident adults and youth to highlight their dreams for local children and then incorporating strategies that encouraged residents to design and develop activities to encourage those dreams, this community has made first steps to increasing the opportunities for youth to be successful.

THE YES WE CAN! INITIATIVE

Yes We Can! (YWC!) was launched in the spring of 2001 by the W. K. Kellogg Foundation (WKKF) in its home city of Battle Creek, Michigan. YWC! is a community building initiative funded by the W. K. Kellogg Foundation that aims to improve educational and economic outcomes in Battle Creek by mobilizing low-income communities and resident leaders and building their capacity to influence the decisions and policies that impact their lives. Here, we focus on the design phase and Phase 1 of this initiative, which emphasized building community capacity and readiness to increase resident mobilization for community change (Foster-Fishman et al., under review).

According to 2000 U.S. Census Bureau data, Battle Creek is a city of 53,364 residents where the main sources of employment for residents are manufacturing (25 percent of workers), educational, health, and social services (21 percent of workers), and retail trade (11 percent of workers). Of the majority of residents (97 percent) who indicated that their race is of one category, most were Caucasian (75 percent), followed by Black/African American (18 percent) and Hispanic/Latino(a) (5 percent). The majority of housing is occupied by owners (66 percent) rather than renters. Across the city, 11 percent of families and 14 percent of individuals live below poverty. Eighty-two percent of residents age 25 and older have a high school diploma. However, according to results of state standardized tests, an average of only 41 percent of students in the local school district had satisfactory test results in 2002 according to analysis of data available from the Michigan State Department of Education. These demographic characteristics varied within different parts of the city. Within the city, seven economically distressed neighborhoods (e.g., elementary school catchment areas, or ESCAs) were invited to be the initial neighborhood partners. These ESCAs were characterized by high levels of unemployment and poverty (e.g., 31 to 95 percent of students eligible for free and reduced lunches, many neighborhoods with 20 to 43 percent of residents living in poverty) as well as poor educational outcomes for youth (e.g., an average of 62 to 79 percent of fourth- and fifth-graders had unsatisfactory scores across four tests in 1999).

From the beginning, WKKF emphasized the importance of building sustainable change, and therefore incorporated input from community residents into the design phase—and even in the early stages, youth participation formed an essential value of the initiative. Focus groups were conducted with resident leaders, including youth, from the seven targeted neighborhoods to hear directly from the community about their concerns, hopes and dreams, and processes through which the initiative could succeed in their neighborhoods—with the intention that residents would play a key role in designing the nature of the YWC! partnership.

Out of these conversations with local adults and youth emerged three key strategies that residents recommended to provide a critical foundation for mobilization efforts: (1) providing opportunities for small wins that would increase feelings of empowerment and hope through residents' initiation of relatively small neighborhood-based projects that would produce immediate and observable changes; (2) building social capital within the neighborhoods and between neighborhoods and community organizations; and (3) expanding resident adult and youth leadership (Berkowitz & Foster-Fishman, 2002). To accomplish these goals, three resident-focused approaches were implemented in Phase 1: (1) a neighborhood minigrant program, including a resident steering committee that included youth; (2) creation of a community connections office staffed by local neighborhood organizers, called connectors; and (3) a photovoice evaluation project. (See Foster-Fishman, Nowell, Deacon, Nievar, McCann, in press for more details on these programming components.)

Early in the planning stages, the developers recognized the importance of incorporating youth input if the YWC! initiative were to be successful. Youth were considered to be true stakeholders in the process, critical to identifying relevant issues for young people living in these communities and to shaping strategies that would mobilize youth in developmentally appropriate ways. Moreover, both to ensure that the initiative addressed fundamental youth issues and as a result of what residents expressed about the history of and potential for youth involvement in their neighborhoods, youth were recruited to be part of the minigrant steering committee and encouraged to apply for neighborhood minigrants. Below, we describe how and what we learned when youth and adult residents described their experiences of and dreams for their community.

YOUTH NEEDS AND DESIRES: FOCUS GROUPS AND PHOTOVOICE

While committed to gaining youth input into the early design phases of YWC!, the W. K. Kellogg Foundation also faced a significant challenge: there was a long history in the community of youth either not attending or minimally participating in planning activities and focus groups. YWC! staff explained that youth often complained that these activities were "boring" or "unengaging." For this reason, YWC! staff and the evaluation team worked to design innovative processes that would attract youth (and adults) to be involved and actively engage them in expressing their opinions and ideas. Two innovative forums were implemented—a focus group process that modeled open space technology and a photovoice project utilizing photography, personal journals, and shared reflections (Wang & Burris, 1994). These creative methods were implemented and became venues for both adult and youth residents to express their concerns, needs, and hopes around the youth in these economically distressed neighborhoods.

Focus Groups

Between January and April of 2002, 90 youth resident leaders and 140 adult resident leaders participated in focus groups to provide critical input to inform the design of Phase I. Because previous experiences had indicated that youth often find "traditional" focus groups boring and facilitators experience difficulty in getting youth to speak up and become active participants, we designed an alternative youth focus group format to allow us to work with the natural energies of young people in an active way. In contrast to traditional focus group formats, where questions are asked verbally by facilitators who then manage group discussions around the topics, this technique presented questions visually and engaged youth interactively in writing their own responses in a series of "stations" hung on the wall. This format, similar to open-space technology, increased youth control over the content of what was discussed and the process by which youth shared information. For example, some youth chose to only participate via written notes they pasted on the wall; others engaged in interactive discussions with other youth and the facilitators about the topics at each station.

Photovoice

In addition to focus groups, the evaluation team designed participatory evaluation strategies intended both to collect baseline evaluation data and to develop resident readiness and capacity for affecting change. One such strategy was photovoice (Wang & Burris, 1994), which places cameras in the hands of residents to document meaningful details of daily life and facilitates empowerment by incorporating group reflection. In late summer of 2002, a racially diverse group of 12 youth and 17 adults were recruited by YWC! staff from the targeted neighborhoods to participate in the photovoice project. Over five weeks, participants shot one roll of film each week. Participants were given significant latitude and freedom to express what they felt was important in their photos, but they were asked to focus their photography and reflections around answering the following three questions: "What is your life like?" "What is good about your life?" "What needs to change?" Participants then selected three images that they found particularly meaningful and wrote thoughts about each photo that expand on statements and questions such as: "I want to share this photo because ..." "What's the real story this photo tells?" "How does this story relate to your life and/or the lives of people in your neighborhood?" Participants brought these written reflections with them to weekly reflective sessions where they met with up to six other participants from their neighborhood. An evaluation team member facilitated each meeting. At the beginning of each session, participants shared their interpretations, thoughts, and beliefs regarding the meaning and significance of their selected images. Group members would then jointly select up to five photos to discuss as a group. Throughout the photovoice project, youth members were observed to be strongly committed to the overall process. Youth members attended regularly and participated in the dialogue sessions extensively, and even the youngest members showed profound insights into the meaning of the photographs.

What Did (Youth and Adult) Residents Want for Youth?

Strikingly, although focus group and photovoice participants were not specifically asked to speak to issues related to local youth, adult and youth residents from every neighborhood described their desire for expanded opportunities to ensure success for neighborhood children. Adult residents talked about developing centers, programs, and recreational areas that would provide safe, stimulating havens for their children and build their chances for a good education and employment, while youth reported visions of a bright future in which they could succeed in school, get the job of their dreams, live well and in a safe, clean, and desirable neighborhood, and have and support a family.

Adults were committed to success for youth. What emerged especially clearly through these discussions was the potentially powerful motivating force for action that youth issues constituted in this community. Both focus group and photovoice participants indicated that community residents were highly concerned about and committed to their children:

> The neighborhood is very interested in creating positive change for youth. Parents want better educational opportunities for kids and know education means economic gain. (adult focus group participant)

I think we need to be more involved with the kids…sometimes, parents, we don't have time for the kids. We need to stay all the time, focus on the family…not on other things. There's the future of tomorrow, have time for the kids. You need to work, and I know you [are] tired, but this is nothing to do with your kids. If you want to have better kids, you need to support your kids. (adult photovoice participant)

Adults described wanting their children to have a better life, to have goals and dreams that can be achieved through educational success:

That's what I'm pushing to them because I'm not finished my schooling in my country … and I told them you don't have school, you don't have a future. You don't have the same level, you know like other people. You don't have GED … you don't got a good job. You can go clean offices or [do] hard jobs … because you don't have experience, you don't have school … so that's what happened [to me]. (adult photovoice participant)

The importance and value of supporting youth within these neighborhoods was so central that focus group and photovoice participants noted that the best way to engage residents in the YWC! initiative was through local youth: "Create programs and opportunities for the youth. Parents will work for their children. If you get the youth to come, their parents will come too."

However, both adults and youth described challenges to youth achieving their dreams, and they identified ways to increase the chances of success that support the use of a community youth development approach.

Out-of-school activities. A major theme that emerged from focus group conversations in every neighborhood was the need for more out-of-school activities—in fact, we received dozens of comments from the focus groups and photovoice participants, particularly from adults, who were greatly concerned with the current state of resources for their children. This comment by a photovoice participant summarizes the fears many adults expressed about the lack of recreational resources for their children:

We need some things in our community. I wish we had a playground. What happens is when you don't have what you need in your community … you got your kids getting into trouble. When they get bored, they get angry 'cause there's nothing to do. They get into trouble. (adult photovoice participant)

One photographer who took a picture of a Sony PlayStation® reflected on the lack of other activities for teenagers and wrote:

Teenagers don't have much to do here. And they want to do things. Most of the kids between 7th grade and 9th grade are too young for jobs, but yet too old for everything else that's offered, and those are the trouble ages, 'cause they're tryin' to figure out who they are. (adult photovoice participant)

Both adults and youth reported significant problems with the recreational activities and areas that did exist. For example, several focus group and photovoice participants described parks that were frequented by drug dealers or lacked playground equipment. As one youth photovoice participant poignantly described a picture she had taken of a boy standing in a park (see Photo 1):

Photo 1 It's a picture of my nephew. He looked, like, lonely since there was nothing to do there. There's nothing for him to do there. He could just stand. There's not even, like, any benches or anything where you could sit. (Youth photovoice participant)

Residents reported a need for free or subsidized activities, since activities that did exist tended to be unaffordable for poor families. In addition, many discussed other barriers to using available activities, including limited hours and lack of transportation:

> We have a lot of latchkey kids so that's really important that they have something to do. Programs like Scouts only last an hour. We need programs that go through the afternoon. We need programs that help kids with their homework. Programs that help the kids learn to use technology. These programs need to be wrapped around the whole school system. (adult focus group participant)
>
> [The kids who need out-of-school programs] are living in poor sections of town; they have no way to get there. They have parents, a lot of them are single-parent homes, and ... no one to take the kids to where they need to be. (adult photovoice participant)

When asked what types of out-of-school programming they would hope to see for youth, residents responded with a wide range of activities. Although policymakers have recently emphasized out-of-school programming as a strategy to increase academic achievement, residents had more expansive goals for the youth of the community. Although these residents mentioned academic improvement as one potential goal, they tended to be more concerned about supporting the development of their children's broader interests and assets. Residents envisioned opportunities to learn about finances and career development, engage in art and sports activities, participate in drug and alcohol resistance programs, and simply have fun in a safe environment. One representative comment of this sentiment is highlighted:

> There should be a Girls and Boys Club. It deals with working on the entire child and not just the educational needs of the child. Kids [would] learn social skills and communication skills. (adult focus group participant)

Additionally, several focus group respondents expressed their desire to use out-of school activities to enhance youth connections to family and community through parent participation, running programs through local faith-based organizations, and facilitating community service activities. Residents supported the development of out-of-school programs in the community, believing that the programs could provide many types of positive opportunities for youth.

Role models and mentors. Youth were especially insightful about the importance of role models to provide support and examples for youth—but also noted that role models and mentors were not readily available in their neighborhoods. One youth who participated in photovoice took a picture of a poster of a rapper on her wall:

> I chose this picture because it's [someone] who I really like and who I look up to. ... [It] just shows that there's always somebody in the world that somebody can look up to, you know, there's just always somebody out there doing something positive. Someone who inspires you.
> You wanna be like them...I don't think that a lot of kids got enough good role models. (Youth photovoice participant)

During the subsequent group discussion, another youth commented on the need for local youth to have a greater and more consistent adult presence in their lives:

> A lot of people have to look up to somebody that they don't even know. It's sort of sad that people can't have somebody that they know personally—like their mom or their dad or somebody like their grandpa—that they can look up to. The people that's in your life, like, in your life like right now, mentors like that, I think they're more important because you know they're gonna be there. (Youth photovoice participant)

In both photovoice and focus groups, participants desired adults to provide not only support and guidance, but a vision of possibility for the future—and saw today's youth as role models for the adolescents of tomorrow. Reflecting on another youth's photograph of his sports awards, one youth commented:

> He can be a role model to somebody like his little brother or little sister; something like that. Like, when he goes to his wrestlin' and it be a lot a people there. Like, if he went, like, every time, it could be like a role model thing. And the little kids look at him, like, I want to do that. (Youth photovoice participant)

In addition to seeing youth as catalysts for younger participants, one youth who had participated in a mentoring program also viewed mentoring programs as levers to launch youth into action:

> Something that would help out a lot more is more successful programs ... and more dedicated mentors to, like, sort of persuade young people my age to wanna do more and wanna give their free time to help out the community and the city as a whole. ... I been in the program since the 4th grade, and I'm a senior now. I haven't gotten tired of it yet. I'm forever doing

something, I mean, it's better than sitting at home watching TV to me. (Youth photovoice participant)

These comments indicated that community youth were keenly aware of the importance of mentors and the opportunities that they could foster in the lives of youth. Youth identified a need to foster more mentors and mentoring relationships in the community. In identifying this need, youth recognized that both youth and adults were responsible for mentoring others.

Youth leadership and action. Focus group and photovoice participants had many positive comments about community service in which youth were engaged and how it demonstrated youths' role as leaders of change. Photovoice youth were eager to present photos that represented their involvement in community improvements, expressing their pride in successfully making even small corners of their neighborhoods safer, more pleasant places. Moreover, some youth discussed fairly sophisticated ways to garner support for their efforts (see Photo 2):

Photo 2 A group of my friends and I got together and we totally renovated this area, this ground. We planted flowers about two years ago, and then last year we did a cleanup and made it all a lot better. Each fall we come and look at it and then decide what to do for the springtime. We've kept it up so far. We got a very little bit of money from the school, we put in that grants application financed through the Kellogg Foundation, and one local business donated time. (Youth photovoice participant)

Although some youth felt capable of making change happen, photovoice youth expressed some frustration with the change process. They were frustrated with inaction on the part of their peers as well as with lack of recognition and respect from community adults for their work.

> We are interested in buying a building to start our own youth program. Right now, I mean, it's all just pretty much dreams and hopes, because we really can't afford to do it. Not too many people hear about us and then not too many people will take us seriously either. (Youth photovoice participant)

Adults acknowledged the frustration that youth felt in not being respected or recognized for their leadership activities and showed awareness of how adults participate in this situation:

> Most of what you hear today is that youth is mis[-]spent, and what they're doing wrong. We don't spend enough time talking about the good things that the youth are doing. I'd like to see it—more pictures in the paper, spotlight that we do have youth that are caring, intelligent, and dedicated people. (adult photovoice participant)

Through these photovoice and focus group activities, youth and adults acknowledged the need for youth leadership activities to be fully recognized and appreciated. Interestingly, an actual by-product of the photovoice activities was support and recognition of youth leadership activities. The very process of reflecting on this need to honor youths' role as community decision-makers and leaders of change helped to establish these roles for youth. This process gave youth an opportunity to voice their ideas, have them affirmed by other youth and adults, and to see themselves as active participants in a community based decision-making process. Several of the youth involved in the process took on expanded leader roles within their community.

Adults and youth photovoice participants were provided with unique opportunities for mutual reflection about each others' experiences in the community. A representative sample of photovoice participants were interviewed after the completion of this project (Foster-Fishman et al., in press). Results suggest that participants were significantly affected by their experiences as photographers and as members of the neighborhood dialogue groups in which they reflected on their photographs. Participants reported an increased sense of competence and a growing critical consciousness, expanded relationships and increased efficacy that facilitated their ability to become community change agents.

Youth and adults' comments showed a strong desire for improved out-of-school activities, more mentors, and greater recognition for youths' roles as community leaders. Having these opportunities to express their concerns, youth further established their roles as community leaders, and adults were exposed to the powerful capacity of youth in these roles.

YOUTH GOVERNANCE AND YOUTH-ADULT PARTNERSHIPS: THE NEIGHBORHOOD MINIGRANT PROGRAM AND YOUTH STEERING COMMITTEE

In response to the issues and suggestions shared by residents through the focus group process, a minigrant program was initiated in June 2002. This program was designed to provide opportunities for community residents to develop projects that would have a meaningful and visible impact on the neighborhood, promote partnerships between residents and local organizations, and increase residents' leadership capacity. Program guidelines were developed by a steering committee comprised of adult residents from the seven neighborhoods, which was given freedom to design the minigrant program within the constraints set by the foundation for total budgeting amounts and applicant eligibility (e.g., target neighborhood residence). Given the concern that programs desired by and for youth programs may not be fully addressed by an adult-run minigrant program, a separate minigranting process for youth was also established. This included the development of a youth-only minigrant steering committee and a separate funding allocation for youth-led minigrant programs. Minigrant funds of up to $2,500 each were available to individuals or groups of residents from the targeted neighborhoods to support projects that would have visible effects in the neighborhood and the potential for long-term change. Projects were funded that could target increasing residents' capacity to help children learn, opportunities to support economic self-sufficiency, or strengthening neighborhood relationships. The minigrant application was a simple two-page form, and both adults and youth were encouraged to apply for funds. Minigrant applications were designated as either "youth" or "adult" minigrants by the applicant.

YOUTH MINIGRANTS: THE VISION

As mentioned, the initial strategy to support youth involvement in the minigrants was to establish separate review and award processes for youth and adults. The initial expectation was that youth grants would be those submitted and led by youth and would be distinguished from adult-led minigrants. Therefore, the adult minigrant steering committee would review grant applications and make award decisions for adult-led minigrants, and a youth minigrant committee would be created to review and award funds for youth-led minigrants. In keeping the two groups separate, the youth minigrant program aimed to make funds for youth-sponsored projects easily accessible so that youth would be free to express themselves and make decisions without being "overrun" by adults. The initial hope was that the separate youth committee would also offer youth opportunities for both formal leadership—through committee membership and training seminars—and informal leadership—through applying for and implementing minigrant projects.

YOUTH MINIGRANTS: THE REALITY

While some of the initial vision for youth minigranting was fulfilled, in other areas it was not. Although the minigrant process had been conceived as one avenue to expand youth action and leadership, in the end, few youth actually applied for minigrants, and most of the youth-focused minigrants were initiated by adults in the community or at YWC!. By the time the minigranting program had been implemented for nearly a year, only eight minigrant applications had been submitted by youth. And in only five of those grant applications were youth the primary leaders. In the three other applications, youth submitted the grant with a parent or were token participants. Youth grants were later expanded to include "youth-focused" grants, which could be submitted by adults with youth as the intended recipients. Although youth themselves did not initiate many grants, the majority of grants approved by the minigrant program through October 2004 were youth-focused, with 58 percent (n = 110) being youth-focused minigrants and 42 percent (n = 79) of the minigrants targeting both adults and youth. The majority of these youth-focused grants were adult-initiated.

The youth-focused minigrants included those focused on enhancing academic achievement, providing material needs, promoting self-esteem, providing recreational opportunities, upgrading computers, enhancing parent participation in children's education, and increasing earning opportunities and training (e.g., babysitter certification). Although few youth-led minigrants were submitted, the successful ones did show the impact the youth could have on their community. In addition, more successes were evident in the impact that youth participation in the minigrant steering committees had upon youths' own development as well as their partnerships with adults.

THE YOUTH STEERING COMMITTEE

Impacts of Youth Participation

For most of these youth, participating on the youth steering committee was their first formal leadership experience. In December 2002 (approximately six months after YWC! started), interviews were conducted with 23 adult and 5 youth neighborhood leaders (i.e., minigrant recipients, YWC! minigrant steering committee members, neighborhood activists and leaders), YWC! staff and administrators (8 interviews), and relevant Battle Creek Community Foundation management and staff (2 interviews). In addition, observations were made of adult and youth steering committee meetings during their first four months of operation, minigrant recipient evaluation forms were analyzed, and relevant YWC! documents were reviewed (Berkowitz & Foster-Fishman, 2002).

Overall, the data from those interviews suggests that participation in the youth steering committee and the development of minigranting activities provides valued outcomes for the youth involved. For many youth, these activities were their first forays into leadership positions, and they found their experiences to be rewarding and at times even "life altering." Not only had the minigranting process exposed youth to the possibilities of leadership, but it had also exposed the community to the possibility of youth as leaders. As one youth minigrant leader reported:

> [Yes We Can!] is taking care of the neighborhood and making sure everything's fine ... you guys come here and say questions that are really important to know, like "How is the neighborhood doing?" It makes me feel good because I want to tell other people my ideas and my feelings. (Berkowitz & Foster-Fishman, 2002)

Impacts on Youth Development

The impacts most frequently cited by respondents were the positive effects of involvement on the youth themselves. These effects are noticed widely across respondents—not only by the youth themselves, but also by adult leaders and youth staff members. Respondents note multiple positive developments emerging through youth minigrant steering committee participation or direct work on a minigrant (see Table 7.1):

Youth Impacts on Community

Youth were involved in making changes in their neighborhoods both directly—through developing and implementing minigrant ideas—and

Table 7.1
Reported Impacts of Youth Involvement

• Increased self-confidence and self-esteem	• "I'm not that shy anymore to go places or do things or talk to people—because of talking to different people and being around the people that are there. It's good because you can't be shy during a job interview . . . you gotta learn to speak up." —Youth Minigrant Steering Committee Member
• Improved communication skills and gaining experience in speaking confidently in public and with adults	• "It's got me speaking more—like out in public. For example, the time we went to San Francisco with the minigrant team, and I did most of the talking. Before I probably would have said three things and then quit." —Youth Minigrant Steering Committee Member
	• "Our kids like it. It makes them more involved, instead of being shy. Like our daughter—it's helped her start communicating better . . . Being around other people with other opinions is good for them." —Parent of Youth Minigrant Leader
• Literacy skills	• "Kids who couldn't read a whole paragraph at the beginning have improved their reading skills. It's [the minigrant steering committee] had an impact on their academic success in school." —Youth Committee Staff Member
• Leadership skills and a sense of themselves as leaders. This sense of self as a leader emerges most strongly in the interviews with youth who were on the minigrant steering committee—a more formalized leadership role. Youth who have entered these roles embrace them and carry this sense of leadership into multiple arenas of their lives.	• "It's impacted my whole life experience . . . I would never have thought I'd be a leader. And I needed it for what I want to do in life." —Youth Minigrant Steering Committee Member
	• "We're learning as a committee—how to read minigrants, and how to decide which to keep and which to throw back, and how to hold an important discussion." —Youth Minigrant Steering Committee Member
	• "Being able to write grants is a leadership opportunity. When you organize around a grant you have to take on a leadership role in making it all come together." —Youth Minigrant Leader.
	• "We go to meetings as who we are, what we want our future to be for our brothers and sisters . . . In school, I look at myself as a leader—I'm a leader to my brother, sister, etc. I'm not going to go to the mall and act differently (than I act in a meeting)." —Youth Minigrant Steering Committee Member
• Exposure to new experiences that they might not ordinarily have.	• "The San Francisco trip—three or four people came from the youth steering committee . . . San Francisco is such a big city . . . to see all the youth programs there—wow! We have three or four and they have hundreds. It was a good experience." —Youth Minigrant Steering Committee Member

indirectly—through making decisions around minigrants for youth. Several of the youth-led minigrants focused on providing fun, positive activities for youth—e.g., after-school dance classes or transportation to the library for story hour—or in helping youth develop skills, such as a certified babysitting class through the Red Cross. These activities have primarily impacted the youth who have participated directly in them. However, other youth have implemented—or are in the process of developing—minigrant activities comparable to the kinds of projects submitted by their adult counterparts, with neighborhood-level impacts. For example, three teens used a minigrant to help coordinate a neighborhood cleanup effort that spanned 10 days and filled six large dumpsters with trash from the neighborhood. In another neighborhood, a fifth-grader used minigrant funds to coordinate an ice cream social to bring residents together. These activities suggest the potential of youth to lead activities in their neighborhoods that have broad impacts for both youth and adults. One barrier to effective youth-adult partnerships can be an assumption on the part of adults that youth are primarily interested in having a good time. However, many of the young people we spoke with, in describing their ideas, expressed interest in and dedication toward projects and goals that went far beyond immediate self-interest:

> I'm hoping to get a field developed—a basketball court/playground. … Lots of kids in the neighborhood have no place to play but the street—and one kid almost got hit [by a car]. (youth minigrant leader)
>
> At school I'm planning—during my fourth hour [study hall], I'm drawing maps of the neighborhood and showing the [street] lights. And then I draw you guys doing the street lights. (youth minigrant leader)

Impacts on Adult-Youth Partnerships

Bringing youth and adults to work together as partners in addressing common issues can be a challenge. As one youth minigrant steering committee member stated: "It's a challenge to [work with adults], because adults don't really understand youth, and youth don't understand adults and the decisions they make." Both youth and adult informants gave positive indications that youth involvement in YWC! activities was promoting respect for youth among adults and shifting the way that neighborhood adults view youth:

> You know, if these teenage boys … can do this huge cleanup … if these kids can do this and are willing to do this, that says a lot. If we can get kids like that interested and at their age level, then they've done a wonderful job. … I was so impressed by the cleanup that these boys did. They

pulled together and pulled off some of these huge working projects. (adult neighborhood leader)

It makes me feel happy—that somebody is looking at the youth in a different perspective—that's real cool. (youth minigrant steering committee member)

Through their participation in these activities and committees, additional opportunities emerged:

Adults in my neighborhood might be ready to work with youth, because in my neighborhood, a lot of people are so proud of us ... the neighborhood—they see us, see the achievements we have made, and they have respect for us...the neighbors ask us questions now, and we answer them. (youth minigrant steering committee member)

Through these many comments, it is clear that youth involvement in the minigrant steering committee embodied many of the components of best practices in asset strategies reviewed earlier. This included opportunities for youth to fund out-of-school activities and other programs of priority to youth, to work in partnership with adults, and to solidify their role as leaders and change agents in the community. Youth gained specific skills to enhance their roles as leaders and change agents, and adults became more aware of youth's ability to serve in these capacities and to respect their contributions.

LESSONS LEARNED

The focus groups, photovoice sessions, and the minigrant steering committee provided many opportunities to engage youth and invest in their development. The initiatives began with high hopes for youth involvement, and many of the dreams came to fruition. Other hopes were not realized as strongly as desired, but through it all many lessons were learned. The key lessons focused on understanding the challenges faced when engaging youth and the supports needed to retain their involvement in meaningful ways.

Creativity Proved Useful in Engaging Youth

Both the photovoice activities and the focus groups tapped into youth creativity and energy while eliciting their thoughts and reflections. The photovoice process allowed youth to express themselves through photographs, written journals, and shared reflections in intimate group settings. Youth were active contributing members to the photovoice group. The experience proved to be powerful and personally transforming for participants, and youth were highly engaged in all phases of this process

(Foster-Fishman, Nowell, Deacon, Nievar, & McCann, in press). One important lesson learned during this effort was the effectiveness of using multiple ways for youth to express themselves. In the photovoice project, youth used photos, written reflections, and dialogue during group conversations to share their points of view and express their opinions. Follow-up conversations with participating youth indicated that having these multiple modes for expression was important to them, allowing their diverse strengths to emerge and be highlighted in the process.

Similarly, the creative use of "fun stations" as a youth-centered method of conducting focus groups turned out to be a successful strategy for engaging youth and gathering their input (Berkowitz, Hughes, & Foster-Fishman, 2002). In contrast to traditional focus groups, which tend to be sedentary and potentially uncomfortable for youth who do not want to speak up in front of others, this process was highly energetic and fun. Youth indicated that, "This is the most fun project I've been in," and "I wish school were more like this." This enthusiasm was reflected in their high level of involvement and interest in the overall process. Additionally, most participants in these groups were highly engaged in contributing ideas at each station, which stands in contrast to many focus groups where a few participants occupy most of the discussion and it is challenging to make sure quieter voices are heard. This alternative focus group format also provided useful data. Through this process, evaluators gathered a large number of ideas and insights from a broad array of young people in a relatively short period of time. This method also contained some limitations that should be taken into consideration for future use. In particular, low literacy levels—especially among younger participants—proved to be problematic. More specific technical details regarding tips for success at the design and implementation stages are available for those wishing to duplicate these methods (Berkowitz, Hughes, & Foster Fishman, 2002).

Recognize Challenges of Youth Involvement

In contrast to the focus group "fun stations" and the photovoice activities, the minigrant program struggled much more to engage youth and maintain their involvement. Very few youth-initiated minigrants were submitted. The majority of youth minigrants that were funded were led by adults and involved youth as token participants or as intended recipients of the programmatic efforts. Furthermore, youth involvement in the minigrant steering committee often waned (Berkowitz & Foster-Fishman, 2002).

> We're trying to get [a stronger membership]—some of the people aren't coming, but we get two more members for every person we let go ... so it's kind of bad and kind of good. (youth minigrant steering committee member)

Similar to research on other organizations seeking to engage youth in pro-grammatic efforts, this particular minigrant initiative found itself challenged to successfully engage youth in programming strategies based on adult-initiated concepts and traditional adult operations (Young & Sazama, 1999). In reflecting on reasons for low youth involvement, several factors were iden-tified. Description of those challenges and responses are presented elsewhere (Berkowitz & Foster-Fishman, 2002), but key points are highlighted below.

Understand youth time constraints. First, although adults expected that youth would be more available to submit grants during the summer, adults were unaware of how busy youth continued to be during the summer because of jobs, extracurricular activities, and involvement in other groups. Consistent with other findings, adults are not often aware of the time con-straints that youth face in their daily lives (Young & Sazama, 1999).

Understand how youth organize differently. Second, youth did not organize themselves for collective action in the same manner as adults for whom the minigrant process was initially structured. The minigrants were designed to help residents work assertively to learn to know their neigh-bors and organize efforts within their neighborhoods. Likewise, minigrant funds were allocated to be disbursed evenly across each of the seven neighborhoods. However, youth tended to feel more comfortable organiz-ing with their peers, and those social relationships were not aligned with neighborhood boundaries. Although youth demonstrated the ability to impact their neighborhoods in meaningful ways, as have others across the nation (Checkoway, 1998), the focus on neighborhood-based strategies for minigranting did not have broad appeal with youth residents.

Equip youth with the necessary tools to succeed in organizations. Third, youth did not have the necessary supports in place to undertake the prepara-tion and submission of minigrants. While the minigrant application process was designed with simplicity in mind, the tasks of designing an activity, creating a budget, and gathering support letters or signatures appeared to be overwhelming to some youth given their lack of previous experience in these areas. This is not unlike other youth-focused programs that have discovered that well-intentioned strategies to empower youth by giving them opportunities to be self-directing fail when adequate supports are not in place to compensate for their lack of experience (Hart, 1992). Not want-ing to intrude on youth initiative, adults often fail to offer youth tangible assistance when it is desired. While youth do not want adults to take over decision-making or planning, they do desire to have adults invest in their personal development by teaching them the tools and skills needed to func-tion within an organization. This is one of the many reasons for suggesting that youth and adults work together in combined committees rather than in separate youth and adult committees. Best practices suggest that the most empowering results for youth occur when youth and adults make decisions together and in numbers that do not overly represent adults. In fact, given this insight and the strong recommendations made by adult and youth steering committee members, less than one year into the minigranting program, the youth and adult committees were merged into one decision-making body. Although this integrated approach is preferred, even the inclusion of youth in a separate committee is a first step toward the ultimate goal of shared decision-making (Zeldin, McDaniel, Topitzes, & Calvert, 2000).

Equip youth and adults with the tools to maintain positive decision-making partnerships. Fourth, not only did community youth not have the tools they needed to successfully navigate the minigrant application process, neither youth nor adult supporters on the youth minigrant steering committee had the comprehensive preparation they needed to successfully work together. Many have noted that the process of integrating youth and adults together as co-decision-makers involves a steep learning curve for both groups (Young & Sazama, 1999; Zeldin et al., 2001). Youth often lack the skills they need to function with an adult-centered organization. Adults might forget that youth have not yet learned how to read ledgers or prepare budgets, understand annual reports, conduct meetings according to protocol, or understand rules for group decision-making. At the same time, adults often underestimate the decision-making and leadership capacities of youth and try to dominate meetings or decisions (Camino, 2000b; Young & Sazama, 1999; Zeldin et al., 2000; see Huber, Frommeyer, Weisenbach, & Sazama, 2003, for a more extensive review). As one youth minigrant steering committee member reported,

> Sometimes at the meeting [a staff member] was at the side of me, telling me, "I would approve this" or "I would deny this." It was confusing to me—if I were [in that position], I don't think I'd be telling people [that].

As a result, youth often fear speaking up to offer their opinions or to ask questions when the setting is heavily weighted with adults or appears intimidating. Even adults have doubts about their own capacities to work effectively with youth. Levels of discomfort and uncertainty may plague youth and adult members alike, although the youth members are generally more vulnerable in their ability to insist on necessary changes.

Consider the Best Practices and Lessons Learned from Others

Clearly, many issues presented challenges to engaging youth as active participants in programmatic activities and decision-making roles. Many of these struggles are predictable and have been faced by others. For these reasons, researchers and practitioners in youth governance and youth-adult partnerships have suggested the following strategies that have helped to prepare adults and youth for these new roles (Camino, 2000a; Young & Sazama, 1999):

1. *The organization and its leaders must have a deep commitment to honor youth and adult input equally enough to overcome barriers.* The value must be embedded strongly enough in the culture to overcome the hierarchy typically present between youth and adults as well as to overcome tokenism, attitudes, and institutional barriers that support that hierarchy and exclude youth (e.g., meeting times, locations, number of youth members). Functionally, this means that at least two or more youth members will be included on the board, and more if necessary, to balance the weight of power between youth and adults. The merged adult-youth steering committee includes such a composition.

2. *Organizations must seek and provide intergenerational training and education for youth and adults.* Both groups will need training in the skills, competencies, and new ways of thinking that they will need to employ to understand each other's experiences and perspectives. The training provides an opportunity for youth and adults to reflect on their own and others' competencies, stereotypes, and fears in working together. An example of youth-partnership training for organizations is that which has been developed and implemented by Youth on Board (www.youthonboard.org).

3. *Establish support systems.* Youth, adults, and their parents may need ongoing support in the newly established youth-adult partnerships. Youth may require additional orientation and training to level the playing field so they are able to perform successfully on tasks that are new to them but familiar to adults (e.g., reading budgets and ledger sheets) and to understand their roles and responsibilities. Parents may benefit from orientation programs to help them understand their child's new role as well. Adults in the organization may gain from ongoing support from one another to process and reflect on their new experiences in working with youth

This initiative to engage youth was undertaken at a time of growing support for the inclusion of youth in community research and evaluation. Some of the key issues that have arisen in this new movement have been to determine what methods should be used when involving youth and to ascertain what roles youth should play in community research. The methods employed in this initiative allowed youth to move beyond subjects to become consultants and at times even partners on the continuum toward youth as directors in the community evaluation process (Checkoway &

Richards-Schuster, 2003). In experimenting with youth involvement in these creative ways, the program initiators learned many lessons specific to the unique tasks of this project and some experienced in other communities trying to effectively engage and support youth.

In summary, each of the unique components of the Yes We Can! initiative contained the three asset strategies reviewed here. The focus groups, photovoice project, and the minigranting program with its steering committee each touched on at least one or more of the issues of out-of-school-time, mentoring, and youth decision-making and governance. The overlap and continuity of these components may have been an important factor in why these activities had such profound effects on youth, adults, and their communities.

REFERENCES

Beker, J., Eisikovits, Z., & Guttmann, E. (1987). Economic considerations in supporting preventive services for troubled youth: The case of adolescents on the farm. *Children & Youth Services Review, 9*(3), 187–206.

Berkowitz, S., & Foster-Fishman, P. (2002). *Yes We Can! process evaluation report: 2002—First year implementation.* [Available from W. K. Kellogg Foundation, One Michigan Avenue East, Battle Creek, MI 49017.]

Berkowitz, S., Hughes, H., & Foster-Fishman, P. (2002). *Yes We Can! methods brief: A new strategy for conducting focus groups with youth.* [Available from W. K. Kellogg Foundation, One Michigan Avenue East, Battle Creek, MI 49017.]

Brown, R., & Evans, W. P. (2002). Extracurricular activity and ethnicity: Creating greater school connection among diverse student populations. *Urban Education, 37*(1), 41–58.

Calabrese, R. L., & Schumer, H. (1986). The effects of service activities on adolescent alienation. *Adolescence, 21*(83), 675–687.

Camino, L. (2000a). Putting youth-adult partnerships to work for community change: Lessons from volunteers across the country. *CYD Journal, 1*(4), 27–31.

Camino, L. (2000b). Youth-adult partnership: Entering new territory in community work and research. *Applied Developmental Science, 4*(Suppl.1), 11–20.

Carnegie Council on Adolescent Development. (1992). *A matter of time: Risk and opportunity in the non-school hours.* New York: Carnegie Corporation of New York.

Checkoway, B. (1998). Involving young people in neighborhood development. *Children and Youth Services Review, 20*(9/10), 765–795.

Checkoway, B., & Richards-Schuster, K. (2003). Youth participation in community evaluation research. *American Journal of Evaluation, 24*(1): 21–33.

Cooper, H., Valentine, J., Nye, B., & Lindsay, J. (1999). Relationships between five after-school activities and academic achievement. *Journal of Educational Psychology 91*(2), 369–378.

DuBois, D. L., Holloway, B. E., Valentine, J. C., & Cooper, H. (2002). Effectiveness of mentoring programs for youth: A meta-analytic review. *American Journal of Community Psychology, 30*(2), 157–197.

Eccles, J. S., & Barber, B. L. (1999). Student council, volunteering, basketball, or marching band: What kind of extracurricular involvement matters? *Journal of Adolescent Research, 14,* 10–43.

Foster-Fishman, P., Fitzgerald, K., Brandell, C., Nowell, B., Chavis, D., & Van Egeren, L. A. (Under review). Building a community of possibility: The role of small wins and community organizing.

Foster-Fishman, P., Nowell, B., Deacon, Z., Nievar, A., & McCann, P. (In press). Using methods that matter: The impact of reflection, dialogue, and voice. *American Journal of Community Psychology.*

Grossman, J. B., & Rhodes, J. E. (2002). The test of time: Predictors and effects of duration in youth mentoring relationships, *American Journal of Community Psychology, 30*(2),199–219.

Hart, R. A. (1992). *Children's participation: From tokenism to citizenship.* Innocenti Essays No. 4. [Available from United Nations Children's Fund, UNICEF, International Child Development Centre, Piazza S.S. Annunziata 12, 50122 Florence, Italy.]

Herrera, C., Sipe, C. L., McClanahan, W. S., Arbreton, A. J. A., & Pepper, S. K. (2000). *Mentoring school-age children: Relationship development in community-based and school-based programs.* [Available from Public Private Ventures, One Commerce Square, 2005 Market Street, Suite 900, Philadelphia, PA 19103, Tel: (215) 557-4400, Fax: (215) 557–4469, http://www.ppv.org.] Retrieved September 19, 2004, from http://www. mentoring.org/resources/pdf/relationship_dev.pdf.

Hersch, P. (1998). A tribe apart: *A journey into the heart of American adolescence.* New York: Ballantine.

Hoover, A. B., & Weisenbach, A. (1999). Youth leading now!: Securing a place at the table. *New designs for youth development, 15*(3). Retrieved October 31, 2004, from http://www.cydjournal.org/NewDesigns/ND_99Sum/Hoover.html.

Huber, M. S., & Kossek, E. E. (1999). Community distress predicting welfare exits: The under-examined factor for families in the United States. *Community, Work, and Family, 2*(2), 173–186.

Huber, M.S.Q., Frommeyer, J., Weisenbach, A., & Sazama, J. (2003). Giving youth a voice in their own community and personal development: Strategies and impacts of bringing youth to the table. In F.A. Villarruel, D.F. Perkins, L.M. Borden, & J.G. Keith (Eds.), *Community youth development: Programs, policies, and practices.* Thousand Oaks, CA: Sage.

Jekielek, S. M., Moore, K. A., Hair, E. C., & Scarupa, H. J. (2002). *Mentoring: A promising strategy for youth development.* Research Brief. [Available from Child Trends, 4301 Connecticut Avenue, NW, Suite 100, Washington, DC 20008, Tel: (202) 362-5580, Fax: (202) 362-5533, http://www. childtrends.org.] Retrieved September 19, 2004, from http://12.109.133.224/ Files/MentoringBrief2002.pdf.

Keith, J.G., Huber, M.Q., Griffin, A., & Villarruel, F.A. (2001). *Building best lives: Profiles of 24,000 Michigan youth from 2 asset approaches.* [Available from Community Youth Development Program, 203 Human Ecology, Department of Family & Child Ecology, Michigan State University, East Lansing, MI 48824, Tel: (517) 355-7732.]

Kingsley, T.G., McNeely, J.B., & Gibson, J.O. (1997). *Community building: Coming of age.* [Available from Development Training Institute, 2510 St. Paul Street, Baltimore, MD 21218, Tel: (410) 338-2512, Fax: (410) 338-2751, info@dtinational.org.]

Kirby, D., & Coyle, K. (1997). Youth development programs. *Children and Youth Services Review, 19*(5/6), 437–454.

Klindera, K., & Menderweld, J. (2001). Youth involvement in prevention programming. Issues at a Glance. Retrieved October 31, 2004, from http://www.advocatesforyouth.org/publications/iag/involvement.htm.

Kubisch, A.C., Weiss, C.H., Schorr, L.B., & Connell, J.P., (1995). Introduction. In J.P. Connell, A.C. Kubisch, L.B. Schorr, & E.H. Weiss (Eds.), New *approaches to evaluating community initiatives: Concepts, methods, and contexts* (pp. 1–21). Washington, DC: Aspen Institute.

Larson, R.W. (2000). Toward a psychology of positive youth development. *American Psychologist, 55,* 170–183.

Le Menestrel, S. (2003). *In the good old summertime: What do parents want for their kids?* (ERIC Document Reproduction Service No. ED476571).

Markstrom, C. A. (1999). Religious involvement and adolescent psychosocial development. *Journal of Adolescence, 22,* 205–221.

Miller, B.M. (2003). *Critical hours: Executive summary.* Nellie Mae Foundation.

Perkins, D.F., Borden, L.M., Villarruel, F.A., Carlton-Hug, A., & Stone, M. (under review). Why ethnic minority urban youth choose to participate— or not to participate.

Quinn, J. (1999). Where need meets opportunity: Youth development programs for early teens. *The Future of Children, 9,* 96–116.

Scales, P.C., Benson, P.L., Leffert, N., & Blyth, D.A. (2000). Contribution of developmental assets to the prediction of thriving among adolescents. *Applied Developmental Science, 4,* 27–46.

Scales, P.C., & Leffert, N. (1999). *Developmental assets: A synthesis of the scientific research on adolescent development.* Minneapolis: Search Institute.

Shinke, S.P., Cole, K.C., & Poulin, S.R. (2000). Enhancing the educational achievement of at-risk youth. *Prevention Science, 1*(1), 51–60.

Shonkoff, J.P., & Phillips, D.A. (Eds.). (2000). *From neurons to neighborhoods, The science of early childhood development.* Washington, DC: National Academy Press.

Sipe, C.L. (2002). Mentoring programs for adolescents: A research summary. *Journal of Adolescent Health, 31*(Supplemental Article), 251–260.

Sipe, C.L., Ma, P., & Gambone, M.S. (1988). *Support for youth: A profile of three communities.* [Available from Public Private Ventures, One

Commerce Square, 2005 Market Street, Suite 900, Philadelphia, PA 19103, Tel: (215) 557-4400, Fax: (215) 557-4469, http://www.ppv.org.] Retrieved September 19, 2004, from http://www.mentoring.org/resources/ pdf/relationship_dev.pdf.

Smock, K. (1997). *Comprehensive community initiatives: A new generation of urban revitalization strategies.* Unpublished paper presented on COMM-ORG: The Online Conference on Community Organizing and Development. [Available at http://comm-org.utoledo.edu/papers97/smock/smockintro.]

Traynor, W. (1995, September/October). Community building hope and caution. *Shelterforce Magazine,* 12–16.

Villarruel, F. A., Perkins, D. F., Borden, L. M., & Keith, J. G. (2003). *Community youth development: Programs, policies, and practices.* Thousand Oaks, CA: Sage.

Wang, C., & Burris, M. A. (1994). Empowerment through photo novella: Portraits of participation. *Health Education Quarterly, 21*(2), 171–186.

Whalen, S. P., & Wynn, J. R. (1995). Enhancing primary services for youth through an infrastructure of social services. *Journal of Adolescent Research, 10,* 88–110.

Young, K. S., & Sazama, J. (1999). *Fourteen points: Successfully involving youth in decision-making.* [Available from Youth on Board, 58 Day Street, Third Floor, PO Box 440322, Somerville, MA 02144.]

Zeldin, S., McDaniel, A. K., Topitzes, D., & Calvert, M. (2000). *Youth in decision-making; A study on the impact of youth and adults on organizations.* Unpublished manuscript. Commissioned by The Innovation Center for Youth and Community Development A Division of National 4-H Council in partnership with the Youth in Governance Taskforce of the National Association of Extension 4-H Agents and supported by the Surdna Foundation. [Available from University of Wisconsin-Madison, Department of Human Development and Family Studies.]

Zeldin, S., McDaniel, A., Topitzes, D., & Lorens, M. B. (2001). Bringing young people to the table: Effects on adults and youth organizations. *CYD Journal, 2*(2), 20–27.

Ziazi, Z. (2003, July). *Middle Eastern communities & youth in the U.S.: An online course module: Community youth development.* Unpublished document. Michigan State University, Department of Family and Child Ecology, East Lansing: [Available from Community Youth Development Program, 203 Human Ecology, Department of Family & Child Ecology, Michigan State University, East Lansing, MI 48824, Tel: (517) 355-7732.]

Chapter 8

SCHOOL-BASED SEXUAL VIOLENCE PREVENTION PROGRAMS: CURRENT EVALUATION FINDINGS AND POLICY IMPLICATIONS

Stephanie M. Townsend and Rebecca Campbell

Sexual violence is perpetrated against women at an alarming rate in the United States. Studies have found that 15 to 36 percent of women report being victims of at least one completed rape in their lifetime (Desai & Saltzman, 2001). Young women and girls are the most vulnerable to sexual violence. The National Women's Study found that almost two-thirds of completed rapes occurred before age 18 years and slightly more than one-fifth between 18 and 24 years (Kilpatrick, Edmunds, & Seymour, 1992). As communities have become more aware of the risks that their youth face, they have begun implementing prevention programs. Most of these programs are conducted in schools not only because they offer economy of scale, but they also provide opportunities to promote discussion and reflection (Rispens, Aleman, & Goudena, 1997). Most school-based rape prevention programs emphasize basic education about sexual violence, and these interventions have been found to increase youths' knowledge about sexual violence and for older youth to increase the degree to which they view the perpetrator, rather than the victim, as responsible for the assault. However, there is little evidence that commonly employed practices actually change behaviors related to the perpetration of sexual violence or significantly reduce the risk of victimization. This chapter provides a critical overview of the most common types of rape prevention programs being used in K-12 settings and findings about their impact. Case examples are included to illustrate the types of curricula being used. This is followed by a discussion of alternative approaches that may be more effective as preventive interventions. Finally, policy reforms that are necessary for the development and implementation of such alternatives are identified.

COMMON SEXUAL VIOLENCE PREVENTION PROGRAMS

Elementary School Programs

Programs to prevent sexual victimization are widely implemented with elementary school–age children. A national survey of youth and their parents suggested that most programming is focused on elementary-age children (Finkelhor & Dziuba-Leatherman, 1995). However, most programming starts in grade four, which is contrary to expert recommendations that prevention education should start earlier. The national survey found that most programs address similar content, including the continuum of touch, strategies for stopping abuse attempts, sexual abuse in the family, admonitions to tell an adult, and reassurances that abuse is never the child's fault. Some of the content was found to vary according to the age of children, with sexual abuse in the family being addressed more with older children and kidnapping being stressed more with younger children. These topics are most often covered on multiple occasions, and the programs were taught in an interactive manner. Slightly more than half of the children reported that the programs included opportunities to practice the skills they were being taught.

Case Example: Beldingville Sexual Abuse Prevention Program

A recent study of community-based rape prevention programs provides a rich description of common practices in rape prevention (Townsend & Campbell, under review). Elementary school programs are exemplified by the Beldingville Sexual Abuse Prevention Program. This program is funded by private foundation grants made to the local rape crisis center and has been operating for approximately 10 years. It was developed in response to a community needs assessment that indicated a need for sexual assault prevention programming.

The curriculum was grafted together from different programs that the agency thought had been proven effective, although the evidence for effectiveness was vague. The prevention program is staffed by five full-time positions, which is unusually high for these types of programs. The curriculum consists of four related but independent curricula: one each for preschool through second grade, third through fifth grade, middle school, and high school. The curriculum for the youngest children is designed to help them understand child sexual abuse with a focus on teaching children avoidance skills. Abuse avoidance is promoted by teaching the children about body ownership, the differences between "good touch" and "bad touch," and the importance of telling a safe adult if anyone tries to touch them inappropriately. The teaching methods rely on gaining children's attention by having them interact with a staff person who is dressed in a costume of a big, purple bird. The bird reads to the children from a book that tells the story of her experience with feeling what they call an "uh-oh" feeling when her uncle touched her inappropriately and how she told her parents. The following week the character returns to the classroom and asks the children questions about what they learned and hands out treats. The curriculum for the third through fifth grade students focuses on conflict resolution and issues related to domestic violence. It does not directly address sexual assault, although the concepts of healthy, cooperative relationships lays the groundwork for the middle school and high school programs that address sexual harassment and acquaintance rape. The Beldingville program performs outcomes evaluations on all of its curricula. The staff have developed pre- and posttest measures to see if students understand the basic facts about what sexual abuse is and what they should do if anyone tries to harm them.

Effectiveness of Elementary School Programs

A number of reviews of child sexual abuse prevention programs have summarized common practices and have generally concluded that most children benefit from these types of programs insofar as they learn the concepts and acquire the self-protection skills that are being taught (e.g., Carroll, Miltenberger, & O'Neill, 1992; Finkelhor & Strapko, 1992). A meta-analysis of published evaluations concurred with these conclusions and additionally found that the programs are effective even for younger children (age five and younger) who appear to benefit more initially than do older children, although over time they are more likely to forget what they have learned (Rispens, Aleman, & Goudena, 1997). The effects of the programs decrease over time for all children, but even at follow-up assessments there was a considerable positive effect. It is important to note that these programs are targeting potential victims and not potential perpetrators. They may be effective at helping children to respond in a self-protective way when faced with attempted victimization. However, they do not reduce the frequency of those attempts.

Middle School and High School Programs

Community-based rape crisis centers have also made substantial in-roads into the educational system for older youth. A national study found that

96 percent of rape crisis centers offer community education in high schools (Campbell, Baker, & Mazurek, 1998). Middle school and high school programs are quite similar, although the older students tend to receive more detailed instruction about sexual assault, whereas sexual harassment is emphasized more with middle school students. These programs focus on reducing the risk of victimization and they seek to reduce the psychological distress of victimization. Although a variety of topics are covered by rape prevention programs, some topics are mainstays. These include basic sexual assault facts (e.g., myths, definitions, prevalence, legal statutes); how to reduce the risk of being assaulted (e.g., risk factors, alcohol, drug-facilitated rapes); what to do after someone has been assaulted (e.g., community resources, how to be supportive, medical exams, how to avoid blaming the victim); what constitutes a healthy relationship; and what sexual harassment is. These topics are covered in relatively short programs, typically between one- and three-hour sessions that are implemented in classrooms. Increasingly, programs rely on didactic presentations and interactive activities. Few community programs rely on a lecture-style format.

Although there are common practices and programs frequently share materials, rape prevention curricula are not standardized. Unlike an area such as substance use prevention in which there are some curricula that are widely used, community-based programs tend to develop their own materials as well as adapt ideas and curricula from other programs. Some states are moving toward standardizing their prevention curricula. However, as discussed below, this approach may diminish the ability to develop programs that respond to local needs.

Case Example: River City Rape Prevention Program

Again drawing from a study of community-based programs (Townsend & Campbell, under review), the most common type of program found in middle schools and high schools were short programs that are exemplified by the River City Rape Prevention Program. This program is funded from a combination of state and federal funds allocated specifically for rape prevention education. The program has been operating for six years. Prior to its development there was no rape prevention information in the schools, so the local rape crisis center developed the program in order to fill the unmet need of educating youth about sexual violence. The availability of funding was a significant factor in its creation.

The curriculum used in the River City program was created by the local agency. It looked at what other programs were doing and pulled together pieces from various places plus added their own ideas. The agency did not adopt a predeveloped curriculum because the curricula available for purchase generally were too long and incorporated too many other issues besides sexual assault. Additionally, the current staff person prefers doing interactive activities that fit her own style and that allow her to emphasize what she thinks is the most important information. The program is staffed by one full-time person who does all of the presentations in the schools. The curriculum consists of two sessions, each lasting approximately 60 minutes. It targets students in grades 9 and 10, with most of the presentations being done in health classes with mixed-gender groups.

The goals of the River City program focus on increasing knowledge about sexual assault issues, educating students about risky behaviors, and educating them about the services that are available if a rape occurs. Topics covered include basic definitions related to sexual assault, what to do after a rape, sexual assault laws, sex offender registration, date rape drugs, assertiveness, and sexual harassment. The staff person who teaches this program uses a variety of teaching methods including didactic presentations, an anonymous question box, and interactive activities. The activities change each year according to what issues seem to be most important. One activity that has been used is a matching exercise in which blue index cards have a word or statement related to sexual assault and yellow index cards have the corresponding definition or explanation. She hands out the cards to the students and they move around the classroom trying to find the match for their cards. Once they all think they have their matches, they go over the words and definitions, talking about why the matches were correct or incorrect. Another exercise the River City program has used is giving the students various rape scenarios and asking them to come up with ways they could assertively respond in each situation. These scenarios also have addressed the issue of victim blaming by asking students how they would feel if they were in the situation and what kinds of responses would be helpful.

The River City program, like all of the state-funded programs in its state, is required to do outcomes evaluations. The staff have developed their own pre- and posttest measures to see if the students are better informed about sexual assault and hold fewer victim-blaming attitudes following the program.

Effectiveness of Common Practices in Middle School and High School

Regrettably, the effects of school-based rape prevention programs have been very limited. This has been most clearly documented with researcher-developed programs that are similar to those used in middle schools and high schools. Evaluations of these types of programs have documented significant intervention effects on rape-supportive attitudes as evidenced by comparing pretest and posttest scores (e.g., Black, Weisz, Coats, & Patterson, 2000; Frazier, Valtinson, & Candell, 1994; Heppner, Humphrey, Hillenbrand-Gund, & DeBord, 1995; Hilton, Harris, Rice, Smith Krans, & Lavigne, 1998; Lanier, Elliott, Martin, & Kapadia, 1998; Lenihan & Rawlins, 1994). However, changes in attitudes do not necessarily predict changes in behavior related to perpetration of sexual violence (cf. review of debate in Eagly & Chaiken, 1993). The importance of this distinction is underscored by evaluations that have demonstrated that although students receiving the programs showed significantly less rape myth acceptance, there were no changes in the rates of perpetration (Foshee, Bauman, Greene, et al., 2000; Gidycz et al., 2001). As has been noted, "It may simply be unrealistic to expect that long-held, deeply ingrained attitudes and beliefs will be changed in any lasting way as the result of a 1 or 2 hour program. *The danger of such programs is that they can make us think that we are doing something, even if we are not*" (Frazier et al., 1994, p. 156, emphasis added).

Even with longer programs, behavioral effects have been short-lived. One of the most comprehensive programs that has been evaluated is the Safe Dates program, a prolonged intervention with eighth and ninth grade students at 14 schools in rural North Carolina (Foshee, Bauman, Arriaga, et al., 1998; Foshee et al., 2000). Half of the schools received both school activities and community activities, while half received only community activities. School activities included a theater production by peers, a 10-session interactive curriculum taught by teachers who received 20 hours of training, and a school poster contest. Community activities included services for adolescents in abusive relationships and training given to community service providers. Pretest to posttest analyses showed promising program effects, including significant attitude and behavior changes in schools that received the full intervention. These effects included 60 percent less sexual violence perpetration in the full intervention schools compared to the schools that only received community activities. However, follow-up analyses one year later failed to show any long-term behavioral effects. Although effects on dating violence norms, conflict management skills, and awareness of community services for dating violence were maintained, the differences in sexual violence perpetration attenuated.

Summary

The current state of affairs in rape prevention is a combination of hard-earned success and disappointing outcomes. Community-based rape crisis centers have worked to gain access to schools and to develop positive relationships with school staff. Increasingly, the prevention of sexual violence is moving from the periphery to being an accepted function of schools. Having rape prevention in schools has helped to change youths' knowledge and attitudes about sexual violence. However, these successes are offset by the fact that to date there have been no demonstrated changes in perpetration or victimization rates as a result of these programs. Although behavioral changes are infrequently studied, when they are the best outcomes have been short-lived. Clearly, alternative approaches need to be developed and tested. Current programs should continue to promote increased awareness of sexual violence, help-seeking, and compassionate response to victims. However, the present programs must be augmented with a different approach to decrease the incidence of sexual violence.

ALTERNATIVE APPROACHES TO SEXUAL VIOLENCE PREVENTION

Current intervention approaches to reduce sexual violence among school-aged youth have not been able to demonstrate sustainable behavioral change, which means that it is important to consider new ways to address these issues. An alternative model proposed here has three distinguishing characteristics. Preventive interventions need to (1) *change settings* rather than individuals, (2) *be locally specific,* and (3) *build community capacity* to respond to sexual violence as a social problem.

Changing Settings

School-based interventions typically target *individuals* as the unit of intervention. This is seen in the way programs measure their outcomes. The most common assessment technique is to administer a questionnaire before and after the program in which students are asked questions about basic sexual assault facts and their own attitudes about sexual assault. The results are compared to see whether students' knowledge and attitudes changed in the intended ways. Even when the *content* of the program includes topics about how society condones sexual violence or how some settings present more risks, the programs do not usually attempt to change those social and environmental factors. For example, although the role of alcohol and the risks posed by being in isolated settings are often discussed in rape prevention programs, directly changing social and dating settings is not attempted as a preventive intervention. Similarly, although some programs discuss social factors such as how gender socialization contributes to sexual violence, they do so by making students more aware of what gender socialization is and its consequences. It is the rare intervention that attempts to change the social-ization process itself. Like most curricula in our educational system, effects are looked for in the individuals who receive the curriculum. In this way, rape prevention falls into the same trap as other preventive interventions: they focus too much on individual program recipients and not enough on social settings as the context for intervention (Elias, 1987). What is needed is a shift beyond the narrow scope of increasing individuals' knowledge and changing their attitudes about sexual violence to the broader task of transforming what has been called *rape culture:* the "complex of beliefs that encourages male sexual aggression and supports violence against women" (Buchwald, Fletcher, & Roth, 1993, p. i). This requires changing settings, social structures, cultural patterns, and institutions.

Obviously, transforming the culture in which we live extends far beyond interventions in schools. However, the question can also be asked: How do we change our schools to promote what Peggy Reeves Sanday (1996) calls a rape-free rather than a rape-prone culture? A detailed discussion of strategies for changing rape culture is beyond the scope of this chapter. However, some general themes are worth highlighting. First, schools must *redefine their role* to go beyond academic instruction to providing for the needs of the whole child. This shift has already begun with schools taking on social problems such as drug and alcohol use and even their current inclusion of rape prevention in the curriculum. However, social issues are still predominantly addressed through traditional educational approaches. Schools need to take on a greater role in providing mental health support, changing settings both within and outside of school, and activating students to be agents of social change. Second, these types of changes reflect a radi-cal *restructuring of relationships* between the school, students, families, and other community institutions. Developing interventions based on students' experiences, family involvement as active and equal partners, and the inte-gration of schools and other community agencies will build on indigenous resources, change the balance of power, and alter decision-making pro-cesses. Third, the *school staff must also become the focus* for intervention. Typically, training school staff merely consists of making a presentation to inform them of what will be done with students. In focusing on school staff as the locus of intervention, it is they who must become aware of the issues, who may need to evaluate and change their own attitudes, and who must develop new skills for working with students to address gender violence.

Case Example: Mentors in Violence Prevention Program

The Mentors in Violence Prevention (MVP) Program is one recent attempt to change the culture within schools by reducing male peer support for sexual violence. It is an example of changing the setting within the school by activating students to be agents of social change and redefining their relationships with one another. This program trains athletes and other student leaders to be *empowered bystanders* who confront sexist and abusive peers (Ward, 2003). The overarching goal is for students to show other students, through example and mentoring, that sexism and gender violence are not acceptable and will not be tolerated in the school culture. The program is unique in two aspects. First, it is one of the few programs that focuses on the relationship between masculinity and violence and that recognizes the potential for males to be change agents in responding to gender violence. Second, while other programs have used peers to present rape prevention information with the belief that increased awareness will change behavior, MVP attempts to change norms in the school more directly by empowering students to speak out when they witness sexist or abusive behavior. As such, MVP seeks to change the culture within the school to one that does not tolerate sexism or gender violence by promoting immediate peer intervention.

The MVP program begins with 12 to 14 hours of initial training, conducted over two to three months. In this training student leaders explore the ways they have been socialized into gender roles, learn to recognize and be critical of society's acceptance of violence against women, and practice how to confront sexist and violent behavior and attitudes. In addition to using the skills they acquire in their daily interactions, MVP participants are also given additional training on how to conduct their own awareness-raising workshops in their schools.

The MVP program is currently undergoing a three-year evaluation. The findings from Year 1 (Ward, 2003) have documented the need for this type of programming. Data indicate that MVP influences a positive change in students' knowledge and awareness about gender violence, their attitudes toward the issues, and their confidence in confronting male violence against women when they see it among their peers. However, the program has not yet been evaluated in terms of its impact on students' experiences with gender violence, so conclusions about whether this approach is more effective than typical prevention programs cannot yet be made. The program is highlighted here because it represents a new approach that attempts to change the setting's norms.

Locally Specific Interventions

As noted earlier, while there are prevention practices that are common in terms of curriculum content and teaching techniques, rape prevention has not seen the same type of standardization as have efforts to address other social and developmental issues. There is not yet any equivalent to the Substance Abuse and Mental Health Services Administration's list of model drug prevention programs (SAMHSA, 2004). However, the current funding climate, especially for schools in the context of the No Child Left Behind Act, creates pressure to use programs that have been rigorously evaluated and that are implemented with fidelity to the curriculum as written. The standardization of rape prevention should be approached with caution, however, and the needs for locally specific interventions should be seriously considered.

Implementing rape prevention in schools is often a difficult task, especially in the initial efforts to gain the cooperation of administrators and faculty and to obtain access to students. In a study of community-based rape prevention programs, staff reported many challenges in their negotiations with the schools (Townsend, 2003). For example, the length of programs was typically determined not by curriculum design but by the access the school was willing to provide. For example, although one program has a 12-session curriculum available, in all but one school they present only two sessions because that is all the time the schools will allow. Additionally, 80 percent of program staff reported that school policies about sex education both proscribed and prescribed certain topics in the programs. Prohibited topics included contraception (including the type offered as a standard part of post-rape medical treatment), pregnancy, general questions about sex, same-sex relationships, and use of the word "sex." Programs must have the flexibility to respond to these local norms as well as to community-specific needs. Standardized curricula may not afford such flexibility.

In addition to influences from schools, staff who were interviewed in Townsend's (2003) study also reported limitations placed on them by community attitudes that affect both access to youth and what can be done in an intervention. For example, communities may have a history of not prosecuting sexual assaults, think that sexual assault is irrelevant to their community, place a higher priority on other social problems, not support the questioning of gender roles and socialization, or be fraught with tension between schools and social service agencies. These issues can impact not only the process of implementing an intervention, but also the form and content of it. Again, programs must have the flexibility to work within these contexts and to address community attitudes that may be barriers to further prevention efforts.

The presence of local norms requires that interventions be designed to match the local setting and that they be responsive to cultural and institutional diversity (O'Neill & Trickett, 1982). Doing so can increase the validity of the intervention by reflecting the setting as experienced by and perceived by participants (Bronfenbrenner, 1977). It is also important to take into account the individuals and systems that will operate the intervention. Because interventions are operator-dependent, they cannot be separated from the settings in which they are implemented (Elias, 1987). This is a very different view than the push for standardized curricula that assumes the key to success is implementing an effective curriculum with fidelity.

Community Development

Closely related to interventions that change settings and that are locally specific is the idea that rape prevention should be done in a way that develops the community's capacity and resources in responding to sexual violence. Rather than thinking of preventive intervention as developing the right curriculum, it should be thought of as developing community resources and competencies (Kelly, 1971, 1988; Trickett, Kelly, & Vincent, 1985) so that the community can be more effective in addressing its social problems (Argyris, 1970).

The typical use of curricula that are designed and taught by staff from the local rape crisis center does little to develop the school's own capacity and resources. If the rape crisis center is unable to continue providing the curriculum, the school reverts to the status quo. Although individual students may have learned or changed, there is nothing in place to continue the social change process. What is needed is more support for developing the school community. Specifically, five areas of development should be considered.

First, schools can increase their capacity for identifying and intervening with potential perpetrators. This might involve training faculty and staff to identify students who are living in aggressive households, who have been victims of child abuse, or who harbor hostile attitudes, especially when those attitudes are expressed through sexual antagonism. It is important to note that what is being suggested here is broader than the basic training many schools provide for their staff on their legal obligations as mandated reporters of suspected child abuse. Staff need to be trained on how to identify a broader range of experiences, how to respond to disclosures effectively, and how to be an effective bridge between children and counseling staff. In addition to establishing effective internal referral and follow-up processes, the school might create links to therapeutic services that are formalized to include appropriate feedback loops and on-campus services.

Second, schools can increase their capacity to teach students how to reject verbal pressure. This would need to start with assessments that identify when, where, and how students experience verbal pressure in school, with particular attention paid to gender-based and sexually nuanced pressures. Again, the training of faculty and staff is critical to community development in a school setting. A model for training staff to create norms that reject verbal pressure might include increasing awareness of types of aggression, risk factors, role of the classroom teacher, and the influence of the school climate on student behavior; developing strategies to prevent aggression; improving teacher management skills to reduce power struggles; and enhancing skills to assist students who are the targets of aggression (Orpinas & Horne, 2004).

Third, schools can increase their capacity to promote gender equity. Assessment, training, and supervision regarding gender equity is a particularly challenging task for many schools because it requires critical self-assessment. The need for development in this area is underscored by a study that found that although teachers consistently reported that boys and girls were not different in their behavior, abilities, or needs and they treated them the same, observations of teacher-student communication indicated that teachers interacted with boys approximately three times more often than girls (Auxer, 2002).

Fourth, schools can further develop their institutional capacity by reviewing and amending their discipline policies. Three specific discipline issues should be examined. (1) Discipline policies can be used to reduce delinquent peer associations by including prohibitions against encouraging another person to violate school rules and censuring those who fail to report a violation. Additionally, while communication with parents and guardians about discipline issues is typically done on an individual basis, intensive group interventions with families of students who are acting out can decrease delinquent associations by reconnecting youth, families, and schools (Schoenwald, Henggeler, Brondino, & Donkervoet, 1997; Smith et al., 2004). (2) Discipline policies may also need to be revised to include the censuring of verbal pressure. It is common for codes of conduct to prohibit only explicit threats and not other forms of verbal coercion. (3) Schools may also benefit from revising their sexual harassment policies to allow for third-party complaints registered by staff or faculty and for informal reporting mechanisms. Additionally, policies should protect against sexual harassment based on hostile environment and not only one-on-one acts.

Fifth, the school can increase its capacity to work with families. By exploring new ways to mutually support what is being done at both school and home, schools can tap into and augment family resources, thereby increasing the capacity for meeting students' needs on a broad array of issues, including sexual violence. Building successful partnerships with families may, however, require that schools redefine parental involvement to include not only the familiar idea of getting parents into schools, but also the idea of the schools going proactively into homes and bringing the school to families (Lopez, 2001). Additionally, rather than seeing marginalized parents as not having the resources or education to be partners in education, schools need to recognize the cultural and educational strengths of families even if the parents lack the social capital to negotiate the school system and social services on their own (Lopez, 2001). While school-family partnerships have been effectively used for addressing academic concerns and social issues such as conflict resolution (e.g., Aber, Jones, Brown, Churdry, & Samples, 1998; Leblanc & Lacey, 2000), drug abuse (e.g., Shope, Copeland, Kamp, & Lang, 1998; Shope, Copeland, Marcoux, & Kamp, 1996), and general violence prevention (Laird, Syropoulos, & Black, 1996), little has been done to enlist families as a resource for preventing sexual violence. This is an important area for intervention given the importance of families in child and adolescent development.

Summary

We have made a case here for developing interventions for rape prevention that go beyond curricula that promote increased knowledge and attitude changes in individuals. The school setting needs to become an explicit focus for intervention. While curricula have their role in raising community awareness about sexual violence, they are not sufficient. Interventions must go beyond raising awareness and instead must focus on changing the systems and the culture that permit and condone sexual violence. This is a large task and one that schools and community-based rape crisis programs must be supported in if they are to succeed.

PUBLIC POLICIES TO SUPPORT MORE EFFECTIVE RAPE PREVENTION

While the work of developing and implementing new approaches to rape prevention must be done locally, it can be supported by policies at both the state and federal levels. Four initiatives may be effective strategies for achieving this goal: (1) increased funding, (2) technical assistance for evaluation, (3) more flexibility from funders, and (4) differentiation between rape prevention and sex education.

Increased Funding

From a fiscal standpoint, investing in prevention is a cost-effective strategy. The Centers for Disease Control and Prevention (CDC, 2003) estimate the medical and mental health costs of rape to be $270 million annually. As large as these estimated costs are, the CDC acknowledges that they are conservative underestimates. They exclude important monetary costs, including criminal justice costs, use of social services such as women's shelters and counseling clinics, medical costs related to indirect physical symptoms (e.g., chronic pain, sleep disturbances), and mental health costs when the violence was not the presenting issue.

As part of the response to the social and economic costs of sexual violence, the Violence Against Women Act of 1994 initially authorized $35 million per year for the federal Rape Prevention Education program in 1996 and 1997 with an increase to $45 million per year in 1998 through 2000. Reauthorization increased the funding to $80 million per year for the next five years. Although this represents unprecedented governmental support for rape prevention, it is important to consider the authorizations in the context of the actual appropriations and what is meant by "rape prevention education." For the 2003 and 2004 fiscal years, only $44.2 million were appropriated into the budget for the Rape Prevention Education funds, representing slightly more than half of the authorized level. Furthermore, a percentage of the funds are used at the federal level for administrative purposes and additional administrative costs are taken out at the state level, diminishing the funds that are available to programs.

It is important to understand what the federal Rape Prevention Education funds can be used for at the local level. Permitted uses are educational seminars, hotline operations, training programs for professionals, informational materials, and other efforts to increase awareness about sexual assault, including in underserved minority communities and on college campuses. Of particular importance is the fact that the funds can be used for operating hotlines. Hotlines are a mainstay of community-based rape crisis centers and are a critically important service. However, they are primarily a resource for victims and their family and friends following an assault. In this regard, the support they afford may be useful at preventing additional psychological distress but has little impact on preventing sexual violence. Yet many rape crisis centers rely on the federal Rape Prevention Education funds to support operation of their hotlines. This reduces the money available for programs that are more directly related to prevention. It is imperative that funds continue to be available for the operation of crisis hotlines. What is needed are higher levels of funding so that more resources are available for primary prevention.

Technical Assistance for Evaluation

The call for accountability in nonprofit organizations is often institutionalized as required program evaluation that demonstrates the effectiveness of programs. For example, the state agencies that administer the federal Rape Prevention Education funds and private funders such as the United Way of America require that grantees have plans for how to evaluate their programs and that performance outcomes are regularly reported. However, few program staff have formal training in program evaluation and those that do still have to cope with the fact that resources put into evaluation often take away from resources that would otherwise be put into providing services. Both funding and technical assistance are needed to assist programs in planning and carrying out meaningful evaluations.

One model for this type of assistance is seen in the Sexual Assault and Rape Prevention (SARP) Evaluation Project (Campbell et al., 2004). In order to build the evaluation capacity of rape prevention programs in Michigan, the state funder brought together multiple stakeholders to provide evaluation training and consultation to all state-funded rape prevention and victim services programs in the state. Because they recognized the diversity of programs, they opted for locally developed evaluations that could be tailored to specific programs rather than standardized evaluation protocols. Over six years, the SARP team assessed the evaluation needs of the agencies, developed training materials that were flexible enough for multiple programs and purposes, and provided training and technical assistance. An assessment of this approach indicates that it was successful at teaching evaluation skills and building and sustaining the organizations' evaluation capacity.

Flexibility from Funders

Developing interventions that change settings, are locally specific, and that increase community capacity to respond to sexual violence requires greater flexibility than many rape prevention programs currently have. Although there has been a shift in many funders' language away from an individualized approach to a public health perspective on prevention, in practice funding agencies often impose requirements that limit the structure and content of prevention programs.

For example, the proposal guidelines for rape prevention and education issued by the Kentucky Department for Mental Health and Mental Retardation (2004) include criteria for using evidence-based and promising practices. The highest scores are awarded for programs that "have had successful findings published in a professional journal, are approved or accredited by a University or National Agency or have supportive data related to effectiveness and clear method of evaluation." To date, the only programs that have positive published findings are the common practices described at the beginning of this chapter. Although these programs may be effective at raising awareness, there is little evidence that they are effective as universal or primary prevention. Therefore, the funding criteria are giving preference to common but limited practices and allowing little room for innovative approaches. A similar limit can be seen in the department's performance objectives and quarterly report forms for fiscal year 2005 which measure program performance by the number of education programs, the number of education participants, and the outcomes assessments from at least half of the educational program participants. These objectives and reports are clearly based on the premise that prevention is being provided in a structured educational format that is conducive to counting programs and participants. However, preventive interventions that change structures and norms are not measurable in this way. For example, working with a school to revise its policies and procedures for responding to sexual harassment cannot be counted as an educational program with participants. Even change strategies such as the MVP program would be underestimated in such reports. Although it would be easy to count the initial training sessions and participants, the ongoing intervention that happens through the student leaders' example and mentoring cannot be captured in this way. Therefore, funders need to consider the ways their requirements result in greater limitations on programs than the funders intended. Even apparently reasonable preferences and requirements can lead to unintended limitations that dramatically shape and limit interventions.

Differentiation Between Rape Prevention and Sex Education

Finally, state and local policies concerning sex education need to be evaluated and in some cases amended to allow schools to engage in rape prevention more easily. In a study of community-based rape prevention programs in one state, Townsend (2003) found that the content of rape prevention programming was limited by state law, which requires that if a school chooses to teach sex education, all components of the curriculum must: include the teaching of abstinence, be presented in at least two public hearings, receive school board approval, be periodically reviewed by an advisory committee, be overseen by a supervisor who is approved by the state department of education, and be explained in advance to parents and guardians who have the right to excuse their child from such instruction. As a consequence of the state law and how it is implemented at the local level, 90 percent of programs in this study reported not being able to talk about anything perceived as being about sex and/or having to justify why rape prevention is not sex education. Correcting the confusion between sexual violence and sexual activity can be assisted by policies that make a clear distinction between the two and that allow for rape prevention programs to be implemented in schools without being subject to policies about sex education.

CONCLUSIONS

Sexual violence is perpetrated at an alarming rate, with young women and girls being at the highest risk for victimization. In response, increasing attention is being paid to school-based rape prevention programs. Many communities have implemented such programs, with elementary age children being educated about child abuse prevention and older youths receiving information about sexual violence with a particular emphasis on acquaintance rape. These programs tend to be short in duration and to be implemented with mixed-gender audiences of students. For elementary age children, common approaches focus on appropriate and inappropriate forms of touch, strategies for stopping abuse attempts, sexual abuse in the family, the importance of telling an adult when abuse occurs, and reassurances that abuse is never the child's fault. In middle schools and high schools, common approaches focus on disseminating basic information about sexual violence, dispelling myths, changing victim-blaming attitudes, and raising awareness of local resources for victims. Not surprisingly, research that has evaluated these types of programs suggests that they do not have long-lasting effects. Although elementary age children are taught important information, many children forget what they have learned when it is not reinforced over time. Additionally, it is questionable whether children can translate skills they may learn in the classroom to abusive situations. While older youths have been shown to change their attitudes about sexual violence, no sustained behavioral changes have been demonstrated.

To make prevention programs more effective, the following strategies are suggested. First, interventions need to focus on changing settings rather than merely changing individuals' knowledge and attitudes. Changing settings allows for transforming the context of rape culture that supports and condones sexual aggression. Second, interventions need to be locally specific. This would allow programs to respond to local norms, community-specific needs, and local attitudes that may be barriers to prevention efforts. Third, rape prevention should emphasize community development, not just curriculum development. Preventive interventions should develop the community's capacity and resources for responding to sexual violence.

As part of a comprehensive prevention strategy, policy reforms are also needed to increase funding, increase communication between funders and programs so that programs can develop innovative approaches and the capacity to evaluate them, and examine how other school policies may hinder efforts for sexual violence prevention.

REFERENCES

Aber, J. L., Jones, S. M., Brown, J. L., Churdry, N., & Samples, F. (1998). Resolving conflict creatively: Evaluating the developmental effects of a school-based violence prevention program in neighborhood and classroom context. *Development and Psychopathology, 10,* 187–213.

Argyris, C. (1970). *Intervention theory and method: A behavioral science view.* Reading, MA: Addison-Wesley.

Auxer, R. (2002). *Science teachers' attitudes toward male and female students in middle school.* Unpublished Master's thesis, Barat College, River Forest, IL.

Black, B., Weisz, A., Coats, S., & Patterson, D. (2000). Evaluating a psycho-educational sexual assault prevention program incorporating theatrical presentation, peer education, and social work. *Research on Social Work Practice, 10,* 589–606.

Bronfenbrenner, U. (1977). Toward an experimental ecology of human development. *American Psychologist, 32,* 513–531.

Buchwald, E., Fletcher, P. R., & Roth, M. (Eds.). (1993). *Transforming a rape culture.* Minneapolis: Milkweed Editions.

Campbell, R., Baker, C. K., & Mazurek, T. (1998). Remaining radical? Organizational predictors of rape crisis centers' social change initiatives. *American Journal of Community Psychology, 26,* 465–491.

Campbell, R., Dorey, H., Naegeli, M., Grubstein, L., Bennett, K., Bonter, F., Smith, P., Grzywacz, J., Baker, P., & Davidson, W. (2004). An empowerment evaluation model for sexual assault programs: Empirical evidence of effectiveness. *American Journal of Community Psychology, 34,* 251–262.

Carroll, L. A., Miltenberger, R. G., & O'Neill, H. K. (1992). A review and critique of research evaluating child sexual abuse prevention programs. *Education and Treatment of Children, 15,* 335–354.

Centers for Disease Control and Prevention. (2003). *Costs of intimate partner violence against women in the United States.* Atlanta: Centers for Disease Control and Prevention.

Desai, S., & Saltzman, L. E. (2001). Measurement issues for violence against women. In C. M. Renzetti, J. L. Edleson, & R. K. Bergen (Eds.), *Sourcebook on violence against women* (pp. 35–52). Thousand Oaks, CA: Sage.

Eagly, A. H., & Chaiken, S. (1993). *The psychology of attitudes.* New York: Harcourt Brace Jovanovich.

Elias, M. J. (1987). Establishing enduring prevention programs: Advancing the legacy of Swampscott. *American Journal of Community Psychology, 15,* 539–553.

Finkelhor, D., & Dziuba-Leatherman, J. (1995). Victimization prevention programs: A national survey of children's exposure and reactions. *Child Abuse & Neglect, 19,* 129–139.

Finkelhor, D., & Strapko, N. (1992). Sexual abuse prevention programs: A review of evaluation studies. In D. J. Willis, E. W. Holden, & M. Rosenberg (Eds.), *Prevention of child maltreatment* (pp. 150–167). New York: Wiley.

Foshee, V. A., Bauman, K. E., Arriaga, X. B., Helms, R. W., Koch, G. G., & Linder, G. F. (1998). An evaluation of Safe Dates, an adolescent dating violence prevention program. *American Journal of Public Health, 88,* 45–50.

Foshee, V. A., Bauman, K. E., Greene, W. F., Koch, G. G., Linder, G. F., & MacDougall, J. E. (2000). The Safe Dates program: 1-year follow-up results. *American Journal of Public Health, 90,* 1619–1622.

Frazier, P., Valtinson, G., & Candell, S. (1994). Evaluation of a coeducational interactive rape prevention program. *Journal of Counseling and Development, 73,* 153–158.

Gidycz, C. A., Layman, J. M., Rich, C. L., Crothers, M., Bylys, J., Matorin, A., & Jacobs, C. D. (2001). An evaluation of an acquaintance rape prevention program: Impact on attitudes, sexual aggression, and sexual victimization. *Journal of Interpersonal Violence, 16,* 1120–1138.

Heppner, M. J., Humphrey, C. F., Hillenbrand-Gunn, T. L., & DeBord, K. A. (1995). The differential effects of rape prevention programming on attitudes, behavior, and knowledge. *Journal of Counseling Psychology, 42,* 508–518.

Hilton, N. Z., Harris, G. T., Rice, M. E., Smith Krans, T., & Lavigne, S. E. (1998). Antiviolence education in high schools. *Journal of Interpersonal Violence, 13,* 726–742.

Kelly, J. G. (1971). Qualities for the community psychologist. *American Psychologist, 26,* 897–903.

Kelly, J. G. (1988). A guide to conducting prevention research in the community: First steps. *Prevention in Human Services, 6,* 11–81.

Kentucky Department for Mental Health and Mental Retardation. (2004). *FY 2005 plan and budget: Proposal guidelines and objectives – Rape prevention and education.* Retrieved August 10, 2004, from http://mhmr.ky.gov.

Kilpatrick, D., Edmunds, C. N., & Seymour, A. K. (1992). *Rape in America: A report to the nation* Arlington, VA: National Victim Center.

Laird, M., Syropoulos, M., & Black, S. (1996). *What works in violence prevention: Findings from an evaluation study of Lions-Quest Working Toward Peace in Detroit Schools.* Newark, OH: Question International.

Lanier, C. A., Elliott, M. N., Martin, D. W., & Kapadia, A. (1998). Evaluation of an intervention to change attitudes toward date rape. *Journal of American College Health, 46,* 177–180.

Leblanc, P., & Lacey, C. (2000). *Evaluation report on the Alleghany Foundation grant "Making Peace Work in the Miami-Dade County Public Schools."* Miami: Peace Education Foundation.

Lenihan, G.O., & Rawlins, M.E. (1994). Rape supportive attitudes among Greek students before and after a date rape prevention program. *Journal of College Student Development, 35,* 450–455.

Lopez, G.R. (2001). Redefining parental involvement: Lessons from high-performing migrant-impacted schools. *American Educational Research Journal, 38,* 253–289.

O'Neill, P.T., & Trickett, E.J. (1982). *Community consultation.* San Francisco: Jossey-Bass.

Orpinas, P., & Horne, A. M. (2004). A teacher-focused approach to prevent and reduce students' aggressive behavior: The GREAT Teacher Program. *American Journal of Preventive Medicine, 26,* 29–38.

Rispens, J., Aleman, A., & Goudena, P.P. (1997). Prevention of child sexual abuse victimizations: A meta-analysis of school programs. *Child Abuse & Neglect, 21,* 975–987.

SAMHSA. (2004). *Model programs.* Retrieved August 17, 2004, from http://modelprograms.samhsa.gov.

Sanday, P.R. (1996). Rape-prone versus rape-free campus cultures. *Violence Against Women, 2,* 191–208.

Schoenwald, S. W., Henggeler, S. W., Brondino, M. J., & Donkervoet, J. C. (1997). Reconnecting schools with families of juvenile offenders. In J. L. Schwartz & W. E. Martin, Jr. (Eds.), *Applied ecological psychology for schools within communities: Assessment and intervention* (pp. 187–205). Mahwah, NJ: Lawrence Erlbaum.

Shope, J., Copeland, L., Kamp, M., & Lang, S. (1998). Twelfth grade follow-up of the effectiveness of a middle school-based substance abuse prevention program. *Journal of Drug Education, 28,* 185–197.

Shope, J., Copeland, L., Marcoux, B., & Kamp, M. (1996). Effectiveness of a school-based substance abuse prevention program. *Journal of Drug Education, 26,* 323–337.

Smith, E. P., Gorman-Smith, D., Quinn, W. H., Rabiner, D. L., Tolan, P. H., & Winn, D. (2004). Community-based multiple family groups to prevent and reduce violent and aggressive behavior: The GREAT Families Program. *American Journal of Preventive Medicine, 26,* 39–47.

Townsend, S.M. (2003). *Isomorphic pressures on community-based rape prevention programs.* Unpublished master's thesis, University of Illinois at Chicago.

Townsend, S.M., & Campbell, R. (under review). Common practices in community-based rape prevention programs: Implications for practice.

Trickett, E.J., Kelly, J.G., & Vincent, T.A. (1985). The spirit of ecological inquiry in community research. In D. Klein and E. Susskind (Eds.), *Knowledge building in community psychology.* New York: Praeger.

Ward, K.J. (2003). *Mentors in violence prevention: Evaluation.* Boston: Northeastern University, Mentors in Violence Prevention.

Chapter 9

SEXUAL BEHAVIOR AMONG ADOLESCENTS: THE ROLE OF THE FAMILY, SCHOOLS, AND MEDIA IN PROMOTING SEXUAL HEALTH

Margaret Rosario and Eric W. Schrimshaw

At the beginning of the twentieth century, Freud (1905/1962) outlined several critical observations that scientists and lay people alike now take for granted. He affirmed the importance of sexuality in the individual's life. He detailed how disturbances in the sexual arena profoundly influence the individual's mental health. He added that the disturbances could occur as early as the beginning of life. In essence, Freud not only retrieved sexuality from the repression of the Victorian era, he also highlighted its effects on the individual's mental health and general functioning. His theoretical proclamations and empirical observations, so radical at the time, did not stop here.

Freud (1905/1962) argued that psychosexual development begins at birth, that puberty coincides with a reawakening of repressed sexual urges, and that these sexual urges and desires focus on a human object and eventually result in sexual activity with another human being. Freud's arguments have been validated and extended to include the psychosexual development of the fetus (e.g., Money, 1988; Zucker, 2001). And, everyone, from parents to marketing executives, knows that puberty marks a major life transition from a presumed asexual childhood to the sexually charged adolescent years. The secondary sexual characteristics that emerge (e.g., growth spurt, breast development for girls and facial hair for boys), the compulsions that attend grooming and are aimed at being physically attractive, and the acquisition of a real, desired, or imagined love object that consumes attention (i.e., "the crush") are just some examples of the changes that occur and foretell sexual involvement of the youth with another individual.

The question concerning adults is not whether sexual activity will occur, but rather when and under what circumstances. Anxieties abound, including, for example, that sexual debut may happen when the adolescent is too young, involved in a relationship considered undesirable by parents or others, or occur outside the confines of marriage. We add some other potential and tangible negative consequences of sexual activity: pregnancy and sexually transmitted infections (STI).

In this chapter, we acknowledge that sexual activity usually begins in adolescence (from puberty to approximately age 25 years) and that this reality must guide efforts to reduce the potential negative consequences of sexual activity for youths, namely, pregnancy and STI. We review what is known about protecting youths from the negative consequences of sexual activity, using an ecological perspective. Specifically, we review the roles that families, schools, and society, by means of the media, play in reducing or increasing the potential negative consequences of sexual activity among youths. We conclude with a set of recommendations for protecting youths from such consequences. Before beginning this process, we review what is known about sexual activity among youths. We focus attention on American youths, but provide a context in which to understand their sexual activity by comparing them with peers from other developed countries. More specifically, we focus primarily on youths in early and middle adolescence (i.e., from puberty through the teenage years).

PREVALENCE OF SEXUAL ACTIVITY

There have been historical changes in the sexual activity of American youths. The number of youths engaging in sexual intercourse before age 18 years was greater for those reaching puberty during or after the sexual revolution of the late 1960s and early 1970s (60 percent males and 53 percent females) than for those reaching sexual maturity before the sexual revolution (47 percent males and 31 percent females), according to the National Health and Social Life Survey (Joyner & Laumann, 2001). However, since the late 1980s, the number of youths reporting sexual intercourse has decreased according to representative national surveys (Abma & Sonenstein, 2001; Brener et al., 2002; Santelli, Londberg, Abma, McNeeley, & Resnick, 2000). For example, over six administrations between 1991 and 2001 of the Youth Risk Behavior Survey, the number of high school students reporting ever having sexual intercourse significantly decreased from 51 percent to 43 percent for girls and from 57 percent to 49 percent for boys (Brener et al., 2002). Despite the recent decrease, the number of sexually experienced youths constitutes 52 percent of the population, aged 15 to 19 years (Abma & Sonenstein, 2001).[1]

The numbers of American youths ever having sexual intercourse are comparable with youths from other developed countries. In the 1990s, 51 percent of American girls aged 15 to 19 years reported such experience as compared with 49 percent, 51 percent, and 61 percent of French, Canadian, and British girls, respectively (Darroch, Singh, & Frost, 2001). The median age at initiating sexual intercourse was 17.2 years among American girls, 17.1 through 17.5 years among Swedish, Canadian, and British girls, and 18 years for French girls (Darroch et al., 2001). Similarly, the number of youths having sex recently was comparable across most of the groups: 59 percent American, 62 percent British, 64 percent French, and 79 percent Swedish girls (Darroch et al., 2001).

The similarity of these data has two related implications. First, the data suggest that sexual activity is prevalent and normative among teenagers. Second, the similarity of the cross-cultural data indicates that biological factors explain sexual activity among youths to a great extent (Halpern, 2003; Rogol, Roemmich, & Clark, 2002; Weisfeld & Woodward, 2004).

NEGATIVE CONSEQUENCES OF SEXUAL ACTIVITY

Despite the cross-cultural similarities in rates of sexual activity, large discrepancies exist with respect to pregnancy and, by implication, all related outcomes (e.g., births, abortions). American girls, aged 15 to 19 years, are 64 percent to four times more likely to be pregnant than girls from Canada, France, Great Britain, and Sweden, with 84 cases per 1,000 among Americans, compared with a high of 47 cases among Britons and a low of 20 among French girls (Darroch et al., 2001). In fact, when all European countries from the Atlantic to the Urals are considered, as well as Canada, Israel, and Japan, the pregnancy rate of the United States is only exceeded by that of the Russian Federation (Singh & Darroch, 2000).

Like the pregnancy rate, STI rates are higher among American youths than among peers from other developed countries, with the exception of the Russian Federation (Panchaud, Singh, Feivelson, & Darroch, 2000). For example, the annual number of cases of gonorrhea per 100,000 teenagers equals 572 for Americans and 77 for Britons, the third highest rate after Russia and the United States. In addition, the teenage population in America has STI rates that are 50 percent to six times greater than those of adult Americans (Panchaud et al., 2000). Human papillomavirus (HPV), trichomoniasis, and chlamydia accounted for 88 percent of all new STI among youths 15 to 24 years in 2000 (Weinstock, Berman, & Cates,

2004). HPV accounted for 51 percent of all new STI cases (Weinstock et al., 2004), a worrisome rate given the causal link between HPV and subsequent cervical cancer. Indeed, the direct medical costs in 2000 of STI among American youths aged 15 to 24 years were estimated at $6.5 billion (Chesson, Blandford, Gift, Tao, & Irwin, 2004).

SEXUAL RISK BEHAVIORS

Certain sexual behaviors are necessarily responsible for the elevated pregnancy and STI rates just outlined. From a review of available data from representative national samples, we have identified sexual behaviors that place American youths directly or indirectly at risk for pregnancy and STI. Although the following list is not exhaustive, it represents, in our opinion, the nine sexual risk behaviors that are most prevalent and worrisome.

First, many youths initiate sexual intercourse early when their judgment and rational thinking processes are still problematic. By age 17 years, 47 percent of girls and 53 percent of boys report having sexual intercourse (Abma & Sonenstein, 2001). Second, not only are multiple sexual partners relatively common among sexually experienced youths, but each partner increases the overall probability of exposure to an STI. By age 15 to 17 years, 20 to 25 percent of sexual experienced girls and 38 to 47 percent of sexually experienced boys report four or more lifetime numbers of partners (Santelli et al., 2000). Third, once youths become sexually active, they are likely to continue being sexually active, as the number of partners just cited indicates and as evidenced by the prevalence of recent sexual intercourse. Among 15- to 17-year-old youths, 71 to 78 percent of girls engaged in sex during the past three months, as did 60 to 65 percent of boys (Santelli et al., 2000).

Fourth, pregnancy is likely because contraceptive methods are not used consistently. Similarly, STIs are likely because condoms are used inconsistently. During the most recent episode of sexual intercourse, approximately 20 percent of girls aged 15 to 17 years used oral contraceptives, and approximately 45 percent had a partner who used condoms (Santelli et al., 2000). Of youths, 49 percent did not discuss contraception with their first partner before having sex (Manlove, Ryan, & Franzetta, 2003).

Relationship or partner characteristics are related to risk to the extent that they increase the likelihood of pregnancy or STI. Fifth, consistent contraceptive use decreases by 14 percent for every month that a romantic relationship endures among youths, after controlling for a host of related factors (Manlove et al., 2003). Sixth, the age of the sexual partner is important. Consistent contraceptive use decreases by 11 percent with every year that a partner is older than the youth (Manlove et al., 2003). Nearly 50 percent of girls have a partner who is two or more years older than they are (Manlove et al., 2003).

Seventh, youths engage in multiple sexual practices, all of which pose risk for STI. The cumulative prevalence increased from 55 percent of youths engaging in sexual intercourse to 64 percent when oral and anal sex were included, according to a representative national survey restricted to male youths (Gates & Sonenstein, 2000). Of these male youths, 11 percent reported anal sex, one of the riskiest activities for STI, including HIV, for the receptive partner (Gates & Sonenstein, 2000). Yet, eighth, many youths consider sexual intercourse to be the only activity that defines "sex" (Remez, 2000). Consequently, "abstinence" for many youths allows for any sexual activity other than sexual intercourse (Remez, 2000). Among ostensibly knowledgeable and sophisticated college students, a survey found that 37 percent defined oral sex and 24 percent defined anal sex as abstinence (Horan, Phillips, & Hagan, 1998).

The last sexual risk behavior for pregnancy and STI among youths involves using alcohol or other drugs before sex, which, necessarily, compromises judgment and impulse control. Among high school students, there was an increase of 18 percent from 1991 to 2001 in alcohol and drug use before the last episode of sexual intercourse (Brener et al., 2002).

In summary, American youths are sexually active and often at risk for negative consequences such as pregnancy and STI. It is essential to reduce the prevalence of these potential negative consequences. To meet this goal, one must acknowledge the reality in which American youths find themselves and dispassionately examine the factors that either elevate or reduce the negative consequences of pregnancy and STI among these youths.

To understand pregnancy and STI among American youths, we assume an ecological perspective in which the individual is surrounded by the social systems with which he or she interacts and which influence his or her behaviors and cognitions (e.g., Bronfenbrenner, 1979; Revenson, 1990). We focus on three social systems in which youths are enmeshed: the family, schools, and mass media. Youths spend substantial amounts of time interacting with these systems and these systems strongly influence youths.

The relations among the systems are such that we are able to offer some hypotheses concerning their effect. To the extent that the systems provide a consistent and realistic message to protect youths from the possibilities of pregnancy and STI, one should obtain reduced rates of negative consequences. On the other hand, increased rates would be expected if one or more systems provide unrealistic messages or contradict what another system advances. The cross-cultural data reviewed earlier, in which American youths had elevated rates of pregnancy and STI relative to youths in other developed countries, indicate that the American family, schools, and/or mass media are not being as effective as possible in protecting youths from negative consequences. Below, we review the role that families, schools, and mass media play in reducing or amplifying sexual behaviors, including those that place youths at risk for pregnancy and STI.

THE FAMILY

Although lay people have long believed that parents play a critical role in shaping their children's behavior, it has only been in the past two decades that scientific research has begun to examine the extent to which parents influence their children's initiation of sexual behavior and their sexual risk behaviors after initiation. Research has identified several aspects of family and parent-child relationships that are related to sexual initiation or risk behavior.

The role of family structure—that is, whether the child lives in a two-parent or single-parent household—has been examined in a number of large-scale studies. The evidence indicates that male and female youths who live in two-parent families are less likely to have had sexual intercourse and less likely to initiate sex than youths in single-parent families headed either by a mother or father (Flewelling & Bauman, 1990; Santelli, Lowry, Brener, & Robin, 2000; Smith, 1997). Nevertheless, research has found that family structure does not predict sexual initiation or sexual risk behaviors after taking into account other parent-child relationship factors, such as level of communication, parental monitoring, and parental attitudes (Dittus, Jaccard, & Gordon, 1997; Miller, Forehand, & Kotchick, 1999; Ramirez-Valles, Zimmerman, & Newcomb, 1998). This suggests that family structure may have an indirect influence on sexual behavior or mask more important issues, such as parent-child relationships. As compared with sexual initiation, the role of family structure on adolescent sexual risk behaviors appears to be unexamined.

Many parents have strongly held attitudes about both whether their child(ren) should engage in sexual behavior and about the use of birth control by their youth(s). These attitudes have been found to predict adolescent sexuality. Specifically, maternal disapproval of adolescent sexual behavior and beliefs that adolescents should abstain from sexual behavior until marriage have been found to be associated with a lower likelihood of adolescents reporting sexual intercourse (Carvajal et al., 1999; Dittus et al., 1997; Hovell et al., 1994; Sieving, McNeely, & Blum, 2000). However, parental attitudes about sexual abstinence must be communicated to adolescents if they are to influence behavior. Moreover, conversations about delaying sex must occur prior to sexual initiation for them to be effective (Clawson & Reese-Weber, 2003). Although parental attitudes have been related to adolescent sexual behavior, to date, communication of these attitudes has been little examined. However, some research has found that greater communication between adolescents and mothers about nonsexual topics has been associated with a lower likelihood of sexual initiation (Karofsky, Zeng, & Kosorok, 2000). This suggests that the quality of parent-adolescent relationships may also be a critical factor in delaying sexual debut.

In contrast, a substantial body of research has examined the role of parental communication of safer sex beliefs and the role this has on subsequent sexual risk behavior. Specifically, greater communication about the risks of unsafe sexual behavior is associated with fewer sexual episodes, greater condom use, and consistent condom use (Hutchinson, Jemmott, Jemmott, Braverman, & Fong, 2003; Kotchick, Dorsey, Miller, & Forehand, 1999; Romer et al., 1999). Although most of this research has focused on communication by mothers, at least one study has suggested that communication by fathers also is beneficial (Clawson & Reese-Weber, 2003). The timing of these conversations is critical. For adolescents to use condoms during their first sexual encounter, parents must discuss condoms before sexual initiation (Miller, Levin, Whitaker, & Xu, 1998). Even conversations about condom use that occur after sexual initiation have been found to increase subsequent condom use. There is also evidence that greater parent-adolescent communication in general is associated with lower sexual risk, including fewer sexual episodes and fewer sexual partners (but not condom use; Miller et al., 1999), suggesting the importance of strong parent-adolescent relationships.

Despite the critical nature of parental communication, honest communication about sexual information by parents with their adolescent children is rare. Indeed, there appear to be misunderstandings or differences of opinion about such communication. For example, when mothers and their teenagers were asked whether they had talked about sex, 72 percent of mothers believed they had, but only 45 percent of their teenagers believed they had such a conversation (Jaccard, Dittus, & Gordon, 1998). Further, when conversations about delaying sexual intercourse take place, about half the time (42 to 58 percent) they happen after sexual initiation has already occurred, obviating any effect on delaying initiation (Clawson & Reese-Weber, 2003). These low levels of communication or mistimed communications may be attributed to parents' evaluation that their adolescents are at low risk for sexual activity. Parents have been found to grossly underestimate their children's sexual risk and behavior (Jaccard et al.,

1998; Stanton et al., 1999). For example, whereas 58 percent of middle school students reported having had sexual intercourse, only 2 percent of their parents reported that they believed their child had initiated sex (Young & Zimmerman, 1998). Parental misconceptions about their youth's probable sexual activity may result in decreased parent-child communication about sexual behavior and its consequences.

Finally, parental monitoring and supervision of adolescents' activities have been found to delay sexual initiation. Several studies have found that high levels of parental monitoring were associated with delays in sexual initiation and a lower likelihood of engaging in sexual intercourse (Miller et al., 1999; Romer et al., 1999; Smith, 1997). In addition, some evidence has suggested that low levels of parental monitoring of a child's activities may lead to substance use, which, in turn, may lead to sexual initiation (Mandara, Murray, & Bangi, 2003). Although less consistent, some research also has found that parental monitoring is associated with fewer sexual risk behaviors (e.g., increased condom use, fewer sexual partners; Heubner & Howell, 2003; Rodgers, 1999) and lower likelihood of having a diagnosed STI (Crosby, DiClemente, Wingood, Lang, & Harrington, 2003).

SCHOOL PROGRAMS

Over the years, intervention programs have been developed and implemented in American schools to delay sexual debut among sexually inexperienced youths and/or to reduce sexual risk behaviors among sexually active youths. Two types of programs have been developed and their effectiveness is reviewed here. First, sex-education programs are based on psychological theories; provide factual data on, for example, pregnancy, contraceptive methods, HIV and other STIs; as well as sometimes provide condoms and instruction on condom use. Sex-education programs contain an abstinence component for youths who are sexually inexperienced. Second, abstinence-only programs aim to delay sexual debut by having youths refuse sex. Such programs may address sexually active youths by inviting them to become abstinent until some future event, such as marriage. Whereas sex-education programs usually target high school students, abstinence-only programs often focus on middle school students.

Sex-Education Programs

Studies of large representative samples of the American youth population, to be reviewed shortly, consistently demonstrate that sex-education programs in high schools do not promote sexual activity among youths who are virgins, contrary to concerns expressed by parents and others. Furthermore, among sexually active youths, the programs promote behaviors that decrease the likelihood of pregnancy and STI.

In a national survey of female youths, participation in mandated sex-education programs focusing on HIV education or correct use of condoms was unrelated to being sexually active (Averett, Rees, & Argys, 2002). Safer Choices, a complex and curriculum-intensive program to delay sexual debut and reduce pregnancy, HIV, and other STIs by promoting condom use, was implemented in high schools in California and Texas. Safer Choices did not increase the number of youths who were sexually active relative to youths in the control schools (Basen-Engquist et al., 2001). However, the sexually active youths in the prevention program engaged in fewer numbers of sexual encounters unprotected by condoms and had fewer sexual partners with whom condoms were not used than did youths in the control schools. In Massachusetts high schools, all youths were exposed to HIV education, but some youths were in schools where condoms were made available along with instruction on condom use. Youths in condom-available schools were less likely to have ever had sex than youths in schools that did not provide condoms (Blake et al., 2003). In addition, youths in the condom-available schools were less likely to have had sex recently (in the past three months) than youths in the control schools. And youths who recently had sex were more likely to use condoms, if their schools made condoms available. Similar results have been found in New York City (Guttmacher et al., 1997) and Seattle (Kirby et al., 1999). The beneficial effects of sex-education programs extend to youths in middle school (O'Donnell et al., 1999).

In addition to the effectiveness findings just mentioned, a review of the literature found that no school-based, sex-education programs hastened sexual debut, increased the frequency of sexual intercourse, or increased the number of sexual partners (Kirby, 2000). Furthermore, the cost-effectiveness of sex-education programs has been demonstrated. An economics analysis of Safer Choices found that $2.65 were saved in medical and social costs for every dollar expended on the program (Wang et al., 2000).

Investigations demonstrate why sex-education programs have such beneficial effects as delaying sexual debut among virgins and increasing condom use among sexually active youths. The programs are based on psychological theories (e.g., Ajzen & Fishbein, 1980; Bandura, 1997; Fisher & Fisher, 1992). Consequently, the youths' knowledge about HIV and other STIs increases, as does the youths' self-efficacy with respect to refusing sex (Basen-Engquist et al., 2001). In addition, positive attitudes toward condom use improve, self-efficacy in using condoms increases, and barriers to using condoms decrease. Similar findings have been found by others (e.g., Guttmacher et al., 1997), including youths' demonstrated behavioral skills (e.g., obtaining condoms, carrying condoms, requesting that a partner use condoms: Fisher, Fisher, Bryan, & Misovich, 2002). Detailed reviews of explanatory factors in the sociocognitive and behavioral domains are available (e.g., Albarracín, Johnson, Fishbein, & Muellerleile, 2001; Jemmott & Jemmott, 2000; Kirby, 2002).

Abstinence-Only Programs

School-based abstinence programs have been developed and implemented to delay sexual debut among the uninitiated and to promote a return to abstinence among youths who are sexually experienced. Abstinence efforts would necessarily reduce pregnancy and STI rates, if successful. At the other extreme, such efforts could be associated with increased pregnancy and STI rates, if they failed to provide the sex education necessary to prevent pregnancy and STI outcomes among youths who continue to be sexually active or who become sexually active.

The abstinence-only programs suffer from a number of factors that makes evaluation of their effectiveness difficult. Surprisingly, many programs do not assess sexual behavioral outcomes (e.g., engaging in sexual intercourse); instead, they assess attitudes, intentions, or knowledge (e.g., Carter-Jessop, Franklin, Heath, Jimenez-Irizarry, & Peace, 2000; Sather & Zinn, 2002; for a review, see Thomas, 2000). Some studies are methodologically suspect—for example, lacking a control group (e.g., Barnett & Hurst, 2003). In fact, a recent meta-analytic study found only 12 intervention programs between 1985 and 2000 that met adequate design standards for effectiveness evaluations (Silva, 2002). Among these studies, Silva (2002) found that differences between the abstinence and control groups were essentially nonexistent (Cohen's $d = 0.05$). The nonsignificant differences on sexual activity have been found across communities (rural, suburban, and urban) and among youths of diverse ethnic or racial backgrounds (Barnett & Hurst, 2003; Blinn-Pike, 1996; Denny, Young, & Spear, 1999; Lieberman, Gray, Wier, Fiorentino, & Maloney, 2000). Therefore, and as reported in an earlier literature review (Kirby, 2000), abstinence-only programs do not delay sexual debut. However, as discussed earlier, intervention programs that combine abstinence and sex education have proven effective in, for example, delaying sex for sexually inexperienced youths, especially girls, and increasing contraceptive or condom use at last sex (e.g., Aarons et al., 2000; Basen-Engquist et al., 2001).

Why freestanding abstinence programs do poorly with respect to delaying sexual debut among virgins, relative to abstinence components that are part of sex-education programs, is understandable, if a recent evaluation of abstinence-only programs is accurate. The report (Wingfield, 2004) found that some programs provide false information (e.g., condoms do not protect against HIV infection, pregnancy is possible if genitals are touched), misrepresent biological facts (e.g., humans receive 58 chromosomes from their parents), or spend time on matters unrelated to sexual behavior (e.g., stereotypic information, such as women need to be financially supported). Any one of these three categories of misinformation may work against delaying sexual debut by engendering mistrust of any information (including any valid information) that may be provided by the intervention program.

MASS MEDIA

By nearly all accounts, both popular and scientific, adolescents are active consumers of mass media, including television, music, videos, and various teen magazines. Despite the widespread belief that the overuse of these media is bad for adolescents and the long history of scientific research documenting the role of these media in promoting violent behavior (Anderson & Bushman, 2001; Anderson et al., 2003; Bandura, Ross, & Ross, 1963; Donnerstein, Slaby, & Eron, 1994), the effects of media consumption on adolescent sexual initiation and sexual risk behavior have been relatively unexamined. However, given the heavy consumption of television, music, videos, and magazines by adolescents—and the often sexualized content of these media—they each may serve as important influences on the sexual norms and behaviors of adolescents.

Television programming viewed by adolescents has been found to contain high levels of both sexual behaviors and discussion of sexuality (Kunkel, Cope, & Biely, 1999; Ward, 1995). For example, in a series of three separate studies, Kunkel and colleagues found that nearly 60 percent of television programming contained talk about sex, and over 60 percent of programming contained sexual behaviors (e.g., provocative flirting, passionate kissing, sexually suggestive portrayals of characters in bed). Similar prevalence was found among both prime-time and teen-focused programming. Daytime programming such as soap operas and television talk shows also was found to have high levels of sexual talk or behavior (Greenberg & Busselle, 1996; Greenberg, Sherry, Busselle, Hnilo, & Smith, 1997). The major problem with the discussion or depiction of sexuality on television concerns its unrealistic characterization. The portrayal focuses largely on the pleasurable and recreational aspects of sex, but rarely on the risks, responsibilities, or consequences of sexual behavior (Aubrey, 2004; Kunkel et al., 1999; Ward, 1995).

Despite the well-documented sexual content of television programming, research examining the potential effects of viewing television on sexual behavior remains little examined. Indeed, much of the research has focused not on the relation of television viewing to sexual behavior, but rather its effects on attitudes about sex and perceived norms about others' sexual behavior (Aubrey, Harrison, Kramer, & Yellin, 2003; Davis & Mares, 1998; Ward, 2002; Ward & Rvadeneyra, 1999). This research, however, does demonstrate that youths who are more frequent television watchers or who are more "involved" in their television viewing (e.g., self-identify or empathize with television characters) are more likely to endorse sexual stereotypes (e.g., view women as sex objects and men as sex driven; Ward, 2002), expect to initiate sexual activities early in a relationship (Aubrey et al., 2003), and provide higher estimates of how sexually active people are (Davis & Mares, 1998). Although most research has not examined sexual behavior itself, a large longitudinal study did provide support for the adverse effects of television on sexual behavior. Collins and colleagues (2004) found that adolescents who watched more sexual content (either sexual talk or sexual behavior) were more likely to initiate sexual intercourse.

Concerns about the adverse effects of music and music videos on various adolescent behaviors have been raised repeatedly. Indeed, the highly sexualized content of various forms of music (e.g., rock, rap) and the sexual imagery of music videos have been documented (Arnett, 2002; Sommers-Flanagan, Sommers-Flanagan, & Davis, 1993). Furthermore, increased frequency of watching rock music videos has been found to be associated with greater sexual permissiveness and having sexual intercourse among adolescents (Strouse, Buerkel-Rothfuss, & Long, 1995). The relation of music videos to sexual behavior was stronger among adolescent females and among those in poorly functioning families (Strouse et al., 1995). More recently, African American adolescent females with greater frequency of watching rap music videos were found to be more likely to have multiple sexual partners and to have acquired an STI than peers with lower frequency of watching rap videos, even after controlling for parental monitoring (Wingood et al., 2003).

Finally, adolescents, particularly young women, are avid consumers of magazines and the advertising contained within them. In particular, a number of teen magazines actively target this young, predominantly female audience. As with other forms of media, magazine content and magazine advertising have become over time significantly more sexual and explicit in their depictions of sex (Carpenter, 1998; Reichert, Lambiase, Morgan, Carstephen, & Zavoina, 1999). Women, in particular, are portrayed in a sexually explicit manner in magazine advertising, although men too have been portrayed more sexually over time (e.g., Reichert et al., 1999).

Teen magazines, in particular, have been documented as becoming highly sexualized over time (Carpenter, 1998). In her analysis of the content of *Seventeen* magazine, which typically targets an audience less than age 17 years, Carpenter found that discussions of sexual desire, masturbation, oral sex, and recreational sexual activity were commonplace. Furthermore, like the content of television, portrayals of sexual behavior in magazines have focused on the pleasures of sexual activity, but rarely depict or discuss the consequences (e.g., abortion, STI; Johnson, Gotthoffer, & Lauffer, 1999). Despite the sexual content of magazines and their avid consumption by adolescents, no studies were found that had examined the role of reading magazines on adolescents' initiation of sexual activity, number of sexual partners, or use of contraceptives or condoms during sexual activities. However, if one may generalize from research on television, music, and videos, then magazines targeting (and popular with) adolescents may increase the youths' sexual risk behaviors, rendering youths vulnerable to such negative consequences as pregnancy and STI.

SUMMARY AND CONCLUSION

As parents and/or members of society, we must recognize and accept that many adolescents are sexually active. Indeed, nearly half of all high school girls and more than half of all high school boys have initiated sexual intercourse (Brener et al., 2002), many before age 17 years (Darroch et al., 2001). Denying that adolescents are sexually active, although common among parents (e.g., Young & Zimmerman, 1998), may prevent or distort intervention efforts to delay sexual debut and to reduce risk for such negative consequences as pregnancy and STI. By failing to address the reality of sexual activity among adolescents, we may set youths on a trajectory toward a lifetime of difficulties. Indeed, we invest substantial resources as a society to promote the educational, psychological, and social development of youths. However, the opportunities made possible by these investments prove problematic if adolescents have a child and turn toward caring for that child rather than pursuing their goals. Young women who become pregnant as teenagers are subsequently more likely to have lower educational attainment, to be unemployed or employed in unskilled occupations, to be a single parent, and to receive welfare (Olausson, Haglund, Weitoft, & Cnattignius, 2001). Opportunities also may be squandered if youths contract an STI because they have not been provided with the skills to protect themselves. Such STIs as HIV and HPV have serious long-term consequences for physical health and longevity.

Given the profound consequences that may result from adolescent sexuality, it is imperative that we acknowledge adolescent sexuality and make efforts to delay sexual debut and provide youths with the skills to protect themselves when they become sexually active. Here, we have provided a review of the roles that families, schools, and the media play in adolescent sexual initiation, sexual risk behaviors, pregnancy, and STI. Despite the array of potential strategies for reducing the prevalence of these sexual outcomes, evaluation of the effectiveness of intervention programs has demonstrated that some programs are more effective than others.

Although much attention and effort have been focused on school-based abstinence-only programs, the research reviewed here demonstrates that these programs have failed to delay sexual debut. On the other hand, comprehensive sex-education programs have been found to delay sexual initiation. In addition, parental involvement in their children's lives appears critical in delaying sexual debut, given that parental monitoring of adolescent activities, communication of parental attitudes about adolescent sexuality, and communication about the potential consequences of sexual initiation have each been shown to be associated with a lower likelihood of sexual initiation. Further, some evidence suggests that reducing adolescent viewing of television and music videos may delay sexual initiation among adolescents.

Delay of sexual debut, while important, cannot be the only goal because initiation of sexual activity is common during adolescence and such activity continues once initiated. Thus, solely offering sexual abstinence is unrealistic and irrelevant, except for youths who have not initiated sexual activity. Moreover, abstinence-only information may increase risk for pregnancy and STI because youths are not provided with the knowledge and skills to protect themselves from such potential negative consequences.

Parents, schools, and communities are critical participants in promoting safer sexual behaviors among adolescents to prevent negative consequences, such as pregnancy and STI. Scientific research has found that comprehensive sex-education programs that provide the knowledge and skills to engage in safer sexual behaviors are effective. Such programs improve the youths' efficacy in refusing sex and increase youths' positive attitudes toward condom use, ability to use a condom correctly, and prevalence of condom use during sex. Although school-based, sex-education programs are effective, parents and communities should not rely solely on schools to encourage safer sexual behaviors. Indeed, communication from parents about the risks of unsafe sexual behaviors are strongly associated with fewer sexual partners, greater condom use, and consistent condom use. Further, parental monitoring of adolescent activities also is associated with fewer sexual risks and fewer STI diagnoses. Finally, increased viewing of television and music videos has been associated with sexual risk, which is unsurprising considering the media's ubiquitous portrayal of sex as pleasurable and without negative consequences. Parental monitoring of adolescent use of television and other media may provide another means by which to reduce sexual risk behaviors and prevent negative consequences such as pregnancy and STI.

Denying or ignoring adolescents' developing sexuality by parents, schools, and communities places adolescents at risk for both early sexual debut and unsafe sexual behaviors. The individuals and systems involved in each of these domains must work to address adolescent sexuality and foster its safe development. Here, we have outlined directly or by implication the strategies that parents, schools, and the media can employ to prevent sexual risk and promote healthy sexuality. We have not addressed the influence of peers in the adolescent's sexual activity for two reasons. First, peers are not adults and, therefore, not responsible for providing accurate information and skills to protect youths. Second, youths select their friends as much as their friends select them, rendering any influence between an adolescent and friends bi-directional.

We conclude with several critical facts. As we work toward delaying sexual debut and reducing sexual risk behaviors, we must bear in mind the normality of sexuality, its importance for humans, and its connection to such strong emotions as love. We should avoid scaring our children or casting sexuality as wrong or unacceptable, given that we do not know the short- or long-term impact that such messages may have on youths' attitudes and reactions to their own sexuality and that of others. Similarly, we should avoid the media's misrepresentation of sexuality as devoid of responsibility and serious consequences. As a society, we should strive to provide youths with consistent and accurate messages about sexuality, rather than false or contradictory messages. Thus, we must acknowledge that sexual development begins long before puberty and continues throughout life, such as changes brought about by menopause or prostate cancer. Sexuality plays an important role in the mental and physical health of the individual and ensures the survival of the species. Sexual activity between two humans represents the normative mode of sexual expression and frequently makes its debut during adolescence. Like any behavior, sexual activity carries risks that require preventive actions. Therefore, the information, attitudes, and skills conveyed to adolescents about sexuality may influence their relations to their own and others' sexuality, as well as their immediate and long-term health.

NOTE

1. Slight differences exist in the prevalence rates of sexual activity among the various representative national surveys that have to do with methodological issues,

such as whether the sample was recruited from high schools or households. The former necessarily excludes school dropouts, whereas the latter captures such youths.

REFERENCES

Aarons, S.J., Jenkins, R.R., Raine, T.R., El-Khorazaty, M.N., Woodward, K.M., Williams, R.L., Clark, M.C., & Wingrove, B.K. (2000). Postponing sexual intercourse among urban junior high school students—A randomized controlled evaluation. *Journal of Adolescent Health, 27,* 236–247.

Abma, J.C., & Sonenstein, F.L. (2001). Sexual activity and contraceptive practices among teenagers in the United States, 1988 and 1995. National Center for Health Statistics. *Vital Health Statistics, 23*(21), 1–80.

Ajzen, I., & Fishbein, M. (1980). *Understanding attitudes and predicting social behavior.* Englewood Cliffs, NJ: Prentice-Hall.

Albarracín, D., Johnson, B.T., Fishbein, M., & Muellerleile, P.A. (2001). Theories of reasoned action and planned behavior as models of condom use: A meta-analysis. *Psychological Bulletin, 127,* 142–161.

Anderson, C.A., Berkowitz, L., Donnerstein, E., Huesmann, L.R., Johnson, J.D., Linz, D., Malamuth, N.M., & Wartella, E. (2003). The influence of media violence on youth. *Psychological Science in the Public Interest, 4,* 81–110.

Anderson, C.A., & Bushman, B.J. (2001). Effects of violent video games on aggressive behavior, aggressive cognition, aggressive affect, physiological arousal, and prosocial behavior: A meta-analytic review of the scientific literature. *Psychological Science, 12,* 353–359.

Arnett, J.J. (2002). The sounds of sex: Sex in teens' music and music videos. In J.D. Brown & J.R. Steele (Eds.), *Sexual teens, sexual media: Investigating media's influence on adolescent sexuality* (pp. 253–264). Mahwah, NJ: Lawrence Erlbaum.

Aubrey, J.S. (2004). Sex and punishment: An examination of sexual consequences and the sexual double standard in teen programming. *Sex Roles, 50,* 505–514.

Aubrey, J.S., Harrison, K., Kramer, L., & Yellin, J. (2003). Variety versus timing: Gender differences in college students' sexual expectations as predicted by exposure to sexual oriented television. *Communication Research, 30,* 432–460.

Averett, S.L., Rees, D.I., & Argys, L.M. (2002). The impact of government policies and neighborhood characteristics on teenage sexual activity and contraceptive use. *American Journal of Public Health, 92,* 1773–1778.

Bandura, A. (1997). *Self-efficacy: The exercise of control.* New York: Freeman.

Bandura, A., Ross, D., & Ross, S.A. (1963). Imitation of film-mediated aggressive models. *Journal of Abnormal and Social Psychology, 66,* 3–11.

Barnett, J.E., & Hurst, C.S. (2003). Abstinence education for rural youth: An evaluation of the Life's Walk Program. *Journal of School Health, 73,* 264–268.

Basen-Engquist, K., Coyle, K. K., Parcel, G. S., Kirby, D., Banspach, S. W., Carvajal, S. C., & Baumler, E. (2001). Schoolwide effects of a multicomponent HIV, STD, and pregnancy prevention program for high school students. *Health Education and Behavior, 28,* 166–185.

Blake, S. M., Ledsky, R., Goodenow, C., Sawyer, R., Lohrmann, D., & Windsor, R. (2003). Condom availability programs in Massachusetts high schools: Relationships with condom use and sexual behavior. *American Journal of Public Health, 93,* 955–962.

Blinn-Pike, L. (1996). Preteen enrichment: Evaluation of a program to delay sexual activity among female adolescents in rural Appalachia. *Family Relations, 45,* 380–386.

Brener, N., Lowry, R., Kann, L., Kolbe, L., Lehnherr, J., Janssen, R., & Jaffe, H. (2002). Trends in sexual risk behaviors among high school students— United States, 1991–2001. *Morbidity and Mortality Weekly Report, 51*(38), 856–859.

Bronfenbrenner, U. (1979). *The ecology of human development: Experiments by nature and design.* Boston: Harvard University Press.

Carpenter, L. M. (1998). From girls to women: Scripts for sexuality and romance in "Seventeen" magazine, 1974–1994. *Journal of Sex Research, 35,* 158–168.

Carter-Jessop, L., Franklin, L. N., Heath, J. W., Jimenez-Irizarry, G., & Peace, M. D. (2000). Abstinence education for urban youth. *Journal of Community Health, 25,* 293–304.

Carvajal, S. C., Parcel, G. S., Basen-Engquist, K., Banspach, S. W., Coyle, K. K., Kirby, D., & Chan, W. (1999). Psychosocial predictors of delay of first sexual intercourse by adolescents. *Health Psychology, 18,* 443–452.

Chesson, H. W., Blandford, J. M., Gift, T. L., Tao, G., & Irwin, K. L. (2004). The estimated direct medical cost of sexually transmitted diseases among American youth, 2000. *Perspectives on Sexual and Reproductive Health, 36,* 11–19.

Clawson, C. L., & Reese-Weber, M. (2003). The amount and time of parent-adolescent sexual communication as predictors of late adolescent sexual risk-taking behaviors. *Journal of Sex Research, 40,* 256–265.

Collins, R. L., Elliott, M. N., Berry S. H., Kanouse, D. E., Kunkel, D., Hunter, S. B., & Miu, A. (2004). Watching sex on television predicts adolescent initiation of sexual behavior. *Pediatrics, 114,* 280–289.

Crosby, R. A., DiClemente, R. J., Wingood, G. M., Lang, D. L., & Harrington, K. (2003). Infrequent parental monitoring predicts sexual transmitted infections among low-income African American female adolescents. *Archives of Pediatric and Adolescent Medicine, 157,* 169–173.

Darroch, J. E., Singh, S., & Frost, J. J. (2001). Differences in teenage pregnancy rates among five developed countries: The roles of sexual activity and contraceptive use. *Family Planning Perspectives, 33,* 244–250, 281.

Davis, S., & Mares, M-L. (1998). Effects of talk show viewing on adolescents. *Journal of Communication, 48,* 69–86.

Denny, G., Young, M., & Spear, C.E. (1999). An evaluation of the Sex Can Wait abstinence education curriculum series. *American Journal of Health Behavior, 23,* 134–144.

Dittus, P.J., Jaccard, J., & Gordon, V.V. (1997). The impact of African American fathers on adolescent sexual behavior. *Journal of Youth and Adolescence, 26,* 445–465.

Donnerstein, E., Slaby, R.G., & Eron, L.D. (1994). The mass media and youth aggression. In L.D. Eron, J.H. Gentry, & P. Schlegel (Eds.), *Reason to hope: A psychological perspective on violence and youth* (pp. 219–250). Washington, DC: American Psychological Association.

Fisher, J.D., & Fisher, W.A. (1992). Changing AIDS-risk behavior. *Psychological Bulletin, 111,* 455–474.

Fisher, J.D., Fisher, W.A., Bryan, A.D., & Misovich, S.J. (2002). Information-motivation-behavioral skills model-based HIV risk behavior change intervention for inner-city high school youth. *Health Psychology, 21,* 177–186.

Flewelling, R.L., & Bauman, K.E. (1990). Family structure as a predictor of initial substance use and sexual intercourse in early adolescence. *Journal of Marriage and the Family, 52,* 171–181.

Freud, S. (1905/1962). *Three essays on the theory of sexuality.* Translated and edited by James Strachey. New York: Basic Books.

Gates, G.J., & Sonenstein, F.L. (2000). Heterosexual genital sexual activity among adolescent males: 1988 and 1995. *Family Planning Perspectives, 32,* 295–297, 304.

Greenberg, B.S., & Busselle, R.W. (1996). Soap operas and sexual activity: A decade later. *Journal of Communication, 46,* 153–160.

Greenberg, B.S., Sherry, J.L., Busselle, R.W., Hnilo, L.R., & Smith, S.W. (1997). Daytime television shows: Guests, content, and interactions. *Journal of Broadcasting & Electronic Media, 41,* 412–426.

Guttmacher, S., Lieberman, L., Ward, D., Freudenberg, N., Radosh, A., & DesJarlais, D. (1997). Condom availability in New York City public high schools: Relationships to condom use and sexual behavior. *American Journal of Public Health, 87,* 1427–1433.

Halpern, C.T. (2003). Biological influences on adolescent romantic and sexual behavior. In P. Florsheim (Ed.), *Adolescent romantic relations and sexual behavior: Theory, research, and practical implications* (pp. 57–84). Mahwah, NJ: Lawrence Erlbaum.

Heubner, A.J., & Howell, L.W. (2003). Examining the relationship between adolescent sexual risk-taking and perceptions of monitoring, communication, and parenting styles. *Journal of Adolescent Health, 33,* 71–78.

Horan, P.F., Phillips, J., & Hagan, N.E. (1998). The meaning of abstinence for college students. *Journal of HIV/AIDS Prevention and Education for Adolescents and Children, 2,* 51–66.

Hovell, M., Sipan, C., Blumberg, E., Atkins, C., Hofstetter, C.R., & Kreitner, S. (1994). Family influences on Latino and Anglo adolescents' sexual behavior. *Journal of Marriage and the Family, 56,* 973–986.

Hutchinson, M. K., Jemmott, J. B., Jemmott, L. S., Braverman, P., & Fong, G. T. (2003). The role of mother-daughter sexual risk communication in reducing sexual risk behaviors among urban adolescent females: A prospective study. *Journal of Adolescent Health, 33,* 98–107.

Jaccard, J., Dittus, P. J., & Gordon, V. V. (1998). Parent-adolescent congruency in reports of adolescent sexual behavior and in communications about sexual behavior. *Child Development, 69,* 247–261.

Jemmott, J. B., & Jemmott, L. S. (2000). HIV risk reduction behavioral interventions with heterosexual adolescents. *AIDS, 14*(suppl. 2), S40–S52.

Johnson, M. A., Gotthoffer, A. R., & Lauffer, K. A. (1999). The sexual and reproductive health content of African American and Latino magazines. *Howard Journal of Communications, 10,* 169–187.

Joyner, K., & Laumann, E. O. (2001). Teenage sex and the sexual revolution. In E. O. Laumann & R. T. Michael (Eds.), *Sex, love, and health in America: Private choices and public policies* (pp. 41–71). Chicago: University of Chicago Press.

Karofsky, P. S., Zeng, L., & Kosorok, M. R. (2000). Relationship between adolescent-parental communication and initiation of first intercourse by adolescents. *Journal of Adolescent Health, 28,* 41–45.

Kirby, D. (2000). School-based interventions to prevent unprotected sex and HIV among adolescents. In J. Peterson and R. DiClemente (Eds.), *Handbook of HIV prevention* (pp. 83–101). New York: Plenum.

Kirby, D. (2002). Effective approaches to reducing adolescent unprotected sex, pregnancy and childbearing. *Journal of Sex Research, 39,* 51–57.

Kirby, D., Brener, N. D., Brown, N. L., Peterfreund, N., Hillard, P., & Harrist, R. (1999). The impact of condom availability in Seattle schools on sexual behavior and condom use. *American Journal of Public Health, 89,* 182–187.

Kotchick, B. A., Dorsey, S., Miller, K. S., & Forehand, R. (1999). Adolescent sexual risk-taking behavior in single-parent ethnic minority families. *Journal of Family Psychology, 13,* 93–102.

Kunkel, D., Cope, K. M., & Biely, E. (1999). Sexual messages on television: Comparing findings from three studies. *Journal of Sex Research, 36,* 230–236.

Lieberman, L. D., Gray, H., Wier, M., Fiorentino, R., & Maloney, P. (2000). Long-term outcomes of an abstinence-based, small-group pregnancy prevention program in New York City schools. *Family Planning Perspectives, 32,* 237–245.

Mandara, J., Murray, C. B., & Bangi, A. K. (2003). Predictors of African American adolescent sexual activity: An ecological framework. *Journal of Black Psychology, 29,* 337–356.

Manlove, J., Ryan, S., & Franzetta, K. (2003). Patterns of contraceptive use within teenagers' first sexual relationships. *Perspectives on Sexual and Reproductive Health, 35,* 246–255.

Miller, K. S., Forehand, R., & Kotchick, B. A. (1999). Adolescent sexual behavior in two ethnic minority samples: The role of family variables. *Journal of Marriage and the Family, 61,* 85–98.

Miller, K. S., Levin, M. L., Whitaker, D. J., & Xu, X. (1998). Patterns of condom use among adolescents: The impact of mother-adolescent communication. *American Journal of Public Health, 88,* 1542–1544.

Money, J. (1988). *Gay, straight, and in-between: The sexology of erotic orientation.* New York: Oxford University Press.

O'Donnell, L., Stueve, A., San Doval, A., Duran, R., Haber, D., Atnafou, R., Johnson, N., Grant, U., Murray, H., Juhn, G., Tang, J., & Piessens, P. (1999). The effectiveness of the Reach for Health community youth service learning program in reducing early and unprotected sex among urban middle school students. *American Journal of Public Health, 89,* 176–181.

Olausson, P. O., Haglund, B., Weitoft, G. R., & Cnattingius, S. (2001). Teenage childbearing and long-term socioeconomic consequences: A case study in Sweden. *Family Planning Perspectives, 33,* 70–74.

Panchaud, C., Singh, S., Feivelson, D., & Darroch, J. E. (2000). Sexually transmitted diseases among adolescents in developed countries. *Family Planning Perspectives, 32,* 24–32, 45.

Ramirez-Valles, J., Zimmerman, M. A., & Newcomb, M. D. (1998). Sexual risk behavior among youth: Modeling the influence of prosocial activities and socioeconomic factors. *Journal of Health and Social Behavior, 39,* 237–253.

Reichert, T., Lambiase, J., Morgan, S., Carstephen, M., & Zavoina, S. (1999). Cheesecake and beefcake: No matter how you slice it, sexual explicitness in advertising continues to increase. *Journalism and Mass Media Communication Quarterly, 76,* 7–20.

Remez, L. (2000). Oral sex among adolescents: Is it sex or is it abstinence? *Family Planning Perspectives, 32,* 298–304.

Revenson, T. A. (1990). All other things are *not* equal: An ecological perspective on the relation between personality and disease. In H. S. Friedman (Ed.), *Personality and disease* (pp. 65–94). New York: Wiley.

Rodgers, K. B. (1999). Parenting processes related to sexual risk-taking behaviors of adolescent males and females. *Journal of Marriage and the Family, 61,* 99–109.

Rogol, A. D., Roemmich, J. N., & Clark, P. A. (2002). Growth at puberty. *Journal of Adolescent Health, 31,* 192–200.

Romer, D., Stanton, B., Galbraith, J., Feigelman, S., Black, M. M., & Li, X. (1999). Parental influence on adolescent sexual behavior in high-poverty settings. *Archives of Pediatric and Adolescent Medicine, 153,* 1055–1062.

Santelli, J. S., Lindberg, L. D., Abma, J., McNeely, C. S., & Resnick, M. (2000). Adolescent sexual behavior: Estimates and trends from four nationally representative surveys. *Family Planning Perspectives, 32,* 156–165, 194.

Santelli, J. S., Lowry, R., Brener, N. D., & Robin, L. (2000). The associations of sexual behaviors with socioeconomic status, family structure, and race/ethnicity among US adolescents. *American Journal of Public Health, 90,* 1582–1588.

Sather, L., & Zinn, K. (2002). Effects of abstinence-only education on adolescent attitudes and values concerning premarital sexual intercourse. *Family Community Health, 25,* 1–15.

Sieving, R.E., McNeely, C.S., & Blum, R.W. (2000). Maternal expectations, mother-child connectedness, and adolescent sexual debut. *Archives of Pediatric and Adolescent Medicine, 154,* 809–816.

Silva, M. (2002). The effectiveness of school-based sex education programs in the promotion of abstinent behavior: A meta-analysis. *Health Education Research, 17,* 471–481.

Singh, S., & Darroch, J.E. (2000). Adolescent pregnancy and childbearing: Levels and trends in developed countries. *Family Planning Perspectives, 32,* 14–23.

Smith, C.A. (1997). Factors associated with early sexual activity among urban adolescents. *Social Work, 42,* 334–346.

Sommers-Flanagan, R., Sommers-Flanagan, J., & Davis, B. (1993). What's happening on music television? A gender role content analysis. *Sex Roles, 28,* 745–753.

Stanton, B.F., Li, X., Galbraith, J., Cornick, G., Feigelman, S., Kaljee, L., & Zhou, Y. (1999). Parental underestimates of adolescent risk behavior: A randomized, controlled trial of a parental monitoring intervention. *Journal of Adolescent Health, 26,* 18–26.

Strouse, J.S., Buerkel-Rothfuss, N., & Long, E.C.J. (1995). Gender and family as moderators of the relationship between music video exposure and adolescent sexual permissiveness. *Adolescence, 30,* 505–521.

Thomas, M.H. (2000). Abstinence-based programs for prevention of adolescent pregnancies. *Journal of Adolescent Health, 26,* 5–17.

Wang, L.Y., Davis, M., Robin, L., Collins, J., Coyle, K., & Baumler, E. (2000). Economic evaluation of Safer Choices: A school-based human immunodeficiency virus, other sexually transmitted diseases, and pregnancy prevention program. *Archives of Pediatric and Adolescent Medicine, 154,* 1017–1024.

Ward, L.M. (1995). Talking about sex: Common themes about sexuality in the prime-time television programs children and adolescents watch most. *Journal of Youth and Adolescence, 24,* 595–615.

Ward, L.M. (2002). Does television exposure affect emerging adults' attitudes and assumptions about sexual relationships? Correlational and experimental confirmation. *Journal of Youth and Adolescence, 31,* 1–15.

Ward, L.M., & Rvadeneyra, R. (1999). Contributions of entertainment television to adolescents' sexual attitudes and expectations: The role of viewing among versus viewer involvement. *Journal of Sex Research, 36,* 237–249.

Weinstock, H., Berman, S., & Cates, W., Jr. (2004). Sexually transmitted diseases among American youth: Incidence and prevalence estimates, 2000. *Perspectives on Sexual and Reproductive Health, 36,* 6–10.

Weisfeld, G.E., & Woodward, L. (2004). Current evolutionary perspectives on adolescent romantic relations and sexuality. *Journal of the American Academy of Child and Adolescent Psychiatry, 43,* 11–19.

Wingfield, B. (2004, December 3). Study faults abstinence courses. *New York Times, 154,* A22.

Wingood, G.M., DiClemente, R.J., Bernhardt, J.M., Harrington, K., Davies, S.L., Robillard, A., & Hook, E.W. (2003). A prospective study of exposure to rap music videos and African American female adolescents' health. *American Journal of Public Health, 93,* 437–439.

Young, T.L., & Zimmerman, R. (1998). Clueless: Parental knowledge of risk behaviors of middle school students. *Archives of Pediatric and Adolescent Medicine, 152,* 1137–1139.

Zucker, K. (2001). Biological influences on psychosexual differentiation. In R.K. Unger (Ed.), *Handbook of the psychology of women and gender* (pp. 101–115). New York: Wiley.

Chapter 10

CRIMINALIZING CHILDHOOD: THE SHIFTING BOUNDARIES OF RESPONSIBILITY IN THE JUSTICE AND SCHOOL SYSTEMS

Jessica R. Meyer, N. Dickon Reppucci, and Jessica A. Owen

Like many social constructs, the conception of childhood has evolved over time in the United States. In several social realms, recent shifts involve movement away from thinking about childhood as a distinct developmental stage, in which youth under 18 years of age constitute a specific category of inexperienced and vulnerable individuals with special needs. In response to public and legal policy changes within the past few decades, exacerbated by sensational media reports and misinformed public perceptions of increasing juvenile violent crime rates (Males, 1996; Sickmund, Snyder, & Poe-Yamagata, 1997), the developmentally oriented understanding of childhood as a time of growth and maturity has been largely swallowed by fear. Cultural conceptions of children as naïve innocents have morphed into impressions of youth as "superpredators" who commit adult crimes. Young people are less likely to be viewed as malleable individuals deserving protection and rehabilitation. Rather, the focus is on holding them accountable for their individual behavior via punishment and tends to obscure the previous consideration of protective and rehabilitative ideals. This shift is particularly evident in the juvenile justice and school systems. The juvenile justice system has shifted from a rehabilitative ideal that considers troubled youth as misguided and impressionable, to one that characterizes youth as culpable for their conduct as adults and thus deserving of the same punitive criminal sanctions. Likewise, the school system has shifted from a paternalistic model of fairness and provision of equal education to all students, to one that increasingly utilizes strict, zero tolerance standards and expulsion procedures for disciplinary action.

In this chapter, we argue that policies within juvenile justice and school systems, driven by public and political fears of social disorder, and reflecting notions of inflated levels of culpability in youth, are unwarranted. First, we discuss traditional ideas of childhood and adolescence, their evolution into the contemporary view of youth, and the mechanisms behind this evolution. Then, we present the historical context of the U.S. school system, its recent shift to get-tough policies for students—including zero tolerance and heavy use of expulsion procedures—and difficulties with public school reenrollment of children transitioning out of the juvenile justice system. This is followed by a discussion of the evidence (or lack thereof) of the efficacy of these policies. Then we outline a brief history of the juvenile justice system and its shift into a more adversarial criminal justice system that uses Draconian measures such as adult transfers, sentences of life without parole, the death penalty (until 2005), and municipal ordinances to combat youth crime. We also present empirical evidence that suggests that the progressive transformation of the juvenile justice system may have iatrogenic effects on youth crime. We conclude with an argument against the unwarranted and extreme increase in the responsibility that these changes have put on youth in schools and courts and provide suggestions for future policies and research to inform such policies.

TRADITIONAL CONCEPTUALIZATIONS OF CHILDHOOD AND ADOLESCENCE

In the United States, attitudes toward children and the concept of childhood have been subject to remarkable change over time. In the eighteenth and nineteenth centuries, high mortality rates prevented many children from entering adulthood. As a result, young individuals were often treated with indifference; those children who survived and emerged from infancy and physical dependency, usually around seven years of age, were integrated into intergenerational groups for work and recreation. Parents allowed children to participate in most adult activities, including drinking, gambling, and engaging in sexual behavior, and made no efforts to protect their innocence. Children became adults simply by working with and functioning like adults. Thus, children were viewed as miniature adults rather than as qualitatively different from their elders (Feld, 1999). The responsibility as well as the autonomy to provide for the best interests of children was left to families, and *social* responsibility for child welfare was largely ignored (Schmidt & Reppucci, 2002).

However, industrialization and urbanization in the second half of the 1800s led to a dramatic transformation of these notions of childhood. Industrial modernization encouraged migration and the separation of work from the home, which consigned women to a life of domesticity and care-taking of children. These changes altered the conception and vision of childhood, especially within the middle and upper classes; children were viewed as innocent and malleable (Feld, 1999). Social structural changes associated with modernization also spawned an era of reform (1890–1914), the "century of the child," at which point *societal* concern with the experience of childhood became relatively new phenomena. Reformers passed child labor and welfare laws and created formal education requirements and other social institutions, such as the juvenile court, to differentiate and separate children from adults. By the end of World War I, nearly all states had enacted legal measures and institutional programs to enforce the segregation of children from adults. For example, community child guidance clinics were developed to prevent juvenile delinquency (Feld, 1999). These actions and the evolving conception of childhood were increasingly refined through the 1960s, when attention toward the juvenile court, prevention of delinquency, and child guidance and school problems were in the public limelight (Levine & Levine, 1992).

Adolescence as a label and a construct was created at the turn of the twentieth century (Hall, 1904) and was considered an extension of childhood. Whereas before this time, youth age 14 and older were legally considered adults, by the 1920s the juvenile court's jurisdiction extended to all youth under the age of 18. Thus, most adolescents were classified with younger children as minors. Legal privileges given to adults were not afforded to youth of any age; in exchange, minors were not held as accountable as adults for their actions. However, in the past few decades, society has witnessed a partial abandonment of the concept of adolescents as children in several realms.

PROGRESSIVE VIEWS OF CHILDHOOD AND ADOLESCENCE

Due to the efforts of reformers in the child-saving era at the beginning of the twentieth century and later in the 1960s, Americans no longer left the well-being of children to families alone. The ideas that youth possess rights, that the "best interests of the child" are not always represented by the family, and that society has a responsibility to safeguard these rights and interests have emerged relatively recently in U.S. history (Schmidt & Reppucci, 2002). For example, legislation was enacted to prohibit the use of children as fiscal resources for exploitation. The state was permitted to intervene when parents demonstrated that they were not able to serve in the best interests of their children. Protections were afforded to youth due to the widespread recognition that young children are developmentally immature and without the capacity to make independent choices that reflect their own well-being (Melton, 1983; Reppucci & Crosby, 1993; Schmidt & Reppucci, 2002).

The relatively progressive, paternalistic role of states in the provision of protections to youth initiated new struggles and dilemmas about how to balance fairly the rights of children, family, and the state. In particular, two groups—sometimes characterized as "kiddie libbers" and "child savers"—illustrate differences in beliefs about serving child, family, and state interests: child savers believe that legislation should protect children, while kiddie libbers believe that efforts should be made to facilitate children's autonomy and self-determination (Mnookin, 1980). In efforts to reconcile these disparate ideas when making legal decisions, the justice system has found it necessary to distinguish adolescents as a separate category, distinct from children and adults. Thus, courts repeatedly face the question of whether adolescents' cognitive developmental capacities require that they be granted the protection of children or the autonomy of adults (Schmidt & Reppucci, 2002).

Unfortunately, a coherent philosophy spanning social contexts regarding differences between children, adolescents, and adults is nonexistent. Developmental differences between children and adults are often acknowledged; for example, it is widely accepted that children and preadolescents demonstrate less reasoning capabilities than adults (Keating, 1990). This understanding is reflected in policies that regulate the rights of children and adolescents to drive, vote, drink, and make autonomous medical decisions. However, a consensus concerning distinctions between adolescents and adults has not yet been reached.

Researchers have generally concluded that adolescents 14 years of age and older are similar to adults with regard to cognitive capacities for decision-making in some realms but not in others (Britner, LaFleur, & Whitehead, 1998). Yet those that favor the more traditional beliefs of childhood and adolescence as developmental stages of vulnerability and malleability suggest that many youth of all ages lack the experience, maturity, and judgment of older people (Reppucci, 1999). Several commentators have suggested that, despite the cognitive capacity of youth, differences in psychosocial maturity continue to develop during the adolescent years and may affect judgment and decision-making (Scott, Reppucci, & Woolard, 1995; Steinberg & Cauffman, 1996). Examples abound.

Substantial evidence exists that even into middle adolescence, youth are more *susceptible to peer influence* than adults (Moffitt, 1993; Steinberg & Silverberg, 1986). Between childhood and young adulthood, individuals become more *future-oriented* (Greene, 1986; Nurmi, 1991). In addition, when asked about their *perceptions of short- versus long-term consequences,* teens tend to discount the future more than adults do and focus more on short-term consequences (Gardner, 1993). Adolescents differ from adults in their *perceptions and attitudes about risk* (Scott et al., 1995), with teens often placing relatively less weight on risk than adults (Halpern-Felsher & Cauffman, 2001). Finally, over the course of adolescence, youth tend to be more *impulsive* than adults (Greenberger, 1982; Steinberg & Cauffman, 1996).

In contrast, some policymakers believe that notions of youth as immature, dependent, and deficient in decision-making are less valid among older age groups in adolescence. They argue that adolescents should be held equally as responsible as adults for criminal acts, even though they may be considered less competent in other areas (e.g., abortion and medical decision-making). This view has extended into ideas about children and preadolescents as culpable beings, and it dominates present-day beliefs and policies regarding the treatment of youth in courts and schools. For example, courts now deem youth to be as culpable and responsible as adults for many types of criminal behavior, without the consideration of developmental factors. Courts are not putting much weight, if any, on the immaturity and lack of long-term planning abilities of adolescents (Cauffman & Steinberg, 2000) when they commit a crime. The age at which adolescents may be transferred to adult court and until 2005, sentenced with the death penalty were lowered (Reppucci, 1999). The following discussion presents some reasons why adolescents, and to some extent even preadolescents, have been conceptualized as adults in the predominant cultural view.

PATTERNS OF JUVENILE CRIME AND SCHOOL VIOLENCE

Although concerns about juvenile crime have surfaced and resurfaced over the past century, violent crime by youth became viewed as a serious social problem in the mid 1980s. FBI Crime Index reports indicate that between 1980 and 1996, the juvenile (under 18 years of age) arrest rate for violent crime increased 58 percent and 12 percent just between 1991 and 1995, which is a much sharper increase than it was for adults (FBI, 1996, 1997). Between 1986 and 1995, homicide arrests of juveniles increased 89.9 percent, while the homicide arrest rate for adults actually declined 0.3 percent (FBI, 1996). Certainly, juvenile crime rates indicate that attention and resources should be geared toward the prevention and reduction of youth delinquency.

However, in the plight to address youth crime, a number of additional statistics often go unnoticed by policymakers and reporters. First, juveniles only account for a minority (e.g., 18.7 percent in 1995) of all offenders arrested for violent crime. Second, although juvenile homicide rates increased until 1995, juveniles accounted for only 15 percent of homicides in 1995 (FBI, 1996). Therefore, despite increases in juvenile violent crime rates during the 1980s and early 1990s, adult offenders committed the vast majority of violent crime. Third, although there has been a dramatic increase in violent crime rates over the past couple of decades, violent crimes constitute only a small component of all criminal offenses (approximately 10 to 15 percent). Property crimes, on the other hand, are disproportionately committed by juveniles and were relatively stable during this same time period. Thus, contrary to popular belief, the *overall* rate of juvenile crime did not increase substantially during the 1990s.

More recent data indicate that juvenile arrests for violent crimes peaked in 1994, following a more general pattern of diminishing overall crime arrests between 1993 and 2002 (FBI, 2003; Sickmund, Snyder, & Poe-Yamagata, 1997). The 2002 estimate of juvenile violent crimes was 7 percent lower than the 1998 approximation and 25.9 percent below the 1993 figure. Likewise, even though arrests for adults for all offenses in 2002 rose 1.5 percent over the previous year's arrests, arrests for juveniles fell 3.5 percent (FBI, 2003). Similar to the rates in 1995 (18.7 percent), youth accounted for only 14.9 percent of arrestees for violent crime in 2002.

A similar misconception about the frequency of youth violence *within school environments* exists. From 1997 to 1999 a couple of highly publicized school shootings generated some copycat shootings. Media inundated the public with frightening images of assaulted children and grief-stricken peers and parents. Leading news sources misstated statistics and suggested that violent juvenile crime was soaring in the mid-1990s (Cornell, 2003). As a result, the general public has considerable fear and concern about school violence. Seven out of 10 Americans in recent surveys said they believed a shooting was likely in their school, and Americans were 49 percent more likely to express fears of their schools in 1999 than in 1998 (Center on Juvenile and Criminal Justice, 2000). In the late 1990s, nearly two-thirds of poll respondents (62 percent) believed that juvenile crime was on the increase (Center on Juvenile and Criminal Justice, 2000).

Contrary to public perception, frequency of school violence has been decreasing and has always been relatively rare. Overall crime in schools has declined dramatically since 1994 (National Crime Victimization Survey, 2003), and homicides in schools declined during the 1990s (National School Safety Center, 2003). Although the number of student homicides on school property ranged from 23 to 35 during the years of the copycat shootings (1997 to 1999), in the following four years there was an average of only 5.75 student homicides on school property (http://youth-violence.edschool.virginia.edu/violence-in-schools/school-shootings. html). Similarly, the overall percentage of students who reported being threatened or injured with a weapon at school has remained relatively stable since 1993 (Youth Risk Behavior Survey, 2003). A report drawn on data from sources including the U.S. Department of Education's National Center for Education Statistics and the U.S. Department of Justice states that, "The number of children killed by gun violence in schools is about half the number of Americans killed annually by lightning strikes" (Center on Juvenile and Criminal Justice, 1998, p. 1). In a later report, statistics indicated that in 1999, there was a one in two million chance of being killed in one of America's schools (Center on Juvenile and Criminal Justice, 2000). Indeed, more children die of the flu and pneumonia than are killed at school (National Vital Statistics Report, 1998). Schools remain one of the safer environments for young people in the community. Less than one percent of homicides and suicides among school-age children occur in or around school grounds (Kachur et al., 1996), and the rate of crimes committed by youth is low during school hours (Snyder & Sickmund, 1999). None of these statistics have changed the perception of the general public that schools are unsafe, and this may be largely due to the mass media extensive coverage of the Columbine school shooting in Colorado in 1999 when 12 students and 1 teacher were killed by two disturbed classmates.

HISTORY OF THE AMERICAN SCHOOL SYSTEM
AND SCHOOL SAFETY POLICIES

In colonial America and well into the nineteenth century, children were socialized and educated in the family. Later in the 1800s, during the inception of the child-saving era, formal education became more important to society. Thus, the right for free and universal education became largely established by the time of the Civil War. During this time, the school population drastically increased due to immigration, industrialization, urbanization, and new compulsory attendance laws (Levine & Levine, 1992). Schools took action by implementing rigid systems for promotion into grade levels and supervision of instruction, which were often antithetical to the individual needs of students. However, social structural changes related to modernization at the turn of the century marked the beginning of the progressive social reform period; reformers initiated the progressive education movement to make public education more relevant to industrial society (Feld, 1999). Visiting teachers were introduced into the public school system to deal with the needs of individual children, by intervening on a more ecological level with families, courts, social agencies, and welfare systems. These teachers explained the child's behavior to the school in order to modify the school's behavior to the child. Nevertheless, by the 1920s, efforts toward social reform had waned, and visiting teachers were replaced by professionals trained to focus on inner psychological problems. The nation became more conservative, and attention shifted from social reform efforts to a focus on individual responsibility. It was not until the Soviets launched Sputnik in 1957 that Americans felt a blow to their pride and turned their attention again toward ways to improve schools, which spawned new social reform efforts to advance the links between schools and community agencies (Levine & Levine, 1992).

In the past few decades, schools have again shifted their focus away from social responsibility for the prevention of youth problems and individualized treatment for troubled youth; instead, schools are focused on promoting school safety after a threat by a student has been made, and typically schools implement standard, one-size-fits-all punitive sanctions for all youth. This change in approach has largely been in response to the aforementioned increase in sensational imagery of school violence on television, prompted by a series of copycat school shootings in the 1990s (Cornell, 2003). Although a few egregious school shootings took place in a relatively short period of time, the epidemic of school violence presented by the media is unsubstantiated by statistics. There is virtually no difference between the rates of crime in schools in 1989 and the school crime rates in 1995 (Snyder & Sickmund, 1999). Despite the facts and statistics, media and public reaction to school shootings have sparked the adoption of "safe school" policies to identify and intervene proactively with potentially violent adolescents. Examples include zero tolerance, mandated school uniforms, surveillance cameras and metal detectors, and compulsory school attendance. Although a discussion of each of these policies is too exhaustive for the purposes of this chapter, we will present a synopsis of the legislation, practices, problems, and research of zero tolerance strategies.

Zero Tolerance Policies

To promote safety in schools, Congress began passing zero tolerance laws in the *Federal Gun-Free Schools Act* (1994), requiring states to pass legislation that mandates implementation of predetermined disciplinary measures for specific offenses. These sanctions began by requiring a one-year expulsion for students carrying firearms on school grounds. However, many states later extended these policies to apply them to a broad range of conduct, including other types of weapons, possession or use of drugs, and less frequently for habitual profanity or defiant/disruptive behavior (Advancement Project and the Civil Rights Project [APCRP], 2000). These policies usually oblige administrators to sanction suspension or expulsion to students for the commission of such acts. As a response to perceptions of disorder and chaos within the schools, the implementation of these strategies has received widespread support; zero tolerance procedures are widely implemented across the nation's schools, and in the year 2000, the vast majority (87 percent) of Americans favored the use of zero tolerance (Rose & Gallup, 2000).

However, others have harshly criticized zero tolerance policies for a number of reasons. The American Bar Association stated that zero tolerance treats all threats of violence as equally dangerous and deserving of the same punishments and fails to provide flexibility for school administrators to consider the seriousness of threats or degree of risks (Cornell, 2003). Unfortunately, the bearers of such predetermined punishment are all too often young students who have committed minor infractions and pose no danger to others. For example, kindergarten students as young as six years of age have been suspended for bringing a nail clipper or toy axe as part of a Halloween costume to school. Other students have been expelled for accidentally bringing a pocketknife (which was packed in the bag for an earlier Boy Scouts trip) or sparklers to school. Additional inadvertent incidents have included bringing a plastic knife in a lunchbox and packing scissors or headache medication in schoolbags. A 17-year-old student in Chicago was arrested and later expelled for shooting a paper clip with a rubber band. Similarly, students have been suspended or expelled for "drug related activity" such as wearing one pants leg up or sniffing "white out" correction fluid in class (APCRP, 2000). Clearly, zero tolerance policies allow limited, if any, opportunity to consider the context and meaning of threats by students.

Given the inflexibility of predetermined responses to perceived threats of school violence, disciplinary actions under the zero tolerance philosophy have been undertaken even when school administrators and others involved recognized that the targeted students intended no harm. In Mississippi, five high school students threw peanuts while on the school bus and accidentally hit the bus driver. The young men were arrested for felony assault, which carries a maximum penalty of five years in prison. They also lost their bus privileges and suspension was recommended. Although community support aided in the dismissal of the charges, all of the students dropped out of school because they lacked a substitute means of transportation to school (APCRP, 2000).

The rigidity of zero tolerance policies has also significantly affected the treatment of disabled children. Despite the *Individuals with Disabilities*

Education Act (1997), which prohibited school administrators from disciplining students with special needs as they would discipline students without disabilities, some administrators respond to disabled students with standard zero tolerance approaches. For example, an autistic child was expelled and charged with battery for kicking a teacher, and a young child with attention deficit hyperactivity disorder was charged with battery for kicking an aide (APCRP, 2000). Clearly, as evidenced in the aforementioned examples, these strict sanctions erroneously include students who do not intend to commit any harm. Indeed, research suggests that this is an inherent weakness in the one-size-fits all approach to school violence. Violent behavior committed by youth is a rare event and is extremely difficult to reliably detect, given that predictive strategies identify a large number of false positives (Mulvey & Cauffman, 2001).

The millions of children left without educational opportunities exemplify the copious number of false positives identified by zero tolerance. Approximately 3.1 million students in America, or nearly 6.8 percent of all students, were suspended or expelled from school in 1997. This is up from 3.7 percent of students in 1974 (Center on Juvenile and Criminal Justice, 2000). This increase appears to be related to the implementation of zero tolerance sanctions—for example, case studies of middle schools in Miami-Dade County, Florida, indicate that suspension rates are higher when zero tolerance sanctions are employed (APCRP, 2000). Unfortunately, harsh disciplinary measures often mandate harsh punishment over education. Many students who receive exclusionary punishments become alienated from the educational process and experience short or long-term deprivation of education. Suspension is a moderate to strong predictor of a student dropping out of school (Skiba & Peterson, 1999). In addition, although some suspended or expelled students are offered alternative schooling, it has been suggested that students attending these schools are often mistreated and/or denied adequate instruction (APCRP, 2000).

Perhaps even more alarming, zero tolerance policies have led to a growing number of criminal charges filed against children for their conduct in school. There are 43 states that necessitate reporting of a commission of a crime on school property to law enforcement agencies. School administrators may interpret these laws differently, and sometimes youth are reported for behavior that would not be considered a criminal act in the community. Students subjected to zero tolerance sanctions are frequently charged with assault or battery for kicking, hitting, or fist fights. Although the law requires serious bodily injury in most criminal charges of aggravated assault, the severity of the behavior in the school system often goes unnoticed. Therefore, students engaging in typical childhood/adolescent behavior may now become enmeshed in the juvenile justice system. Given the increasingly harsh way that youth are treated in this system, it is critical to examine the repercussions of entangling children in it for infractions committed in the school environment.

Interestingly, zero tolerance policies are not effective with youth who are dangerous, because they mandate extremely punitive sanctions for rule-breaking, which oblige unreasoned responses to any reported problem, and thus prohibit at least some information that would be shared with the administration by students. Since students tend to be the best source of information about the activities of other students, violence prevention programs should perhaps aim to encourage an atmosphere in which sharing information is respected and discussed and a sense of belonging is promoted, rather than acted upon in a punitive and unreasoned fashion (Mulvey & Cauffman, 2001). Second, the facilitation of supportive relationships between prosocial adults and troubled youth has been found to be an essential protective factor in resilient at-risk youth (Noam, Winner, & Rhein, 1996). However, punitive responses by adults preclude the development of such relationships. Third, research indicates that exclusionary punishments, such as suspension, may accelerate the process of delinquency by providing at-risk youth with little parental supervision and more time to associate with deviant peers (Skiba & Peterson, 1999). Fourth, troubled youth often view exclusionary punishments, which fail to take into account mitigating factors and do not allow youth opportunities to problem-solve or learn how to develop self-control, as exemplifications of lack of justice or fairness (APCRP, 2000). As a result, they feel rejected and alienated, and often fail to return to school (APCRP, 2000).

Indeed, returning to school is especially problematic for youth who have had criminal charges filed against them for their conduct in school. According to a report by the Office of Juvenile Justice and Delinquency Prevention (OJJDP, 2000), youth exiting juvenile correctional facilities may "become lost in a tangle of bureaucratic agencies that too often share only limited information with each other, resulting in fragmented assistance. In most cases, no single agency or advocate 'looks after' the needs of an adjudicated youth" (p. 3). The lack of a clear definition of roles often leads to duplication of services, or to "guess[ing]" by educators supplied with inadequate information about the services the youth received while in detention. "The time it takes to obtain all the information," the OJJDP report states, "often leads to unnecessary referrals, duplicate services, inaccurate information, and service delays" (p. 3). For many children, re-enrollment involves enrollment in an "alternative school" for students labeled as having disciplinary problems (Tobin & Sprague, 2000), which may exacerbate engagement in the undesirable behaviors. The following discussion presents empirical evidence on the efficacy and indirect effects, such as difficulties with education re-enrollment, of zero tolerance, and other types of school interventions.

Efficacy of School Interventions

The efficacy of zero tolerance policies in ensuring school safety is highly dubious. There is little evidence to suggest that zero tolerance procedures reduce school violence or increase school safety (APCRP, 2000). The National Center for Education Statistics (NCES) study of school violence demonstrates that schools that use zero tolerance are less safe than those without such policies (Skiba & Peterson, 1999). Some schools claim that implementation of zero tolerance philosophies reduced suspensions or expulsions in concurrent years; however, many of these statistics fail to account for the number of expelled students who drop out, become incarcerated, or attend alternative schools (APCRP, 2000). Problem youth are usually repeat offenders and lengthening their suspension times may artificially reduce rates of these types of sanctions (APCRP, 2000).

The limited efficacy of get-tough school sanctions is not surprising, given that most of the single-focus interventions for violent adolescents have demonstrated little effectiveness (McCord, Widom, & Crowell, 2001). In contrast, the most successful interventions have a more multisystemic focus and involve multiple community settings (Lipsey & Wilson, 1998). A meta-analysis suggests that school-based prevention programs focused on enhancing protective factors are effective in reducing aggressive behavior at school (Wilson, Lipsey, & Derzon, 2003). For example, promoting healthy relationships has been shown to be more effective for reducing school crime than implementing punitive policies after a crime has been committed or a threat has been made (Nettles, Mucherah, & Jones, 2000). Social competence programs are the most common type of program demonstrating substantial positive effects in the reduction of delinquency; these programs incorporate instruction on how to resolve conflicts, lessons on communication and negotiation skills, provision of mentors, and training in relaxation and self-monitoring techniques (Cornell, 1999).

Specific to those students for whom zero-tolerance policies have resulted in criminal charges and incarceration, research indicates that increased levels of school attachment are associated with decreased levels of recidivism (Keith & McCray, 2002). Indeed, numerous studies document the connection whereby the incidence of recidivism increases when enrollment is not available soon after release (Geddes & Keenan, 2004). The fact that many states have no organizational structure to support the goals or operations of education re-enrollment suggests that zero-tolerance policies, particularly those that criminalize behavioral problems, put children at risk for decreased school attachment and thus increased rates of recidivism.

HISTORICAL CONTEXT AND TRANSFORMATION OF THE JUVENILE JUSTICE SYSTEM

Before the turn of the century, children under the age of 7 were considered incapable of engaging in criminal activity, youth between 7 and 14 years could be treated as adults if courts determined that they acted as adults, and all individuals 14 years and older were considered to be adults in the judicial system (Reppucci, 1999). These guiding assumptions began to change when the first juvenile court was established in 1899 in Illinois. At this point, reformers were enraged that children as young as 7 years could be tried and punished as adults (Levine & Levine, 1992); therefore, the judicial system was restructured to focus on rehabilitation for youth, rather than punishment. However, several decades later the juvenile court began transforming from an ostensibly social rehabilitative agency into a scaled down adult criminal justice system for youth. Some scholars argue that drastic shifts in the conceptualization and function of the justice system for youth can largely be attributed to changes in social structural ideas and cultural perceptions of youth (Feld, 1999). To understand how these contextual factors may have converted the seminal ideal of the juvenile court as a welfare agency into a punitive system, we outline the development of the juvenile court and the sociostructural and ecological frameworks present during these time periods.

The first juvenile court was created in the "best interests" of the child; the state served as *parens patriae,* a surrogate parent, and separated children from adults to offer them rehabilitative rather than punitive sanctions. An underlying principle was that youth, due to their immaturity, do not bear the same culpability as adults for committing crimes. Thus, judicial proceedings were intended to be informal in order to care for youth, and individual circumstances were usually considered when making determinations of whether to bring them to court. Records and proceedings were to be kept confidential in order to prevent the attachment of stigma to youth, and incarcerated juveniles were to be separated from adult criminals in prison (Reppucci, 1999). To maintain the informality of judicial treatment of youth, due process rights, such as the right to counsel and the privilege against self-incrimination, were also precluded from judicial proceedings.

The lack of due process became the major criticism of the juvenile court in the 1950s, when informal guidelines were resulting in the incarceration of many youth who may have been sheltered from such punishment if they had been afforded due process rights. At this time, the paternalistic juvenile court was criticized for failing to rehabilitate young criminals or reduce juvenile crime (Dean & Reppucci, 1974; Levine & Levine, 1992), and court officials believed that youth were receiving neither procedural safeguards nor effective rehabilitative efforts. In response, the Supreme Court granted juveniles due process rights, including the right to counsel and privilege against self-incrimination, in the landmark case, *In re Gault* (387 U.S. 1[1967]). Accordingly, conceptual and procedural differences between the social control of youth and adults began to erode. The *Gault* case highlighted a fundamental shift in treating juveniles as children toward treating them as adults. Whether it was intended or not, the *Gault* decision also legitimated imposition of harsher sanctions to youth on a larger scale. (For a detailed discussion of this issue, see Manfredi, 1998.)

The need to dictate less punishment to juveniles because of their developmental immaturity was still recognized during the *Gault* era (Scott & Grisso, 1997). This was explicitly demonstrated in Supreme Court rulings that considered the culpability and constitutionality of sentencing young offenders. In *Lockett v. Ohio* (438 U.S. 586, 604 [1978]), the Supreme Court ruled that a sentencing court must consider a youth's age as a mitigating factor. *Eddings v. Oklahoma* (455 U.S. 104 at 116 [1982]) noted that age, mental and emotional development, and background must be considered in sentencing, and ruled that youth "deserve less punishment because (they) may have less capacity to control their conduct and to think in long-rage terms than adults" (455 U.S. at 115 n 11). Similarly, in *Thompson v. Oklahoma* (486 U.S. 815 [1988]), which concerned capital punishment for a 15-year-old, the court ruled that a young person's culpability is not equal to that of an adult's, and therefore youth are not deserving of the same punishment (i.e., death penalty). The *Thompson* court also declared that "adolescents as a class are less mature and responsible than adults ... minors often lack the experience, perspective, and judgment expected of adults ... inexperience, less education, and less intelligence make the teenager less able to evaluate the consequences of his or her conduct while at the same time he or she is much more apt to be motivated by mere emotion or peer pressure than is an adult." (487 U.S. at 834).

However, a year later, *Stanford v. Kentucky* (492 U.S. 361 [1989]) rejected the culpability analysis of the *Thompson* (1988) ruling and declined to prohibit capital punishment for 16- and 17-year-olds. The *Stanford* and *Thompson* rulings, although only one year apart, parallel the shift from the paternalistic, rehabilitative view of youth to the view of youth as adult-like criminals that has occurred over the past few decades. Unfortunately, when the best interests of the child and the demand for public safety were blended into a single institution, as was the case during the reform of the juvenile court, it became very difficult to balance both needs. As a result, the modern changes occurring within the juvenile justice system now threaten to mask developmental differences between children and adults. One notable exception is the recent Supreme Court hearing of *Roper v. Simmons* (125 S.Ct. 1183 [2005]) to determine the constitutionality of the juvenile death penalty. By a vote of 5-4, the Supreme Court on March 1, 2005 held that the Eighth and Fourteenth Amendments forbid the execution of offenders who were under the age of 18 when their crimes were committed.

Some scholars suggest that the current shifts in the juvenile justice system have been largely instigated by macrostructural changes involving deindustrialization, high poverty rates, and dissipation of employment opportunities for young, lower class citizens (Feld, 1999). These societal changes have contributed to the increase in youth violent crime and homicide rates. Indeed, poverty, family background, and locality have been shown to be strongly related to violence; in fact, these factors far better predict violence than young age (Males, 1996). In addition, media depictions solidified the view that juvenile crime was out of control. These perceptions sparked a get-tough, "old enough to do the crime, old enough to do the time" response from public officials in order to promote public safety. Within a five-year period, nearly every state amended its waiver laws in response to real or perceived escalation of urban youth violence (Feld, 1999). Thus, juvenile and criminal court systems have converged, with punishment as the just priority.

THE CURRENT JUVENILE JUSTICE SYSTEM

Today, juvenile courts embody more procedural formality, waive serious young offenders to the adult criminal system, and all too often afford youthful offenders punishment instead of rehabilitation. These changes are largely due to a deemphasis on individualized treatment of the offender, in conjunction with a focus on the seriousness and type of the present offense. Paternalistic, rehabilitative ideals aimed at gaining a fuller understanding of a juvenile's character and circumstances to meet his or her needs have largely disappeared.

Waivers to Adult Court and Draconian Sentencing

The mechanisms to facilitate youth's prosecution under adult criminal laws are commonly known as *waiver* or *transfer to adult court*. The waiver of juveniles to adult court has been an option since the inception of the juvenile court; although in the past, juvenile waivers were based largely on individual differences in adolescents' dangerousness, sophistication/ maturity, and amenability to treatment (Salekin, 2002). This practice has changed significantly over the last decade; transfers have become increasingly automatic, based on the type or seriousness of the crime or the age of the defendant, meaning judges cannot always make decisions on a case-by-case basis. Some states limited waiver to felony offenses and established a minimum age for transfer to adult court, usually 14, 15, or 16 years of age, although a few have lowered the ages to 8, 10, and 13 years. Other states have no restrictions on transfer (Snyder & Sickmund, 1995). Many states also extended the number of crimes that youth could be transferred for without hearings (Reppucci, 1999). As a result, there has been a 71 percent increase in juvenile cases transferred to adult courts between 1985 and 1994 and a 100 percent increase from 1994 to 1998 (Salekin, 2002). Once youth are transferred to adult criminal courts, it is likely that their diminished responsibility and immaturity will not be recognized (Feld, 1999).

Once waived and if convicted, courts often impose Draconian sentences on juveniles. Several studies (McNulty, 1996; Podkopacz & Feld, 1996; Rudman, Hartstone, Fagan, & Moore, 1986) show that criminal courts imprison youth more often and with longer sentences than juvenile courts do. A 1993 California Department of Corrections study found juveniles were consistently confined for 60 percent *longer* than adults for the same crimes (one year longer, on average) (Males, 1996). Nearly all states confine juveniles sentenced in criminal court to adult correctional facilities either with young adult offenders or in the general prison population (Torbet et al., 1996). In addition, waiver strategies rendered at least some juveniles eligible for the death penalty (Feld, 1999; *Kent v. United States,* 383 U.S. 541 [1966]). Waived youth as young as 13 or 14 years of age have been sentenced to life without parole, and those as young as 16 or 17 years of age have been sentenced with the death penalty. Although customary international law explicitly prohibits the execution of juvenile offenders, the United States was the only country in the world that proclaimed its legal right to do so; in fact, 19 states in the United States allowed the execution of minors (Amnesty International, 2004; Streib, 2002). Since 1998, a few rogue executions of juvenile offenders took place in only four other countries—China, the Democratic Republic of the Congo, Iran, and Pakistan. Yet the overwhelming majority of juvenile executions occurred in the United States (Amnesty International, 2004). The imposition of capital punishment on juveniles certainly challenged the idea that youth are less criminally responsible for their actions. Instead, mandatory life and capital sentences embody cultural judgments that youth are as culpable and blameworthy, and thus should be held just as accountable, as adults. These notions were altered by the U.S. Supreme Court in2005, when a 5-4 vote in *Roper v. Simmons* (125 S.Ct. 1183 [2005]) forbid the execution of offenders who were under the age of 18 when their crimes were committed. The Court determined that society should view juveniles as categorically less culpable than the average criminal.

Local Ordinances: Curfew Laws for Youth

As part of the get-tough mentality that has characterized the relatively recent reformation of the juvenile justice system, municipal ordinances have become an increasingly popular way to attempt to combat juvenile crime (Fried, 2001). For example, curfew laws for youth have become a heavily utilized method to control delinquency (Fried, 2001). As of 1995, approximately 77 percent of large U.S. cities employed curfew ordinances, and about half of these were enacted in the early 1990s (Ruefle & Reynolds, 1995). Their common purpose is to reduce juvenile crime and to protect juveniles from harmful influences and crime (Marketos, 1995). To do so, the curfew ordinances restrict the activities and hours that youth may be out on the streets without parental supervision. Offenses usually result in fines, community service, counseling, or probation (Ruefle & Reynolds, 1995). Municipal curfew ordinances have received extensive support from the public and law enforcement. Surveys conducted in the late 1990s indicate that between 77 and 92 percent of citizens espouse favorable opinions of curfew laws and law enforcement and consider curfew programs responsible for changes in crime rate (Fried, 2001).

OBJECTIONS TO RECENT JUVENILE JUSTICE REFORMATIONS

Although drastic transformations in the juvenile justice system have emerged in the past few decades, both developmental theory and research indicate that these changes may not be beneficial to the well-being of youth *or* the protection of society. Harsher sentences do not appear to be effective in deterring violent criminal behavior (Gottfredson & Hirschi, 1995). In New York, evaluations of adult transfers did not find any systematic decline for the included offenses (Singer & McDowall, 1988). In Florida, recidivism rates have been shown to be higher for those who were transferred to adult courts as compared to those who were not transferred for comparable crimes (Bishop, Frazier, Lanza-Kaduce, & Winner, 1996). In regard to curfew laws, Fried (2001) reviewed efficacy research conducted in the late 1990s and the year 2000 in Detroit and New Orleans, as well as cities in California and Texas. These studies concluded that curfew ordinances were ineffective in reducing juvenile crime and victimization, and some actually found that curfews *increased* crime rates, especially in the afternoon hours when curfews were not enforced. Only one study mentioned by Fried (2001) showed small reductions in some types of juvenile arrests as a result of curfews, and the researchers indicated that, at best, they demonstrated extremely weak support for the reduction in crime by curfews (McDowall, Loftin, & Wiersema, 2000).

In contrast to get-tough sanctions, some prevention programs that target groups of individuals *prior* to the occurrence of serious violence have been shown to be effective. Violence is determined by many complex factors, including biological predispositions and familial, contextual, and societal variables, so it is not likely to be prevented by simple, single-faceted fixes (Fried & Reppucci, 2002). Thus, programs that target multiple areas of children's lives are the most likely to be effective (Tate, Reppucci, & Mulvey, 1995).

Under the current one-size-fits-all punitive response system of the courts, individuals receive punishment largely based on the type or seriousness of the crime. However, nearly half of male, juvenile delinquents desist after their initial contact with the court system (Wolfgang, Figlio, & Sellin, 1972) and the vast majority of adolescent offenders desist from crime as they mature into adulthood (Farrington, 1986); moreover, some youthful offenders are chronic in their criminal behavior but others are time-limited (Moffitt, 1993). Although both chronic and time-limited juvenile offenders suffer punitive sanctions, it is the relatively smaller group of chronic career offenders who account for a disproportionate amount of all juvenile crime (Feld, 1999). It is these egregious cases that often become highly visible and fuel widespread fear and get-tough legislative efforts to control crime.

Legal and social science scholars suggest that juveniles should not be held to the same standards of criminal responsibility, and thus not be subjected to the same punishment, as adults who have committed comparable crimes (Steinberg & Scott, 2003). Suggestions have been made to mandate age as a mitigating factor in criminal sentencing, just as mental illness, insanity, duress, and self-defense are regularly considered in the assessment of criminal culpability (Steinberg & Scott, 2003). Three main categories of mitigating circumstances are often used in the culpability analysis of criminal defendants: (1) impairments or deficiencies in decision-making that affect an individual's choice to engage in criminal activity (i.e., mental illness or mental retardation), (2) external circumstances that may have caused any reasonable person to engage in criminal activity (i.e., self-defense, duress), and (3) evidence that the criminal act was out of character for the individual (i.e., first offense). Steinberg and Scott (2003) argue that each of these categories is important to an assessment of the culpability of adolescents, such that adolescents demonstrate diminished cognitive and psychosocial development that may shape their criminal choices, they are more vulnerable to coercive circumstances due to immature decision-making skills and less autonomy, and their criminal behavior is less likely to reflect bad character because they are still in the process of forming their self-identity.

With regard to juvenile transfers to adult court in particular, it appears that the current justice system is failing to place the same weight as the original juvenile court on adolescents' dangerousness, sophistication/ maturity, and amenability to treatment (Salekin, 2002). Treating all individuals the same, based on the type or seriousness of the crime, neglects differences in the likelihood that a given adolescent will persist in criminal activity or be receptive to treatment. Although our understanding in these areas is limited, research generally concludes that: (1) unlike adults who commit crime, many juveniles who engage in criminal behavior will desist and live normal adult lives (Moffitt, 1993), (2) youth may demonstrate different developmental pathways toward sophistication/maturity, and (3) youth are more malleable than adults and thus more amenable to treatment. First, it is more likely that a juvenile delinquent will cease criminal behavior if he or she committed the first offense during mid-adolescence or later. In contrast, life-course persistent juvenile criminals tend to engage in antisocial behavior well before adolescence (Moffitt, 1993). Second, the developmental limitations of youth (i.e., risk perception, time perspective, judgment) (Scott, Reppucci, & Woolard, 1995), would prevent the majority of youth reaching the criterion for sophistication/ maturity necessary for transfer to adult court in the original guidelines; only those youth who are more advanced in their level of sophistication/ maturity would be waived (Salekin, 2002). Third, substantial evidence in the psychological and medical literature indicates that the earlier a disorder is detected, the better the prognosis, which has been the basis for treating rather than punishing delinquent youth (Salekin, 2002). Such research suggests that differential treatment by the juvenile court is necessary.

Finally, there are glaring inconsistencies in the philosophy of the "get tough on crime" approach. As discussed earlier, the current juvenile justice system tends to make waiver and sentencing decisions primarily based on the type and seriousness of the crime, without taking into account developmentally relevant factors that may reduce the culpability of young defendants. However, in the courts' utilization of get-tough local ordinances, such as curfew laws, they make the psychological assumption that youth do not have the decision-making capabilities or competence to exert personal discretion about appropriate activities to be engaged in and time frames while out of the home (Fried, 2001). Such restrictions have also been placed by courts on youth in many other areas of their lives; for example, youth were deemed too "immature" to get a tattoo, drink, smoke, drive, or make autonomous decisions about abortion or commitment to mental hospitals (*Parham v. J.R.,* 1979). Many restrictions have been placed on *all* youth due to the limited development of their autonomy, maturity, judgment, and decision-making capacities in comparison to adults; it is ironic that the current justice system is failing to acknowledge these same developmental limitations when they may be applied to *delinquent* youth for treatment decisions. Policy concerning youth criminal behavior remains isolated from other legal policies regarding youth.

SUMMARY

Despite historical vacillation between a focus on social versus individual responsibility for the welfare of youth (i.e., ecological models targeted at the prevention of youth problems versus a lack of focus on community responsibility for children's well-being), in the past century childhood has been fairly consistently viewed as a distinct developmental stage constituting malleability and vulnerability. However, in the past few decades, children and adolescents have not been viewed as fragile creatures in need of protection; instead, they are often treated like adults and held fully accountable for their personal behavior if they are alleged to have committed a crime. Today, we are faced with a punitive, adult-like justice system and a one-size-fits-all school safety approach that suggest that youth's crimes make them adults. Yet research has shown that differences do exist between youth and adults (Reppucci, 1999). Should these differences vanish because a youth commits or is alleged to have committed a crime?

This shift in the conceptualization of childhood and adolescence is largely related to increased public fears of dangerousness of youth, sparked by highly publicized incidences of a few copycat school shootings during the 1997–1999 school years and a period of escalating juvenile crime from 1985 to 1994 (which has since decreased). The exaggerated media depictions of youth violence (Males, 1996) have contributed to the public fears of the dangerousness of youth. In turn, perceived overwhelming public support for zero tolerance school safety policies and get-tough, Draconian criminal sentencing for young offenders has been the result, despite little evidence that zero tolerance procedures either reduce school violence or increase school safety (APCRP, 2000) or that harsher sentences, adult transfers, and municipal ordinances deter criminal behavior (Fried, 2001; Gottfredson & Hirschi, 1995; Singer & McDowall, 1988).

Unfortunately, the ambiguous boundaries between youth and adults result in extreme reactions, which often lead to adverse consequences for children, families, and communities. Get-tough responses fail to consider the individual characteristics of perpetrators, such as age, and thus treat young people similarly to adults. Zero tolerance in schools treats all threats of violence as equally dangerous and deserving of the same punishments, which prevents administrators from using flexibility in the treatment of disabled youth and students. Likewise, concern about the long-term implications of prohibiting young individuals from educational prospects is masked by public anxiety about school violence. Millions of children are left without educational opportunities (APCRP, 2000), and a growing number of criminal charges are filed against children for their conduct in school. This is problematic, since the recent convergence of the juvenile and adult criminal justice systems has led to harsher sentencing of youth who commit crimes. There has been a significant increase in juvenile cases transferred to adult courts since 1985 (Salekin, 2002), and from 1989 to 2005, more juveniles were rendered eligible for the death penalty.

The authors do not refute the seriousness of juvenile crime or the need to develop innovative approaches to deal with this social problem. Likewise, the authors do not argue that chronic juvenile offenders who commit serious crime should suffer no serious consequences for their actions. We agree with Scott and Grisso (1997) that youth must be punished but that youth in and of itself is a mitigating factor that should reduce culpability. After witnessing devastating school shootings in the mass media, and the increased ease with which youth are able to access guns, the public deservingly feels like a new type of threat to society has arisen. Yet, such public fear should not provoke irrational response. Criminal policy for public protection should be grounded in reality, not in exaggerated depictions. Public safety must be balanced with the facilitation of youth's rehabilitation and their successful transition to adulthood. It is our social responsibility to provide a hopeful future to youth, even to those who have committed a dangerous act and may not be clearly amenable to treatment.

FUTURE DIRECTIONS

Heightened fears of social disorder have masked a rational, objective analysis to the problem of youth crime and aggression and stimulated an ill-advised adoption of exceptionally punitive criminal sanctions and school disciplinary policies for youth that are not evidence-based. The future welfare of children and protection of society depends on our ability to discontinue overreacting to threats, exaggerated media reports, and political conveniences. A well-informed approach that is based in empirical evidence is clearly needed to combat youth violence.

SUGGESTIONS FOR SCHOOL SAFETY

Prevention Strategies

- Given the research that suggests that prevention programs are most effective at reducing youth violence and crime, resources should be focused on school-based prevention programs that target children in early primary grades before they come into contact with the law, with the goal of reducing aggression at an earlier age (Salekin, 2002).

- Given that the majority of school violence involves interpersonal disputes or bullying (APCRP, 2000), schools should make efforts to provide training to teachers and administrators regarding conflict resolution so that they may provide social competence instruction and counseling to students (Cornell, 1999).

- School safety resources should be redirected to the group identified as being at the highest risk. Given that prediction of dangerousness on an individualized basis is often inaccurate and has a high likelihood of identifying false positives, some scholars suggest the use of ongoing risk assessment as an alternative (Mulvey & Cauffman, 2001). Individuals can be grouped into low- or high-risk status and then monitored for transitions that may further increase the likelihood of violence. For example, the FBI has shown that in almost every school shooting case, the perpetrators made threats of violence to other students shortly before committing the crimes (Cornell, 2003).

Intervention Strategies

- In the instances in which monitoring at-risk youth is unsuccessful at preventing threat, schools should consider alternative measures to zero tolerance responses. Schools should employ solutions to school violence that concentrate on developing environments that promote greater connections between students and adults (APCRP, 2000). For example, the FBI recommended student threat assessments, which are standard, practical guidelines for schools to follow to evaluate threats and respond with appropriate interventions, as a viable risk reduction strategy. Guidelines suggest forming threat assessment teams made up of school resource officers, administrators, and school psychologists and counselors, who should interview students who make threats and then consult with each other to make decisions about ways to prevent violence after threats have been made. Teams are advised to consider individual circumstances of potentially dangerous students, including intent and accessibility to weapons. Although most studies had considerable limitations, research has demonstrated the efficacy of such assessment measures in field tests involving 35 schools; many of the students who made threats in these schools exhibited improved behavior at school (Cornell, 2003).

- In the instances in which youth are sentenced to time in correctional and detention facilities for criminal behavior, the school re-enrollment transition should be a smooth one. In a recent *Summary of Best Practices in School Reentry for Incarcerated Youth Returning Home,* Geddes and Keenan (2004) highlight four mechanistic principles that facilitate such transition and provide examples of programs, laws, and regulations that adhere to them. The principles are: (1) inter-agency and community cooperation/clear roles and responsibilities; (2) youth and family involvement; (3) speedy placement; and (4) appropriate placement, which involves insuring that the student is returning to an appropriate education placement in the least restrictive environment. "Continuity is vital, and frustration must be reduced to a minimum. There should be individualized consideration of each student's placement based on the presumption that a young person has been rehabilitated, not automatic placement in alternative programs for students with discipline problems." (p.3)

Research

- Additional financial support should be provided for scientifically rigorous investigation of zero tolerance policies and other types of school safety procedures, alternative school programs, and student threats and threat assessment responses, guidelines, and policies (Cornell, 2001).

Suggestions for Reformations in Juvenile Courts

The ideals of the original juvenile court movement were unfulfilled; reduction in crime and recidivism was not achieved, courts often did not have adequate resources, and some judges were left to rule in an arbitrary fashion. The tradeoff between due process rights and more individualized, treatment-oriented responses was highlighted, and many felt that neither was achieved (Levine & Levine, 1992). As a result, a juvenile justice system more like the adversarial adult system is currently in place, although it is just as ineffective and unsuccessful in achieving protection for either youth or the public at large. These transformations have iterated society's loss of hope for a viable, effective solution to balance youth's need for guidance and rehabilitation and society's need for protection. We urge policymakers and public officials alike to work to develop a renewed commitment to a justice system that may improve opportunity for delinquent youth as well as reduce youth crime.

- We agree with Steinberg & Scott (2003) that policymakers and public officials should renew commitment to a categorical approach in which most youth are dealt with in a separate justice system. The juvenile justice system should maintain rehabilitation as a central aim and prohibit the incarceration of minors in adult facilities. The incarceration of juveniles as adults should be reserved for those who are truly unamenable to treatment and inflict large amounts of social harm, a very narrow category of repeat offenders who provide strong indications of re-offending despite prolonged exposure to ecological prevention and intervention models mentioned above (Slobogin, Fondacaro, & Woolard, 1999). Even in these instances, juveniles should not be incarcerated indefinitely, and precautions should be taken to protect minors from the iatrogenic effects of incarceration in adult prisons. A focus on the categorical approach offers practical advantages over one in which a single individualized assessment must be utilized, given that we cannot reliably detect dangerousness or psychosocial immaturity on an individualized basis; moreover, although there are variations in maturity within the age cohort of adolescence, the 18 year age boundary can be applied confidently to most individuals in the group (Steinberg & Scott, 2003).

- Courts are faced with innumerable psychological assumptions about the immaturity and vulnerability of minors. Social science should inform decisions about differences between children, adolescents, and adults and how these differences may affect treatment of adjudicated youth. In particular, there is need for studies that link developmental changes in decision-making to changes in brain structure and function, and more research that examines age differences in decision-making under ecologically valid contexts (Steinberg & Scott, 2003).
- Similarly, empirical studies about the efficacy of punitive sanctions such as adult transfers, sentences of life without parole, and municipal ordinances to curtail juvenile crime may help courts decide whether these approaches are designed appropriately to address social problems.

CONCLUSIONS

In this chapter, we strongly suggest that public policies of the past few decades have had the effect of criminalizing childhood. They appear to have been developed as a result of fear of youth exacerbated by exaggerated attention from the public media to descriptions of heinous juvenile crimes and school shootings. By blaming the youth themselves, we do not have to address many flaws in society, such as an increasing number of children raised in poverty (Males, 1996), vast discrepancies in resources allocated to schools in higher socioeconomic status communities, which results in less qualified teachers in the poorer school systems (Tuerk, 2005), mass culture that glorifies violence and guns, and materialism. Moreover, we focus the blame on poor and minority youth and their families, and assume that these policies will not affect our children. This is wrong. Criminalizing childhood by introducing zero tolerance policies in the schools and treating youth as adults in our justice system when they commit crime, may make us feel safer but it may also deprive them of the opportunity to make mistakes without suffering undue stigma and punishment that may fit the crime but not the child.

REFERENCES

Advancement Project and the Civil Rights Project (APCRP). (2000, June 21). *Opportunities suspended: The devastating consequences of zero tolerance and school discipline policies.* Boston: Harvard Civil Rights Project, Accessed September 12, 2005 from http://www.civilrightsproject.harvard.edu/research/discipline/opport_suspended.php.

Amnesty International. (2004, September 14). *Stop child executions! Ending the death penalty for child offenders.* Accessed September 12, 2005 from http://www.amnestyusa.org/abolish/juveniles/.

Bellotti v. Baird, 443 U.S. 622 (1979).

Bishop, D., Frazier, C., Lanza-Kaduce, L., & Winner, L. (1996). The transfer of juveniles to criminal court: Does it make a difference? *Crime and Delinquency, 35,* 179–201.

Britner, P. A., LaFleur, S. J., & Whitehead, A. J. (1998). Juvenile right to counsel: A national comparison of state legal codes. *American Journal of Criminal Law, 23,* 611–632.

Cauffman, E., & Steinberg, L. (2000). (Im)maturity of judgment in adolescence: Why adolescents may be less culpable than adults. *Behavioral Sciences & the Law, 18,* 1–21.

Center on Juvenile and Criminal Justice. (1998). School house hype: The school shootings, and the real risk kids face in America. Washington, DC: Accessed September 12, 2005 from http://www.cjcj.org/pubs/shooting/shootings.html.

Center on Juvenile and Criminal Justice. (2000). School house hype: Two years later. Washington, DC: Accessed September 12, 2005 from http://www.cjcj.org/pubs/schoolhouse/shh2pr.html.

Cornell, D. G. (1999, May 13). *Psychology of the school shootings.* Testimony presented at the House Judiciary Committee, Oversight Hearing to Examine Youth Culture and Violence, Accessed September 12, 2005 from http://youthviolence.edschool.virginia.edu.

Cornell, D. G. (2001, March 13). *School violence fear versus facts.* Congressional briefing on understanding and preventing youth violence, Accessed September 12, 2005 from http://youthviolence.edschool.virginia.edu.

Cornell, D. G. (2003). Guidelines for responding to student threats of violence. *Journal of Educational Administration, 41,* 705–719.

Dean, C., & Reppucci, N. D. (1974). Juvenile correctional institutions. In D. Glaser (Ed.), *The handbook of criminology* (pp. 865–895). Chicago: Rand McNally.

Farrington, D. (1986). Age and crime. In M. Tonry & N. Morris (Eds.), *Crime and justice: An annual review of research* (pp. 189–217). Chicago: University of Chicago Press.

Federal Bureau of Investigation (FBI). (1996). *Uniform crime reports.* Washington, DC: U.S. Department of Justice.

Federal Bureau of Investigation (FBI). (1997). *Uniform crime reports.* Washington, DC: U.S. Department of Justice.

Federal Bureau of Investigation (FBI). (2003). *Uniform crime reports.* Washington, DC: U.S. Department of Justice.

Federal Gun-Free Schools Act, 20 U.S.C. 8921 (1994).

Feld, B.C. (1999). *Bad kids: Race and the transformation of the juvenile court.* New York: Oxford University Press.

Fried, C.S. (2001). Juvenile curfews: Are they an effective and constitutional means of combating juvenile violence? *Behavioral Sciences & the Law, 19*(1), 127–141.

Fried, C.S., & Reppucci, N.D. (2002). Youth violence: Correlates, interventions, and legal implications.. In B.L. Bottoms, , M.B. Kovera, & B.D. McAuliff (Eds.), *Children, social science, and the law* (pp. 233–269). Cambridge, England: Cambridge University Press.

Gardner, W. (1993). A life-span rational choice theory of risk taking. In N. Bell & R. Bell (Eds.), *Adolescent risk taking* (pp. 66–83). Newbury Park, CA: Sage.

Geddes, S., & Keenan, K. (2004, November). *A summary of best practices in school reentry for incarcerated youth returning home,* Report to Commonwealth of Virginia Board of Education by Just Children, Legal Aid Justice Center.

Gottfredson, M.R., & Hirschi, T. (1995). National crime control policies. *Society, 32,* 30–36.

Greenberger, E. (1982). Education and the acquisition of psychosocial maturity. In D. McClelland (Ed.), *The development of social maturity* (pp. 155–189). New York: Irvington.

Greene, A. (1986). Future-time perspective in adolescence: The present of things future revisited. *Journal of Youth and Adolescence, 15,* 99–113.

Hall, G.S. (1904). *Adolescence: Its psychology and its relations to physiology, anthropology, Sociology, Sex, Crime, Religion, and Education.* New York: Appleton.

Halpern-Felsher, B., & Cauffman, E. (2001). Costs and benefits of a decision: Decision-making competence in adolescents and adults. *Journal of Applied Developmental Psychology, 22,* 257–273.

Individuals with Disabilities Education Act, 20 U.S.C. 1400 (1997).

In re Gault, 387 U.S. 1 (1967).

Kachur, S.P., Stennies, G., Powell, K., Modzeleski, W., Stephens, R., Murphy, R., Kresnow, M., Sleet, D., & Lowry, R. (1996). School-associated deaths in the United States, 1992–1994. *Journal of the American Medical Association, 275,* 1729–1733.

Keating, D. (1990). Adolescent thinking. In S.S. Feldman & G.R. Elliot (Eds.), *At the threshold: The developing adolescent* (pp. 54–89). Cambridge, MA: Harvard University Press.

Keith, J., & McCray, A. (2002). Juvenile offenders with special needs: Critical issues and bleak outcomes. *Qualitative Studies in Education, 15,* 691–710.

Kent v. United States, 383 U.S. 541 (1966).

Levine, M., & Levine, A. (1992). *Helping children: A social history.* New York: Oxford University Press.

Lipsey, M., & Wilson, D. (1998). Effective intervention for serious juvenile offenders: A synthesis of research. In R. Loeber & D. Farrington (Eds.), *Serious and violent juvenile offenders: Risk factors and successful interventions* (pp. 313–345). Thousand Oaks, CA: Sage.

Lockett v. Ohio, 438 U.S. 586 (1978).

Males, M.A. (1996). *The scapegoat generation: America's war on adolescents.* Monroe, ME: Common Courage Press.

Manfredi, C.P. (1998). *The supreme court and juvenile justice.* Lawrence: University Press of Kansas.

Marketos, A.K. (1995). The constitutionality of juvenile curfews. *Juvenile and Family Court Journal, 46*(2), 17–30.

McCord, J., Widom, C.S., & Crowell, N.A. (Eds.). (2001). *Juvenile crime, juvenile justice.* Washington, DC: National Academy Press.

McDowall, D., Loftin, C., & Wiersema, B. (2000). The impact of youth curfew laws on juvenile crime rates. *Crime & Delinquency, 46,* 76–91.

McNulty, E.W. (1996). The transfer of juvenile offenders to adult court: Panacea or problem? *Law and Policy, 18,* 61–76.

Melton, G.B. (1983). Toward "personhood" for adolescents: Autonomy and privacy as values in public policy. *American Psychologist, 38,* 99–103.

Mnookin, R.H. (1980). Children's rights: Beyond kiddie libbers and child savers. *Journal of Clinical Child Psychology, 7*(3), 163–167.

Moffitt, T. (1993). Adolescence-limited and life-course-persistent antisocial behavior: A developmental taxonomy. *Psychological Review, 100,* 674–701.

Mulvey, E.P., & Cauffman, E. (2001). The inherent limits of predicting school violence. *American Psychologist, 56*(10), 797–802.

National Crime Victimization Survey (NCVS). (2003). Bureau of Justice Statistics, U.S. Department of Justice. Accessed September 12, 2005 from http://youth-violence.edschool.virginia.edu/violence-in-schools/national-statistics.html.

National School Safety Center. (2003). *School associated violent deaths.* Westlake Village, CA: Accessed March 18, 2005 from www.nssc1.org.

National Vital Statistics Report. (1998). Washington, DC: National Center for Health Statistics.

Nettles, S., Mucherah, W., & Jones, D. (2000). Understanding resilience: The role of social resources. *Journal of Education for Students Placed at Risk, 5,* 47–60.

Noam, G., Winner, K., & Rhein, A. (1996). The Harvard Rally program and the prevention practitioner: Comprehensive, school-based intervention to support resiliency in at-risk adolescence. *Journal of Child and Youth Care Work, 1–1*(1), 36.

Nurmi, J. (1991). How do adolescents see their future? A review of the development of future orientation and planning. *Developmental Review, 11,* 1–59.

Parham v. J.R., 442 U.S. 584 (1979).

Podkopacz, M.R., & Feld, B.C. (1996). The end of the line: An empirical study of judicial waiver. *Journal of Criminal Law and Criminology, 86,* 449–492.

Reppucci, N.D. (1999). Adolescent development and juvenile justice. *American Journal of Community Psychology, 27*(3), 307–326.

Reppucci, N.D., & Crosby, C.A. (1993). Law, psychology, and children: Overarching issues. *Law & Human Behavior, 17,* 1–10.

Roper v. Simmons, 125 S.Ct. 1183 (2005).

Rose, L.C., & Gallup, A.M. (2000). The 32nd annual Phi Delta Kappa/Gallup poll of the public's attitudes toward the public schools. *Phi Delta Kappan, 86*(1), 41–52.

Rudman, C., Hartstone, E., Fagan, J., & Moore, M. (1986). Violent youth in adult court: Process and punishment. *Crime & Delinquency, 36,* 75–96.

Ruefle, W., & Reynolds, K.M. (1995). Curfews and delinquency in major American cities. *Crime & Delinquency, 41*(3), 347–363.

Salekin, R.T. (2002). Juvenile transfer to adult court. In Bottoms, B.L., Kovera, M.B., & McAuliff, B.D. (Eds.), *Children, social science, and the law* (pp. 203–232). Cambridge, England: Cambridge University Press.

Schmidt, M.G., & Reppucci, N.D. (2002). Children's rights and capacities. In Bottoms, B.L., Kovera, M.B., & McAuliff, B.D. (Eds.), *Children, social science, and the law* (pp. 76–105). Cambridge, England: Cambridge University Press.

Scott, E., & Grisso, T. (1997). The evolution of adolescence: A developmental perspective on juvenile justice reform. *Journal of Criminal Law and Criminology, 88,* 137–189.

Scott, E., Reppucci, N., & Woolard, J. (1995). Evaluating adolescent decision making in legal contexts. *Law and Human Behavior, 19,* 221–244.

Sickmund, M., Snyder, H.N., & Poe-Yamagata, E. (1997). Juvenile offenders and victims: 1997 update on violence. Washington, DC: Office of Juvenile and Delinquency Prevention.

Singer, S.I., & McDowall, D. (1988). Criminalizing delinquency: The deterrent effects of the New York juvenile offender law. *Law and Society Review, 22,* 521–535.

Skiba, R., & Peterson, R. (1999). The dark side of zero tolerance: Can punishment lead to safe schools? *Phi Delta Kappan, 80*(5), 372–376.

Slobogin, C., Fondacaro, M.R., & Woolard, J. (1999). A prevention model of juvenile justice: The promise of *Kansas v. Hendricks* for children. *Wisconsin Law Review,* 185–226.

Snyder, H., & Sickmund, M. (1995). Juvenile offenders and victims: A focus on violence. U.S. Department of Justice, Office of Juvenile Justice and Delinquency Prevention.

Snyder, H., & Sickmund, M. (1999). Juvenile offenders and victims: 1999 national report. U.S. Department of Justice, Office of Juvenile Justice and Delinquency Prevention.

Stanford v. Kentucky, 492 U.S. 361 (1989).

Steinberg, L., & Cauffman, E. (1996). Maturity of judgment in adolescence: Psychosocial factors in adolescent decision-making. *Law and Human Behavior, 20,* 249–272.

Steinberg, L., & Scott, E. S. (2003). Less guilty by reason of adolescence: Developmental immaturity, diminished responsibility, and the juvenile death penalty. *American Psychologist, 58*(12), 1009–1018.

Steinberg, L., & Silverberg, S. (1986). The vicissitudes of autonomy in early adolescence. *Child Development, 57,* 841–851.

Streib, V. (2002). The juvenile death penalty today: Death sentences and executions for juvenile crimes, January 1, 1973–November 15, 2002. Unpublished report. Accessed September 12, 2005 from http://www.law.onu.edu/faculty/streib/juvdeath.pdf.

Tate, D. C., Reppucci, N. D., & Mulvey, E. P. (1995). Violent juvenile delinquents: Treatment effectiveness and implications for future directions. *American Psychologist, 50*(9), 777–781.

Thompson v. Oklahoma, 487 U.S. 815 (1988).

Tobin, T., & Sprague, J. (2000). Alternative education strategies: Reducing violence in school and the community. *Journal of Emotional and Behavioral Disorders, 8,* 177–186.

Torbet, P., Gable, R., Hurst, H., Montgomery, I., Szymanski, L., & Thomas, D. (1996). *State responses to serious and violent juvenile crime: Research report.* Washington, DC: U.S. Department of Justice, Office of Juvenile Justice and Delinquency Prevention.

Tuerk, P. W. (2005). Research in the high stakes era: Achievement, resources, and No Child Left Behind. *Psychological Science, 16(6),* 419–425.

Wilson, S. J., Lipsey, M. W., & Derzon, J. H. (2003). The effects of school-based intervention programs on aggressive behavior. *Journal of Consulting & Clinical Psychology, 71,* 136–149.

Wolfgang, M., Figlio, R., & Sellin, T. (1972). *Delinquency in a birth cohort.* Chicago: University of Chicago Press.

Youth Risk Behavior Survey. (2003). Washington, DC: National Center for Disease and Prevention and Health Promotion, Bureau of Justice Statistics, Accessed September 12, 2005 from http://youthviolence.edschool.virginia.edu/violence-in-schools/national-statistics.html.

Chapter 11

PATHWAYS OF RISK AGGREGATION FOR ALCOHOL USE DISORDERS

Hiram E. Fitzgerald and Robert A. Zucker

Work reported in this article was supported by NIAAA Grant R37 AA07065.

This chapter is an expanded version of the authors' article "Effets à court et á long terme de l'alcoolism parental sur les enfants" (Short- and long-term effects of parental alcohol use on children) *PRISME, 33,* 28–42.

Early human development is characterized by a sequence of dynamic and systemic reorganizations beginning at conception and continuing throughout postnatal development. These reorganizations occur at fairly well circumscribed intervals: 1–3 postnatal months (shift from external regulation to internal regulation); 7–9 months (emotional and cognitive reorganizations based on significant changes in memory processes); 12–14 months (transition to upright locomotion); 18–24 months (transition to language as the major form of communication); 5–7 years (transition from preschool to formal schooling); 9–14 years (changes associated with puberty, influence of peers, and the shift to "if-then" thinking), and 18–25 years (identity, independence, and the transition to adulthood). Each of these transitions involves biopsychosocial change processes and each is embedded within the context of the individual's experiential world. The experiential embeddedness of human development provides nearly unlimited contexts that can facilitate or interfere with progress toward healthy development. Perhaps the most significant context during the first 18 years of life is the family, and it is within the dynamics of family life that we have been studying etiologic factors that shape risk for alcohol use disorders (AUD), use of other drugs, and/or co-related developmental psychopathologies.

Alcoholism is the most common form of substance abuse in the United States, impacting about 6 million children, of whom about 2,250,000 are under the age of five (SAMSA, 1998). The median age of first use of alcohol is about age 14, and children who begin drinking earlier than the median are four times more likely to become alcohol dependent than are individuals who begin drinking at age 20 (Grant & Dawson, 1997). Although the age of first drink may occur as early as age 9 or 10 (Donovan et al., 2004), findings from the Michigan Longitudinal Study (MLS) suggest that the experiential determinants of onset, use, and abuse originate considerably earlier than that. Moreover, the determinants do not coalesce to form a single pathway resulting in alcohol abuse or alcohol dependence. On the contrary, because development is a dynamic process, the rich diversity of life experiences acts to create multiple pathways of development that begin to differentiate at conception and continue to do so throughout the life course (Fitzgerald, Puttler, Mun, & Zucker, 2000; Zucker, Fitzgerald, & Moses, 1995; Zucker, Chermack, & Curran, 2000).

The Michigan Longitudinal Study was designed to study the development of risk for alcoholism and problems associated with alcoholism, to specify the determinants of diverse pathways over the life course, and, based on knowledge gained from such study, to forge recommendations for prevention. In this chapter, we provide an overview of findings from the MLS, focusing on evidence that underlies the supposition that there are multiple pathways toward alcohol use disorders and that these pathways are constructed from dynamic relationships among risk and protective factors over the life course. One pathway is characterized by strong continuity from the preschool years into adolescence. Children traveling along this pathway evidence risky behaviors very early in development and are surrounded by rearing environments that maintain and solidify risky behavior throughout childhood and adolescence. Two other pathways reflect more discontinuous processes. These pathways are characterized by flow between risk and protective factors, suggesting that children traveling along these pathways have a higher probability of developmental outcomes that will not include substance use disorders as outcomes. Before addressing these issues, however, it will be useful to review some of the background knowledge related to the etiology of alcohol use disorders.

CAUSAL INFLUENCES ON ALCOHOLISM ETIOLOGY

When attempting to specify causal influences on the etiology of alcoholism, it is necessary to account for alcohol-specific and alcohol-nonspecific influences (Table 11.1). Alcohol-specific factors are those that selectively

Table 11.1

Family Risk Factors Affecting the Development of Psychopathology Among Children of Alcoholics (COAs) Compared with Children of Nonalcoholics[1]

Risk Factor	Research Findings
Alcohol-Specific Family Influences[2]	
Modeling of drinking behavior	COAs are more familiar with a wider range of alcoholic beverages at a younger age and develop alcohol-use schemas (i.e., experience-based beliefs) earlier.
Alcohol expectancies	COAs have more positive expectancies regarding the reinforcing value of alcohol (i.e., they are more likely to expect that alcohol will make them feel good).
Ethnicity and drinking practices	COAs from certain ethnic groups may be at increased risk for alcohol abuse because of the interaction between alcohol expectancies and ethnicity.
Alcohol-Nonspecific Family Influences[2]	
Parent psychopathology	Certain subgroups of COAs are raised in families in which parents have psychiatric diagnoses, such as antisocial personality disorder or depression, in addition to alcohol dependence. The comorbidity is related to increased risk.
Socioeconomic status (SES)	COAs whose parents have comorbid diagnoses are more likely to come from lower SES homes in which the families are exposed to financial stress.
General family psychopathology	Alcoholic families are characterized by low cohesion (i.e., little closeness among family members), high conflict, and poor problem-solving skills. COAs are more likely to come from broken homes.
Family aggression/violence	COAs may be more likely to be the targets of physical abuse and to witness family violence.
Parental cognitive impairment	COAs are more likely to be raised by parents with poorer cognitive abilities and in an environment lacking cognitive stimulation.

[1] Adapted from Ellis, D., Zucker, R. A., & Fitzgerald, H. E. (1997). The role of family influences in development and risk. *Alcohol, Health & Research World,* 21, 218–226. In the public domain.

[2] Alcohol-specific family influences selectively predict alcohol abuse and dependence, whereas alcohol-nonspecific family influences predict a variety of psychiatric problems, including alcoholism.

predict alcoholism, whereas alcohol-nonspecific factors are those that predict both alcoholism and other co-occurring types of psychopathology.

Alcohol-specific risk factors range from possible genetic contributions to risk, through prenatal exposure to alcohol, the development of positive (and negative) expectancies about alcohol, and the ease with which alcohol is available, both in the home and elsewhere. Nonspecific risk factors include family socioeconomic status (SES), parental education, parenting practices, and family aggression and conflict. When SES, parental education, and rearing practices are poor, and family aggression and conflict are high, risk for alcohol use disorders increases. It has not been definitively determined how specific and nonspecific factors interact to culminate in alcohol use disorders, but it is clear that these factors contribute to the variety of life-course pathways that result in alcohol dependence and abuse endpoints. The fact that children without positive family histories for alcoholism and without alcoholic parents also become alcohol abusive or dependent, only enriches the diversity of life events that contribute to risk and, therefore, make the task of identifying specific pathways even more difficult. In other words, why low-risk children develop alcohol use disorders is of equal interest to specifying the determinants of such disorders for high-risk children. The importance of specifying the protective factors in development, therefore, parallels the importance of determining explicit risk factors. The pathways of interest in this chapter are those descriptive of the children at highest risk for alcoholism and coactive developmental dysregulation and, therefore, are those most likely to reflect the contributions of genetics, the quality of the prenatal environment, and the early postnatal experiences that contribute to risk.

Biological Contributions to the Etiology of Alcohol Use Disorders

Evidence for the biological basis of alcohol use disorders is strong for both men and women (Heath, 1995). It is estimated that genetic effects and experiential effects each account for about 50 percent of the variance associated with risk for alcoholism. Until specific genes or combinations of genes can be identified, it is not possible to adequately evaluate the full genetic contributions to alcohol use disorders. Nevertheless, there are few investigators today who would argue against the weight of the evidence pointing to genetic components of the diathesis (hereditary predisposition to a disease) related to alcohol use disorders. Within this context, a number of investigators study regulatory functions on the premise that when there are problems with behavioral regulation (difficult temperament, undercontrolled aggressive behavior, depression), such behaviors are symptomatic of risk for the development of psychopathology, including substance use disorders.

One hypothesis is that sons of alcoholics find alcohol to be reinforcing because it heightens the pleasurable, excitatory aspects of initial intoxication but attenuates the feelings of anxiety and depression as blood alcohol levels drop (Newlin & Thompson, 1990). Other investigators suggest that the initial state of central nervous system disinhibition and hyperexcitability results in a number of externalizing disorders among children of alcoholics, and, for these children, the exposure to alcohol provides an initially powerful and immediate normalizing and rewarding effect (Begleiter & Porjesz, 1999); that is, it heightens pleasure. Moreover, because the rewarding effect is transitory, eventually larger and larger amounts of alcohol become necessary to generate and sustain the pleasurable effects. Thus, over time, one would expect that the individual would drink more frequently and in greater quantities in order to re-create the pleasurable effects of alcohol.

One problem with the central nervous system disinhibition/ hyperexcitability hypothesis is that not all children of alcoholics (COAs) develop alcohol use disorders, and not all children exposed to alcohol experience negative long-term effects. Some COAs may lack the central nervous system disinhibition/hyperexcitability vulnerability; others may have it, but have the good fortune to be reared in environments that do not exacerbate, and may even modulate, the initial disinhibitory proclivities. This potential for multiple outcomes would not exist if the etiology of the disorder was determined by a single causative factor. But it is not; in fact, alcoholism is what is in genetic parlance characterized as a complex genetic disorder, requiring multiple genes, operating in concert (or not) with multiple environments. Under conditions of adversity, such risk adds up and produces the problem endpoint. Under protected or nurturing environmental conditions, the risk is moderated. Thus, there is evidence that socioecononmic status influences the effects of alcohol exposure (Day, Richardson, Geva, & Robles, 1994). The combination of low socioeconomic status and heavy alcohol consumption is also associated with smoking, poor nutrition, poor health, increased stress, and use of other drugs. Thus, although alcohol consumption may be reinforcing (alcohol-specific effect), a wide range of non-alcohol–specific factors also play a key role in determining how a genetic susceptibility to alcohol use disorder may express itself over the life course. In short, even when considering etiologic factors related to alcoholism, life experiences matter.

Several investigators have suggested that difficult temperament, evident as early as in the first year of life, is an early indicator of a pathway to alcohol use disorders (Tarter & Vanyukov, 1994). In fact, the pathway may begin prenatally during the time when the central nervous system begins to differentiate and then develop toward its adult structure (Moffitt, 1993). These sensitive prenatal times involve the first and third trimesters when the fetus is particularly vulnerable to prenatal exposure to alcohol. From this perspective, difficult temperament (behavioral dysregulation) would be an early manifestation of genetic or congenital influences, and later manifestations would be in the form of behavioral problems during the toddler and preschool years, and conduct disorder problems in the elementary years. Thus, difficult temperament during infancy and high behavior problems during the preschool period reflect two components of an early forming pathway of risk for developmental psychopathology, including alcohol use disorders. That this pathway seems to be more easily organized in sons of antisocial alcoholic fathers is a reflection of the dynamic relationships among genetic, familial, and experiential forces in development (Zucker, Ellis, Fitzgerald, Bingham, & Sanford, 1996).

We have used the concept of "nesting structure" to guide studies of children who are exposed to risk factors that frequently co-occur. Nesting structure expresses the notion that alcohol-specific and alcohol-nonspecific factors become interconnected within the context of the etiology of risk. Thus, the risks confronting the children of alcoholics are not just related to familial alcoholism, but also to the other factor(s) that "nest" or co-occur with the alcoholism. For example, alcoholic families with co-occurring psychopathology increase the saturation of risk for alcoholism as well as the co-occurring psychopathology among children being reared in such families (Zucker et al., 2000), as might factors such as poor parental education, poor parenting practices, low socioeconomic status, or family conflict.

Evidence suggests that being reared in an alcoholic environment in which one or both parents are alcoholic with co-occurring antisocial personality disorder or depression increases the probability that children will be caught in a developmental pathway that will sustain problem behavior (Fitzgerald et al., 2000; Zucker, Fitzgerald, et al., 2000). But the heterogeneous nature of alcoholism suggests that gene-environment transactions not only structure strong continuity pathways but also structure discontinuous pathways. And, for alcohol researchers, the challenge is to discover which factors contribute to the development of which pathways. Our approach to the study of these pathways has been guided by a systemic risk aggregation, probabilistic model (Zucker, 1987) that allows for the simultaneous study of continuous and discontinuous pathways (Fitzgerald, Zucker, & Yang, 1995; Zucker, Fitzgerald, & Moses, 1995). What this means is that we recognize that the risk for alcohol use disorders may change over the life course and that identification of the factors that promote change (either toward or away from alcoholism) is important for developing effective prevention programs.

THE MICHIGAN LONGITUDINAL STUDY

The MLS has been studying 437 families, with the vast majority having been followed for almost 20 years, in order to isolate risk and protective factors that structure etiologic pathways leading children toward or away from alcoholism and co-occurring psychopathology (Zucker, 1987, 1990). As noted, the MLS is theoretically guided by a risk-cumulation model of aggressive behavior, negative affect, and alcohol involvement that is both probabilistic and dynamic and that, under cumulation conditions, leads to alcohol abuse or alcohol dependence, other drug abuse dependence, and/or co-occurring psychopathology (Fitzgerald, Davies, Zucker, & Klinger, 1994; Fitzgerald et al.,1995; Fitzgerald, Puttler, Mun, & Zucker, 2000; Zucker, Ellis, & Fitzgerald, 1994; Zucker, Fitzgerald, & Moses, 1995; Zucker, Chermack, & Curran, 2000). We recruited the initial families through the courts, searching for families where the father had been convicted of drunken driving with blood alcohol levels of .15 if a first conviction and .12 if a multiple conviction, and who was living in a nuclear family that included a son between the ages of three and five years old. Subsequently, a determination for inclusion was made based on evidence that the court-recruited man met criteria appropriate for an alcoholism diagnosis. As these families were enrolled into the study, we sought to match each family with one from the same community, where the father did not meet criteria for an alcoholism diagnosis. Along the way, some fathers in community-recruited families did meet criteria sufficient for an alcoholic diagnosis. Thus, we ended up with a community-based sample of families that were categorized on the basis of father's alcoholism diagnosis (alcoholic court-recruited, alcoholic community-recruited) or absence of alcoholism (nonalcohol community–recruited) (Zucker, Fitzgerald, et al., 2000).

Participating families agreed to a data collection protocol that consisted of extensive assessments, which would be repeated every three years (child ages 3–5, 6–8, 9–11, 12–14, 15–17, 18–21, and onward to 30–32). In order to establish onset of substance use/abuse, additional information from the children is collected beginning at age 11 and continuing annually through age 17.

As we began to analyze data from Wave 1 (when the children were 3–5), it became evident that our recruitment groupings were not those that reflected the risk cumulation models guiding our work. In short, early on we discovered the impact of alcohol-specific and alcohol-nonspecific influences. This led to a reclassification of the families on the basis of the presence or absence of a sustained lifetime history of antisocial behavior in the fathers. Men with a pattern of alcoholism in adulthood in combination with a lifetime history of antisocial behavior were categorized as antisocial alcoholics (AALs), and men without this sustained history were categorized as non-antisocial alcoholics (NAALs) (Zucker, 1987; Zucker et al., 1996). This classification strategy proved highly effective (Table 11.2). For example, AAL men are more likely to have had a history of childhood behavior problems, illegal behavior, arrests, chronic lying, relationship disturbances, failed relationships, depression and family violence, neuroticism, poor achievement and cognitive functioning, and low socioeconomic status (Fitzgerald et al., 1995; Ichiyama, Zucker, Fitzgerald, & Bingham, 1996; Zucker, Fitzgerald, et al., 2000) than are NAALs or men in the control group.

Subtyping on the basis of the father's co-occurring antisocial symptomatology also provided a strong marker for individual differences in parental risk and an effective indicator of family-level risk aggregation as well. Thus, alcoholic men not only have more other psychopathology, a poorer social adaptation (lower SES), and a denser family history of alcoholism, but they also are downwardly socially mobile from their own parents, they live in families with higher levels of family violence, and experience higher rates of separation and divorce. They also tend to marry women who have similar life histories (Ellis, Zucker, & Fitzgerald, 1997; Fitzgerald, Zucker, Puttler, Caplan, & Mun, 2000; Zucker et al., 1996). Thus, although father criteria were used to recruit and then to specify comparison groups, children are reared in parental environments that offer variation in exposure to parental risk factors. For example, nearly

Table 11.2

Characteristics of the Michigan Longitudinal Study Research Participant Groups Based on Paternal Diagnosis of Antisocial Personality Disorder and/or Alcohol Abuse or Dependence

Antisocial alcoholic (AAL)	Nonantisocial alcoholic (NAAL)	Nonantisocial/nonalcoholic (control)
Father alcoholic; mother commonly alcoholic	Father alcoholic; mother commonly nonalcoholic	Neither parent substance abusing/dependent
High lifetime antisocial behavior	Low or variable lifetime antisocial behavior	Low lifetime antisocial behavior
High parental psychopathology	Moderate parental psychopathology	Moderate to low parental psychopathology
High family history positive for alcoholism	Moderate family history positive for alcoholism	Low family history positive for alcoholism

one-third of the children of alcoholics in the MLS are exposed to two parents with alcohol abuse/dependence diagnoses, and nearly one-half are exposed to parents with some kind of co-occurring psychopathology in at least one parent (e.g., antisocial personality disorder or depression).

Impact of Paternal Alcoholism on Sons

Cross-sectional comparisons at Wave 1 (3–5 years) indicate that sons of male alcoholics have higher levels of hyperactivity, more negative mood, more problematic social relationships, greater deficits in cognitive functioning, higher levels of aggressive behavior, and earlier development of internal schemas about alcohol and other drugs than do boys from nonalcoholic families. Sons of alcoholics also score lower on measures of IQ and are more likely to have higher scores on indicators of impulsivity (Fitzgerald et al., 1993; Poon, Ellis, Fitzgerald, & Zucker, 2000). Negative parental characteristics exacerbate the appearance of child risk factors, such that sons reared in risky environments (heavy load of specific and nonspecific alcohol factors) have even more aggression, delinquent behavior, attention problems, depression, and social problems than do comparison boys.

Externalizing problems are of special interest because of the possibility that they are proxy indicators of later alcohol problems. We have suggested that as early as the preschool years, sons of alcoholics have organized a system of dysfunctional behaviors that seem to be symptomatic of co-occurring psychopathology (Fitzgerald, Puttler, Mun, & Zucker, 2000; Zucker, Fitzgerald, et al., 2000) and, in particular, seem to prime the preschooler for continued expression of dysfunctional behaviors well into the elementary and middle school years (Fitzgerald, Zucker, Puttler, Caplan, & Mun, 2000; Loukas, Fitzgerald, Zucker, & von Eye, 2001; Mun, Fitzgerald, Puttler, Zucker, & von Eye, 2001; Wong, Zucker, Puttler, & Fitzgerald, 1999).

Currently, it is not possible to isolate the unique contributions of genetic, biological, and psychological effects on these developmental outcomes. Nonetheless, findings from the MLS and from the broader literature on alcoholism support the conclusion that both alcohol-specific and alcohol-nonspecific factors are nested within families. In fact, the evidence suggests that in many families, nested risk factors are extremely dense (AAL families in the MLS) and elevate children's risks for a variety of poor outcomes. For example, family environments that are high in the negative expression of emotions and in spousal violence influence the link between child difficult temperament during the preschool years and child externalizing behaviors during the elementary years (Ellis et al., 1997;

Wong et al., 1999). A broad set of studies have documented that children's externalizing behaviors decrease over the elementary years as the effects of socialization and self-regulation begin to take hold. This normative decrease from preschool through the elementary years is evident among the children participating in the MLS as well. However, differences among children from AALs, NAALs, and the control group persist, such that children from AAL families continue to have higher rates of externalizing behavior problems than do children from NAAL or control families, and a higher proportion sustain clinical range scores (Mun et al., 2001; Wong et al., 1999). In addition, children of parents with multiple forms of psychopathology showed elevated levels of distraction and reactivity (Mun et al., 2001). The findings suggest that child temperamental characteristics play different roles in the development of behavior problems depending on the influence of other risk factors.

Differences in cognitive functioning between sons of alcoholics and sons of nonalcoholics are also evident in early childhood. Preschool-age sons of alcoholics were three times more likely to score less than 80 on an IQ test (impaired range). Moreover, these low scores cannot be attributed to the effects of Fetal Alcohol Syndrome because such children were screened out of the MLS during recruitment (Fitzgerald et al., 1993). When we compared parental IQ with that of their children, parental IQ predicted children's intellectual functioning, with verbal IQ particularly negatively affected in sons of antisocial alcoholics. Differences in academic achievement appeared as early as the first and second grades (Poon et al., 2000), with children of antisocial alcoholics scoring lower on the spelling and arithmetic scales of the Wide Range Achievement Test-Revised, and showing poorer abilities in abstract planning and attention. In addition, differences in levels of impulsivity between children from antisocial alcoholic families and the other groups were also present and were suggestive of specific impairments in the part of the brain known to be involved in higher mental processes, executive functioning, and behavioral regulation. In the effort to understand the relative influences of specific and nonspecific factors influencing alcohol use disorders, it is important to note that the effects of paternal alcoholism status still contributed to the child's intellectual functioning even after controlling for socioeconomic status, parental education, and parental IQ (Poon et al., 2000).

Does Biobehavioral Dysregulation Influence Regulatory Processes?

Evidence that we have found thus far clearly supports the critical influence of the rearing environment, parenting practices, family resources, and the presumed underlying diathesis on biobehavioral dysregulation among sons of alcoholics, and especially among sons of antisocial alcoholics. Another set of questions that we are examining concerns the extent to which individual dysregulation begins to regulate developmental processes. In other words, do characteristics of the individual (for example, difficult temperament, high levels of behavior problems, or behavioral inhibition) become causal influences on the rearing environment and parenting practices, such that disorganized behavior begins to influence or regulate the quality of parent-child interaction or peer relationships? What impact do the child's personal characteristics have on relationships with others in the context of high family conflict or parental psychopathology? And, conversely, how do these characteristics influence the child's characteristics?

MLS investigators found that the level of child behavior problems measured during the initial years of elementary school was most strongly predicted by the level of child behavior problems during the preschool period (Loukas, Fitzgerald, Zucker, & von Eye, 2001; Loukas, Piejak, Bingham, Fitzgerald, & Zucker, 2001). However, the child's behavior problems during preschool were not the only predictor of behavior problems during the elementary years. Family conflict was also related to more disruptive behaviors at school entry, and high levels of family conflict were related to slower rates of decline in child behavior problems over the elementary years (Loukas, Zucker, Fitzgerald, & Krull, 2003). When we added paternal psychopathology (antisocial personality disorder) to the mix, it strengthened the relationship between preschool-age behavior problems and school-age behavior problems. Several lines of research indicate that normatively disruptive behavior problems peak during the preschool years and then steadily decline through childhood. The analyses we have just reviewed indicate that factors such as family conflict and parental psychopathology act to maintain high levels of children's behavior problems when one would normally expect them to decline during the elementary years.

Is Behavioral Undercontrol Context Specific?

When studying the etiology of disorganized behavior, it is important to determine the extent to which the behaviors under investigation are context specific or can be generalized to multiple settings. This is important because if behavior problems only are evident in the home, it would suggest that family dynamics should be the focus of prevention or intervention efforts. However, if the behavior generalizes across contexts, then intervention efforts must be more complex and far-reaching. For children, school is the common out-of-home context that provides an opportunity to address the issue of context specificity. So, in the MLS, we ask teachers to provide information about children's school behavior and school achievement. The teachers are aware that the target children are participating in a study of family health, but they are not aware of any of the characteristics that are being studied, nor are they aware of any characteristics of the parents that led to their involvement in the study.

Teacher assessments support the context-general nature of children's problem behavior. First grade teachers differentiated children of AALs, NAALs, and controls on ratings of developmental status, suggesting that the children's behavior is not unique to their home environment. Although teacher ratings of child aggression, activity, likeability, and attractiveness did not significantly differentiate among the groups, in every instance, the means were in the expected direction, with children of AALs scoring lowest. When asked to project child performance in middle school, teachers projected the poorest school performance for children of AALs. Teachers also reported that AAL parents showed less interest in their children's school performance than NAAL parents or control-group parents (Fitzgerald, Davies, & Zucker, 2002). These results are especially interesting because the teachers are completely unaware of the study design and family groupings. Finally, teachers' ratings and perceptions of children's performance are supported by findings indicating that sons of AALs do more poorly on measures of academic achievement and intellectual functioning than do sons of NAALs or controls (Poon et al., 2000).

Mental Representations for Alcoholism and Co-occurring Psychopathology

Mental representations refer to the encoding of experience into memory, with the presumption that the events are encoded into long-term memory. Current evidence suggests that autobiographical memories begin to consolidate into long-term memory during the second year of life. Self-rehearsal and reminders from adults about experienced events help the child to consolidate events in long-term memory, but rehearsal also alters the event. Autobiographical memories are reconstructions of events and, as such, they are subject to embellishment early in the consolidation process. According to Howe and Courage (1997), autobiographical memory for events develops at the same time that children develop "a knowledge structure whose features serve to organize memories of experiences that happened to 'me'" (p. 499).

Our work with MLS children suggests that mental representations or schemas about alcohol begin to develop during the preschool years, and that such schemas include the contextual, motivational, affective, and normative aspects of use (Zucker & Fitzgerald, 1991; Zucker, Kincaid, Fitzgerald, & Bingham, 1995). Sons of male alcoholics are better able to identify specific alcoholic beverages, to correctly identify a larger number of alcoholic beverages, and are more likely to have cognitive schemas that include alcohol consumption as an attribute associated with adult male roles than are sons of nonalcoholics. In addition, preschool-age sons of male alcoholics have mental representations of their fathers that included drinking as part of the father role (Zucker et al., 1995).

In early childhood, the emphasis on mental representations has been two-fold: development of mental representations of attachment objects in children (the initial love objects in the child's life) and the influence of such representations on one's parenting abilities. The representations of adults who have unresolved conflicts with their parents subsequently impact their parenting abilities. Thus, memory for familiar events during early development (mother-infant or father-infant relationships) is related to the development of a working model of self and relationships that is hypothesized to carry over into adulthood and to be evoked when the adult is placed in the parenting context. This work is related to common beliefs that we tend to parent our children more similarly to the ways we were parented rather than in dramatically different ways. Davidson (1996) reports that children remember events that are consistent with gender role stereotypes better than those that are inconsistent, and, remarkably, when events are not consistent with stereotypes, preschool-age children distort the information to make it consistent. Moreover, this is one instance in which boys seem to organize their mental representations of mother-child and father-child relationships more crisply than do girls.

Living with an alcoholic parent provides numerous occasions to model sex-role behavior and to construct a working model of what it is to be a father, mother, or spouse. Thus, when considered in the context of a broader developmental literature, alcohol expectancies of preschool-age children are extremely complex organizational structures. Moreover, they are unique to the individual child's experiences, the autobiographical structures of mind or what memory researchers refer to as autobiographical memory (Schneider & Bjorklund, 1998). The question is, do these early mental structures strengthen over the elementary years so that when children transition to adolescence, the mental models or expectancies related to alcohol and interpersonal relationships play a regulatory role in decisions about drinking, smoking, sexual activity, or other risky behaviors?

Consider, for example, recent findings from studies of the early years of life that are related to the development for memory of familiar events. An explicit assumption of attachment theory (Karlen, 1996) is that memory for familiar events (mother-infant interactions) is related to the development of a working model of self as well as a working model for relationships (Verschuren, Marcven, & Schoefs, 1996). The weight of this literature suggests that children as young as three years of age already have working models or schemas about familiar events. Autobiographical memories are only partially based on experience, however, because they are constructed from experience and are influenced by exposure to others' constructions of experience, particularly those of parents (Schneider & Bjorklund, 1998). Mothers who elaborate their stories and challenge their toddlers with high rates of memory questions tend to have toddlers with richer autobiographical memories (Harley & Reese, 1999). Toddlers who were developmentally more advanced in self-recognition also tended to have richer autobiographical memories of shared events.

Children are able to recall unpleasant events as well as they are able to recall pleasant ones (Merritt, Ornstein, & Spiker, 1994). Although issues related to post-traumatic stress disorder or reactive attachment disorder (Zeanah et al., 1999) do not appear in the alcoholism literature, they seem entirely consistent with the notion that highly conflictual rearing environments can have a powerful effect on the autobiographic events children experience and construct over time. Conway and Pleydell-Pearce (2000) suggest that event-specific knowledge related to traumatic experiences is automatically encoded into long-term memory. Traumatic memories often trigger a stress response that increases glucosteroid release, which in turn has a negative effect on the hippocampus and medial temporal lobe networks (Markowitsch, Thiel, Kessler, von Stockhausen, & Heiss, 1997). The hippocampus is a brain structure that plays a key role in memory processes as well as the regulation of stress. The hippocampus and related limbic structures of the medial temporal lobe mature relatively early in postnatal life and are involved in the development of explicit memory (Nelson, 1995), a component of memory that seems to reach its near-adult level by the preschool years. Thus, damage to the hippocampus and the neural networks to which it is linked, would have direct effects on impulse control and self-regulation of behavior.

Living in a family with an alcoholic parent with or without coactive other psychopathology presents numerous occasions to experience the events of drinking, parenting behavior, and marital relationships. It seems reasonable therefore, to link the literature on the emergence of children's memory for familiar events, including the affective load carried by these events, with studies of alcohol schemas in preschool-age children. This linkage suggests a model of early alcohol schema formation in children that develops in concert with other developmental processes, including emotional differentiation, self-regulation, interpersonal dynamics, social behavior, and motivation forces involving beliefs, wants, and desires. If schemas include multiple components of risk, it heightens the risk that alcohol use disorders will be one possible endpoint on the developmental pathways that unfold.

A Person-centered Approach to Risk and Resilience

Recently, we have structured models to assess etiologic issues related to risk and resilience, where resilience is defined as a successful adaptation despite adversity (Zucker, Wong, Puttler, & Fitzgerald, 2003). Our interest was to identify both individual characteristics and aspects of the rearing environment that relate to positive outcomes (McCord, 1988; Werner, 1986), particularly the impact of the mother-child relationship during the early years. Zucker and his colleagues developed an adversity index that is a summative parental psychopathology measure taking into account both the currency and the severity of alcohol use disorder, as well as the presence or absence of parental antisocial behavior. This approach led to the characterization of four types of children: *resilient* children were defined as those with high adaptation in the context of high adversity;

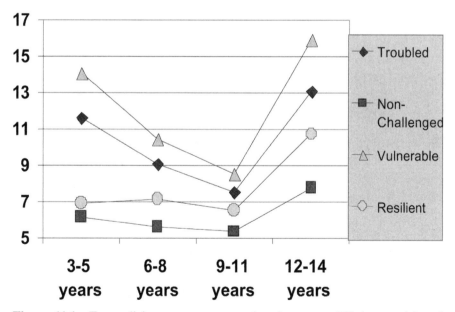

Figure 11.1 Externalizing symptoms over time in groups differing on risk and adversity. Source: p. 88 in Zucker, R. A., Wong, M. M., Puttler, L., & Fitzgerald, H. E. (2003). Resilience and vulnerability among sons of alcoholics: Relationship to developmental outcomes between early childhood and adolescence. In S. Luthar (Ed.), *Resilience and vulnerability: Adaptation in the context of childhood adversities.* New York: Cambridge University Press. Reprinted with permission.

nonchallenged children were defined as having normal adaptation under conditions of low adversity; *vulnerable* children experienced low adaptation (high psychopathology) under conditions of high family adversity; *troubled* children experienced high psychopathology under conditions of low adversity, indicating that they have poor behavioral adaptation even without significant family adversity (see Zucker et al., 2003).

Nonchallenged children had the lowest level of externalizing behavior followed, in order, by the resilient, troubled, and vulnerable children (Figure 11.1). At all ages, vulnerable children had the highest level of externalizing behavior and were significantly different from the least challenged group at all ages. Although resilient children were not different from their nonchallenged peers as preschoolers, they showed a small but reliable higher level of externalizing behavior as they grew older.

Figure 11.2 shows that the nonchallenged children had the lowest levels of internalizing problems, followed by the resilient children. During preschool and the early elementary years, nonchallenged and resilient children had fewer internalizing symptoms than either vulnerable or troubled children, although this pattern changes around puberty. By early adolescence, the nonchallenged group is significantly lower than all other groups. Thus, by early adolescence, vulnerable children are at highest risk, the challenged children are at lowest risk, and the resilient

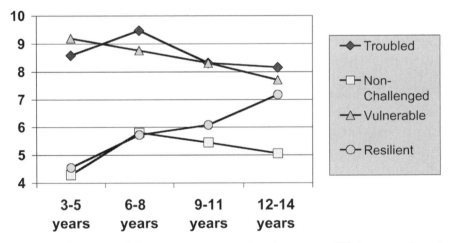

Figure 11.2 Internalizing symptoms over time in groups differing on risk and adversity. Source: p. 88 in Zucker, R. A., Wong, M. M., Puttler, L., & Fitzgerald, H. E. (2003). Resilience and vulnerability among sons of alcoholics: Relationship to developmental outcomes between early childhood and adolescence. In S. Luthar (Ed.), *Resilience and vulnerability: Adaptation in the context of childhood adversities.* New York: Cambridge University Press. Reprinted with permission.

children are at intermediary risk, particularly because of the increase in internalizing symptoms during puberty. Whether this increase is a transitory correlate of puberty or will reflect the pre- and post-pubescent linkages between serotonin and child aggression reported by Twitchell and colleagues (2000) remains to be determined. Nevertheless, with the exception of internalizing symptoms among resilient children, these findings support a pattern of stability of developmental pathways over a 10-year time period, irrespective of the challenge of family adversity. In that regard, the person-centered approach provides support for a set of diatheses that remain stable in the face of substantial differences in rearing environments.

CONCLUSIONS

Our work to date provides support for three hypothesized developmental pathways leading to alcohol use disorders and/or coactive psychopathology. One pathway (Fitzgerald, Puttler, Mun, & Zucker, 2000) describes strong continuity across at least a 15-year span, and it reflects the early emergence of maladaptive behavior that is supported by familial, neighborhood, and peer maintenance structures sufficient to organize biobehavioral dysregulation as a life-course pathway (Table 11.3). This pathway consists of high biobehavioral dysregulation during preschool (difficult temperament, externalizing behavior, poor cognitive functioning) that is maintained in the elementary years and expressed in adolescence by early-onset drinking, smoking, and active sexual behavior, poor school performance, and involvement with the criminal justice system (Mayzer, Puttler, Wong, Fitzgerald, & Zucker, 2003). The other two pathways are marked by greater discontinuity, with strong individual differences and greater heterogeneity in both risk and protective factors (Zucker, Chermack, & Curran, 2000; Zucker, 2003). As indicated in Table 11.4, the preschool and childhood periods for children on these pathways are essentially identical. It is during middle childhood that differentiation begins, as family disorganization, conflict, unemployment, and, perhaps, divorce increases. Discontinuity Pathway I adolescents are more likely to participate in minor delinquency and have more parent relationship problems than are Pathway II adolescents. In addition, they are more likely to be involved with deviant peer networks and have more internalizing problems than are children tracking on Discontinuity Pathway II.

Children reared by alcoholic parents, especially those with co-occurring psychopathology, are at risk for dysfunctions involving behavioral and affect self-regulation, interpersonal relationships, cognitive functioning, and value structures. Over the course of development, many children

Table 11.3
Risk Over Time: The Continuity Pathway

Preschool
    Externalizing behavior problems, social withdrawal, poor school readiness.
Childhood
    Behavior problems, oppositional behavior, impulsivity, social withdrawal, poor school performance.
Late middle childhood
    Family disorganization (divorce/separation, loss of job, health or social problems of other family member); poor parent monitoring.
Adolescence
    Earlier onset of alcohol and other drug involvement, heavier alcohol and other drug problems, delinquency, depression.
Adulthood
    Antisocial personality disorder, mood disorder, substance abuse disorder.

Adapted from Fitzgerald, Zucker, Puttler, Caplan, & Mun (2000).

Table 11.4
Two Discontinuity Pathways Suggesting Differentiation Occurring During the Transition from Elementary to Middle School

Discontinuity Pathway I	*Discontinuity Pathway II*
Preschool	
School readiness, behavior within normal limits, adaptive temperament.	School readiness, behavior within normal, limits, adaptive temperament.
Childhood	
Good school adaptation and performance; good friendship network.	Good school adaptation and performance; good friendship network.
Late middle childhood	
Family disorganization (divorce/ separation, loss of job, health or social problems of other family member); poor parent monitoring; shift in more deviant peer network; increasing emergence of externalizing behavior, developing pattern of internalizing problems.	Family disorganization (divorce/separation, loss of job, health or social problems of other family member) shift in peer network; increasing emergence of externalizing behavior.
Adolescence	
Alcohol and other drug involvement, minor delinquency. Poor or adverse outsider response or parent response; undependability of both parents, less available prosocial network.	Alcohol and other drug involvement, Parent or outsider response and/or clinical course.

Adapted from Zucker, Chermack, & Curran (2000) and Zucker (2003).

encounter what one might refer to as a set of naturally occurring protective factors. A child's life course might bring her or him into contact with a teacher, coach, minister, youth volunteer, or Big Brother or Big Sister, who provides a contrast for the child's existing schema for adults and facilitates a reorganization of that schema. Other children are so surrounded by dysfunction that even naturally occurring resilience opportunities cannot break into the child's developmental pathway. The long-term outcome, therefore, is the construction of a developmental trajectory that resists change and moves the child on a pathway leading to substance abuse and co-occurring psychopathology. Moreover, the more the child moves along this trajectory, the more he or she becomes an active agent in generating maintenance structures though such activities as peer selection, school dropout, drinking, and delinquent behavior. The ultimate challenge facing society will be to translate knowledge of etiologic pathways into effective preventive-intervention programs that are tailor-made to the child's developmental situation.

REFERENCES

Begleiter, H., & Porjesz, B. (1999). What is inherited in the predisposition toward alcoholism? A proposed model. *Alcoholism: Clinical and Experimental Research, 23,* 1125–1135.

Conway, M.A., & Pleydell-Pearce, C. (2000). The construction of autobiographic memories in the self-memory system. *Psychological Review, 107,* 261–288.

Day, N.L., Richardson, G.A., Geva, D. & Robles, N. (1994). Alcohol, marijuana, and tobacco: Effects of prenatal exposure on offspring growth and morphology at age six. *Alcoholism: Clinical and Experimental Research, 18,* 786–794.

Davidson, D. (1996). The role of schemata in children's memory. In H. Reese (Ed.), *Advances in child development and behavior* (Vol. 26, pp. 35–58). New York: Academic Press.

Donovan, J.E., Leech, S.L., Zucker, R.A., Loveland-Cherry, C.J., Jester, J.M., Fitzgerald, H.E., Puttler, L.I., Wong, M.M., & Looman, W.S. (2004). Really underage drinkers: Alcohol use among elementary students. *Alcoholism: Clinical and Experimental Research, 28,* 341–349.

Ellis, D.A., Zucker, R.A., & Fitzgerald, H.E. (1997). The role of family influences in development and risk. *Alcohol Health & Research World, 21,* 218–225.

Fitzgerald, H.E., Davies, W.H., & Zucker, R.A. (Eds.). (2002). Growing up in an alcoholic family: Structuring pathways for risk aggregation and theory-driven intervention. In R. MacMahon & R. deV. Peters (Eds.), *30th Banff Conference on Behaviour Science, Children of disordered parents* (pp. 127–146). Boston: Kluwer.

Fitzgerald, H.E., Davies, W.H., Zucker, R.A., & Klinger, M. (1994). Developmental systems theory and substance abuse: A conceptual and methodological framework for analyzing patterns of variation in families. In L. L'Abate (Ed.), *Handbook of developmental family psychology and psychopathology* (pp. 350–372). New York: Wiley.

Fitzgerald, H.E., Puttler, L.I., Mun, E-Y., & Zucker, R.A. (2000). Prenatal and postnatal exposure to parental alcohol use and abuse. In J.D. Osofsky & H.E. Fitzgerald (Eds.), *WAIMH Handbook of infant mental health: Vol. 4. Infant mental health in groups at high risk* (pp. 126–159). New York: Wiley.

Fitzgerald, H.E., Sullivan, L.A., Ham, H.P., Zucker, R.A., Bruckel, S., & Schneider, A.M. (1993). Predictors of behavioral problems in three-year-old sons of alcoholics: Early evidence for onset of risk. *Child Development, 64,* 110–123.

Fitzgerald, H.E., Zucker, R.A., Puttler, L.I., Caplan, H.M., & Mun, E.-Y. (2000). Alcohol abuse/dependence in women and girls: Aetiology, course, and subtype variations. *Alcoscope: International Review of Alcohol Management, 3*(1), 6–10.

Fitzgerald, H.E., Zucker, R.A., & Yang, H-Y. (1995). Developmental systems theory and alcoholism: Analyzing patterns of variation in high risk families. *Psychology of Addictive Behaviors, 9,* 8–22.

Grant, B.F., & Dawson, D.A. (1997). Age of onset of alcohol use and its association with DSM-IV alcohol abuse and dependence: Results from the National Longitudinal Alcohol Epidemiologic Survey. *Journal of Substance Abuse, 9,* 103–110.

Harley, K., & Reese, E. (1999). Origins of autobiographical memory. *Developmental Psychology, 35,* 1338–1348.

Heath, A.C. (1995). Genetic influences on alcoholism risk: A review of adoption and twin studies. *Alcohol Health and Research World, 19,* 166–171.

Howe, M.L., & Courage, M.L. (1997). The emergence and early development of autobiographical memory. *Psychological Review, 104,* 499–523.

Ichiyama, M.A., Zucker, R.A., Fitzgerald, H.E., & Bingham, C.R. (1996). Articulating subtype differences in self and relational experience among alcoholic men via structural analysis of social behavior. *Journal of Consulting and Clinical Psychology, 64,* 1245–1254.

Karlen, L-R. (1996). Attachment relationships among children with aggressive behavior problems: The role of disorganized early attachment patterns. *Journal of Consulting and Clinical Psychology, 64,* 64–73.

Loukas, A., Fitzgerald, H.E., Zucker, R.A., & von Eye, A. (2001). Alcohol problems and antisocial behavior: Relations to externalizing behavior problems among young sons. *Journal of Abnormal Child Psychology, 29,* 91–106.

Loukas, A., Piejak, L.A., Bingham, C.R., Fitzgerald, H.E., & Zucker, R.A. (2001). Parental distress as a mediator of child problem outcomes in alcoholic families. *Family Relations: Interdisciplinary Journal of Family Studies, 50,* 293–301.

Loukas, A., Zucker, R.A., Fitzgerald, H.E., & Krull, J. (2003). Developmental trajectories of disruptive behavior problems among sons of alcoholics: Effects of parent psychopathology, family conflict, and child under control. *Journal of Abnormal Psychology, 112,* 119–131.

Markowitsch, H.J., Thiel, A., Kessler, J., von Stockhausen, H.M., & Heiss, W.D. (1997). Ecphorising semi-conscious episodic information via the right temporalpolar cortex: A PET study. *Neurocase, 3,* 445–449.

Mayzer, R., Puttler, L.I., Wong, M.M., Fitzgerald, H.E., & Zucker, R.A. (2003). Developmental constancy of social misbehavior from early childhood to adolescence as a predictor of early onset of alcohol use. (Abstract). *Alcoholism: Clinical and Experimental Research Supplement, 27,* 65A.

McCord, J. (1988). Identifying developmental paradigms leading to alcoholism. *Journal of Studies on Alcohol, 49,* 357–362.

Merritt, K.A., Ornstein, P.A., & Spiker, B. (1994). Children's memory for a salient medical procedure: Implications for testimony. *Pediatrics, 94,* 17–23.

Moffitt, T.E. (1993). Adolescence-limited and life-course persistent antisocial behavior: A developmental taxonomy. *Psychological Review, 100,* 674–701.

Mun, E-Y., Fitzgerald, H.E., Puttler, L.I., Zucker, R.A., & von Eye, A. (2001). Temperamental characteristics as predictors of externalizing and internalizing child behavior problems in the contexts of high and low parental psychopathology. *Infant Mental Health Journal. 22,* 393–415.

Nelson, C.A. (1995). The ontogeny of human memory: A cognitive neuroscience perspective. *Developmental Psychology, 31,* 723–738.

Newlin, D.B., & Thompson, J.B. (1990). Alcohol challenge with sons of alcoholics: A critical review and analysis. *Psychological Bulletin, 108,* 383–402.

Poon, E., Ellis, D.A., Fitzgerald, H.E., & Zucker, R.A. (2000). Cognitive functioning of sons of alcoholics during the early elementary school years: Differences related to subtypes of familial alcoholism. *Alcoholism: Clinical and Experimental Research, 23,* 1020–1027.

SAMSA. (1998). Preliminary results from the 1997 National Household Survey on Drug Abuse (DHHS Publications Document No. SMA 98–3251). Rockville, MD.

Schneider, W., & Bjorklund, D.F. (1998). Memory. In D. Kuhn & R.S. Siegler (Eds.), *Handbook of child psychology: Vol. 2. Cognition, perception, and language* (pp. 467–521). New York: Wiley.

Tarter, R.E., & Vanyukov, M. (1994). Alcoholism: A developmental disorder. *Journal of Consulting and Clinical Psychology, 62,* 1096–1107.

Twitchell, G.R., Hanna, G.L., Cook, E.H., Fitzgerald. H.E., & Zucker, R.A. (2000). Serotonergic function, behavioral disinhibition, and negative affect in children of alcoholics: The moderating effects of puberty. *Alcoholism: Clinical and Experimental Research, 24,* 972–979.

Verschuren, K., Marcven, A., & Schoefs, V. (1996). The internal working model of the self: Attachment and competence in five year olds. *Child Development, 67,* 2493–2511.

Werner, E.E. (1986). Resilient offspring of alcoholics: A longitudinal study from birth to age 18. *Journal of Studies on Alcohol, 47,* 34–40.

Wong, M.M., Zucker, R.A., Puttler, L.I., & Fitzgerald, H.E. (1999). Heterogeneity of risk aggregation for alcohol problems between early and middle childhood. *Development and Psychopathology, 11,* 727–744.

Zeanah, C.H., Danis, B., Hirshberg, L., Benoit, D., Miller, D., & Heller, S.S. (1999). Disorganized attachment associated with partner violence: A research note. *Infant Mental Health Journal, 20,* 77–86.

Zucker, R.A. (1987). The four alcoholisms: A developmental account of the etiologic process. In P.C. Rivers (Ed.), *Nebraska symposium on motivation: Alcohol and addictive behaviors.* (Vol. 34, pp. 27–83). Lincoln: University of Nebraska Press.

Zucker, R.A. (1990). The concept of risk and the etiology of alcoholism: A probabilistic-developmental perspective. In D.J. Pittman & H. White (Eds.), *Society, culture and drinking patterns re-examined.* Piscataway, NJ: Rutgers Center of Alcohol Studies.

Zucker, R.A. (2003, October). Risk for addictive disorders early in life: New findings, new models of prevention. Invited address at the American Society for Addiction Medicine, Washington, DC.

Zucker, R.A., Chermack, S.T., & Curran, G.R. (2000). Alcoholism: A life span perspective on etiology and course. In A.J. Sameroff, M. Lewis, & S.M. Miller (Eds.), *Handbook of developmental psychopathology* (pp. 569–587). New York: Kluwer Academic/Plenum.

Zucker, R.A., Ellis, D.A., Fitzgerald, H.E. (1994). Developmental evidence for at least two alcoholisms: 1. Biopsycho social variation among pathways into symptomatic difficulty. Annals of the New York Academy of Science, 708, 134–146.

Zucker, R.A., Ellis, D.A., Fitzgerald, H.E., Bingham, C.R., & Sanford, K.P. (1996). Other evidence for at least two alcoholisms, II. Life course variation in antisociality and heterogeneity of alcoholic outcome. *Developmental Psychopathology, 8,* 831–848.

Zucker, R.A., & Fitzgerald, H.E. (1991). Early developmental factors and risk for alcohol problems. *Alcohol Health & Research World, 15,* 18–24.

Zucker, R.A., Fitzgerald, H.E., & Moses, H. (1995). Emergence of alcohol problems and the several alcoholisms: A developmental perspective on etiologic theory and life course trajectory. In D. Cicchetti & D. Cohen (Eds.), *Manual of Developmental Psychopathology: Vol. 2. Risk, disorder, and adaptation* (pp. 677–711). New York: Wiley.

Zucker, R.A., Fitzgerald, H.E., Refior, S.K., Puttler, L.I., Pallas, D.M., & Ellis, D.A. (2000). The clinical and social ecology of childhood for children of alcoholics: Description of a study and implications for a differentiated social policy. In H.E. Fitzgerald, B.M. Lester, & B. Zuckerman (Eds.), *Children of addiction: Research, health, and public policy issues* (pp.109–141). New York: Garland.

Zucker, R. A., Kincaid, S. B., Fitzgerald, H. E., & Bingham, C. R. (1995). Alcohol schema acquisition in preschoolers: Differences between COAs and non-COAs. *Alcoholism: Clinical and Experimental Research, 19,* 1011–1017.

Zucker, R. A., Wong, M. M., Puttler, L. I., & Fitzgerald, H. W. (2003). Resilience and vulnerability among sons of alcoholics. Relationship to developmental outcomes between early childhood and adolescence. In S. S. Luthar (Ed.), *Resilience and vulnerability: Adaptation in the context of childhood adversities* (pp. 76–103). New York: Cambridge University Press.

INDEX

AACAP (American Academy of Child and Adolescent Psychiatry), members to children ratios of, 29

AALs (antisocial alcoholics): academic achievement v. NAALs, 260; classification subtype of, 256; NAALs v., 256, 260

AAP (American Academy of Pediatrics), 31; ADHD toolkit for primary care physicians of, 37; continuing education activities of, 37

Abused women, parenting style of, 8

Academic achievement: of AALs v. NAALs, 260; by African American youth, 81–82; poverty impact on, 111

Accreditation Council for Graduate Medical Education. *See* ACGME

ACGME (Accreditation Council for Graduate Medical Education), training requirements of, 30

Add Health Survey (National Longitudinal Survey of Adolescent Health), analysis of, 129–30

ADHD (attention deficit hyperactivity disorder): care barriers with, 43; evaluation and treatment of, 39, 42–43; pediatricians' care for, 42–44; pediatricians' collaboration with schools on, 43; pediatricians' difficulties concerning, 43–44; pediatricians' prescription for, 29; pediatricians' training in, 43; prevalence of, 42

Adolescence: childhood v., 221; family life during, 80; label and construct of, 221; peer influence in, 80; racial identity during, 80–81; risks associated with, 79–80

Adolescents. *See* Sexual activity in adolescents; Youth

Adopted adolescents: adjustment difficulties of, 129; culture camps for, 136; family impact on, 132–33, 135; The FOLK Photojournalism Project for, 138–40; identity organization in, 125; international v. domestic, 128; interpersonal challenges of, 126–27; The Latino Photojournalism Project for, 138–42; The Lost and Found Company program for, 136–38; outpatient settings for, 131; overreferral to therapy

CONTRIBUTING
AUTHORS AND EDITORS

G. ANNE BOGAT is a clinical psychologist who received her PhD from DePaul University in 1982. She is currently Professor and Director of Clinical Training in the psychology department at Michigan State University. Her research interests include family violence, youth mentoring, and person-oriented methodologies

REBECCA CAMPBELL, Ph.D. is Associate Professor of Community Psychology and Program Evaluation at Michigan State University. Her current research includes studies on the community response to rape, vicarious trauma among violence against women researchers and service providers, and the evaluation of sexual assault nurse examiner (SANE) programs. She is the author of *Emotionally involved: The impact of researching rape* which won the 2002 Distinguished Publication Award from the Association for Women in Psychology. Dr. Campbell received the 2002 Emerging Leader Award from the Committee on Women in Psychology of the American Psychological Association.

YVETTE C. CLINTON is a doctoral student in the developmental psychology program at the University of Michigan. Her dissertation research focuses on the experiences of Black/White biracial youth; more specifically, how parental messages about racial and interactions with peers relates to youths' Black and biracial racial identities. In addition, she has been involved with studies investigating how African American mothers' racial identity and perceptions of discrimination relate to mental health outcomes, and how mental health and life stress relate to African American mothers' involvement with their children's education.

SHAUNA M. COOPER received her Ph.D. in developmental psychology from the University of Michigan. Her undergraduate degree was earned at the University of North Carolina at Chapel Hill. Dr. Cooper's research involves utilizing integrative and ecological frameworks to understand the socio-contextual factors associated with African American adolescents' psychological and educational outcomes. She is particularly interested in how racially gendered experiences affect the educational trajectories and outcomes of African American male and female adolescents. In addition, she is interested in translating her research into practice.

WILLIAM S. DAVIDSON II is University Distinguished Professor and Chair of the Ecological/Community Psychology Graduate Program at Michigan State University. He is also Editor in Chief of the *American Journal of Community Psychology*. His 30 plus years of research and community involvement have been in the areas of alternative programs for troubled youth, violence prevention, violence against women, and community evaluations.

TARA DONAHUE is a doctoral student in the educational policy program at Michigan State University. Her dissertation research focuses on how after-school programming for youth interface with host schools to enhance teaching and learning. She has worked with the Education Policy Center at MSU and served on the statewide evaluation of 21st Century Community Learning Centers. Currently, she is the Director of Research at the Michigan Coalition of Essential Schools (MCES) where she oversees the evaluation of the Comprehensive School Reform program and coordinates the National Network of Partnership Schools among the MCES schools.

HIRAM E. FITZGERALD received his Ph.D. in developmental psychology in 1967 from the University of Denver. He is a Fellow of the American Psychological Association and the American Psychological Society. Currently, he is Assistant Provost for University Outreach and Engagement and University Distinguished Professor of Psychology at Michigan State University. His research has focused on biobehavioral organization during early infancy, factors regulating father-child relationships, and the impact of community network prevention programs for families with birth to three age children, and the etiology of alcoholism He is Executive Director of the World Association for Infant Mental Health.

PENNIE FOSTER-FISHMAN is an associate professor in the Department of Psychology at Michigan State University. She received her Ph.D. in organizational/community psychology from the University of Illinois at Chicago. Her research interests primarily emphasize systems change, particularly how organizational, inter-organizational, and community systems can improve to better meet the needs of children, youth, and families. She has investigated human service delivery reform, multiple stakeholder collaboration, coalition development, community organizing, and resident empowerment as vehicles for systems change Currently, she is leading a longitudinal evaluation of a comprehensive community initiative intended to promote individual, family, neighborhood, and community well-being.

KRISTINE FREEARK is a clinical psychologist with both research and clinical interests in adoptive family relationships and their impact on children's well-being. Dr. Freeark is also involved in a program of research focused on family factors related to the social and emotional adjustment of young children in internationally adoptive families. This research seeks to identify protective factors in the adoptive family, particularly in the area of parent-child communication about adoption, their co-constructed processing of adoption information, and related emotions. She is affiliated with the University of Michigan's Center for Human Growth and Development at the University of Michigan and also maintains a clinical practice in Ann Arbor, Michigan.

ALANE GAHAGAN MSW is a child psychotherapist at Four Winds Hospital in Katonah, New York. She grew up in a large family in Michigan where she developed a love for children, nature and art. She received a bachelor's degree from Michigan State University and studied Visual Communication at Pratt Institute. After working in art and design for over 20 years, she returned to graduate school at Fordham University for a Master's in Clinical Social Work. In her current position, she combines her passions for children and creativity. Her treatment utilizes a three-pronged approach merging psychodynamic, behavioral modification and family systems theories, buttressed by the power of unconditional support. Her school-age patients set their own treatment goals, and pursue them through a variety of creative methods.

SHEILA GAHAGAN MD MPH is Clinical Professor of Pediatrics and Communicable Diseases and Assistant Research Scientist at the Center for Human Growth and Development at the University of Michigan. Her experience working with American Indian children, urban Mexican American children and low income, urban Midwestern White and African American children has shaped her understanding of the influence of culture and socioeconomic status on health and wellbeing. Her clinical work focuses on behavioral interventions for obesity, failure to thrive, infant eating disorders, infant-toddler regulatory disorders, fetal alcohol syndrome and ADHD.

MELISSA S. QUON HUBER, Ph.D. is a research associate at Michigan State University with over 10 years of experience evaluating community and educational initiatives that impact families and their children. Her research has emphasized the role of geographic location in understanding social characteristics and outcomes of youth and their families. She has utilized Geographic Information Systems to analyze geographic characteristics in relationship to these social characteristics and outcomes. She has conducted research and evaluation training for community youth leaders and K-12 educators, and has published her work in numerous scientific journals.

ALYTIA A. LEVENDOSKY, Ph.D. is an Associate Professor of psychology at Michigan State University. She received her Ph.D. in clinical psychology from University of Michigan in 1995. Her research areas include domestic violence, child abuse, trauma, parenting in high-risk environments, and attachment.

JONATHAN LIVINGSTON is a Research Associate with Michigan State University Outreach and Engagement. He is also a graduate of Florida A&M University's Community Psychology master's program. His areas of research are African American psychological well-being and the cumulative effects of racism and social inequalities on mental health, health disparities, and education in the African American community. Additional areas of interest include cultural competence, community development, empowerment, and activism. Jonathan has co-authored articles in *Current Sociology*, as well as the *International Journal of Cancer Prevention*.

JULIE LUMENG completed her undergraduate degree in English with Distinction at the University of Michigan and received her doctorate of medicine at the University of Michigan Medical School. Dr. Lumeng is currently on the faculty at the University of Michigan Medical School. Clinically, she sees children with developmental and behavioral concerns in Ypsilanti, Michigan, a community in which many children live in poverty. Dr. Lumeng is also on the faculty at the Center for Human Growth and Development, a multidisciplinary research unit of the University of Michigan. Her research addresses the behavioral, social, and cognitive factors affecting children's eating behavior and obesity risk.

JESSICA R. MEYER is a graduate student in the clinical/community psychology doctoral program at the University of Virginia. She is interested in research on children, families and the law, including police interrogation of youth, adolescent development and juvenile justice, and other issues related to the legal system and public policy.

JESSICA A. OWEN is a doctoral candidate in clinical and community psychology at the University of Virginia. She received her B.A. in Psychology and Art History from Williams College in 1999. Her research focuses broadly on children, families and the law. She is currently researching the contexts of juvenile re-entry into communities after incarceration and juvenile interrogation. Ms. Owen is a Fellow in the University of Virginia's Interdisciplinary Pre-Doctoral Training Program in Education Sciences for her work on re-enrollment in schools during re-entry. She has also been awarded The Society for the Psychological Study of Social Issues' applied Social Sciences Internship for her work on police perceptions of juvenile interrogations.

N. DICKON REPPUCCI, Ph.D., received his doctoral degree in clinical psychology from Harvard University, and became Professor of Psychology at the University of Virginia in 1976, where he was Director of Clinical Training from 1976-1980, and Director of the Community Psychology. He is a Fellow of the American Psychological Association and the American Psychological Society. He has served on various editorial boards and on the NIMH Internal Review Committees concerned with violence and antisocial behavior and with life-span development and prevention. His research has focused on children, families and the law. In 1998 he was honored as the recipient of SCRA's Award for Distinguished Contributions in Theory and Research.

MARGARET ROSARIO, Ph.D., is an Associate Professor in the Psychology Department at The City University of New York. She is concerned with the development of identity, the importance of various identities for the individual, their integration into an overarching personal identity, and the associations of identity formation and integration with mental and physical health. Professor Rosario's work in this area primarily targets adolescents and focuses mainly on ethnic, gender, and sexual identities. Her second research area includes the influence of exposure to community violence on a host of adaptational and health-related outcomes among youth. Potential mediators and moderators of these relations are of critical interest.

STEPHANIE J. ROWLEY, Ph.D. is an assistant professor in developmental psychology and the Combined Program in Education and Psychology at the University of Michigan. Her research examines the effects of racial identity and other race-related attitudes and beliefs on the academic self-views and achievement of African American adolescents. She is also interested in identity in pre-adolescent ages and the ways in which race is experienced differently for African American boys and girls.

ERIC W. SCHRIMSHAW, M.A., is a doctoral candidate in health and social-personality psychology at The City University of New York - Graduate Center. His research interests include: (1) the factors that facilitate adaptation to and growth from stress and illness; (2) the factors that influence health risk behaviors (e.g., sexual risk, substance abuse); and, (3) the factors that influence health care behaviors and health care decision-making (e.g., medication adherence). In particular his interests focus on the roles of social and interpersonal relationships—including social support, social conflict, stigma, self-disclosure, and sexual relationships—as they relate to health and health behavior.

LOU ANNA KIMSEY SIMON, Ph.D. is the 20th President of Michigan State University. Prior to assuming the role of president, she was provost and vice president for academic affairs at Michigan State University and provost of the Michigan State University College of Law. She is regarded nationally as a powerful advocate of a research-active, student-centered university that is an engaged partner with society, in the land grant tradition. Dr. Simon is deeply committed to the development of effective university-community partnerships that focus on solution-based approaches to the problems of children, youth, and families. Most recently, she co-edited with Maureen Kenny, Karen Kiley-Brabeck and Richard Lerner, *Learning to Serve: Promoting Civil Society Through Service Learning*.

STEPHANIE M. TOWNSEND, M.A., is a doctoral candidate in community psychology at the University of Illinois at Chicago. Her research examines community responses to sexual violence with an emphasis on community-based prevention. She previously served on the Board of Directors of the National Coalition Against Sexual Assault and was the coordinator of a community-based rape crisis program.

LAURIE A. VAN EGEREN, Ph.D, is the Assistant Director of University-Community Partnerships, in charge of Research and Evaluation at Michigan State University. She is the Principal Investigator for the state evaluation of the 21st Century Community Learning Centers programs. A developmental psychologist. Dr. Van Egeren has expertise in program evaluation, quantitative data analysis, development from infancy through adolescence, and evaluation capacity building in communities, early childhood programs, and human service organizations. She conducts both basic and applied research in the areas of family relations, school readiness, and socioemotional development. Dr. Van Egeren is an Education Policy Fellowship program fellow.

ROBERT A. ZUCKER is Professor of Psychology in the Departments of Psychiatry and Psychology, Director of the University of Michigan Addiction Research Center, and Director of the Substance Abuse Section, Department of Psychiatry. His research has focused on three questions: (1) How do people become substance abusers? What factors move them on into alcohol or other drug dependence? (2) What are the precursive factors that mediate these outcomes? (3) What interventive programming, both pharmacotheraputic and behavioral, can be developed that will (a) reduce risk for such substance abusing outcomes, and (b) remediate them, once they are in place? He is a MERIT awardee from the National Institute on Alcohol Abuse and Alcoholism.